The Libertarian Idea

Ethics and Action
A series edited by Tom Regan

The Libertarian Idea

Jan Narveson

Temple University Press
Philadelphia

Temple University Press, Philadelphia 19122
Copyright © 1988 by Temple University. All rights reserved
Published 1988
Printed in the United States of America

The paper used in this publication meets the minimum
requirements of American National Standard for Information
Sciences—Permanence of Paper for Printed Library Materials,
ANSI Z39.48-1984

LIBRARY OF CONGRESS
Library of Congress Cataloging-in-Publication Data

Narveson, Jan, 1936–
    The libertarian idea / Jan Narveson.
    p.   cm.
    Bibliography: p. 355
    Includes index.
    ISBN 0-87722-569-9 (alk. paper) : $34.95
    1. Libertarianism.   I. Title.
JC571.N28   1988
320.5'12—dc19   88-15986
                                                                CIP

CONTENTS

v

PREFACE

The moral and political outlook holding that individual liberty is the only proper concern of coercive social institutions, which has lately become known as libertarianism, is or at least certainly seems, in principle, a very pure and therefore extreme view. It also has a certain appeal, to many of us at least—it lends itself to ringing proclamations and slogans such as animated many of the fathers of the American Revolution and are to be found in the political rhetoric of the day, especially but not exclusively in the United States. Ideas that are both extreme and appealing are always interesting to the theorist, who wishes to see what makes them tick, and indeed how loudly they tick. That is the motivation of the present study.

Libertarianism has a fairly long history, going back over 150 years in the United States, and with antecedents in the writings of John Locke (1632–1704) at least, and some of the anarchists such as William Godwin (1756–1836). But it has recently come to the attention of mainline professional philosophers in the English-speaking world because of the work of the Harvard philosopher Robert Nozick, notably his remarkable and much remarked-on book *Anarchy, State, and Utopia*.[1] The origin of the present study, indeed, was my writing of a critical notice of Nozick's book.[2] I had previously been a convinced utilitarian (summed up in my *Morality and Utility*[3]); but the work of David Gauthier in particular (now come to fruition in his great work, *Morals by Agreement*[4]), as well as Nozick's, persuaded me that utilitarianism was an unsatisfactory theory. Still, libertarianism seemed equally so at the time. In the ensuing decade, however, the libertarian theory has come to seem to me more interesting and plausible in its moral substance.

xi

But it seemed also to be in an important sense unfounded. At any rate, its defenders generally appealed, as did Nozick, to what professional philosophers call "intuition"—the philosopher's word for seat-of-the-pants judgments, that is, judgments lacking a basis in explicit theory and resting simply on whatever immediate appeal they may have. Appeal to intuition has never struck me as philosophically acceptable in moral philosophy, however much it may in some other areas such as the philosophy of pure logic. In addressing myself to the question whether libertarianism might actually have some kind of respectable foundations, I am biting off a considerable hunk of this philosophical carrot; whether it is more than I, or perhaps anyone, can chew remains to be seen. But the theory is too interesting to be left to lie in the unruly embraces of intuition.

In this book I present, in a largely sympathetic light, what I take to be the essentials of the libertarian theory, and inquire how far it might issue from a more satisfactory view of the foundations of moral theory, namely—in my judgment, at any rate—approximately the version of the contractarian theory developed by Gauthier. The "what I take to be" is important. The reader will not find here a systematic delving into the works of the many libertarian writers, though that could be done with interest. The formulations found here are mine, and if any resemblance to the ideas of genuine libertarians is not wholly coincidental, they are at any rate not guaranteed to coincide with those of any other writer on the subject.

My verdict is that libertarianism emerges, if not entirely unscathed, yet interestingly close to intact. However, I also take up the vexed question of what follows: does libertarianism have the rather extreme implications normally attributed to it? Does it, for example, show that the State is unjustifiable, that such currently popular programs as those of the modern Welfare State are unacceptable violations of basic human rights, and so on? I am inclined to think that its implications for such things may well be considerably less radical than often supposed. "May well", again, is important. As I try to illustrate, factual considerations are inevitably relevant to these questions, and enthusiasts who wish to push on regardless will not long have an audience among those not already ideologically partial. Nevertheless, libertarianism remains a radical theory; certainly a good deal of present-day political practice would have to be drastically revamped if libertarianism were adopted. I am inclined to think this would be largely change for the better. But the point of this book is more nearly to examine than to advocate. If at times it seems adversarial or even promotional, the intent is to get people to think, rather than to rush out and overturn the existing order (which in any case is not easily overturned—and to their credit, few if any libertarians favor overturn by force, even if that were a possibility).

The book is divided into three fairly equal parts. Part One is devoted to exposition, and in particular to a defense of the *coherence* of libertarian theory. Although any theory must be coherent if it is to be acceptable, the coherence problem for libertarianism is a particularly tricky one. It is not to be overlooked, after all, that many writers on what is presently termed "the Left" defend their versions of socialism and allied theories by an appeal to liberty. I shall examine some of what seem to be the basic ideas behind this work in the course of my reconstruction, making as clear as possible why it seems to me that these efforts are misguided. But there are efforts and efforts, of course. The river of socialism is one into which you cannot step twice; to try to keep up with that flow is to preclude any other appreciable scholarly activity. And in fact, socialist theory on its own account gets extremely short shrift in these pages. Giving it the sort of attention that might possibly dislodge the doting socialist from his or her theoretical pipe dreams is not a task to be accomplished in a few pages— even as brilliant and incisive a few pages as Nozick devotes to it in the aforementioned work. But I do hope to have added a little to the case against claiming seriously that what socialists can plausibly defend socialism in the name of is *liberty*.

In Part Two, I consider the question of foundations: why, if at all, should we accept this theory? Especially because of the formidable example of Nozick, I go to some length to explain why intuition should be roundly rejected as a possible foundation of this (or any) view, and why the contractarian approach should instead be employed—and, of course, what I understand to be involved in that approach. Here my mentor is Gauthier, plus or minus a few important details—though again, the reader (and possibly Gauthier!) must hold me and not Gauthier responsible for any shortcomings. I then ask, after a few brief words about utilitarianism, whether contractarianism would lead to libertarianism, concluding that there is a plausible case for the assessment that it would come, at any rate, fairly close.

But the matter is not likely to be settled with a simple and elegant argument—a fact of importance in itself, for any ringing slogans, tending to put argument at rest, will perhaps ring rather less bravely once the real problems in the way of acceptance assert themselves.

The tendency to rush to the barricades under the impetus of ringing slogans is one that has its appeal, to be sure. But it should *bother* people that the slogans may rest on a quagmire of fallacies and confusions. How many people have been killed because of Marx's ringing slogans, which he supposed had the imprimatur of an advanced social science, but which a closer look reveals to be a logical mess? Doesn't that *matter*? (It is beginning to do so, in the sober aftermath of botched economies—which now seem to be having more influence than the disgraceful record of rewritten history, mass murder, and the rest of it. But not to enough people, or soon enough.)

In Part Three the question considered is what (if anything) libertarianism really tells us about concrete political and social issues. Here I consider certain of the main features of present-day "advanced" societies such as ours in the light—if light it should prove to be—of the libertarian theory. Among the main areas are crime, pollution, medicare programs and the like, education, pornography, and antidiscrimination legislation. Libertarianism has been virtually defined in terms of the rejection of the legitimacy of almost all of these things, and perhaps, for that matter, of the State itself. It is, as I shall explain, not so clear that all of those remarkable implications really do flow from the libertarian hypothesis. High-level moral theories do not yield concrete implications in complex real-life situations nearly so readily as that. On the other hand, we must be aware of the dangers of death by a thousand qualifications. Libertarianism does not look like a bland theory, and if our messy and bland society should end up being fully consistent with it, that is prima facie evidence that something has gone wrong in our exposition.

The general conclusion of this book, then, is that we shouldn't head for the barricades tomorrow. But it is not, as will be seen, entirely passive. In the sober (I hope) prose of philosophical analysis, this study may nevertheless give a certain guidance for action, some of it perhaps being at least slightly out of the ordinary. That would be more gratifying to this author than any number of mindless revolutions.

PART ONE

Is Libertarianism Possible?

The Knock at the Door

IT IS 3:00 A.M. There is a knock at the door. A fairly stout knock at first, and then quite deafening. You hastily get into your housecoat and make your way downstairs, with considerable trepidation. It is the police, and they are here to haul you down to the jail. They have guns and are disposed, if need be, to use them.

Why are they after you? Maybe any of the following: Because you inhaled a substance that made you feel good. Because you didn't send your daughter to the right school. Because you have the wrong religious beliefs. Because you didn't help support the building of a particular super-expensive weapon to protect you from people you don't think you need any protecting from, besides which you think that weapon will only increase the likelihood that you may *really* need to be protected from them later. Because you engineered a business deal leaving you in control of 90 percent of some industry. Because someone thinks that certain things are right which you think are wrong. Because some very powerful person doesn't know anything about statistics. Because someone has different tastes in opera than you do. Because you make more money than most people and don't want to give it to others who have less. Because you failed to install a safety device that in your judgment was wholly unnecessary. Because . . . .

The scene should be from some crazy nightmare, but it is not. All of those reasons and more have occasioned the Knock at the Door, and continue to do so in various parts of the globe, at various times. In these more civilized parts of the world, the knock at the door doesn't usually come at 3:00 A.M.; it's more likely to come at 3:00 P.M., and the police might not even be armed. If it's the tax collectors, they might not even be interested in hauling you off to jail. Instead, they'll

3

merely haul off your car, your house, your collection of oil paintings, or anything else you thought was yours that they can get their hands on.

Shift the focus quite a bit, and we have a rather different specter, one that many will view as quite benign. This is the specter of the People in Uniform—or more likely, in fact, just in ordinary business suits—insisting that you fill out forms, make trips to see officials, and in general institute procedures that quintuple the time it takes to perform what seemed to you wholly routine and mundane activities.

These people have *power* over us. They have the police at their bidding, and the rest of it—the cumbersome machinery of the Law, the Legislature, the Executive. And they don't like back-talk. If you exclaim in protest, they will add another couple of hours to the toll of your time devoted to interests in which you have no interest, another couple of hundred dollars to the bill for doing things you see no point in doing. Including, of course, paying the salaries of these very officials.

People are in the habit, nowadays, of supposing that arbitrary tyranny, at least in the decent, enlightened places in the world such as you and I have been fortunate enough to live our entire lives in, is a thing of the past. After all, government is now generally understood to be a servant of The People, is it not? Don't we have the vote? Can we reasonably expect any more?

Democracy has certainly supplanted the one or a dozen or a few hundred arbitrary tyrants of the monarchies, oligarchies, aristocracies—the ancien régime, the Communist Party of the Soviet Union, and so on. But how much better off are we if those tyrants are replaced by millions of tyrants, pettier but probably no more virtuous, on average, than the monsters of times past or places distant? Arbitrary despotism is not limited to those remote awful examples: it is a property quite capable of being exemplified by The Common Man (whose hitherto near monopoly on them is now strongly challenged as well by The Uncommon Woman). Indeed, it may well be at fullest tide when people are trying to protect you, as they so often are when they find themselves with the Reins of Power in their hands. The style, of course, is different. The classical tyrant can send you off to the dungeons or to the block; The People, on the other hand, will probably send you to . . . the Office! And there shalt thou fill out forms, wait in line, and be told that you are in the wrong office and the right one won't be open 'til Wednesday, during hours when you had hoped to be getting something done or at least spending your life in some pleasanter fashion.

Actually, there is a certain recognition that a majority vote of your fellows maybe isn't *quite* enough to justify the Knock on the Door. Democratic theory, it is admitted, has to do better than that. There are things people can do to you which they ought not, no matter how many people would approve of it if they did. Thus the written constitutions of modern democratic states often have bills of rights appended, and in those that don't, it is nevertheless understood that people are not to be treated in certain ways. There is a modest threat of paradox here: for constitutions are understood to become law by virtue of procedures tantamount to plebiscites, and if the laws in question are attempts to provide people with rights that even large majorities are not to override, what is to keep another plebiscite from being held the day after tomorrow, revoking all those nice protections? Thus may these constraints in democratic constitutions be attempts to do the impossible. Yet they have effect, and—undoubtedly more important—they give a sense of direction to the mind of the citizen. Whatever the niceties and fine print, we feel that there are important principles involved in these proclamations, the general purport of which may perhaps be well summarized in a motto making its rounds a few years back: "Illegitimi non carborandum!" (Don't let the bastards wear you down!). Can this be made a slogan for a new revolution: the antibureaucratic revolution? The revolution that says, "Get off my back!"?

This is merely a philosophical inquiry. It is the business of philosophers to formulate and to subject to disciplined criticism proposed formulations of the general principles underlying the major subject matters of thought. The rallying cry of individual liberty has not lacked standard-bearers over the years. Most interesting among them, because most serious and thorough about their attention to principles, have been the libertarians of recent times. Most notable among professional philosophers has been Robert Nozick in his brilliant work, *Anarchy, State, and Utopia*—a work of which it may certainly be said, as Kant said of Hume's *Treatise*, that it woke a number of us from our dogmatic slumbers. The only trouble is that it threatened to replace one dogma with another: to expound, however inimitably and unforgettably, a "Libertarianism Without Foundations", as one critic has put it.

It was almost universally thought by philosophers until fairly recently that philosophy was not supposed to get mixed up in concrete issues. That view is largely obsolete by now—indeed, the pendulum may have swung rather too far in the other direction. Few meetings of the American Philosophical Association are without their share of political resolutions, and an uncomfortable number of the papers presented at them sound rather too much like sermons. Reality, however, is *there*, and it must be a rather irresponsible, not to say unrecognizable, moral philosophy that can seriously intend to have no bearing on it. In the ensuing chapters I hope to have struck a reasonable balance between what may seem excessively high theory and an unseemly immersion in empirical matters requiring expertise I do not possess. Here are required the knowledge of the economist, the skills of the statistician, the experience of the city planner, and the rest. (Is what has been "struck" a balance, or is it instead an unsteady teetering from one to the other? The reader shall judge.)

Let us begin.

CHAPTER 1

Liberalism, Conservatism, Libertarianism

A Preliminary Definition

A T THE OUTSET let us say that "Libertarianism", as the term is used in current moral and political philosophy (as distinct from a view about freedom of the will), is the doctrine that the only relevant consideration in political matters is individual liberty: that there is a delimitable sphere of action for each person, the person's "rightful liberty," such that one may be forced to do or refrain from what one wants to do only if what one would do or not do would violate, or at least infringe, the rightful liberty of some other person(s). No other reasons for compelling people are allowable: other actions touching on the life of that individual require his or her consent. In the course of this study the idea will get some refinement. But it is always refinement of that idea, rather than some hybrid or evolutionary version.

Although stated at a very general and abstract level, what is thus defined is nevertheless intended to be a substantive moral and political theory, not an exercise in definition or pure conceptual analysis. A great deal of such analysis is, as will be seen in the ensuing pages, necessary before we can claim a decent understanding of this theory and thus be in position to assess its credentials. Is it the true theory of this matter or not? That question will be asked, and tentatively answered, much later in this book. Meanwhile, we turn to the task of giving the theory a reasonably satisfactory and thorough exposition.

Liberal/Conservative

Libertarianism is one kind of liberalism. It is interesting that it is often thought of as a kind of conservatism, as when libertarian defenders of private property are contemptuously referred to as "right-wing" by leftish writers, as though to defend private property in the name of liberty were exactly on all fours with defending genuinely right-wing military dictatorships. The assimilation in question might be understandable in journalists or cracker-barrel pundits, but to find professional philosophers doing so is inexcusable. However, let us admit that the usage of these terms has not been uniform of late. Some attention to definition is needed.

I shall follow the lead of Ronald Dworkin in identifying *liberalism* with the view that "political decisions must be, so far as is possible, independent of any particular conception of the good life, or of what gives value to life."[1] Thus, the goods recognized by a political and moral order may only be the goods of the members of that order, marshaled in some fair way behind public institutions. Appeals to a supposed "absolute" good, standing over and above every individual and over which no individual has any choice or authority, or over which only an elite class has such choice or authority, are ruled out. Thus the liberal must justify principles, policies, and institutions, to any person affected by them, by showing that person they are for his or her good *as seen by that person;* or at any rate, that only the goods of other persons as seen by those other persons can be appealed to in argument purporting to justify those policies, together with some sufficient reason, as seen by that person, for permitting his or her interests to be outweighed for that purpose by those of the others. In this sense (and only this sense), we may accept Dworkin's dictum that for the liberal, everyone counts and, moreover, counts, in some sense needing to be further explained, equally. The alleged goods of unanalyzed groups, for instance, or of the universe at large, will not do, any more than the whims or even the earnest ideological proclivities of some privileged class.

David Gauthier does not use the term 'liberal' in this context, but he presents what we may regard as an excellent statement of the idea nevertheless: "In saying that an essentially just society is neutral with respect to the aims of its members, we deny that justice is linked to any substantive conceptions of what is good, either for the individual or for society. A just society has no aim beyond those given in the preferences of its members."[2]

A *conservative* view, by contrast, does invoke precisely such a conception, insisting that the individual must sacrifice his or her own interests to this august purpose. Alternatively, the conservative will have it that the individual's own interests really are quite other than the individual in question thinks they are, irrespective of inclination or belief to the contrary, adding that policy is to be guided by his "real" or "true" interests, rather than by the shallow conception of those interests held by the individual concerned. On the liberal view, by contrast, every individual has a realm over which he or she is the absolute monarch.

Dworkin's usage departs from a frequent employment of these expressions in which they refer to the relation of the view or policy in question to current practice: if it departs substantially, it is said to be "liberal"; if it purports to uphold that practice, or perhaps its underlying principles, then it is "conservative". Conservatives, in this usage, are opposed to change, whereas liberals are in favor of change. Plainly, that can't be all there is to it in any case, for we would want, usually, to distinguish between "progressive" changes and "reactionary" changes—changes "forward" verses changes "backward". This requires that in addition to the idea signifying change or the lack of it, some further idea is intended. Moreover, this usage becomes confusing when the society in question is, for example, a liberal society and has been for a long time—such as the United States, which may reasonably be thought of as the world's oldest liberal society. What does a conservative in this sense advocate in America? Or in the Soviet Union—which some seem to want to classify as liberal in some sense, though only, I suppose, because it is on the "left". The point is that this sense of the terms doesn't correlate with anything of conceptual interest. We want to know, not whether to support the status quo or not, but *why* we should or should not do so. Nobody, I hope, thinks that any and all change is *necessarily* for the better, nor again that it is necessarily for the worse. Some may, however, think that we owe a duty of loyalty to our roots, our origins, the society that reared us, and so forth; and if they also think that this is our supreme duty, or that because of this we have no rights against the state, then we indeed have a form of conservatism in the sense here discussed. It is typical for conservatives in this sense, however, to be opposed to changes within their society that clearly have a wide social base of support. They have to think, then, that the "society" or "state" to which our fundamental allegiance is owed may not be simply identical with the one we happen to live in.

The two have this in common, though: both hold that there is an entity we must respect simply because it is the locus, as it were, of ultimate authority. But whereas conservatives identify this locus with the State or the larger society or the like, liberals identify it with the individual person, as he or she may be, here and now. Or at least with the person insofar as rationally accessible to others: my reasonable concern with you cannot follow you all the way into the possibly incomprehensible, hidden recesses of your soul. But it can, I believe, follow you far enough so that the rest of your soul can meditate in peace.

Why be a liberal? That is an important and profound issue, which we will in effect be grappling with in Part Two of this book. Is it possible, really, to be a liberal? That will be part of our concern in Part One and now. Liberalism requires a certain impartiality, as Thomas Nagel has pointed out in a superb recent essay, "Moral Conflict and Political Legitimacy".[3] It says that only individuals' values count, and it says that none of them count, as such, for more than any others'. The poorest beggar has rights that the richest and most powerful must respect, and the intellectual nonentity has ideas that, however lacking in any shred of rational merit, he is nevertheless entitled to hold, even when those ideas are flatly inconsistent with one's own obviously superior ones. This raises the question whether one can be sincerely liberal. Must a liberal deny the truth of liberalism when dealing with someone of a different political hue? This is an important question, to which the answer is happily in the negative, once we see what is involved. The liberal need not deny the truth of liberalism in that or any context: but her liberalism requires her to move over and accommodate the conservative and the radical nevertheless—not because their views are true, nor even because they are "just as true as one's own" (they aren't, after all); but rather, because the conservative and the radical are entitled to hold them; their right to hold their views is to be respected just because the views are *theirs*. Further implicit attachment to and explicit articulation of this outlook will be found throughout these pages. But the reader is referred to Nagel's brilliant essay for an insightful account of the issue in its own right.

Left, Center, Right

This is a good place to enter an initial complaint about the use of the terms 'left', 'right', and 'center' in current political discussions. The usage implies that there is a single spectrum along which any particular packet of political views may be located. Are you in favor of free trade and against high import duties? This, apparently, puts you on the "right". Are you in favor of extending the franchise in South Africa to black persons? Ah! You are on the "left"! And if you favor both, then what? What if you disapprove of socialism (that puts you on the "right") but also disapprove of dictatorships (which puts you on the "left"—unless the dictatorships in question happen to be Marxist, in which case, somehow, your disapproval now puts you back with the "right")? Plainly, this usage is futile.

Liberal Individualism as One Kind of Conservatism

The political premises of liberal individualism are often characterized as being very remote from actual life: the individual is supposed, according to these caricatures, to spring full-blown from the womb, complete with a priori political theory and sans any allegiance or even any attachment to his community. The reality of political theory, however, is, according to this criticism, to be found in real communities, where loyalties and attachments form a strong bond between every individual and every other one, and abstract rights have little sway. Political theory, according to this critique, stems from the life of the community and cannot be detached therefrom. And the morality issuing from these reflections will be "My Station and its Duties" (the slogan comes from the title of F. H. Bradley's celebrated essay) rather than any kind of abstract commitment to universal reason.

It is not entirely clear what the thread of argument is in this view, but if I understand it aright, there is at least a threat of fallacy. For the output of this reasoning is supposed to be support for conservatism— *support* for the policies and institutions that actually prevail in whatever society is in question. The snag is, however, that in many communities we have mavericks, people who topple the idols and stick their tongues out at some of the local institutions. Yet if the claims made by these thinkers were right, we shouldn't expect this to happen. If the community has such strong appeal, if its bonds are so efficacious, how did these misfits come to be engendered in it? And how much of a reply to them is it if one merely cites the existing ways as if they were unquestionable? To those who have questioned and are still questioning them, the "argument" that they are what they are will not cut much ice.

But we should agree with one facet of this kind of view: there is indeed such a thing as a community ethos, a moral outlook, that has its hold on the members of the tribe in question and informs many of their attitudes. It is not beyond question and can be founded on thin air or prejudice—or it can be founded on solid considerations that will endear the community to the more thoughtful among its members as well as to the intellectual *hoi polloi*. However, the characterization in question doesn't tell us what the content of the community's ethos may be. That is a variable in the analysis. And once we realize that, we can raise the possibility that the community outlook might itself be liberal. Liberalism, and even libertarianism, could be the conservatism of community X. What that community rams down the throats of its members from infancy onward could be the universal right of everyone to the maximum freedom compatible with a like freedom for all. Nothing in the premises of this criticism preclude this, once one sees what is going on. And we may therefore proceed in our analysis. If libertarianism turns out to be a viable and coherent theory, then it could also become the dogma of the community—in the sense of 'dogma', however, that is compatible with the doctrine so called being rationally supportable rather than a *mere* dogma. And indeed, it is not going too far to suggest that there are at least appreciable elements of this theory woven into the fabric of Western society even now. One does not have to wander far in the streets of Toronto or New York to appreciate that the native proclivities of Canadians and Americans are rather far removed from those of the individuals one is likely to encounter on the streets of Moscow. This could be due, no doubt, in part to the past theorizing of the Lockes and the Jeffersons who formulated their intellectual heritage, just as the attitudes of the Muscovites have likely been shaped by their heritage of Marx and Lenin. But then, that is testimony to the power of intellectual theorizing, given time and the right readers. On one reading of the communitarian critique, such stuff should have no influence whatever. The facts, I think, do not bear out such a verdict. And given that they do not, it clearly behooves us to continue doing political theory and, let us hope, to do it well.

CHAPTER 2

Liberty

Another Preliminary Definition

IN PROPOSING THAT individual liberty is the fundamental and only legitimate concern of any just society, libertarianism assumes the burden of explaining what liberty is, and then in particular what a fundamental right to liberty would look like. The situation, as we will see, is extremely complicated.

A great deal of philosophical ink is spilled on the first of these questions, and rightly so. (*a*) There is the question, What is the subject of liberty: what is it whose freedom is in question? Of course we want to know what it is for a *human* to be free; but humans are complicated entities, and there are many different features of them that might figure in our account of liberty. Some will want to say it is the "whole person", others the strictly rational aspect of the person, others the "will", perhaps in some highly rarefied conception of it, and so on. And (*b*), there is the question of what it is for that entity, or the person as so characterized, to be free or unfree. Luckily, both questions have obvious partial answers—but only partial, and obvious only because incomplete. The obvious answer to the first is that anything with a rational will to act, and enough in the way of a physical body to be at least inherently capable of putting that will into effect, may be free or unfree. What is free or unfree is the *practical agent*, the acting individual who has intentions and interests and makes decisions with a view to bringing about what is intended or realizing those interests. And the obvious answer to the second is that one is free if nothing impedes the operation of the will in question. Both seem to me not only obvious but even right—basically. Yet both need considerable discussion, and both are in important ways incomplete.

The Subject of Liberty

Regarding the first question, the "obvious answer", I have said, is the practical agent, the individual with a rational will, who is free or unfree in the sense relevant to our concerns here. The answer may be obvious, but nevertheless it needs further consideration, for two reasons. In the first place, there will be questions, in some cases very difficult and very practical, of just who is to be said to be rational or even to have a will. One of these questions concerns the precision of our demarcation between those who do and those who don't have the requisite rational wills: if the strong rights associated with the libertarian view belong only to beings endowed with rational wills, then consider those, for instance, with extremely low IQs, or with extreme schizophrenia, and so on. These are marginal cases, those concerning whom it is doubtful whether we should even say that they have "rational wills". The question whether a given marginal case falls above or below the line could literally be a matter of life and death in contexts of medical ethics, for instance. Still, the fact that there will be marginal cases is no reason for thinking the answer is wrong, for any sensible answer to such a question will inevitably spawn marginal cases. We simply have to live with those.

The second problem is much more urgent for purposes of theory construction: Are our concepts of rationality sufficiently value-free to enable us to frame a basic moral principle in terms of them? If in order to apply our supposedly fundamental principle it proved necessary to make another value judgment of the very kind that that principle is supposed to be providing, then obviously its claim to fundamentality is undermined.

Rationality is, of course, a value: it's something we value. And when we assess the rationality of an argument or, in the appropriate sense, of an individual, we are no doubt making judgments relevant to value judgments: "How good is he at logic?" is a natural way to put a question about logical competence. However, even if judgments about rationality do involve value judgments, those judgments need not be in any distinctive sense *moral* judgments, of the very kind that the principle is intended to generate. And it is certain that culturally modulated concepts enter into such judgments. Whether such considerations do anything to damage the status of such principles as the libertarian one is a question we will consider later in this treatment, though not at great length. I shall be operating almost entirely with what I take to be an everyday, intuitively manageable concept of rationality, and only in part with refinements or with special senses of the term; it is in this rather ordinary sense of the term that freedom requires, I take it, the capacity for rationality.

Second, and more basically, we have the question why the notion of a *rational* will should be the right one for talking about liberty. Rabbits, for example, can evidently be free or unfree: a rabbit caught in a trap is not free; one that is bounding gaily about in the meadow is, by contrast, free. But for that matter, we can say that squid are not free to swim into an area closed off by a concrete wall, that a tree wired firmly to stakes is not free to sway in the breeze, and that a stone trapped on a ledge is not free to fall into the canyon below. We are not tempted to say that wiring the tree is an infringement of its rights, nor even an infringement of its liberty (though in the case of some of the more enthusiastic environmental ethicists nowadays, one begins to wonder!) We do not say these things even though a notion of liberty can more or less be applied in each case; we don't say them, because the liberty of these other things is of no general concern or interest to us. Their liberty does not, in general, matter.

Libertarianism is concerned with human liberty; it is the liberty of humans that, morally speaking, matters. Why does it matter? And why doesn't the liberty of these other things matter? An important question, to which we will devote more, and more explicit, attention later on. But meanwhile, we should first ask: *To whom* does it matter? The liberty of some trees, some animals, probably some comets for that matter, does matter to some people. But it doesn't matter to everybody. Neither, however, does the liberty of people in general matter to everybody. Clearly there are those who have no aversion to restricting the liberty of others.

It seems much more plausible, though, to say that the liberty of each rational being matters to that rational being: Smith's liberty matters to Smith, and in general the liberty of person A matters to A.[1] And why is this more plausible? Because not to be at liberty is to be unable to do what we want to do, to achieve our ends, to realize our values—in short, to live, in this or that respect, our lives. This must matter as much as, and because, those wants, ends, and values—those lives—matter. Liberty is essential. But we will go no further with such reflections at this point.

Liberty and Autonomy

Recent writers have made much of the idea of *autonomy* as an important, indeed perhaps fundamental, concept in the moral arena. The emphasis is on self-directedness, as the term implies (in Latin):

the "autonomous" individual is self-directed. Lawrence Haworth expounds a particularly clear and perspicuous account of this elusive concept.[2] On his analysis there are, in brief, three traits necessary for autonomy: (1) competence, (2) procedural independence (not just borrowing one's motivations straight from others), (3) self-control (not being exclusively subject to one's passions and impulses—acting reflectively, with ability to choose whether one will follow a given impulse or not). The second is self-rule vis-à-vis others—as distinct from other-rule; the third is self-rule vis-à-vis oneself—as distinct from rule by one's "baser elements" (not Haworth's term); one's person, not just one's passions, is in charge.[3] These traits are independent and each is necessary. The necessity of "procedural" independence, that is, of thinking for oneself and not simply acting on others' directives or desires with no further mental processing of one's own, is obvious. Regarding the other two, Haworth points out that "No amount of competence can make up for a tendency to yield to every impulse; no amount of independence can compensate for inability to carry out the simplest projects."[4]

He sums up as follows: "The one notion that best catches up the positive dimensions of all three traits . . . is "critical competence". Having critical *competence*, a person is first of all active and his activity succeeds in giving effect to his intentions. Having *critical* competence, the active person is sensitive to the results of his own deliberation; his activity is guided by purposes he has thought through and found reasons of his own for pursuing. Normal autonomy is critical competence."[5]

How does the Haworthian analysis, which is very compelling, affect our deliberations here? Their implications for the doctrine of libertarianism will be considered more closely in Part Two. Meanwhile, we should note that autonomy is plainly, as Haworth says, a matter of degree and indeed, one with no clear upper bound; thus the pursuit of total autonomy could become a hobby, an unattainable ideal. But our doctrine is for everybody, not just autonomy aficionados. There is a normal level of autonomy, as Haworth agrees, and we should accept that our discussion here applies to such normal persons in the first instance. What to do about those below the line will be a specific problem, about which something will be said (quite a bit, actually) in Part Three.

Meanwhile, the specific question raised at present by taking autonomy seriously is this. Clearly, there can be situations in which we could be faced with the question to interfere or not interfere with the actions of some person of at least normal autonomy but who in this case seems to be acting under the influence of what we take to be nonautonomous motivations. A might be drunk, for instance, or acting thoughtlessly, or contrary to what A has previously represented to be A's own best interests. Does the right to liberty that libertarianism posits permit or forbid interference in such cases? The matter can be very tricky in particular cases, but the general principle, it seems to me, is clear enough. As suggested in an earlier account of mine,[6] we should act toward person A on the basis of what A has given us to understand are A's highest motivations: A's view of the good, and not simply A's occurrent desires. Not easy advice to follow in practice, and especially difficult where the question is whether interference is justified by the State or by miscellaneous persons as distinct from friends. But the rationale is clear enough: we want to respect *A's* liberty, and when A is autonomous, person A *wants to be identified by* these higher level, reflected-upon values. (That's A's right, after all, on the libertarian view.) The values to be respected in relation to person A are the values person A has identified with.

In so adapting the present interpretation to the idea of autonomy, notice, there is still no foisting of values by one person upon another. If I try to prevent A from doing x, where x is what A currently seems to want to do but is contrary to what A has clearly insisted are A's own deeper desires or best interests, I am still respecting *A's* liberty by respecting (or rather, trying to respect) A's own values, which after all are a function of A's freedom to form those values. I do not, in principle, impose my values on A in the process—even though it may be granted that it will sometimes be difficult to interpret A's values without some help from my own as a source of evidence about what A's might possibly be when there are unclarities, as there often are.

The Nonatomic Individual

In saying that the subject of liberty is the acting subject, the individual with "practical reason", we do not further assume that that subject is, as we might put it, an "individualistic" individual. We do not assume detachment, either metaphysical or otherwise, from the society this subject was raised in. Individuals make their decisions, do their choosing and deliberating, on the basis of values largely if not entirely absorbed from the surrounding society. Their very personalities are defined by relation to their peers, their acquaintances, their loved ones, and so on. It is not to be supposed that individuals must be, as a rather misplaced metaphor has it, "atomic." Presumably what was meant by 'atomic' is that people don't really affect each other, but just, so to say, bounce off each other—their characters and personalities are fixed entirely by internal causes operating independently of all others. The unfortunateness of this metaphor becomes apparent when we reflect that atoms have no individuality—one atom of a given kind of element is absolutely similar to any other atom of that element, and, indeed, the only individuation possible for an atom is by its spatial relation to all others. It is interesting that doctrines of individual liberty should have been thought to depend on "atomism" under the circumstances, for if any of those things were true, we could have no intelligible morality at all: If people can't affect each other at all, they can hardly do so by the familiar methods of moral training, praising and blaming, and the like. And if we are all identical, what could be the point of advocating as a supreme right that of being allowed to be the particular individual one is, distinct from all others?

What Is Liberty?

To be free is, to begin with, to be free to do what one wants. We are sometimes said to be free or unfree to *have* various things or even to *be* various things, for example, to "be the person one is", as in my last sentence. Later in this study (pages 80–82), it will be argued that the right to have may be analyzed in terms of rights to do: "having-rights" will be reduced to "action-rights". If that is right, it implies that freedom-to-have is a case of freedom-to-do. Freedom-to-be would succumb to this as well if we take the line that "being" a certain way means having certain properties, qualities, characteristics, and that 'having' in the latter phrase has the same sense as when we speak of "having" various kinds of property. But all such reductions require at least some linguistic strain, and probably some conceptual strain as well.

Liberty: Freedom to Bring About

I believe we can minimize such strain by adopting the view that freedom is fundamentally the freedom to *determine*, namely, to determine what is the case. I suggest we can do this by thinking of freedom as defined over pairs consisting of persons and states of affairs. Thus

'Person A is [completely] free with respect to S' = 'S obtains if and only if A chooses that S'.

In other words, whether S obtains is entirely up to A. S happens if A wants it to, and x doesn't happen if A doesn't want it to. Obviously, this is an idealization: so far as macroscopic events in the externally observable world are concerned, this perfect concomitance between will and world is hardly universal. But it is not unheard of either: practically speaking, for instance, it is at present true of each of my fingers that it will fall upon a particular key on the keyboard of my computer if and only if I "tell" it to, and indeed that the appropriate character will appear on the screen if and only if I convey the command in question to the finger in question. If I leave the vicinity, or the computer fails, or any number of other possible occurrences disrupt the proceedings, then this correlation will likewise cease; but when everything is in place, we do come very close to "perfect" freedom in restricted cases such as this. For certain very specific movements of one's body and for certain even more specific states of affairs outside one's body, the movement takes place if and only if one wills that it does, and that external state of affairs obtains if and only if that bodily movement occurs. (The range of such movements of which this very close concomitance between will and act obtains can be quite high for the youngish person in superb physical condition. When one gets a touch of arthritis, like the author, the realization that we are not Superman becomes only too painfully clear. We tell the limb to be just *there*, but in fact it is perhaps a quarter-inch short of being precisely "there", with concomitant dire effects on the dishes. Unfreedom even in this very intimate and restricted area of life has set in. But very considerable freedom at the level of bodily movements is normal. For those more global actions with which so much of so many of our lives is concerned, perfect freedom is so much less than universal that perhaps unfreedom is more nearly the norm.)

Freedom From and Freedom To

There has been considerable discussion in the literature on the subject of 'freedom from' versus 'freedom to'. Is freedom fundamentally freedom *from* some kind of interference? Or is it fundamentally more "positive," consisting in freedom *to* do or have this or that? Fortunately, the horrible muddle implicit in this contrast has been largely cleared up with the recognition that all freedom has to be both: freedom must be freedom to bring something or other about, and in that sense to do something; and freedom-to-do-something simply has to be, while it's at it, freedom *from* whatever interfering factor or factors may be pertinent, since obviously if those factors have their way, then we do not do as we wish. Note that on our above analysis, no interfering factor is mentioned. But this is only because if S's coming about is due entirely to A's wanting it to do so—that is, if A's wanting S is literally a *sufficient condition* for S, then by definition there has been no interfering factor, or none with effect: nothing can have prevented A from bringing about S if A's ordaining of S simply brings S about, with, as it were, no back-talk from the world at large.

Utter Freedom

Let us now, in fancy, remove all restrictions to very specific states of affairs. Thus we produce a definition of complete, or total, or "utter" freedom: to be utterly free is to be such that one could bring about absolutely any state of affairs one wished—for all S, S occurs if and only if A wills S. Such is supposed to be the case with God, I presume. It can also be managed readily for much lesser entities, by default: if an individual doesn't want to do anything, then it will never be the case that it is impeded from doing as it wants. The case of us humans comes in between: there are plenty of things each of us wants, even if there are plenty of others which we do not; and for those we do want, there are obstacles a-plenty to our bringing them about.

Interferences: Where the Action Is

What we should now recognize is that everything interesting about freedom concerns these interfering factors. To be free is for it to be the case that something or other doesn't keep you from achieving whatever it is you wanted to achieve, the "something or other" awaiting specification. We don't bring up the question of Jones's *freedom* unless some possible or actual interfering factor is envisaged. And of course in moral and political contexts, interferences are what all the talk is about. When A presses for the liberty to do x, A is insisting that somebody or other refrain from preventing A from doing x.

But we very soon come upon the need to make some distinctions here, one of which might reasonably be aligned with the 'to' and 'from' distinction, rather than marshaled under the general heading of interferences. Consider the two cases:

(1) Sam's arthritis prevented him from playing football.
(2) Sam's wife prevented him from playing football.

Are these two different *senses* of the term 'prevent'? This is not easy to say, and really doesn't matter. What does matter is that the "preventing" condition in (1) is simply a medical fact about Sam, whereas the condition in (2) is under some human's intentional control. Thus we can ask whether Sam's wife is justified in not permitting Sam to play ball, but we cannot ask Sam's arthritis whether *it* is justified in not permitting him to do so. If someone somehow managed to give Sam arthritis, then that person might be blamed for it and could be said to have prevented him from playing. In the more usual case where no one is to blame, because the condition simply happened as a result of the usual natural causes, then the statement "Sam is not at liberty to play" would be rather misleading if arthritis was the intended problem, but apt enough if his wife's insistence was responsible.

CHAPTER 3

Liberty: Negative versus Positive

Negative and Positive Liberty: Freedom versus Power

LATER IN THIS STUDY a distinction between negative and positive rights will loom large. Here we may make a parallel distinction concerning sorts of liberty. If we are, *simpliciter*, at liberty to do x, then nothing at all prevents us from doing it. This doesn't necessarily mean that we *do* it: it means rather, as the general definition given above implies, that if we don't do it, it's because we don't want to do it, or at any rate haven't decided to do it. But we can divide the sorts of situations in which we are prevented from doing x, even if it should be the case that we do want to do x, into two general classes, exemplifying *positive* and *negative* liberty.

(1) Positive liberty: We can identify positive liberty with the *presence* of those conditions, such as the means of doing x, that enable you to do something, if circumstances permit; one way of being unfree to do it would be for one or more of those conditions not to obtain. These conditions can be either internal or external to the body or mind of the agent. To continue our football example, such things as adequate cardiovascular capability and some skill or knowledge would be examples of internal conditions; a suitable place to play and enough fellow players to form the requisite teams would exemplify external ones. The internal conditions are your *powers*: to have the requisite internal enabling conditions, granted absence of obstacles, is to have, in one main respect, the power to do the thing in question. (Depending on what the thing is, you may well need other conditions or even other types of powers—political, perhaps.)

(2) Negative liberty: this, by contrast, refers simply to the *absence*

of factors that would prevent you from doing x: you've got what it takes to do x, but something stands in your way, blocks your path—interferes, in short. The word of Sam's wife or his doctor are examples in the case of our particular hero (they wouldn't be in some others); the presence of another team on the available playing space would be another, as would someone's tying Sam to a tree, or a lightning bolt's suddenly obliterating the poor fellow.

The presence of various conditions would *enable* Sam to play ball if he so wished—physical factors, such as appropriate muscular structures in good working condition, and psychological, such as possession of the relevant skills, a bit of courage, and so on. If Sam lacks some of these—a team to play with, for instance—then he doesn't play; he needs more resources than he currently has. On the other hand, he might have everything it takes, and yet some further condition arises that prevents him from getting the intended activity going: another team has taken the only available space, or a city ordinance is passed prohibiting its utilization, or a fleet of germs moves in and lays Sam low. In all these cases, of course, the preventing factor renders inoperable or unavailable one or another of the positive conditions. Eliminating the alien factor restores freedom, by restoring a necessary condition for performance. This is the sort of thing that makes it difficult to maintain a sharp distinction between positive and negative freedom in general.

Lack of Desire: A Constraint?

Consider the case where you simply don't *want* to do x. Should this be said to exemplify unfreedom? Not ordinarily, it seems to me: freedom is the condition of being able to do x *if* you want to. Philosophers through the ages have worried about free will and determinism, as though the sheer fact of being subject to general causal laws is ipso facto a constraint on freedom. But the idea that there is a general incompatibility here is surely nonsense. The very idea of my will's "effecting" anything in the external world would seem to involve the idea of causality, which I take it is likewise the idea of general natural laws' connecting types of happenings with other types of happenings.

When should we say that lack of a certain sort of desire is a case of unfreedom? Answer: when you desire to have that sort of desire and can't bring it about that you have it. That we aren't *able* to bring such a thing off, at least in the very short term, is utterly unsurprising. But let us confine ourselves to the logic of the matter. Why do we ever "want to desire" something?[1] Here's a case: you are at a friend's house for dinner, he prides himself on his cooking, and, alas, you find yourself rather averse to what is offered. You would prefer to like it, for you like the friend and want to please him: you desire to desire the products of his culinary labors, but you simply don't—they just don't appeal to you. The desire for a desire in this situation makes sense: we can see how if we desired a certain thing, that would come in very handy for the smooth running of our lives in some respect. It is only because we desire that life situation that it makes sense to say that absence of the more specific desire is an *impediment to freedom*. But this sort of thing must have a stopper somewhere. If I desire x in order to get y, this implies that I desire y; but why do I desire y? Possibly because I desire z. As Aristotle long ago observed,[2] we must come eventually to some desire that you do not have only because its object satisfies some still further desire. Now consider these ultimate desires, which are not desires that we have because we desire something else, but simply desires arising from the way we are—genetic, as may be. *Can* we desire to have desires other than those? Perhaps in some sense we can, though it is unclear what would this mean. But in any case, how could the presence of that fundamental character be conceived as an *impediment* to the actions of the *very person whose character it is?* The "I" who is impeded must *want* something, and if the want is identical with that agent—if wanting that object is an inseparable part of being that agent—then to say that that agent is *unfree* just by virtue of being so constituted is to talk nonsense. The mouse is not unfree because she is not a rooster or a logician or, for that matter, a mountain or a toaster. (Am I "unfree" to toast because I am not a toaster?) Mouse that she is, a cat may well limit her freedom, but not her mousehood.

Can we want to be somebody else? We would have to make a distinction here. When Selma says, "I want to be Woodrow Wilson", does she mean that she wants to continue to be Selma, only with all the outward properties of Wilson? Or does she literally mean that she wants to be that very particular person Wilson is (was), body and soul? In the latter case, however, we have a totally meaningless and empty desire, and not only because Woodrow Wilson has been dead for many a decade. For if Selma ≠ Wilson, then the claim that Selma = Wilson would be, as near as these things can be, logically false. The terms 'Selma' and 'Woodrow Wilson' are proper names whose sense, insofar as we can speak of 'sense' here, lies in their designation of the particular objects in the world to which they are attached. So long as the terms bear that sense (there could be other persons named 'Selma'), then it is a semantical truth, a truth arising from the use of these terms, that Selma ≠ Woodrow Wilson. Thus Selma's "desire" to be Wilson is one that it is logically impossible to fulfill. So if Selma's desire to "be" Wilson is of the former sort—she wants to be a Selma-sheep in Woodrow Wilson–wolf's clothing—then getting what she wants is merely impossible, depending on how thorough a job she wants to make of it (bringing it about that she is born in 1856 and dies in 1924, for instance, is out of the question), but not logically so. However, the impossibility of doing the sort of job Selma presumably wants is enough to make it highly inadvisable for her to try. The asylums are full of those who suppose they have succeeded at this kind of thing. They are right to think that they are not "free" to be Napoleon or whoever. But this is not because there is some impediment to *their* freedom, blocking their way in that direction.

Lack of Reason: Another Constraint?

We are exploring, at the outset, the coherence of libertarianism: can we get off the ground with a theory that the sole basic human right is a general right to liberty? Plainly, one of the major requirements here is noncircularity. We don't, for example, get off the ground if we proclaim such a right, only to turn around to define liberty as "what you have a right to" or some such thing. But how many "such things" will count toward circularity? One question to consider here is whether we must eschew every and any normative or evaluative concept in our definition of 'liberty'. The idea that we can expunge every such element from our analysis is termed 'restrictivism' in a recent treatment by the very able writer John Gray. Restrictivists, he says, have in common a "rejection of the claim that freedom is what has been called an *essentially contestable concept.*"[3] Is this something we wish to deny? Perhaps not. I have, indeed, been proceeding rather as though the concept of liberty was purely descriptive, in some extremely narrow sense of 'descriptive', such as what Gray is trying to express in this passage. But it is time to repudiate this intention. In particular, for instance, it will certainly be extremely difficult to disassociate the notion of liberty entirely from that of rational action. And as we know, we run a risk of opening the Pandora's box of holism, idealism, and eventually every brand of authoritarian or totalitarian ideology if we press very hard on this notion. Fortunately, it is not necessary to go that far. We can keep the lid on Pandora's box by confining our attention to the vestibule, as it were. Here lies not the notion of a richly "rational" self according to some philosopher's special conception thereof, but only of an agent whose actions are at all intelligible, so that we have at any rate *some* idea that she is indeed doing something.

On this difficult and vexed question, we must agree, in the end, with John Gray, who insists that "there is something at least problematic about counting as a freedom an opportunity to act which no reasonable man would ever take. Are we not approaching a conflation of acting freely with acting reasonably?" But Gray goes on to answer this question: "Repudiating any view of freedom as the non-restriction of options which incorporates such a rationalist picture of practical deliberation . . . is not the same as denying the relevance to questions of social freedom of any of the requirements of rational choice. Further, I suggest that the conception of rational choice that is appropriate there is a minimalist and meagre one, stipulating only that an agent *have a reason* for what he does. What such a requirement disqualifies as rational conduct is only the behaviour of a delirious agent, where no goal or end may be imputed to him which renders intelligible what he does. My claims are, first, that we need to invoke this difficult notion since no viable conception of social freedom can altogether dispense with it."[4]

For purposes of this book, I believe, it will not be necessary to inquire too minutely into this matter. In Part Three more will be said about rational choice, which will also offer some further insight into the matter of the sort of liberty we ought to be concerned to defend.

Our Subject: Social Freedom

Some factors preventing the doing of what we wish are within the control of people, and some are not. Moral philosophy generally, and political philosophy in particular, being normative theories concerned with the direction of human action, are therefore concerned only with what is within our control. What is beyond our control may certainly affect our liberty—having terminal cancer will disenable you from doing a great deal that you want to do, most likely; but insofar as it is beyond our control, it is certainly not within the province of moral philosophy. Thus in the current state of the art—though possibly this may change in the not-too-distant future—our genetic makeup determines many of our properties. No amount of special diet and exercise will turn a short adult into a tall one, for instance (and what can be done on a rack isn't quite what the short person has in mind as an improvement in this respect). Is the short person, then, not *free* to do the things that great height enables one to do? Yes, if you like. But on the other hand, no one *made* him thus unfree. This particular kind of unfreedom is not something that any reorganization of society, any remarshaling of anyone's actions, can do anything about. The "freedom" to be as tall as you like is not one that anyone can provide anyone with. People can be arbitrarily penalized for being tall, or short, or whatever, of course, and the very unchangeableness of the quality for which they are thus penalized is a large part of what makes such penalties arbitrary. Our reactions to unchangeable conditions are, of course, within our control.

More generally, what is within our control are actions. The subject of freedom, then, for purposes of moral philosophy, is the subject of how we ought to act vis-à-vis freedom. The libertarian holds that freedom matters a great deal for moral and political purposes—that considerations of freedom are of first importance in determining what we ought to do. Others differ—or seem to. To adjudicate these differences requires precision in identifying their subject. The difference made by observing this obvious point, that our subject is freedom insofar as affectable by our actions, may be considerable.

At this stage it may be well to add that actions affecting freedom may do so directly or indirectly, obviously or subtly, and individually or only in concert with others, perhaps numerous others. We are not assuming that the ambit of liberty-restricting actions is confined to those whose effects are as obvious and immediate as armed robbery, rape, or murder. How significant the less direct ones may be remains to be seen, and will be considered in some detail in Part Two of this book.

A Note on Slavery

There is an exceptionally interesting and important long-standing problem in defining liberty in the relatively simple way we have, viz., as absence of constraints to what one wants (at least on consideration) to do. Thus John Gray, in discussing Berlin, remarks, "Since, on Berlin's original account, the degree of a man's freedom is the extent to which his desires are frustrated by the interferences of others, a man may always increase his freedom by trimming his desires. And this has the consequence that we are precluded from describing as

unfree the wholly contented slave . . . or, more generally, from la-
menting the lack of liberty in a perfectly engineered *brave new world* in
which desires and opportunities always coincide. . . . Only by invoking some norm of human nature which is discriminatory as to the
wants which are to be counted, and which includes evaluations of the
agent's states of mind, can the intuition that the wholly contented
slave remains unfree be supported."[5]

But is this so? Without entirely denying the reasonableness of the
complaint, we can raise two questions at least. First, there is the matter of how the slave came to be such in the first place. Second, what
about the particular means by which his condition is reinforced? Regarding the first: it will certainly be true that at some time in the past,
at least the progenitors of our slave, if he was born into the condition,
were enslaved by a process clearly contrary to their desires at the
time. This does count for something, surely. And about the second, it
seems scarcely possible that a person could come to look forward to
being beaten whenever she deviated in the slightest from some imposed routine, or for that matter that she would never have any desire so to deviate. What we know of American slavery certainly confirms that those enslaved were intensely aware of their condition and
strongly desirous of getting out of it, at least in many of its more
onerous aspects. I think we should allow that in logically and perhaps
even really possible cases, what we term 'slavery' would not in fact be
in violation of the wishes of the agent; but this possibility is insufficient to resuscitate any argument for the legitimacy of it as an institution even on this simple notion of freedom.

We must also ask what a "norm of human nature" is here. The fact
that we don't know anybody who would make a wholly contented
slave, and the various facts about people that make it extremely implausible to suppose that they are living as they wholly desire to
when in the condition we refer to under the name of slavery, seem to
me to constitute a strong case for the norm in question. It is a norm in
the sense of a statement about normalcy: people will not normally—
not ordinarily—be interested in such a condition. We count contrary
instances, if any, as pathological, to be sure. But that about them
which counts as pathological may well be the same as what makes us
count a masochist as pathological: they act contrary to their *own* desires, and not just to the desires of others or of theorists insisting that
they be other than they are. As components of the foundation of a
social rule to the effect that people are not to be enslaved, these considerations surely count heavily. The norm informs and counts to-

ward a belief that liberty is indeed violated in slavery in its paradig-
matic instances; any putative instance of slavery that somehow
managed to constitute a style of life wholly in accord with the de
facto, considered desires of the slave would be sufficiently surprising,
sufficiently far from the central features we intend by this idea, that it
would be unuseful to appeal to as an instance. To defend slavery qua
institution living up to those specifications is like defending the "separate but equal" idea of education struck down, and with reason, by
the American Supreme Court.

Is "Positive Liberty" Liberty?

At least at first sight, many other things are valued besides liberty:
food, for example, and in general the means to achieve what we aim
to achieve, including not only various specific means, material and
otherwise, but also, more generally, the inherent capability to do
those things. Yet, at second sight there is a temptation to marshal
these as well under the heading of liberty, by pointing out, for instance, that one who lacks food is unable to live and thus unable to do
(for long, anyway) what that individual wants to do. Philosophers
tend to contrast freedom and welfare; yet each particular contribution
to welfare may also be viewed as a contribution to the repertoire of
abilities of the person enjoying it, and thus to freedom. If someone
gives me a slice of apple pie, I am now free to eat apple pie in a way
that I was not before: at the minimum, trivially, I have the ability to
eat this pie now, even if in the absence of your giving me this piece on
this occasion I should have been able to have another, or even that
same one, a little later; or, still more trivially, your giving me this piece
of pie now gives me the "liberty" to eat a piece-of-pie-given-to-me-
now-by-you, which I couldn't otherwise do. (Not that that is always
trivial, actually—ask any loved one.) This way of thinking about it
will lead to the conclusion that any and every good is a part of or a
contribution to "liberty": given any good G, you are now at liberty to
lead a life which includes G.

If that seems wrongheaded, as it does, then we need either some
relevant restriction on the *range* of liberties that are in question, or
some refinement of the sense of 'liberty' we are concerned with. But it
is difficult to discern a difference, literally, in the *meaning* of 'liberty'
between the cases where your liberty is affected by lack of means on
the one hand or by the presence of inhibiting factors on the other; or
by natural causes on the one hand or human interference on the

other. Thus the former would seem to be the right option: we must limit the relevant range of liberties. The appropriate restriction is that whereas all sorts of things may interfere with or contribute to my liberty, our concern is social—in particular, with the structure of society. We are concerned with the cases where our liberty is affected by the actions of some other person or persons, and not with the case where some natural condition, for instance, does so. You are at liberty in the social sense when others do not, by their actions, prevent you from doing what you want. You are at liberty in this sense when nobody is interfering with your liberty.

Your liberty to do x, on the other hand, is not *interfered with* when someone else, even if that someone could do so if she chose, fails to provide you with something that would enable you to do x. Ms. A's refusal to play tennis with Mr. B does not interfere with B's liberty, though it may well keep him from getting what he wants. Her refusal is a nonproviding of a service that would enable B to do as he pleases if it were provided; but it is not the putting of an obstacle in his path, preventing him from doing what he otherwise could. If Ms. A did not exist at all, for example, her tennis partnership would likewise not be provided; but the particular service of Ms.-A-in-particular's playing tennis with Mr.-B-in-particular is one that could not be provided at all if she did not exist: the particular actions that B currently would like to perform, requiring as they do the participation of Ms. A, could not be performed at all if she didn't exist. It is therefore wrong to say that she "interferes with" his freedom by refusing to play tennis with B, however frustrating this may be for the latter. And so if we think that people have a duty not to interfere with people's freedom, it will follow that Ms. A does not violate this duty by refraining from playing tennis with Mr. B; or by refraining from whatever other activity requiring her participation she may choose to refrain from—consider the case where B wishes to marry A, as a particularly interesting case.

The point here may be summed up as follows.

(1) For a person, A, to "interfere with" the liberty of some other person, B, is for A to bring it about that B is unable to do what B would otherwise be able to do even without A's assistance. If A prevents B from playing chess with C, A is interfering with B's liberty; but if A prevents B from playing chess with A, namely, by refusing to play with him, then A is not interfering with B's liberty.

(2) For A to *promote* B's liberty is for A to bring it about that B can perform at will some action or actions that B would otherwise be unable to perform. A could do this, for instance, by preventing C from

interfering with B's efforts to do x. Or she could do it by giving him some necessary means to do x. She can even do it simply by agreeing to engage in activity x with B, as our examples illustrate.

Thus (3) *Not promoting the liberty of others does not constitute interfering with their liberty.* It may well constitute *not promoting their good:* life for B may well be worse, and even less free, for A's nonassistance, than it would be with A's assistance. Even so, A does not interfere with B's liberty by refusing it.

Interference with liberty, in short, requires positive action on the part of the interferer. The mere nondoing of what would, if done, promote your ability to do what you want is not sufficient. The "positive action" in question may be somewhere in the background: if on Tuesday I promise you that on Wednesday I will assist you in moving some furniture and then fail to show up, my inaction on Wednesday is indeed part of a train of action on my part that does interfere with your liberty. But my nonappearance on Wednesday, in and of itself, is not what has thus interfered—no matter how much help it would have been if I had shown up, and even if otherwise you would have been unable to move your furniture at all.

It would perhaps be better if we had another word for what I have thus far been referring to as 'positive liberty'. Perhaps 'power' would do: you have the positive liberty to do x if you have the power to do x. This usage, which follows that of Isaiah Berlin in his classic discussion of this subject,[6] has the merit of indicating in a compendious way the area in which the ideas collected by the term 'positive liberty' lie. But it can be misleading in that we are apt to use the term "power" also in its narrower sense in which it refers to the capability on the part of one person to make others do what they don't want to do.

CHAPTER 4

Two Conceptions of Liberty as a Social Concern

The Two Ideas

W E ARE THUS BROUGHT to the point where before us loom two very different ways in which we might understand the idea that the only proper concern of political institutions is human liberty.

(1) On the one hand, we might take "Positive Liberty" as our object: society should, for instance, *maximize* liberty, or perhaps do so subject to a constraint that we distribute it in some way or other (equally, for instance). Our maxim would be: Let us do whatever we can to bring it about that people have as much liberty as possible.

(2) Alternatively, the idea might be: let us insist that people *interfere* with each other's liberty as *little* as possible.

Why aren't these the same? Why isn't maximizing liberty the same thing as minimizing nonliberty? Of course they can be defined that way; it's a matter of clarifying our terms here—which we can do only when we have clarified our ideas, of course. However, 'minimizing interference with liberty' is not quite what (2) says. Insisting that people refrain from such interference is not the same as insisting that they do what they can to bring it about that as little interference with liberty as possible comes about.[1] By "maximizing liberty", what (2) means is *having everyone do whatever would bring it about that everyone was able to do, as nearly as possible, whatever that person wants to do,* and of course doing his part to minimize noninterferences would be part of that goal.

32

What would be involved in maximizing liberty, especially if we count the provision of means to doing what one wants as promoting it? Here are some examples. Is Jones sick? Can you make him well by doing something for him? Very well: then that is what you ought to do, since it thereby enables Jones to do a great deal that he otherwise will not be able to do. Does Smith lack eyesight, which you can rectify by giving him one of your good eyes? Very well: then you are to supply him with that eye (to take an apt example of Nozick's).[2] And so on.

Naturally there would, on this view of the matter, be the question of *how much* you have to give up in order to supply people with these things. The terminology of 'maximizing' suggests a utilitarian formulation. If we maximize some variable F over some group G, then whatever produces the greatest net increment of F is what we are to do. Take 'F' to be 'Liberty'. Then if giving Smith my right eye increases what he can do more than it decreases what I can do, and does so more than any alternative possible distribution of eyes, then out it goes! This is standardly objected to as violating individuals' rights, and the objection is pressed nowhere more strongly than in libertarian circles. The trouble with the enthusiast for "positive liberty" is that to bring about the no doubt excellent goals he profess, he is willing to violate negative liberty. But as we have seen, 'positive liberty' might as well be replaced with 'welfare' or some such term. If we think people's liberty important, we should think it important enough not to violate it for the sake of promoting any such goal, even if it be called 'liberty'.

What Constitutes Interference?

This brings us to the question of what constitutes interference with a course of action. This matter is rendered especially difficult because most assessments of interference are made against a background of already established property rights. Thus, A parks his 10-ton truck in B's driveway, making it impossible for B to get her car out of her garage (efficiently, anyway). This would count as a clear example of interference, but clearly it matters whose driveway A does this in, and why. Even so, perhaps we could say that A has interfered with B in that case, without making a judgment of the rights and wrongs of the matter. Other simple and clear cases: A locks B securely in a room, depriving B of the freedom to move more than about 6 feet in a straight line; A shoots B, making it impossible for B to do anything. But let us admit also that many, and perhaps even most, cases are not so simple and clear. For example, suppose I call you bad names if you do x. This might inhibit your doing x, even though it doesn't outrightly prevent you from doing it. Is it *interference*? It is an outright interference, an intervention, in your psychoacoustic space; but its interference with your actions is a function of your psychology.[3] Which cases are appropriate to the liberty principle and which are matters of etiquette only will not be easy to say.

Next, suppose that someone charges you $5 for doing x. You can still do x, provided you pay the $5. Is this an interference? I think the answer is a short "Yes." Note that even though you can still do x, you cannot do x *simpliciter* any more: instead, you may do x *and* y only. Where y is something you wouldn't have done if you had your choice, we may certainly count the requirement that you do y if you do x as an interference with your freedom to do x.

We should also keep in mind that actions are not necessarily simple, all-at-once occurrences. Humans often act as parts of longer sequences, and what unites them are plans and intentions. We cannot omit this factor, but taking it into account in a fully satisfactory way is difficult. For example, you stand 50 feet down the pathway, but that is just where I wanted to go. You have interfered, perhaps unbeknownst to you, if in consequence I must change my plans. But where does this end? Do you interfere if I plan to take over the whole of North America, but your house is in the way? These discussions will affect our deliberations about appropriation in the State of Nature (Chapter 6).

Coercion

This takes us to the vexed question of coercion. In threatening to shoot you if you fail to do x, I am not making it impossible for you to do x, but merely making it extremely undesirable for you to do so. What if A threatens to show photographs of B in a compromising situation with C to B's enemy/spouse/boss/whatever? The pressure to define coercion in terms of threats to do what one has no *right* to do is great; but if we want to claim that one's fundamental right is a right of liberty, that route is apparently unavailable, or at any rate will require some fine and fairly intricate hedging. I prefer to say that coercion is a matter of bringing it about that the coerced person's alternatives are considerably worse than in the status quo ante, and that some of the ways of making them worse will be interferences with his or her freedom if they are performed. Coercion is not necessarily un-justified. Neither, for that matter, is interference with freedom, once the appropriate structures of right are in place. We arrived at those structures by considerations of *basic* freedom, plus negotiations. Those will give us a sphere of rightful liberty, thus making it possible to talk about wrongful freedom, which can be legitimately interfered with.

Pressuring

Another major problem area here is that of "pressures"—related to but not quite identical with coercion. If the government puts a tax on activity x, is it interfering with freedom? It is making it more diffi-cult to do x—more trouble and more costly—but not making it im-possible. (Forbidding x by law also doesn't make x impossible, of course; that comes under the heading of coercion.) At some point a tax becomes confiscatory or prohibitive, and few would deny that it then constitutes a genuine infringement of freedom. But before that point, what do we say?

An important special case is that of moral pressure. Suppose I am a friend of yours and you know that I won't like it if you do x. This doesn't keep you from doing x at all, but it increases, as it were, the psychological price of doing it. Libertarians have a real problem here, for on the one hand they want to say that an individual has freedom of conscience (itself a vexed area); yet on the other, they can't easily say that we may blame anyone we please for just anything. If Jones has a perfect right to do x, can we *blame* Jones for doing x? If we do, are we not denying in some way or to some degree his freedom to do x? Moral blame and praise consists in psychological punishments or costs and rewards or payments. If I will praise and admire you for doing y and you value my good opinion, then the "psychic profit" of y for you is greater than if I were indifferent to it; if instead I condemn and despise you, then the "psychic cost" of y for you is greater than if I were indifferent. People can be oppressed by expressions of these attitudes. Aren't they in some degree less free to do what they do if such expressions are part of the cost of doing them?

Nor need this be "moral" pressure in any narrow sense. Suppose that Alfreda simply finds Burton unattractive; but it may be that her reporting this simple truth to him would make Burton's existence quite miserable. Yet we (practically all of us, libertarian or not) surely want to say that people must have the right to find others attractive or not, and on appropriate occasions to convey their judgments. But if such expressions interfere with liberty, then we can't easily say that they have such a right if we think everyone has a fundamental right to liberty.

It is urgent that we be able to manage this range of cases. A thought about how to handle it is, first, just to deny the "right of conscience" altogether. If Jones blames Smith for doing x, then what Jones does is wrong unless x is in fact blameworthy. He does *not* have the right to go around blaming people for just anything he likes. Our social behavior in this respect is subject to moral control, unlike our behavior in respect of judging the taste of lima beans.

Second: we should distinguish between being at liberty to do x, and being at liberty to do x without a certain range of consequences of x being imposed by others. Isn't Gilroy free to dislike me, even though I have done no wrong, either to Gilroy or anyone else? Suppose he dislikes me for doing certain things. Must I not then expect to encounter his dislike when doing those things? Clearly, we need to distinguish between those manifestations of his dislike that would actually impede me in the course of my pursuing activity x and those that would not, even though they otherwise make my life less desirable than it might otherwise be. Richard Taylor proposes that we must simply eliminate attitudes from the scope of these principles.[4] Whether this is workable is one question—can we prise attitudes entirely off from the doing of the things we wish to do? But even if it will, there is reason, as will be argued later in this book, to keep the expression of moral and political attitudes within the scope of the principle. We ought not to express condemnation of those who are doing nothing wrong, nor praise and admiration for those who are. If x is morally permissible, then those who do x are entitled to freedom from expressions of moral attitude to the contrary. But obviously, those who make such expressions are normally convinced that their view of what is right is the right view; in their view, therefore, they *are* entitled to engage in such expressions, while those whose behavior they condemn are the ones who should not be entitled to the freedom to do the thing in question.

All of this requires that we tread a delicate line. Consider as a case in point the current abortion controversy. Every weekend, for instance, a group of right-to-life protestors with picket signs walk back and forth on the public sidewalks by a hospital where abortions are carried on. Obviously, they think that the practice of abortion is morally intolerable. What do we who think it is acceptable do by way of permitting expressions of protest? How much use of public facilities such as sidewalks is to be permitted in protests that one thinks unreasonable? Such difficult issues will concern us further later in this book (Part Three).

Interference versus Nonassistance

Though sorting out just what constitutes interference is no easy matter, there is one tempting theoretical assimilation in this area that we should firmly resist. I have proposed to define social liberty in terms of noninterference by others. That noninterference may indeed do you no good, in many cases. If you lack the physical constitution to run the mile in four minutes, then the fact that nobody will stop you from doing so if you try is not of much interest. If you lack food and starve to death, the fact that no *person* prevented you from eating is small consolation. Yet if they indeed haven't, then libertarians will say that you have no complaint against your fellow people—not on the score of liberty, at any rate.

But many social philosophers would insist that you do have a complaint. Whether you do is, of course, one thing; but they also insist that you have this complaint on the score of *liberty*, as libertarians deny. Whether this is a legitimate complaint at all is important, and to examine sympathetically the libertarian view about this— that it is not—is a main object of this essay. We will go into that later. But whether this complaint comes properly under the heading of interference with liberty is a question to consider here and now.

Suppose that even though no one prevented you from eating, no one helped you out either, when they perfectly well could have. Some philosophers, in fact, will insist that these are equivalent cases: that it *was* an interference with your liberty that others didn't feed you when they could. The absence of food prevented you from doing what you wanted to do (stay alive, say), and this absence was due to the nonsupplying of food by others. This nonsupplying is an action on their part, an action that interferes with your liberty—so they will say. Why not go along with them in talking like that?

Let's go back to Sam, our would-be football player. He is prevented from playing by his arthritis, let us suppose. A doctor might be able to "liberate" Sam from his arthritis. Suppose that Dr. X could do this but has not currently done so. Should we say, in the meanwhile, that *she* is *preventing* Sam from playing ball? We should not, and normally would not. By contrast, take the case where Sam could indeed go out onto the field and give it a try, but Dr. X orders him to refrain, on the ground that it would worsen his condition. That would constitute a case like (2): Sam's doctor won't *let* him play ball. In that case his social negative liberty is, to some extent, abridged by his doctor; her orders constitute an externally preventing condition for his football-playing propensities.

Why should we say that Dr. X has not interfered with his freedom when she doesn't cure his arthritis, though she could, or that you have not murdered anyone in Ethiopia when you refrained from sending food to them? One reason is that this refraining is *not* an action, but a nonaction. If we are to say that a nonaction is nevertheless an action, then such "actions" are being "performed" all the time and everywhere by everyone who is not currently doing the particular thing that would, in the present case, relieve your starvation. When one considers all the things I conceivably could be doing right now, and proposes to account each of them an "action", then I am one exceedingly busy person just now, as are we all—and equally so, too, since the membership of this set is no doubt infinite. But we should not say that Jones, who is currently fast asleep, is infinitely busy doing all of those nonactions he is currently nondoing.

Agreed, there is a difference between the cases where we do nothing because we do not realize that there is anything we could be doing and those where we face the question whether to do it and deliberately decline. Real-life cases of the type intended to be exemplified by Dr. X are complicated by the fact that doctors in general have often assumed obligations to render medical assistance where needed. If Dr. X simply refuses to fix Sam's arthritis when she could, and refuses to do so just because she doesn't happen to feel like it, that might be in violation of her official duties as a doctor. We would have to assume that no such undertaking has been made on her part in order to make the point. But we can easily imagine a medical system in which that undertaking has not been made. If not, then her case would illustrate the point: in not operating on Sam, she is not causing his arithritis, not bringing it about that Sam has arthritis. She is only refraining from curing it—a very different matter. Similarly, if you fail to feed the starving peasant in Ethiopia, even though you had the opportunity and knew that you could help, it is still true that you did not murder that unfortunate individual, for you did not kill him.

Another, though related, reason for resisting the assimilation of nonhelping to harming is that it leaves us with no contrast at all between such things as liberty and welfare. To speak this way is to assimilate the many different reasons why a given person, A, at a given time, *t*, is failing to do x or to be in condition C, leaving us with no distinction between the case where A isn't doing x because B tied A to a tree, the case where A simply wasn't able to do x no matter how he tried because A's physical or mental equipment wasn't such as to enable A to do x, and the case where no one supplied A with the equipment necessary for A to do x. But these *are* different.

Most fundamentally of all, however, is that we shouldn't speak this way because to speak this way is to eliminate the most important consideration of all: viz., that to insist that there is no difference between B's actually preventing A from doing x and B's merely not doing what might have enabled A to do x is to trample *B's* freedom into the dust. In actively preventing A from doing x, B is interfering with A's liberty. But in insisting that if B *can* help A, then B *must* help A, we are saying that we may interfere with B's liberty in the matter—that B's liberty doesn't count or doesn't matter. The libertarian wants to say that it *does* matter, and in saying this is certainly picking out a distinguishable aspect of the social scene, asking us to put a certain weight on that aspect rather than ignoring it or putting a wholly different one on it. It's one thing to disagree with her in this; it's quite another to do so by redefining the language in such a way as to refuse to allow that position to be formulated in the first place.

Still, the distinction between doings and nondoings may seem to be getting more weight than it merits here. Can we not cause important effects by our inactions as well as by our actions? If A doesn't water the plants, they will die; if B doesn't leap in to rescue this drowning boy, he will die; if the nurse doesn't give Diana her daily injection, she will go into a coma; and so on. In all of these cases, however, there is an antecedently initiated causal process that will lead to the results in question unless the person in question, or someone else, intervenes. The nonsupplying of Diana with her injection only "causes" her coma in the sense that the advancing condition—diabetes, say—which actually brings about that coma will not be arrested unless the nurse acts. Obviously such interventions can be important, even crucial. It remains that the agent's inaction is not what literally causes the unfortunate outcome. When we nevertheless ascribe responsibility to the inactions of such persons, it will be on the basis of a background expectation that they are to do that thing. And sometimes, the situation is that other people are quite reasonably depending on that crucially situated agent to make the intervention in question. That might be what they are being paid to do, what they

have agreed to do, or what is called for by a role they have intentionally assumed and given other people to believe that they have
committed themselves to acting on. In such cases, the ascription of
responsibility is apt, and blame for nonperformance is warranted. But
the basis of this ascription and this blame is not to be found in the
implausible claim that their inactions cause the results in question; it
is that there is a clear moral case for insisting on their performing the
needed actions. This moral case, however, does not necessarily rest
on a general obligation to bring about good consequences (it doesn't
rest on that in any of the above, notice) any more than it rests on a
faulty causal analysis. Rather, it may rest on commitments voluntarily
undertaken by the agent in question. It may, of course, rest on duties
not so undertaken that nevertheless aren't based on a general duty to
do good or anything of the sort. Many options are theoretically enter-
tainable here (as well as practically instantiated in various societies);
the argument of the libertarian is that the others should be rejected in
favor of this preferred model. But the claim that there literally is no
distinction between causing harm and failing to cause good, if used as
an argument on behalf of one of the other views, is one we should
reject.

CHAPTER 5

Rights

Rights Defined

WHAT IS IT for someone to have a right? This has been regarded as a large question, and in a way, it is. If we confuse this with the question of what our fundamental rights are and why we have them, then it is a very large question indeed, and one to which this book is largely devoted. At this point, however, I am addressing only the question of how we are to understand what it is that someone who claims a right is claiming to have, whether she be justified or no in her claim. This is, in other words, the question of meaning—of how we are to *use* the term 'right' in such expressions as 'A has a right to so-and-so'. If two people disagree about whether someone has a certain right, what are they disagreeing about? That is our question here.

There has now come to be considerable agreement in usage among thinkers on this subject on one major point. This is that there is a *logical* connection between statements about *rights* and statements about *right* (and wrong) or *duties:* the statment 'A has the right to do x' entails a statement about right and wrong action. The catch is that this entailed statement is not a statement about *A's* action being right or wrong. It is, rather, a statement about the actions of some or all *other* people. These people are not always the same, however. If Jones has promised me $5, then Jones has the duty to pay me $5, but nobody else does. On the other hand, everyone has the duty to refrain from killing me, so long as I am innocent of any capital crime. Thus we need a place, or variable, in our definition, to be filled out in particular cases with the names of those whose actions are affected in moral

status by the right being asserted if what is asserted is true. These are
the people whom the right is a right "against". We will designate
these people by the letter 'B', understanding that B could be either
one person or more, ranging up to everybody:

'A has a right' entails 'A has a right *against* B'.

When A has a right against B, what are we saying about B? Specifically, that some possible actions of B's are required, or alternatively
are not to be done, that is, that B has a *duty* to do or not to do certain
things. We will in general take the statement that B has this duty to
refrain from those actions to be equivalent to the claim that they are
wrong, and the statement that B has the duty to do them as equivalent
to the claim that it would be wrong for B *not* to do them. These actions
of B's are, of course, different from the actions of A that the claim
about rights we are defining says A has a right to do. We'll call B's
actions 'y'. Thus we have:

'A has a right against B to do x' entails 'B has the duty to do y'.

This is known as the "correlativity" of rights and duties: claims
about rights entail claims about duties. We should note, however,
that there is a stronger and a weaker version of the thesis. According
to the stronger one, A has a right against B if *and only if* B has a duty
with respect to A. The weaker view has it only that if A has a right,
then B has a duty; it does not claim in addition that every duty we
have is a duty grounded in someone else's right. We shall discuss this
further below, but for the moment we are insisting only on the weaker version.

The next question is: just which claims about duties of B are entailed by statements about A's rights against B? Where A's right is a
right to do something, one answer is clear enough: B may not *prevent*
or, in ways that may have to be further specified, *interfere* with A's
doing of x. In short, whatever else y may be in the above formula, it
will at least include the nondoing of whatever would prevent A from
doing what A has the right to do. Thus:

'A has the right to do x' entails 'B has the duty to refrain from
preventing A from doing x'.

Instead of the somewhat cumbersome 'refrain from preventing
from doing x', we could say, more briefly, that B has the duty to *let* A
do x. It is important to appreciate, however, that "letting" is not the
name of an action itself. There is no such action as allowing, permit-

ting, or letting someone do something. Rather, to allow, permit, or let is simply to refrain (or to announce a definite decision or intention that one is going to refrain) from doing what would prevent, preclude, or make impossible the doing of the thing in question; or in cases where there was some previous obstacle to A's doing what one had the power to undo, then 'let' could be used to designate the act of undoing that, as when a legislature repeals a law against x.

As we have seen above, there is a difficult and important question about preventing and interfering vis-à-vis liberty. Just how much and what sort of interference with x infringes A's right to do it? Ideally, we would have a perfectly neat, crisp statement of precisely what B must or must not do if B is to respect A's right. But we rarely do have this neat statement. We normally have in mind a range of possible interfering actions, running all the way from those that add a mere jot of friction to A's doing x to those that straightforwardly render it impossible for A to do it. We have adverted to this matter above, briefly, and will return to it again (less briefly). Here we shall simply say that although we can also specify the particular range of interferences specifically understood to be proscribed by adding these to the content of the particular right being claimed, what is always understood is that actions by B rendering it impossible for A to do x are ruled out thereby.

This last point is sufficiently important to add a discussion of one putative counterexample widely employed, or rather, misemployed, in the literature. Consider competitive sports, such as chess or football. Do we not have the right to tackle the fellow with the ball, preventing him from making the goal he is striving mightily to achieve? Of course we do. But then, he does not have the right to *make* the goal. He could have that right: imagine a ruling by the umpire that the penalty for some kind of misdeed on the part of team B is that a representative of team A may walk across the goal line unopposed. *That* would be a right to make the goal. Normally, however, the teams have the right only to *try* to make the goal, viz., by any number of maneuvers permitted by the rules of the game. And that right does entail, as our formula says it does, the duty to refrain from rendering impossible or preventing. Thus if some members of team B poison the opposing quarterback by shooting a secret dart at him during the huddle, *that* would violate the quarterback's rights. Or if they build a brick wall across the goal line. And so on. In general, our right is to play the game; it is not a right to win, but only a right to do our best, within the rules, to win. We do often speak loosely in such contexts, for the distinction just made is one that usually doesn't need mentioning. But things that don't often need mentioning do need mentioning in philosophical contexts—not because philosophers are dummies, but because they have an inordinate, and wholly legitimate, interest in being clear. And the obvious can nevertheless be overlooked, to our conceptual peril.

Rights and Duties: Definition or Mere Correlation?

Should we think that the term 'right' in 'having a right' has been *defined* above? Or is it only a truth *about* rights that if you have one, then somebody else has a duty? This has been thought to be a vexed question, but I think there is a simple solution: we may define rights as follows:

> 'A has the right to x' = 'there is some property, F, true of individual A, such that the fact that A is F affords prima facie sufficient moral reason why B ought to do y in relation to A (at a minimum, to refrain from outrightly preventing A from doing x)'.

We certainly do want to say all the things specified in this proposed definition. (1) There certainly must be some *reason* why A is to be thought to have this right; (2) the reason can consist only in some or other fact about A; and (3) whatever else, the duty devolving on B from this right has to be the duty not to prevent A from doing x.

The philosophical "action" here will have to come in providing a satisfactory theory about the connection between F and the related duties for B, which is to say, a satisfactory theory about the reasons for requiring people to do the things they are required to do by virtue of whatever true assertions there are about rights. This book takes a shot at such a theory in Part Two.

Rights without Duties? So-called "Liberty Rights"

There is a tradition, going back at least to Hobbes, of using the term "right" to designate actions that we have no obligation to refrain from doing, with no further normative significance implied. No correlative duty on anyone else is supposed to be involved. This is certainly a different *use* of the term 'right' from the one we are employing here. In this book, 'right' is always a normative term, and its normativity consists precisely in the fact that it *does* entail a duty or obligation on someone to do or refrain from something. Hobbes's usage leads to great confusion. For example, his idea that there is a "right of nature" that is, in effect, the right to do anything one pleases is puzzling, since a condition in which absolutely anybody may do absolutely anything is simply a condition in which nobody has any rights at all. What is supposed to be the significance of describing this situation of total moral as well as political anarchy in terms of "rights," one wonders?

There is something of an answer to this, however. If we ask what the correlative obligation on others may be of a right to do anything, the answer is perhaps this: that others may not, or at any rate it would be rationally unjustifiable for them to, *criticize*. If all actions are permissible, then none are criticizable. But notice how this immediately implies that the action of criticizing is not permissible, in some sense, which already means that "everything is permissible" is contradicted.

Then consider Hobbes's fundamental doctrine about the origin of justice. We come to have duties of justice by virtue of what he calls the "transferring of rights". But unfortunately, as M. T. Dalgarno has pointed out,[1] the sort of "right" Hobbes is talking about here isn't actually transferred, for it is this so-called liberty-right, the right consisting in the lack of obligation to do anything, and you don't transfer this, because the person to whom you transfer it doesn't end up with something that you had before and he didn't. Since everybody has this so-called "right" to do everything, the other person always already has it. What you in fact do is to assume an obligation by *laying down* this antecedent liberty. Naturally if I "give up" a nonobligation, I end up with an obligation. But plainly this is just double-talk for assuming an obligation.

Duties without Rights? Rights, Duties, and Justice

In defining these notions as they apply to rights, I have invoked the concept of *correlativity*. There may still be some occasion for misunderstanding about this, so it will be well to explain further the sense in which I understand such correlations to obtain. The connection between a right and a duty is not incidental but essential. To have a right to someone else's action or inaction is for that person to have a duty to act or refrain (unless the right holder waives his claim): my right to your doing x is your duty to do x, unless I permit you to do otherwise. Rights are not peculiar, esoteric facts that we may merely note and pass on (that is one of the troubles with the theory that there are "natural" rights). Rights reach out and grab us. For you to recognize that I have a right over you *is* for you to acknowledge that you have a duty of the relevant kind. Rights, as we have seen, are always rights "against" some class of persons, persons who are grabbed by them, viz., by thus having the relevant duties. To say that A has a right to do x is to say that B, a member of that class, has a duty, for example, to refrain from interference with A's doing of x; or to do something to enable or help A to do X if A can't do x unaided (this distinction to be discussed below).

More fully, to say that A has a right is to say that there is some fact about A that is such as to constitute a reason for charging B with the duties in question. It is perhaps this feature that makes some people talk as though rights are "peculiar facts". But the facts in question aren't, or anyway needn't be, peculiar. We do need a theory about the relation between those facts and those duties, a theory explaining why those facts constitute or give rise to a good reason for those assignments of duties—and in too many cases the proposed theory is indeed, "peculiar." But what we want, and what I hope to supply later, is a nonpeculiar, common-sense theory with real bite.

Meanwhile, we must recognize the fact that the correlation does not work in the other direction. For one thing, we can clearly have duties toward A that are not due to rights of A. Still, such duties might be due to the rights of some other person, C, whose right is such that we discharge our duty to C by doing something for A, as when I promise to take care of your child if *p* obtains, and then it turns out that *p* does obtain. One might, however, argue that in such cases, the recipient A gets a sort of right nevertheless—an "indirect" right. The question then is whether there are duties toward A that are not due to anyone's rights to anything. Many people think that we have a duty to relieve starvation, for instance, even though neither the starving nor anyone else has the right that we help feed those people. If we accept some such thing, then we need an explanation of the difference between the sort of duties that are and those that are not engendered by rights.

Two suggestions about this are worth considering. One is *enforceability.* Duties that are owed to someone or other on account of someone or other's rights are enforceable, whereas duties not thus grounded are not, but must instead be left to individual choice and discretion. The other is that when rights are in question, our duties are to *specific* persons, whereas when they are not, they are owed not to particular persons but to indefinite classes of persons, or "to oneself," or perhaps not "to" anyone at all.

Duties to No One in Particular?

Let's begin with the last point. Suppose I think that as a matter of justice I have the duty to feed the hungry. What, then, is the relation of this duty of mine to that particular individual over there, who is hungry? It seems to me I cannot claim that there is none whatever, on the ground that my duty is only to the starving "in general" but not to any starving person in particular. Surely, if I have a duty to feed the starving in general, then I have the duty to feed each particular starveling *if* such things as my resources and opportunity permit. In the case where the starveling is right over there, sitting on that bench fifteen feet away, and (1) I know her to be such, (2) I have, let us say, a sandwich in my briefcase, and (3) I can easily replace it without appreciable inconvenience or discomfort, then I am not acting consistently with my sense of duty if I just walk right by: I owe *that person*, here and now, this sandwich.

What is true, in other words, is that in order to get specific duties to specific persons out of this general duty, owed to an indefinite class of persons, we need more information and some clarification. We need, for one thing, information about the circumstances of particular cases. But we also need clarification of just what duty we supposedly have here. For instance, we would need a fairly precise understanding of just how *strong* this duty is: how much is "my share" in carrying out this duty, which includes such things as how much of my resources I must assign to this cause; and this in turn will translate in part into the amount of inconvenience I must be willing to endure or how much trouble I must go to in order to supply the share in question. This is something we rarely have at a high level of precision, of course; and thus the sense that we "owe it to an indefinite class of persons but to no one of them in particular" can be understood in that way. It can hardly, however, be understood in such a way that no duty to any particular person can ever issue from it; that would negate the sense that it was a duty altogether.

Let us see what right the starving might have, if any at all. Suppose there are n hungry persons eligible for your assistance. And suppose you can usefully assist a small fraction, such as $1/n$. True, no one of those hungry persons has a right to your entire supply of assistance, which by hypothesis is not nearly enough to go around. But the group of starving persons as a whole has such a right, according to the thesis we are considering. Now, groups are simply groups, and only individuals have rights and duties as such. When some group is said to have a right or duty, then, we need to know what this says about any particular member of that group. Why can't one who held this be understood to have the belief that each of those hungry persons had a claim, though rebuttable—a *prima facie* right to his assistance? (As we will call it below, pages 50–53.)

So our question becomes this: which of those who believe they have this duty also believe that that duty is grounded on a right of the recipients, and which do not?

Enforceability

And this, it seems to me, may reasonably be explicated in terms of enforceability after all. For me to believe that the starving have the *right* to my assistance is for me to believe that it is okay for someone— "society", I shall be content to call it for the moment—to *force* me to pay up should I at the moment be disinclined to. Thus, such a person might believe that the government may appropriately tax me in order to feed the hungry in question—and do so simply on the ground that those people are in fact hungry and that our resources, including mine, are of such-and-such a level; whereas the person who doesn't believe that this is a matter of rights would not believe that people may be forced to do this, but instead that only voluntary contribution was appropriate.

John Stuart Mill suggested that enforceability is not the differentia we seek, on the ground that *all* duties are enforceable: "We do not call anything wrong, unless we mean to imply that a person ought to be punished in some way or other for doing it; if not by law, by the opinion of his fellow-creatures; if not by opinion, by the reproaches of his own conscience."[2] He went on to suggest that justice should be identified with the duties that are owed to individuals as a matter of their rights. One trouble with this is that the idea of a duty that is not a duty to anyone in particular is unclear or ambiguous, in ways we have just considered above. Another is that we would, if we use Mill's proposal, be back to explaining duties in terms of rights rather than vice versa. This is antithetical to the general line I am taking here and is to be rejected on grounds of obscurity. Still another is that the range of methods of enforcement appealed to is very broad. Let us see if we can sort out this last problem a bit further.

Enforcement and Force

Even the person who believes that he has an unenforceable duty leaving him freedom to choose, however, may be responding to one of the sorts of incentives to performance that Mill lists as a type of "enforcement": to wit, the "reproaches of his own conscience". Now, conscience is one's sense of right and wrong, and Mill purported to be defining the notion of wrongness in general, viz., as that which may be enforced. But if the particular type of enforcement we want can only be explicated in terms of conscience, then we would be going in a circle.

But if we consider carefully, we will find that it is unnecessary to so explicate it. One suggestion would be to identify the "reproaches of conscience" with certain phenomenologically identifiable unpleasant feelings—perhaps equivalent to the unique unanalyzable notions of the intuitionists. However, I think that we would lose the sense of these being *moral* reproaches if they were not also understood as being a part of the appropriate psychological makeup of any normal person, or at any rate, any normal member of the society whose morality is in question. One's internal adverse reaction to one's own poor performance is, in the case where it is properly termed "moral," one's personal contribution to what one thinks ought also to be the "opinion of one's fellows" and not just oneself.

What remains, however, is that we still have a distinction between those methods of enforcement that literally force or coerce, and those that do not. And we can identify the area of justice with that in which literally coercive methods are, at least ultimately, in order, and other areas of morality with those in which they are not.

But we cannot then simply "identify" the area of justice with that of individual rights as well. For this is no longer a matter of definition. If justice is that which may be enforced, then it is one *view* of justice that the only proper use of enforcement is on behalf of the rights of some or other individual(s). Libertarians certainly hold this view. For they hold that everyone's sole fundamental right is the right to liberty, and the use of force, at least prima facie, contravenes that right. To use force is to preclude voluntary action; to coerce is to impede the operation of individual choice by revising the options available to someone without that individual's consent.

Other social philosophies deny this, holding instead that people may properly be forced or coerced into doing various things for others' good, or in order to equalize the welfares or opportunities (or whatever) of various people, or for some cause having no particular connection with public welfare, or for a "general welfare" that has no connection with the well being of any particular persons as seen by those persons. Later we will take up the fundamental question of why we should choose the libertartian's theory of justice rather than some other; for the present, we are concerned only to try to identify that theory. It is in essence a theory about the use of force. Its claim is that the use of force for anything other than the securing of liberty is wrongful, but it does and must claim that the use of force for securing that is in principle justifiable.

A Paradox: My Freedom Is Your Unfreedom?

The connection of rights and duties with enforcement may seem to threaten the aspiring libertarian with a fundamental paradox. For to have a right is, according to the view I have proposed, ipso facto for the liberty of others to be limited, since for one person to have a right is for others to have a duty, and to have a duty is to be eligible for enforcement. But there is no paradox. One can fight fire with fire, and one can protect liberty by limiting liberty. We protect the liberty of any given person by restricing the liberty of everyone else. Protecting everyone's liberty, therefore, means limiting everyone's liberty; a universal right to unlimited liberty is nonsense, as in Hobbes's claim that in the "condition of mere Nature" "every man has a Right to every thing; even to one anothers body."[3] This, if it means anything, is equivalent, as argued above, to the claim that there are in such a condition no rights at all.

But the libertarian has his work cut out for him: he must show that these limitations on liberty are the ones essential to the interest in liberty. And this must take one or the other of two forms. Either he can argue that there is a net gain in liberty from the restrictions in question: that our liberty is *greater* on balance when we impose these restrictions than it would be in the unrestricted condition. Or he can argue that there is a fundamental sphere or area of liberty necessarily attached, so to speak, to each person, such that the proposed restrictions are not within this essential area but outside it. The first idea requires some kind of quantification of liberty so that we can say that one situation involved "more" liberty than another. The other seems to get us into a metaphysically problematic sort of essentialism. Producing a satisfactory theory about this matter is perhaps the greatest single theoretical challenge confronting the aspiring libertarian. Below (pages 73–78, 82–85), we will take up the challenge in the specific form of a claim that property rights restrict liberty.

Rights Prima Facie or Rights Absolute?

For at least fifty years there has been a familiar distinction in the philosophical industry pertinent to the present inquiry: the distinction between what is right "absolutely", or "tout court", or "sans phrase" (or simply, "right, period"), and what is right only "prima facie." The distinction may be carried over into talk of rights: a right of the first sort would be, simply, a right. To say that individual A has a right against B to do a particular act x at a particular time *t* in actual circumstances C is to say, simply—"no ifs, ands, or buts," as the saying goes—that B ought to allow A to do x at that time in those circumstances; whereas to say that A has a prima facie right to do x would be to say that B ought to do that (or whatever) *unless* some consideration "outweighs" or "overrides" the right in question. What are we to say about this?

First: if it is possible to specify some totally general right that is the sole fundamental right anyone has, then the claim that a person, in the circumstances in question, had *that* right would plainly be non-overridable or outweighable: there simply wouldn't be anything to outweigh it. Rights, it has been said, are "trumps,"[4] and if there is only one trump, then no card can stand against it. But life is not so simple. Even if there is only one basic *type* of right, how do we know that it is present in a particular case? Suppose this right is the right to do an action of type F. But now, the circumstances are such that one set of facts about the situation and the agent suggests that x exemplifies F; however, another set of facts suggests that a different action, y, exemplifies this property. So is A's right to do x, or to do y? Well, prima facie, it is to do x; but also prima (or perhaps secunda) facie, it's to do y. We may then have to look to see which set of facts under the circumstances makes for the stronger case on behalf of the action it points to being the one to which A has a right.

For example: do we suppose there is an absolute, nonoverridable right not to be pronounced guilty of some crime if one is in fact innocent of it?[5] One would like to think so. But suppose that if we don't make this false pronouncement, the poor woman will be subjected to yet worse treatment than if convicted? Is her right to nonconviction if innocent stronger than her right to the least noxious treatment deserved in the circumstances? Or what if the alternative to pronouncing her guilty is that a thousand other innocent persons will be pronounced guilty and subjected to far worse treatment as a result? Will our proposed absolute right stand against that? Or will we say that the case in question is totally hypothetical and impossible? Well, let us hope it is: no doubt there is a "possible world" in which it definitely is. But is our actual world that possible world? I wouldn't want to bet on it.

A distinction here may help. Consider a particular case, in the strict sense of 'particular': that is, one that is definitely located in space/time, and all of whose properties are, thus, in fact recorded in the stone of the universe, known by whatever gods there are (and all the pertinent ones known, we think, by us). If we now say that, all things taken together, this act was right, then our statement makes a claim to absoluteness: for we have said, remember, "all" things considered. How we could know that we have them all is an interesting question indeed—but we have made the claim, so we are now either right or wrong about it. As soon as one fact is uncovered that we didn't consider, and that fact is seen to support a different judgment, our claim will have been falsified. Whereas if we say, "well, insofar as the case is of type C, the act is right; but further investigation might reveal that it is also of type D, in which case that might overturn the claim that it is right", then we have made a claim that does not straightforwardly cash out into a judgment about the particular act and is not necessarily proven wrong by further findings.

The logical situation on this matter is as follows. If we think there is more than one single ultimate principle of duty, then it will be at least logically conceivable that there should be cases where they will come into conflict. We shouldn't lie, but we shouldn't assist a murderer: but what about the case where, if we tell anything but a lie, we inevitably assist a murderer?[6] On the other hand, if we suppose there is but one ultimate principle, then of course there will be nothing else to conflict with it. But on further thought, any such principle that has any plausibility at all will be so abstract that we will only be able to apply it to particular cases in the light of considerations that themselves point to opposite conclusions from this one principle. If you are a utilitarian, for instance, you will note some features of an act suggesting that it would maximize overall utility, but others suggesting that it would not. And if you are a libertarian, you will be hard pressed to avoid trying to "measure" interferences in some way or other, or even measuring amounts of liberty. An interesting case in point is provided by Hillel Steiner, who proposes an ingenious system that founders on the following obstacle: it requires being able to count actions. But how *many* actions have I forbidden if I forbid you to wave your hand? There being no end of specifically different motions in which the waving of a hand consists, we are unable to get off the ground with even so simple a case.[7]

There is no assurance that things will be simple. Life is not kind enough, in general, to await the final reckoning. We must act in the light of our best information so far as we can know at the time, and similarly must others. Any or all can be wrong. We can do only our best. But this is true both of the making of absolute judgments *and* of prima facie ones. Error about the former means error in our judgment about the case; error about the latter may not, but truth in the latter, on the other hand, may nevertheless not lead to a definite judgment about the case.

The libertarian would like to say that her preferred fundamental right to liberty outweighs all else: no incursion on liberty can be justified by anything—except where the alternative is a still greater incursion on liberty. Already we are back to ifs and buts! Still, it would be important if one could establish (1) that we can identify fairly clearly what constitutes an interference with liberty—not in the hopeless sense noted above, of trying to identify how much counts as precisely "one" such interference, but simply of whether a given act does or doesn't interfere with it; and (2) that nothing else could count more than the fact that some act was of that description. This could offer considerable guidance. It would mean, in particular, that a reduction of A's liberty could be justified only if what A was proposing to do would interfere with someone else's liberty. If we are driven to say that it would interfere *more* with someone else's liberty, we would be committed to making interpersonal comparisons of degrees or amounts of liberty. This would be unfortunate for the same reasons that it is unfortunate concerning utilitarianism. Ideally, we would avoid this by having the parties negotiate, their bargaining chips being definite rights to particular liberties. Provided we can isolate the subject of liberty from other considerations, we would then have a respectably usable theory on this matter. It is unlikely we can do better. It is, let us admit, also unlikely that we will be able to do that well!

"Side Constraints"

In view of the prominence accorded to it in many discussions and in the book itself, we should say something here about Robert Nozick's notion of "side constraints".[8] His *Anarchy, State, and Utopia* opens with the famous assertion that "persons have rights, and there are things no one may do to violate those rights." This curious passage, which can and surely should be taken to pronounce a truism (that rights oughtn't to be violated, a truism since that is the point of rights-talk), has also been taken to foreshadow the doctrine of "side constraints", further spelled out in such passages as these: "A specific side constraint upon action toward others expresses the fact that others may not be used in the specific ways the side constraint excludes. Side constraints express the inviolability of others, in the ways they specify. These modes of inviolability are expressed by the following injunction: 'Don't use people in specified ways' ".[9]

I take these passages to convey, in rather oracular fashion, at least two entirely distinct suggestions.

(1) On the one hand, there is what we may call the *anti-utilitarian* component: we can't justify doing x to person A *simply* for the purpose of promoting the (supposedly greater) good of person B.

(2) On the other hand, there is what I shall call the "rigorist" component. What this says, roughly, is that if doing x would deprive A of something to which A is entitled by right, then there are *absolutely* no circumstances in which it would be right to do x. Judith Jarvis Thomson points out that Nozick himself doesn't really believe this, since he wonders, for example, whether we couldn't maybe "inflict some slight discomfort" on someone to save "excruciating suffering" in 10,000 cows, leaving the reader with the impression that the answer is in the affirmative. ("The question of whether these side constraints are absolute, or whether they may be violated in order to avoid catastrophic moral horror, and if the latter, what the resulting structure might look like, is one I hope largely to avoid."[10]) It is hard to see how one could avoid that question, though; for we simply do not know what the view is until we have an answer to it. (Much the same may be said of Charles Fried's view as expounded in his *Right and Wrong*: "we can imagine extreme cases where killing an innocent person may save a whole nation. In such cases it seems fanatical to maintain the absoluteness of the judgment . . . even then it would be a *non sequitur* to argue (as consequentialists are fond of doing) that this proves judgments of right and wrong are always a a matter of degree. . . . I believe, on the contrary, that the concept of the catastrophic is a distinct concept."[11] And he, too, vaguely suggests that "the term absolute is really only suggestive of a more complex structure"[12]—without, however, shedding any light on the matter of just what the structure is.

Thomson uses the term 'stringency' to designate the variable, whatever it is, that would tell us how much weight a certain right has in a certain circumstance, the implication being that if it doesn't have very much, then some other moral consideration might outweigh it and permit what would otherwise be violation of a right. She refers to such justified doing of what someone has a right that it not be done, "infringing" as distinct from "violating". Then this interpretation of the doctrine of "side constraints" may be expressed by saying that all rights are "infinitely stringent". This doctrine she rightly takes to be preposterous, as do I.[13]

Both Nozick and Fried state their views in opposition, most especially, to utilitarianism and/or to "consequentialism". But the contrast between acts and consequences is one that will not bear very much theoretical weight[14]—certainly not enough to support doctrines that are literally "absolutist" in the sense of disallowing any appeals whatever to "consequences". If I raise my right arm, have I performed an act? Or have I brought about a consequence (my arm's being in a higher position that it was)? We don't know, and we shouldn't care. If I do something that violates your rights, what does it matter whether I do so by "performing an act" or instead by bringing about something which you have the right that I not bring about? What does matter is having the correct schedule of rights in the first place. It is *not* clear that we have the right not to be killed even when the lives of many others are doomed if we are spared; nor is it clear that we don't. It may well depend on further facts about the situation. What does seem absurd is to imagine that we could identify any sphere of action, the right to which is inviolable under any conceivable circumstances. But this is not because some form of utilitarianism is right after all. There is indeed a "more complex structure"—but not an arcane one, not one in which all matters of degree and all appeals to consequences are ruled out. No nonsuicidal moral theory can court such results.

At very least, then, it should be appreciated that these are two very different claims, the one of which simply does not imply the other. Just because the general form of rights, and their conceptual derivation, isn't utilitarian or, more generally, not teleological, it surely doesn't follow that each particular right thus justified, implying that a certain act x is not to be done, is thereby one that could not under any conceivable circumstances be justifiably done.

Note, for example, that one could well enough *write in* all sorts of circumstances under which x could, after all, be done. This would make the statement of the right more complicated: "Those against whom this right obtains are not to do x, *unless* circumstances C_1 . . . C_n obtain." This could *still* be a "side-constraint", arising from the separateness of the person whose right it is, and so forth. But it would not have the infinite-stringency implication.

In Part Two we will say considerably more about matters related to this. The reader should merely be warned that the theory investigated in this book does not—for better or worse—slavishly imitate that of the work which mainly inspired it.

'General' and 'Particular'; 'Natural' and 'Conventional'

Philosophers have made various distinctions about rights. Some are theoretical distinctions about the ground or "origin" of rights, others are distinctions in content. Two related distinctions that fall one on either side of this line are those between *general* and *particular* rights, and between *natural* and *conventional* rights.

(1) General/particular: this is now an easy one, given the analysis we have just come up with. A "general" right, as the name implies, is a right against *everyone*, that is, against people "in general." My right not to be murdered is not a right that certain particular people not murder me, but rather that everyone capable of murdering me refrain therefrom. This brings up the question of just who "everyone" is, to be sure, and that is not as silly a question as might at first seem. It is an important question in ethical theory whether and how and why there could be rights of this type, and whether "everyone" is, for instance, every rational creature there could possibly be (Kant's view), every normal human of reasonable understanding (approximately my view), or every fellow member of some lesser group such as one's nation or tribe (Gilbert Harman's view,[15] and probably most people's, if they realized it). We will not discuss that here but will do so later (pages 133–135). Meanwhile, there certainly are particular rights whether or not there are general ones: rights we have over particular people to do certain specific actions. The typical example is the right that other parties to arrangements and agreements do their part as promised or agreed. But perhaps there are others. Perhaps our children have rights against us in particular that they do not have against anyone else; or our parents; and surely our friends, lovers, perhaps our neighbors, and so on.

(2) Natural/conventional. This distinction *can* be simply equated with the previous one. We can't have made particular arrangements with everyone, nor can everyone be our mother or friends or whatever; so if there are general rights at all, it might be suggested, these must be "natural".

There are two ways to think of natural rights. One is as the rights we would have in what is sometimes called the "state of nature", though even that term is ambiguous. The standard usage, as in Hobbes and Locke, defines a state of nature simply as an apolitical state, a condition where there is no government. Hobbes denies that there are any rights (in the normatively meaningful sense of 'rights' used here) in such a state, whereas Locke insists that there are. Who is right will be considered in Part Two (and decided in favor of Locke). In that sense, however, it is a logically open question how we came by those rights.

But we might also use the term 'natural right' in another sense: to refer to rights that we "have by nature", as though in addition to our arms and legs, eyes and brains, we also have a further property called "rights". This tends to be allied with an intuitionist view: we just *know* that there are these rights, perhaps by some nonsensuous process of "seeing". Proponents of this view will tend also to claim that our fundamental rights are "self-evident." In this sense, 'natural' is opposed to 'conventional' as designating (presumably) different and contrary theories about the foundation of rights. This question will also be considered in Part Two (where we will find in favor of Hobbes and against Locke—so it comes out a draw!). Meanwhile, we note only that libertarians speak, overwhelmingly, as though the general right to liberty, which it is of the essence of their view to proclaim, is also a natural right in at least the first, but very often also in the second, of these two senses. That fact, as will become evident, provides one of the principal motivations of this book.

Negative versus Positive Rights

This brings us to the very important distinction between "negative" and "positive" rights. This is a distinction in substance and not in form, and a distinction not in what we have the right to do by virtue of having one or another such right, but, rather, a distinction concerning which duties fall upon those against whom they are rights. Rights, as we have seen in the preceding analysis, essentially give rise to duties, and we may accordingly proceed by distinguishing the duties that these different kinds of rights would entail. The distinction, in form at least, is easy enough to make: a *negative* duty is a duty to *refrain* from some specified sort of action or from any action that would bring about a certain specified sort of result, whereas a *positive* duty is to *perform* some specified action, or any action that would bring about a certain specified sort of result. A *negative right*, then, is one that correlates with a negative duty on the part of those against whom it is a right; a *positive right* is one that correlates with a positive duty on the part of those against whom it is a right.[16]

Thus suppose, to take our standard formula, that A has the right to do x. Then the negative form of this right would entail upon B the duty to refrain from preventing A from doing x (or: from interfering, in ways to be further specified). The positive version, on the other hand, would entail upon B the duty to do something (again, to be specified further) to *enable* or *empower* B to do x. To summarize, then:

(1) 'A has the negative right against B to do x' means 'B has the duty to refrain from preventing A's doing of x'.
(2) 'A has the positive right against B to do x' means 'B has the duty to assist A to do x'.

These are the simplest, skeletal versions. But both, and more especially the second, would need to be supplemented. Just which activities on B's part count as actually "preventing" A from doing x? As we have seen, this may be hard to say. And what about activities that merely interfere to various degrees with A's doing of x? Interfere to what extent? And so on. In the case of positive rights, there is the obvious need to say how much. The theoretical need is considerably more urgent and essential in the case of positive rights, for it is of their essence that B perform various actions—that B *do something;* and in particular, that B bring about or contribute to the bringing about of certain results. We thus have to give B some idea which actions, and/or how great a contribution B must make. In the case of negative rights, by contrast, B can typically satisfy the demands in question by doing nothing at all. At this very moment, to use an oft-noted example, I am refraining from murdering every single person in the entire world—and all this without so much as the shadow of a thought being necessary to accomplish the fulfillment of this requirement! However, insofar as my duty is to help, I must get off my bottom and do something; and then the questions, What? and How much? logically must arise, since it is impossible to do something that is of no particular kind, and impossible to accomplish something toward a certain end that is of no particular degree. On the other hand, I might be quite strongly tempted to do some of the things prohibited by another person's negative rights. In that case a negative right would also need further specification: just which sorts of interfering actions are disallowed, and what degree of interference is permitted?

Negative versus Positive Rights to Liberty

If our sole fundamental right is the right to liberty, there is still the question whether *this* is to be construed negatively or positively. It is wrong to think, as some appear to, that a negative right is identical with a liberty right. The *negative* version of a right to liberty would say that our sole right is, in effect, the right not to be interfered with in doing what we want, so that our sole fundamental duty of justice would be the duty not to interfere with the liberty of others. In its positive version, on the other hand, we would have not only that duty but also the duty to *promote* the liberty of others, that is, to bring it about that, or do something to help to maintain the situation in which, they were free from one or another interference with their liberty. The positive construal might, for instance, be used to ground a duty to promote equal opportunity, or to contribute to the common defense. It might even be used to support a welfare state, on the ground that persons not enjoying certain levels of income and so on could hardly be said to be "free" to do various things they wished to do.

But this "positive" sense of the right of liberty cannot be fundamental. For positive rights entail positive duties, and positive duties of justice mean that you may be forced to do them, hence that you may be forced to do something you don't, even on due consideration, want to do. At least on the face of it that is an interference with your liberty, whereas failure to supply Jones with the artificial lung he needs for continued life is not, as argued above, an *interference* with his liberty, even though supplying him with one could reasonably be argued to increase his liberty.

There is an argument, which we will later consider in more detail, that allowing some positive rights, perhaps including this one, would "increase" our liberty overall. That argument assumes that liberty is a sort of social goal or general value that is to be maximized. But it may be that it doesn't work like that. Robert Nozick's view in *Anarchy, State, and Utopia* was, as we have seen, that our fundamental rights are to be respected as "side constraints" rather than "goals". We are enjoined to refrain from certain types of acts, not because this will bring about a desirable state of affairs but instead because those acts are intrinsically wrong. Though side constraints are rejected here, so are social goals.

Libertarianism and Negative Rights

Libertarianism has generally been identified with the thesis that our fundamental moral rights are exclusively negative. The fundamental general right, according to it, is the right to do whatever we wish, unhindered, as nearly as possible, by others—subject, of course, to the restrictions inherent in the similar right of others.

Positive rights, by contrast, must be justified by a procedure that "hitches" them to the basic negative ones.

To take an important example of the latter process, consider the duty to keep promises. No one need *make* any promises to anyone, in principle: that's the individual's business. Once made, however, she now has a positive duty, namely, to do whatever she has promised to do. It will be argued later that nevertheless, the duty to keep promises stems from a negative right—that same basic general right to do whatever we wish, in fact—which therefore includes the undertaking of commitments. It then becomes the case that you prevent or interfere with others doing as they wish if you fail to do as you have agreed with them that you will do. But then, of course, we are into the whole question of what constitutes a sufficient excuse, and what constitutes an overriding justification, for failure to perform.

Why should libertarianism be thus identified? Why shouldn't the libertarian try to maximize positive rights to liberty, as in the version described in Chapter 4 above? The answer is that there is a libertarian case against positive rights that is based on the aforementioned consideration: viz., that they violate liberty in a way that negative rights do not. If our root idea is that the individual—*any* individual—is to be allowed to do, as nearly as possible, what that individual wants with his or her life, then we have already given the ground for restricting individuals from acts preventing others from doing what they please with their lives. It would be self-contradictory to say of everyone that all *may* do as they please, as a matter of right, even though some may go ahead and force others to do one thing rather than another. But it is not self-contradictory to say that no one may be forced to promote anyone else's good, even if that good consists in an expansion of that other person's liberty. Not only is it not self-contradictory but the implication seems straightforward and inevitable, once we are aware that liberty and not something else is what's at stake.

In a recent book-length treatment Kai Nielsen proposes to defend the claim that liberty is compatible with equality. The gist of the "defense" seems to be that everyone could indeed be doing just as he or she wanted and yet everyone have rough economic equality: namely, that is how it would be in a socialist order in which everyone thought that economic equality and so forth were terrific goals.[17] So far, so good. But what if some of them didn't think that? Well, "What [radical egalitarianism] will not do is to protect our unrestricted liberties to invest, retain and bequeath in the economic realm, and it will not protect our unrestricted freedom to buy and sell. . . . The actual liberties that are curtailed in a radically egalitarian social order are inessential liberties whose restriction in contemporary circumstances enhances human well-being and indeed makes for a firmer entrenchment of basic liberties and for their greater extension globally."[18] Nielsen does say that "I am not trying . . . to force or impose any egalitarian social order on anyone." Still, he then talks of workers having "the revolutionary motivation to risk their necks and those of their families in the struggle to achieve it [socialism]" and of how workers "shouldn't wait until that moral authority is established to struggle for their emancipation."[19] It seems that Nielsen isn't advocating the use of force to get us to accept his *theory*, but apparently he is willing to have people use force to get the social system advocated by his theory instantiated—even if that *will* involve interfering with a whole lot of (capitalist) liberties. But then, you see, those are only "capitalist" liberties, and such liberties don't matter anyway, do they? So much for "egalitarianism"!

Whether such talk illustrates what seems to me obvious, that in fact egalitarians aren't much concerned about liberty, and that liberty really is incompatible with so-called radical egalitarianism, is yet to be shown, however, for everything depends on the theory of private property. Most Western radicals are very enthusiastic, at least on paper, about such traditional Western liberties as freedom of speech, the press, and religion, and on the various procedural safeguards we more or less take for granted in criminal trials—though not very many revolutionary socialist regimes manage to maintain more than a semblance of most of these liberties anyway. But property is the watershed issue, dividing libertarians from those leftists who claim also to be liberals. We turn next to this topic.

CHAPTER **6**

Liberty and Property

How Liberty and Property Are Related

IS THERE ANY CONNECTION, or a very close one, between liberty and property? Many evidently think not. Thus from Professor Nielsen: "He [Nozick] seems to be arbitrarily, and in a suspiciously ideological fashion, taking these particular property rights as the fundamental things morally".[1] "Nozick must show, to make his argument stick, *that the only morally justified liberty-respecting property rights are full capitalist property rights.* That that is so is anything but obvious and requires an argument."[2] "Nozick thinks that he has shown, O'Neill argues, that if we have these rights that it follows that individuals may justly acquire complete control over unlimited resources without needing the consent of all whose liberty will be restricted by these property rights."[3] These quotations certainly express dissent with the ideas described, but not arguments against them. It behooves us to have a look at these concepts to see whether there is any reason to think them closely connected. We shall see that there is, indeed.

Now, it is not clear, as I shall be concerned to argue at length in later portions of this book, just what "full capitalistic property rights" are. But whatever they are, it is obviously impossible that a libertarian could consistently defend them if, as Nielsen claims, all sorts of other people's *liberty* would be *restricted* by them. But at any rate it will be conducive to clarity if we appreciate that there are two theoretically distinguishable questions here.

(1) One is whether Nozick, for instance, has correctly specified just what property rights do flow from the libertarian conception, if any—whether, for instance, Nozick mistakenly thinks that most or all

of the activities of General Dynamics or of Henry Ford, Sr., and so on should have been fully protected by the laws. A crucial issue in such arguments will certainly be whether the liberties of third parties, say—or even of some of the second parties in the innumerable actual historical transactions that have taken place in purportedly "cap-italist" societies—were properly respected by all concerned. People being what they are, it would hardly be surprising to find that they at least sometimes were not. And on the theoretical side there will be the very important question whether certain kinds of property ac-quisition would necessarily violate liberty, in a plausible construal of what constitutes liberty. If they would, then of course the libertarian must say that *those* acquisitions are illegitimate, or may be regulated, or whatever. Finally, there is the even more interesting theoretical question whether virtually *any* property transaction violates some-one's liberty, for example, whether any transaction that upsets "equality" must do so. If this last could be made out, then of course the libertarian would simply have to become an egalitarian, and that would be that. But it must be made out in some more interesting sense than that in which, as we have noted, every right ipso facto restricts liberty. To restrict liberty is not necessarily to violate it: if the liberty restricted is not one to which we have a right, then its re-striction is not a violation. The question is whether we can generate this particular restriction on the basis of a fundamental concern for liberty itself. As I have pointed out above, this paradoxical-seeming idea is so far from inconsistent as to be virtually platitudinous. The critic of property must do better than that.

But (2) another and quite different (I insist) issue is whether liberty is all that matters. If it isn't, it is odd that socialists should be so con-cerned to square their doctrines with liberty. Why don't they just agree that their system does cut into liberty but argue that liberty isn't everything and that some other things matter more than it?[4] (A very few do just that, but most do not. This strikes me as curious, and attests, so far as it goes, to the compellingness of the notion of liberty, if not to its implications for practice as claimed by most of its ad-herants.) Libertarians need to answer this second question, and I shall be discussing it in the second section of this treatment.

Property Rights

Meanwhile, however, let us turn to the prior question of just what liberty implies about property. Who is right here—the defenders of the free market or the socialist and/or egalitarians—regarding the *im-*

plications of the liberty idea? The only way we can test this is by attempting to reconstruct what society would be like if it recognized only the liberty right and no other, as the libertarian insists. What would be allowed and what wouldn't?

Robert Nozick has most usefully divided the space for principles on the subject of property into three classes: (1) *initial acquisition*, that is, the acquisition of property rights in external things from a previous condition in which they were unowned by anyone in particular; (2) *transfer*, that is, the passing of property (that is to say, property rights) from one rightholder to another; and (3) *rectification*, which is the business of restoring just distributions of property when they have been upset by admittedly unjust practices such as theft and fraud. Nozick holds that there are legitimate acquisitions, giving rise to full property rights, from the "natural state", and that any fully voluntary transfers of such rights are legitimate.[5] These subjects we must discuss carefully here; the third we will for the most part leave to Part Three of this book.

What is property? A good deal of controversy has surrounded this subject, much of it needless. It is not difficult to get at what we might call the root notion or root definition of property. This general definition will apply to all sorts of property, public and private. All property must be defined in terms of rights—property consists in rights—but the specific rights in which a given case of ownership of property consists can vary greatly in extent. The definition must contain, then, a variable or variables. Let us begin with what we might call the "out-and-out" version, thus:

> 'x is A's property' means 'A has the right to determine the disposition of x'.

We could equally well use as our definiendum the expressions "A owns x" or 'x belongs to A". And when in our definiens we talk of 'determining the disposition of', we could perhaps equally say "controls." The idea is that insofar as the characteristics of item x, values of the predicate-variable F, are brought about by the actions of moral agents, then A has the right that x have characteristic F if and only if A permits it to be the case that x has F. Of course this is an idealization, and moreover a vague one in some respect. For example, many things will probably be done to x that A doesn't know or care about. We could adopt the convention that whenever A is indifferent to x's having F, then A by default, as it were, is understood to permit the action of bringing it about that x has F. But what matters is that in principle, insofar as A is the owner of x, A's view about this is relevant: it is within A's rights to forbid any given action that affects x.

To try to produce a technically satisfactory account we would have to restrict the range of F in some respects. For example, whenever I move from anywhere to anywhere, I make trivial alterations in the *relational* properties of all the material objects in the universe: for example, the vectorial distance from me to the Arc de Triomphe is altered every time I move. But these can hardly be considered even putative infringements of the property rights of those who own whatever of those objects have owners. Yet we could hardly exclude all relational properties in general—notably, for instance, the locations of the objects in question, these being the main properties of most stolen goods that their thieves are interested in altering. How much of this will significantly affect the ensuing discussions is not easy to say in the abstract; I shall simply assume, or perhaps hope, that our intuitive grip on these things is sufficient to enable us to proceed. We could perhaps go a little further and suggest that "ideally" even such properties would be under the thumb of the proprietor of the item in question, but that only an omnipotent personage would be able to take advantage of most of those rights—and such a Personage wouldn't need them anyway!

We must bear in mind that the rights of control and disposition over what is normally called one's "property", for instance, as legally recognized, are usually very much restricted. The kinds of control one could in principle exercise may be divided in various ways. For example, one might be allowed to do anything except damage or destroy the entity in question; one might be permitted to do anything with it during one's lifetime but forbidden the right to determine who gets it after one dies. The class of persons one can sell it to, or the ways in which one might do so, might be restricted in various ways. A tax might have to be paid by the person who purchases it. And so on.[6] These various restrictions are placed on property rights not only by the structure of law but often by parties to particular transactions: A finds it to his interest to transfer some but not other of his rights over x to B in exchange for something or other, and so the ownership of x becomes diluted or fractured. If A begins with the full complement of such rights and then voluntarily transfers some but not others of them, the libertarian cannot complain about this. That it is *possible* to thus fracture these rights is analytically obvious and since the actual implies the possible and these things are actually done, that should lay to rest any tendency to suppose that the libertarian is committed to some notion of ownership that is violated by any such fracturing. This is merely a word of warning at this stage, but perhaps a necessary one.

Independently, and fundamentally, one cannot be understood to have the right to do anything with x that violates the rights of anyone else, whether they be that person's (or corporation's, or State's, or whatever's) property rights or any other sort of rights there may be. Rights constitute a set of boundaries within which one's liberty to use whatever one may use is exercised.

Property in Oneself

In fact, however, the suggestion that there are "other sorts of rights" besides property rights is somewhat misleading, as we shall see. It is plausible to construe *all* rights as property rights. Whenever anyone has a right, Rx, to engage in any sort of actions x, we can find some thing or things y, such that that person must be understood to have, given that he has the right to engage in those actions, the right, Ry, to use that thing or those things: Rx entails Ry. At a minimum, y is some part of that person's body or mind; the agent in question must employ his body and/or mind to do anything, and the liberty to do it will follow automatically from the liberty to use those pieces of human equipment as that person will. Thus it is plausible to suggest that Liberty is Property, and in particular that the libertarian thesis is really the thesis that *a right to our persons as our property is the sole fundamental right there is.*

One can do no better than to quote Murray Rothbard's forthright statement of this view: "in the profoundest sense there *are* no rights but property rights. . . . There are several senses in which this is true. In the first place, each individual, as a natural fact, is the owner of *himself*, the ruler of his own person. Then 'human' rights of the person that are defended in the purely free-market society are, in effect, each man's *property right* in his own being, and from *this* property right stems his right to the material goods that he has produced.

"In the second place, alleged 'human rights' can be boiled down to property rights . . . for example the 'human rights' of free speech. Freedom of speech is supposed to mean the right of everyone to say whatever he likes. But the neglected question is: Where? . . . certainly not on property on which he is trespassing. In short he has this right only either on his *own* property or on the property of someone who has agreed, as a gift or in a rental conract, to allow him on the premises. In fact, then, there is no such thing as a separate 'right to free speech'; there is only a man's *property* right: the right to do as he wills with his own or to make voluntary agreements with other property owners."[7] I cite the passage at this length because the illustration, concerning free speech, so nicely exemplifies the thesis. (I have made similar points in previous essays[8], but came upon Rothbard's passage only recently. For more on freedom of speech, see Part Three.)

If we think that the right to liberty is the most fundamental right there is, then what, after all, do we thereby think? Surely that we may *do* as we want. But doing as we want is doing as we want *with* (various parts of) ourselves; and it is not doing as we want with anything else unless we have in some way acquired the right so to do. Those who have their doubts about the institution of private property usually accept the substance, if not the form, of the thesis that our own bodies and minds are so: here, at any rate, we have entities over which the person is to have control, and which others must gain permission to act upon or with if their use of them is to be morally permissible. Few socialists, to take another Nozickian example, accept that if you are blind and I have two good eyes, then in the interests of equality I am morally bound to part with one of them and turn it over to you, should it be medically possible to do that; or that what should be done with my left arm is properly a matter for majority decision.

Many philosophers, and perhaps most nonphilosophers, are shocked at the suggestion that our bodies or minds are our "property". But it is difficult to see why this should be shocking, unless perhaps at the implication that A could literally sell himself or herself to someone else. That would indeed be a peculiar transaction, since it is hard to see how A could collect once the "goods" had been "delivered". But notoriously people have *given* themselves to others—it was long thought to be standard procedure in marriages, for instance, that at least the female partner give herself, as literally as possible, to the male one. (Some insisted that both give themselves to each other, but there is some difficulty about the logic of that particular exchange!)

What we can say is that in any sense in which selling or otherwise transferring one's right of control over oneself to another person or that person in any other way coming by such right, is conceivable, it is surely also possible, and will likely be found to have actually happened at times. The most notorious example is the occurrence, in times (one hopes) past, of the institution of slavery. It is, of course, an immediate inference from the libertarian idea that slavery, as normally understood, is morally unacceptable. But the libertarian will state the objection to it by insisting that people, any and all of them, are the fundamental owners of their *own* bodies, and of no one else's. The point is that that objection is a coherent and, surely, a powerful one. If it made no sense to talk of ownership of oneself, how could the objection be made?

It is gratifying to find that the essential logic of the position here expounded has been appreciated even by a Marxist philosopher—by reputation (and in fact) one of the most acute of those thinkers at that. G. A. Cohen writes, "Nozick's political philosophy gains much of its polemical power from the attractive thought that . . . each person is the morally rightful owner of himself."[9] He goes on to point out that socialist writers, wanting to defend some very strong positive equality rights in the matter of property, are hard put to it to explain why those rights don't extend also to such things as our arms and eyes. "In my experience, leftists who disparage Nozick's essentially unargued affirmation of each person's rights over himself lose confidence in their unqualified denial of the thesis of self-ownership when they are asked to consider who has the right to decide what should happen to, for example, their own eyes. They do not immediately agree that, were eye transplants easy to achieve, it would then be acceptable for the state to conscribe potential eye donors into a lottery whose losers must yield an eye to beneficiaries who would otherwise be not one-eyed but blind. The fact that they do not deserve their good eyes, that they do not need two good eyes more than blind people need one, and so forth; the fact, in a word, that they are merely lucky to have good eyes does not always convince them that their claim on their own eyes is no stronger than that of some unlucky blind person."[10]

The problem for socialists, as Cohen observes, is how to have both the right of self-ownership, preserving the "attractive thought", and yet a right of equality, getting us the socialism they are so morally enamored of. That there is a problem here is suggested by the fact that "people can do (virtually?) nothing without using parts of the external world. If, then, they require the leave of the community to use it, then, effectively, they do not own themselves, since they can do nothing without communal authorization."[11] It is testimony to the strength of our position that even someone so ideologically opposed gives it clear recognition as an argument that must be confronted.

From Liberty to Property in Things

The above is from the first of two important recent articles in which Cohen contends that even if we accept that people own themselves, which as we have noted he finds an attractive idea, we still don't need to accept the legitimacy (even) of private property in *things*. "It is an intelligible presumption that I alone am entitled to decide about the use of this arm and to benefit from its dexterity, simply because it is my arm. Nor am I therefore confusing the factual truth that this is my arm with the normative claim that I should have exclusive disposal of it. My contention is that the factual truth is a prima facie plausible basis for, not a logical entailer of, the stated normative claim. But there is no comparable presumptive normative tie between any person and any part or portion of the external world."[12]

The argument is developed in the context of reflection on Robert Nozick's views. Nozick proposes a right to acquire property in the "state of nature" which is limited by a "proviso on acquisition", deriving more or less from Locke. The general idea of this proviso is that you can acquire so long as you don't worsen the situation of others. Nozick agrees that the libertarian view would have little appeal if some such condition were not imposed.[13]

But interpreting the intended restriction is not so easy. In particular, the question is, worsen as compared with what? Cohen argues that Nozick's condition amounts to comparing one's situation after the appropriations of others with one's situation had the item appropriated remained unowned. But this condition, he insists, is too weak. He points to conceivable cases in which allowing private ownership might make one, or even the acquirer himself, worse off; and he concludes, after considerable analysis, that "theses about consequences are foundational to Nozick's defense of private property rights, and the rights he asserts consequently lack the clarity and authority he would like us to suppose they have."[14] And he proposes, for instance, that "when assessing A's appropriation we should consider not only what would have happened had B appropriated, but also what would have happened had A and B cooperated under a socialist economic constitution." And reflection along such lines leads him to argue that "once we broaden, in these and other ways, our range of comparison, then, so it seems, a defensibly strong Lockean proviso will forbid the formation of full liberal private property. For there will always be some who would have been better off under an

alternative dispensation that it would be arbitrary to exclude from
consideration. . . . And since, moreover, a defensibly strong Lockean
proviso on the formation and retention of economic systems will rule
that no one should be worse off in the given economic system than he
would have been under some unignorable alternative, it almost certainly follows that not only capitalism but every economic system will
fail to satisfy a defensibly strong Lockean proviso, and that one must
therefore abandon the Lockean way of testing the legitimacy of economic systems."[15]

Then we have the suggestion that "one different alternative is
John Rawl's difference principle, in its strict meaning . . . [which is]
satisfied by a given economic system only if those who are worst off
under it are not more badly off than the worst off would be under any
alternative to it. . . . when it is satisfied one may respond to the complaint of the worst-off group by pointing out that others would suffer
at least as much as they do in any dispensation in which they were
better off than they actually are." And he insists, "it is clear beyond
doubt that an appropriation of private property can contradict an individual's will just as much as levying a tax on him can. Therefore
Nozick cannot claim to be inspired throughout by a desire to protect
freedom, unless he means by 'freedom' what he really does mean by
it: the freedom of private property owners to do as they wish with
their property."[16]

The argument, in short, is that even when we grant that liberty
may be interpreted as property in the person, we don't get from *liberty* to property but, rather, from property to property. Two observa-
tions are in order. First, as Cohen has agreed is an attractive feature of
liberalism, everyone is here assumed to own his or her own person.
Everyone *is* a property owner. Freedom of property owners to do as
they wish with their property is freedom of everybody to use his fundamental property (in his person) as he wishes, consistently with the
like freedom of others. Second, and more crucially for present purposes, in saying that "an appropriation of private property can contradict an individual's will just as much as levying a tax on him can",
we need to know whether an individual *whose will is oriented toward
permitting people to do as they wish unless what they do infringes her own
liberty* would agree with that. The fact that someone might *prefer* that a
particular piece of the world be used in way x rather than way y does
not show that her will is contradicted *in that manner*. That people
would like the world to be in condition C1 rather than C2 shows us
nothing as yet; the question is whether they would like it to be the

case that its being put in condition C1 was done by forcing some people to contribute to C1 rather than something else. Does someone who buys up a piece of property and uses it for something that individual A would prefer it not to be used for *thereby* contravene A's *freedom?* I don't see it. A presumably had the freedom to make a bid on the property if that's what she wanted to do; or to get a number of people together and make a bid, if she can persuade them that that would be a good idea. But—as usual, one is tempted to say—Cohen is subtly assuming that freedom consists in other people's *supplying* you with what you want, rather than, as we have insisted, freedom for you to *do* what you want.

If we bear this in mind, then how does Cohen's proposed test of comparing the worst off in system S with the worst off in S', for all possible alternatives, accomplish? The fact that in a certain system the worst off are spoonfed and end up at higher levels of satisfaction than the worst off in any other system does not prove very much if those who feed them are *forced* to do so. Indeed, since this is an open-ended test, we can posit that the worst off will be, for instance, quasi-vegetables or paraplegics. (We can posit this, because in the actual world there are such individuals.) Why is it relevant to test a system by how much the paraplegics in that system like it? Why should we load the dice in favor of the least able? In a libertarian system, those who wish paraplegics to be better off are free to devote their energies to making them so. How well off they will as a result be is anyone's guess, no doubt. It may or may not be that they will end up better off that way than in any socialist system; but the question is not whether this is so, but why this argument counts *at all*.

In Part II of Cohen's article[17] he proposes to reconcile joint ownership of the external world with private ownership of the self by imaging a pair of two-person worlds. In one, occupied by "Able and Infirm", each owns himself and they jointly own everything else. Cohen argues, in problematic ways, but we need not consider them here, that "without denying self-ownership, and without affirming equality of condition as an underived principle, one may move towards a form of equality of condition by insisting on joint ownership of the external world." The problem is that this seems to be inconsistent with preservation of self-ownership. "For how can I be said to own myself if I may do nothing without the agreement of others? Do not Able and Infirm jointly own not only the world but also, at least in effect, each other?"[18] Cohen's strategy in responding to this obviously plausible objection is to argue that even though their situation "renders self-ownership merely formal", that doesn't really matter, because the situation under capitalism renders self-ownership equally formal. To this end, he conjures up his other two-person world, containing Mr. Z, the abject proletarian, and Mr. C, the capitalist to whom Z "must" sell his labor power. Nozick, after all, thinks that "the circumstances of the most abject proletarian—call him 'Z'—who must either sell his labor power to a capitalist or die, is consistent with nonviolation of the relevant rights. And if that is so, then N could not object that Able's self-ownership is merely formal, since, whether or not it is indeed merely formal, it is not less substantive than Z's."[19]

The argument is that, really, Able's and Z's situations are exactly alike: neither can do anything without another person's agreement, and "it is also true that there is nothing which either need do without his own agreement: neither Infirm nor the capitalist has rights of sheer command which are not grounded in a prior contract to obey."[20]

Is this persuasive? The question before us is whether there is indeed a difference in the situations of Z and Able such that it is reasonable to describe Z's situation as one of liberty and Able's by contrast as lacking it. Cohen's restriction to a two-person situation makes it hard to focus on the issue in many respects. For one thing, we are, of course, given no scenario for the capitalist-Z situation, which in a two-person case is remarkably unrealistic. How, in such a situation, would Capitalist have come by and maintained his command of the resources? And how would Able and Infirm come by their moral trappings? Those details would, I suspect, matter greatly—but more on that below.

Meanwhile, the way in which the two situations mask some of what we would want to bring out is this: Consider the sense in which Z "must" sell his labor to C: granting, as we should not, that for some reason Z has no option of self-employment, then given the circumstance that he must sell his labor to someone and there is only one other person to sell it to, he "must" sell it to C. Were there others, he could knock on the door of *any* capitalist. He "could" do so in precisely the same sense that Able, on the other hand, *cannot* do anything in the external world without the consent of all the other joint owners of that world, of whom there just happens to be only one. And so the incredible difference of situation between them in any remotely plausible real-world scenarios is totally obscured. In a many-person world, Able can do nothing without getting the consent of *everyone*; Z, by contrast, can do whatever he can persuade *someone* to pay him to do. Z's chosen C need ask leave of no other person whether he will hire Z or no; Z need clear it with no one else whether he will work for C, or D, or whoever. In a world of any size, such as any real-life society, Z will have many potential Cs to go to, and Able will have many actual Infirms to get consent from. Were we to take the description literally, that Able must get consent from *each and every* other person *each and every* time Able makes any use of the external world—essentially 100 percent of his actions, after all—then the claim that the difference between Able's and Z's position is "merely formal" would be too far-fetched to be worth advancing for a moment. Indeed, it would not be going too far to suggest that by the time Able got all his approvals—especially when we bear in mind that since everyone is getting everyone's approval, the lines would be of mind-boggling length—he'd likely have starved to death!

Let us return once more to the two-person scenarios. Surely we would be curious to know how on earth C managed to gain control of *all* the resources in the Z-C world. Is Z *completely* incompetent? And if he is, then of course he *is* rather at the mercy of C, but it's hard to see how such a person could avoid that result in any world. Yet in a two-person world, Z would also have a monopoly of what would likely be the most important resource in life for C: human company (and vice versa). In such a situation, whatever the disparity in powers and subsequent resources between them, it is difficult to believe that any very severe inquality of condition will continue, unless C is a complete hermit by inclination. But hermits do not make good capitalists, if exercising severe control over Z's labor is what Cohen is worried about.

In the Able-Infirm world, likewise, we really should ask how this arrangement of having to get general consent for everything came about, anyway. That it would, even in a two-person situation, be less than completely efficient is a fact to which any married person can testify. In real life the unanimity rule in that society could continue only with unanimous support: that is to say, as soon as anyone decided to break it, there would be nothing but the disapproval of the other party to keep him from doing so. Plainly, Cohen's moralities descend from the gods, rather than arising out of the human situation, with its interactions of voluntarily acting more or less rational persons. This is to repeat my complaint that there is no evident reason why the "alternative" of joint ownership should be *available*.

Property Rights and the "Freedom Entails Unfreedom" Paradox

In Chapter 5 we broached the question of whether the fact that rights consist in requirements and thus restrictions on the freedom of others thereby showed that the idea of a right to liberty is inherently paradoxical. Let us now take up the question regarding property rights in particular. Among the most acute of those who raise the specter of this paradox is Allan Gibbard, in an important recent article, "What's Morally Special about Free Exchange?"[21] Though this article deserves further discussion in many ways, we will here focus on his specific version of the criticism that a full private property system cannot be said to flow straightforwardly from a fundamental commitment to a right of liberty.

Gibbard first points out that a fully *free-exchange* system must not be equated with a *price* system. The latter is simply a system in which people have resources (usually in the form of money) that they can exchange for things that have prices. But those prices need not, in turn, be set exclusively by exchanges of property rights among owners of what is exchanged—there could, for instance, be appreciable state intervention in setting the prices. This compares with the free-exchange system, which is, roughly, a system in which ownership rights to things are "transferable by gift or contractual exchange, subject *only* to those restrictions which the parties involved have accepted."[22] The free-exchange system, then, is a full market economy. The question before us is whether the latter system has any special connection with liberty: does it more nearly instantiate the idea that everyone is to be free to do whatever he or she may please, subject only to the restrictions inherent in everyone else's having the same right? Gibbard thinks not.

He points out that "a suitable price system . . . offers a person with sufficient assets a wide range of attractive alternatives for leading his life. It may be highly desirable, then, that everyone face a suitable price system with sufficient assets, and one attraction of free exchange may be that it promises to bring about such a desirable state of affairs." But then he points out that any reasonable price system will have that advantage: "Since, though, we can have a price system without free exchange, the virtues of a price system are not peculiarly virtues of a pure system of free exchange. My question is, is there anything morally special about free exchange itself?"[23]

Gibbard addresses himself to what he calls "intuitionistic" views of free exchange. "These views take moral principles directly pertaining to property rights, or to liberty, as fundamental moral principles. We tend to think of 'ownership' as a primitive, irreducible feature of the world. We were, after all, taught to think of things as 'mine' or 'hers' or 'his' from earliest childhood . . . . We are apt, in careless moments, to think of a person's property as a part of his person, like an arm or a leg. The first step in thinking about property rights is to realize that property is a matter of complex human contrivance, custom, and convention. . . . In thinking about property . . . we must wrench our minds free of the grip of a fetish—the fetish of a primitive 'mine' or 'yours' or 'his' or 'hers' mentality."[24] It is not entirely clear just what point is being made in this at first sight persuasive passage, but perhaps it is that our "primitive" idea of ownership is one in which the various things you could do with anything are thought to be *undecomposable:* that is, you couldn't have, say, the right to use something without also having the right to give it away or whatever. If that is the idea, then of course Gibbard is perfectly right. When you rent a flat, for instance, you have the right to use it but not to give it away. So far so good. But it is not clear what follows from this; in particular, it does not preclude there being a central generating idea—such as our idea of liberty rights—that would not only generate full property rights but *also* the capability of distinguishing the various possible restricted subsets of them that we might find it useful to develop. And that is the claim thai I have made in the foregoing about the liberty principle.

Gibbard continues: "The most promising strategy for defending property rights is that of Locke, who tries to derive property in things from property in one's own person. . . . Now the appeal of appropriation, if we resolutely cast aside ownership as a primitive fetish, seems to me to lie either in considerations of liberty or in considerations of welfare." Again, fair enough; and again, we will table the appeal to welfare until later. We now come to the direct attack on the sort of argument we have certainly been embracing above: "The appeal to liberty, though, cannot be direct, for ownership primarily involves restrictions on liberty—on the liberty of others to make use, without my leave, of the thing I own. What recommends appropriation is that a system of property can, in some ways, enhance liberty and welfare. . . . As for liberty, in an advanced economy a system of property rights can indeed enhance liberty in an important sense of the term. Given a suitable system of exchangeable property rights, each able person will have a choice among a range of reasonably satisfactory ways of life. Liberty in this sense, however, is achievable in a variety of economic orders that yield a price system. It does not require that all property rights be rooted in what I have been calling "extreme ownership".[25]

One further point of interest is made in this connection. Supposing the previous criticisms go through, Gibbard says, "There still remains the question, 'If an exchange of property rights can be made to mutual benefit, why forbid it?' The answer is, to induce a pattern of exchanges that is better on the whole. We forbid employment below the minimum wage because we think that more offers of employment will then be made at or above the minimum wage. We forbid untaxed sales because we think that more people will be then willing to make taxed sales. So put, to be sure, these sound like restrictions on liberty. But they are, for the most part, something more complex: they are restrictions on the exchange of property rights, and property rights are rights to restrict the liberty of others to use a thing. They are a part of a pattern of restrictions on liberty, the pattern constituted by a system of property rights. They are not added restrictions on liberty, over and above the restrictions on liberty involved in a system of pure free exchange. They are restrictions on our legal powers to alter the restrictions on liberty that constitute a system of property rights."[26]

Gibbard sums up as follows: "arguments in favor of extreme ownership for the sake of liberty fail in two ways. If liberty is a matter of having a wide range of reasonably attractive alternatives in one's life, regulated systems of exchange may produce more widespread liberty than would a system of pure free exchange. If, on the other hand, liberty is the lack of legal constraints on action, any system of property rights restricts liberty, and there seems to be no way to identify restrictions on exchange as additional restrictions on action. They are, rather, restrictions on powers to alter restrictions on action."[27]

Here we need to ask two questions. The first has two parts: (a) whether liberty is indeed a matter of what he says it is, and (b) insofar as it is so, whether the defense of liberty consists only in the rather mild characterization he proposes: whether, that is, an exchange system would better exemplify a liberty-regarding system if it merely happened to involve the bringing about of a *wider* range of "attractive alternatives" in one's life, or a range of *more* attractive ones. The second is whether the fact—as it obviously is—that "any system of property rights restricts liberty" means, as he claims, that a system in which prices are dictated by extra-market considerations cannot on that account be shown to involve restrictions of freedom as compared with one in which they are set only by market transactions. We can surely make a stronger case in both respects than Gibbard is willing to allow in these passages—though reminding the reader, for the sake of clarity, that at this point our concern is only with the restricted question whether free exchange is implied by liberty, and not yet with the more fundamental question whether liberty is what we want.

To begin with the first issue: what is the relation between the "amount" of liberty we have and the "range of attractive alternatives among which we can choose"? Not obviously a very direct one, it seems. For one thing, we can easily cite intuitive counterexamples. We can imagine a system, S1, in which we have more, and more attractive, alternatives than another, S2, but *also* a few extremely unattractive nonalternatives over which we have no choice at all. In S2 I may be forced to listen to Billy Graham for one hour a day, whereas in S1 I may choose among fewer operas, cars, and whatnot—but at least I *do* get to choose. Some might find the price worth paying, or even find that hour one of the major advantages of S2; but it is not thereby shown that it better exemplifies liberty.

What would show that a given system better exemplifies liberty would be, it seems to me, that in it there is literally less restriction on liberty. Gibbard would need to count the unavailability of an attractive alternative, L, in Sx a "restriction on liberty" relative to Sy; but I don't. The *liberty* of those in Sx may not be restricted at all—they may simply have too little talent or imagination or luck to have come up with L. But now imagine that in Sx some people are forced to work for others, simply in order to make more attractive alternatives available for those others. That, surely, would involve a restriction literally on the *liberty* of those thus forced.

With this in mind, consider now the claim that "if, on the other hand, liberty is the lack of legal constraints on action, any system of property rights restricts liberty, and there seems to be no way to identify restrictions on exchange as additional restrictions on action. They are, rather, restrictions on powers to alter restrictions on action." Should we be impressed by this? Not at all! This is to talk as though the "restrictions" involved in ownership were nothing but that. But that's absurd! The essence of my having an Apple Macintosh is that I *have* one, at my disposal when and as I wish, which latter of course requires that you not be able simply to use it any time you like; it's *not* that *you can't have one unless I say so*. Imagine that Smerdlovsky is a high party bureaucrat in some benighted Marxist state, and he has the power to prevent you from using an Apple Macintosh, though he doesn't have one himself (and probably wouldn't have any use for it if he did!): does his having that power show that *he* owns the Mac? What is surely essential to our comparison if we are comparing x and y with respect to liberty, in particular, is whether those in Sx who have things *got* them by forcing others to do this or that, that is to say, got them *by* restricting the liberties of others, and whether their use of the things they have is *to restrict* the liberties of others, as when a terrorist uses his Uzi to murder all those who oppose him. But if Jones got a certain item without restricting anyone's liberty in any way in the process, then the fact that having it entails having the right to prevent others from using it does not show that there is *now* a restriction on others' liberty which there wasn't previously. (For an obvious example, consider the case in which you got it by making it, so that if you hadn't done this it would not have existed at all. Now that you have it and won't let others have it, it doesn't follow that they used to be able to use it but now can't!)

CHAPTER *7*

Initial Acquisition

Getting Ownership Started

LOCKE, AS EVERYONE KNOWS, grounded the institution of property on self-ownership. Somehow it is to be because we own ourselves that we come to be able to own items in the world outside our bodies. The question is, how? And it was Locke who held that the central mechanism here was the "mixing of our labour" with the thing that comes to be ours. But also it was Locke who insisted that there were important limits to what we can acquire in a "state of nature", at least: no more than we can use without spoiling, and only what leaves "enough and as good for others". The question quite properly asked by objectors to private property, especially as applying to the "means of production", is how we can suppose that we could, starting with just the premises about self-ownership, wind up with the entire panoply of ownership rights familiar in contemporary nonsocialist societies. It is not clear, as will be seen in Part Three, just what that "panoply" really consists of, but let us suppose that what we are after are the rights of (1) exclusive use, and thus of permitting or refusing use by any others, except only on jointly agreed terms, and (2) transfer in the form of (a) sale, (b) exchange, (c) gift, and (d) bequeathal. This is a list that does substantially approximate what most of us are thought to have in all Western countries with regard to a fairly sizable range of consumer goods. It is also one to which, at least with respect to some kinds of usable things in respect of at least some of its provisions, any socialist will object vigorously. I suggest that the way to the establishment of such rights—not, of course, as rigid and come what may, but as plain presumptions that stand unless collisions with rights of others call for overturning in particular cases—is not all that difficult. That is just what Locke thought, and it seems to me what most of us in practice are inclined to think, though of course objectors will insist that our so thinking is tendentiously ideology-ridden. Let us see.

Rights to Things Are Rights to Act

The first requirement for clarity in this matter is to realize that rights to things are not a separate sort of rights from rights to do, but a genus of them (at least). *All* rights are rights to do various things, in the broad sense identified in Chapter 3, that of intentionally bringing about states of affairs. In the case of the ownership of particular bits of the world, we identify the set of actions in question by relating those actions to the item in question. Here is how I propose to do this. (1) For anything to be eligible for ownership, it must be capable of being in some way affected by someone, at least potentially. The right to use is, I shall say, *primary* in ownership—which does *not* mean that if anyone in any ordinary sense "owns" something, it follows that she even may, let alone can, use it herself. Once we have some ideas of the set of actions that would consist in using the thing x, we also, of course, know what would constitute damaging or destroying x and thus know something about a potential restriction of the rights in (1), if it is the sort of thing that can be damaged or destroyed, should the question arise. Given (1), then, we can also generate (2) a second-level type of action involving x, namely, transferring the (primary) right to use x to some other person(s). Normally this will be done by engaging in some literal act that is only conventionally related to this trans- ference, such as signing a sales slip; but given the conventions, to perform those actions will be to perform the more abstract ones of transferring rights.

Thus all claims about ownership—rights to property—can be ana- lyzed into claims about rights to perform various actions, though sometimes the process will be a bit cumbersome. And Marxists can formulate one of their objections to private property by insisting that type (2) "actions" are in some way a fraud, and that rights to engage in them should be subordinated, in some sense to be specified, to rights to type (1) actions. G. A. Cohen has an interesting explication of a "material/formal" distinction somewhat along the lines of the one just made.[1] Among Cohen's objections to capitalism, the principal one, indeed, seems to be that capitalists don't *do* anything, in some proprietary sense of the word 'do'.[2] But the sense is overly proprietary, since Cohen would prefer a society in which people are not allowed to do the things that capitalists regularly do and finds it very objectionable that in our society as it stands they are so extensively permitted to.

However, we needn't worry about this. For if we begin with the root idea that people are to be allowed to do *whatever* they want to do, then so long as any trains of actions are conceivable and really instantiable, the question can only be whether a given sort of action will collide with the legitimate liberties of others. If it does not, then, given our starting point of a general right to liberty, anyone who *can* do the action described and wants (for whatever reason) to do it is to be allowed to do it.

Suppose, then, that our hypothetical agent does embark on an envisageable train of actions: picking an apple, say (to use a Lockean example), or plowing a bit of land with a view to planting potatoes with a view to eating them, or designing a new piece of computer software. The question, why *allow* him to engage in the second-level acts of selling or giving or bequeathing as well as such first-level acts as eating the apple or the potato or running programs with the software, is properly the question, why *not* allow him to do this? For these are things he wants to do and is able to do. Thus, a right of general liberty will permit him to do them, so long as no good reason of a liberty-restricting type can be found for disallowing these acts.

It may be apropos in this connection to remind ourselves that "allowing" is not the name of any simple act or set of acts; it denotes, rather, refrainings from interferences or preventions of acts. The question "Why allow?" is equivalent to the question "Why not forbid?" Which is to say that it is really the question "Why forbid?" The answer to "Why allow?" is essentially that there is no good reason to forbid: in the absence of such reason, it stands that the action is allowed. Those who wish to make out that there is something *generally* wrong with "capitalist acts among consenting adults" (the delightful phrase is Nozick's[3]) need to find something about those acts that constitutes a good general reason for forbidding them. And if they are attempting to criticize the theory of liberty for its internal *coherence*, then this reason must be specified in terms of restrictions on liberty. It is not, by contrast, necessary for anyone to find good general reasons for *allowing* them. The fact that people want to engage in them is, on the libertarian theory, all the "reason" that takes. Of course, in the case of any action there is a presumption that the agent wants to engage in it; hence the prima facie case is for allowing people to do whatever they do, short of violating the like liberty of others.

Another "Libertarianism Restricts Liberty" Argument

The libertarian will insist, as we put it above, on a "good reason of a liberty-restricting type": that is, to forbid some general type of activity, it must be established that that act interferes with the liberty of others. Critics such as Cohen and O'Neill[4] have in fact concentrated their efforts on precisely that task. Consider, for instance, the following objection by O'Neill, in commenting on Nozick's famous case of Wilt Chamberlain, to whom a hundred thousand people deliberately give a quarter to watch play basketball, thus winding up with a greater income than a large class of hypothetical theorists would wish to allow: "intuitively there seems to be nothing very wrong about premium payments to Wilt Chamberlain. . . . But this will hardly do as an argument against patterned and end-state principles of justice or for entitlement theory. The argument presupposes, so does not demonstrate, that it is wrong to interfere to restore disturbed patterns or end-states. . . . But it is just these property rights which have yet to be established. . . . we do indeed [lack a theory of property], but the lack cannot warrant the assumption[5] that individual property rights are rights to control resources in all ways, to dispose of them however and to whomever the owner wishes, or to accumulate them without limit. This interpretation of property rights must be established *before* the restoration of patterns or end-states by state action can be rejected as unjustified interference which violates individuals' rights."[6]

But we must protest! O'Neill says explicitly that she is, for the sake of argument of course, "assuming that individuals have at least the rights not to be harmed in life, health, or liberty, but that their property rights—rights to control resources—have yet to be established."[7] Very well. But in that case, her charge, in rebutting Nozick's argument, must be to establish in some credible way that the right to have a quarter of a million dollars, which means the right to perform the indefinite array of actions made possible by having that amount of money, got by the above means, constitutes an infringement of the right "not to be harmed in life, health, or liberty." It is clear that Chamberlain's having a whole lot of money does not, as such, harm people's health or take away their lives. It remains, therefore, for her to show that Chamberlain's high income constitutes, somehow, an *infringement of the liberty* of someone or other, and does so *as such,* rather than as an incidental aspect of some of the acts one might thereby be tempted to perform. She is quite right to say that in some sense the other theories need to be refuted before the right to ownership at that level has been established, but that wasn't supposed to be what was in question at this point. What was supposed to be in question was only whether the principle of liberty supports such ownership. And it seems to me that on the face of it, it does. If it could be established that patterning theories, such as the equality theory, were themselves required by the commitment to liberty, then we would have something to worry about. But she doesn't do that, so far as I can see, and the only ways I know of that it can be done involve cheating, notably, by suddenly converting liberty ordinarily so-called, that is, what we termed "negative liberty", into *positive*, and usually positive *equal* liberty and then pointing out that of course if Wilt Chamberlain can do *more* than the rest of us folks—which by virtue of having more money we will suppose that he can—then his actions are "interfering with liberty". But that is not good argument; it is conceptual sleight-of-hand.

O'Neill points to many important questions raised by Nozick but not answered: the "difficulties in the way of assigning complete ownership to the contributor of one factor of production, and the more fundamental problem of understanding why any rights should accrue from mixing one's labour. Why should not labouring be a way of losing one's labour, of improving what is 'in the common state'? Why, at best, should the labourer acquire more than a share in the final product in proportion to his contribution?"[8]

Important and, in a sense, difficult questions, to be sure. But it is wrong to think that they are impossible conundrums. Each of O'Neill's questions has a prima facie answer, in fact; that is, one that stands unless we can establish reasons to think that the actions in question really do interfere with others' right to liberty. (1) The straightforward answer to the general question "Why does labor give one rights to the whole thing that is the product of one's labor?" is that that is what one was *doing* when one exerted oneself in that way. The various things one can do with that whole thing are what the agent saw herself to be in the way of enabling herself to do: that's what her action was *all about*. And if we are accepting the liberty-respecting premise, that is, saying that people have the right to do what they want to do, then *there* is our answer to why the general principle of rights to liberty provides support for ownership of that kind, unless overriding considerations about liberty intervene. (Whether they do, we will discuss anon.) This answer, I appreciate, is rather breathtakingly simple: but it may be the right one, for all that!

(2) And if we want to know why the laborer should get "more than a share in the final product in proportion to his contribution", the answer is that he indeed should not; but then, in the case where he labors in the state of nature, he does not. For there *is* no one else in that hypothetical case—his share is, simply, 100 percent. The laborer in question got there first, luckily for him—or, in most cases, not just "luckily," but with the aid of large amounts of courage, perseverance, ingenuity, and enterprise.

Chamberlain's is not, of course, a state-of-nature case. Still, presumably O'Neill would claim that he gets a disproportionate share of the product of his labor. But does he? I don't see it! For Chamberlain *does* acquire only a share of the "final product"—his teammates, after all, also get paid; and although they don't get paid (we will assume) nearly as much, it's also true that they didn't do nearly as much to attract the box office receipts—if Wilt resigns and is succeeded by no other comparably superb player, we may be sure that the team's gross income would decline by much more than the share Chamberlain has received.

Almost every philosophical reader will, at this point, blanch at this simple argument, which after all ignores the famed "Lockean Proviso". Locke, as we know, held that one was entitled to these things "at least so long as there remains enough and as good for others", and Nozick accepts that some such qualification is in order, though he worries, and very fruitfully, about the exact form it should take. But one must appreciate that Nozick, and probably everyone else who contemplates this problem, is doing two things at once: on the one hand, wondering what the commitment to liberty as such implies about this matter, and on the other, what our rights really are (= really should be). This study will explore both of these issues, indeed, but it is a methodological presumption that they really are two issues and not one. So if we address the first one: what about the "proviso" *if* there is only the single right to liberty—each to have the right to do as he pleases, provided only that he doesn't thereby violate the similar right of others—then we may be able to come up with something of importance about libertariansim, whether it makes this theory look good or bad. Recall, too, my argument that negative rights are fundamental. There are *no fundamental* positive rights if pure liberty is our guide.

With this firmly in mind, let us consider the matter. Meanwhile, back in the State of Nature, we note that this is a wilderness unsullied by positive rights. People may, then, take what they please, so long as what they take, that is to say, what they do there, does not adversely affect the rights that people already have. That my acquisition of a given plot thereby disenables you from having that plot is true enough, but nothing to the point, since you *had no right to that plot*, any more than I did. I acquired the right by getting there first and doing things with it. I did not activate a *claim* I already had, for I had none. Acquisition limits opportunity, to be sure. But nobody had a duty to provide you with that opportunity, nor even to maintain it for you. You simply didn't have a right to it. You did have the right to do whatever would not interfere with the actions of others; but your planting in this plot would do so, alas, for I—you see—am *already here*.

Of course, problems about how your activity involves the things you claim thereby remain. When the first Asian crossed the land bridge to Alaska 11,000 years ago, did she then get title to the whole of North America?[9] Certainly not. That proto-Inuit lady had absolutely no idea what she was getting into; it cannot be plausibly argued that her activity, what she saw herself to be doing, was using a whole continent or anything like it.

"Acquiring" Not an Act

An important point about all this is that just as there is no such action as "allowing", so, too, *there is no such action as "acquiring"*. To acquire an object is to do something that either constitutes, or at any rate is regarded by some relevant people as constituting, good reason for recognizing certain rights of yours in relation to that object. For instance, you enclose a piece of land, you grow beans on it, and in consequence you get to determine the disposition of that piece of land henceforth. Your initial acts of enclosing and planting or whatever yield up a consequent right of that kind, if they do, only because there is some good reason why such acts should get you such rights. That good reason, in the libertarian view, will be whatever good reason there turns out to be for allowing people to do as they please, plus the observation that in engaging in these acts, you were engaging in an ongoing track of activity, allowance of which is just what owning that bit of land consists of.

But what about interferences with liberty when we acquire in the State of Nature? A major consideration relevant to these, I believe, is that ordinarily the first entrant to a previously unowned stretch of territory is not the first person ever to be aware of the existence of that stretch. Suppose that many of us are thus aware, and more or less any of us might go forth. Only you, however, actually do so. If pure intentions were admitted as grounds for land claims, it would be impossible to settle any claim questions that arose. Anyone who did anything would be "interfering with someone's liberty". But for the same reason, we can't let the pure intentions of the actual pioneer sufficiently establish his land claims either. Moreover, as all sorts of authors have recently been at pains to argue, pioneers do not go forth totally detached from the societies they emerged from. Others may well have equipped the expedition, and our pioneer may owe them something for this. And so on. In general, we should accept a good deal of the claim that property rights are conventions. We should accept this because many of them *are* conventions, in the precise sense of understood constraints accepted by those concerned—including the pioneers.

It may well be in the interests of all of us to impose many constraints about initial acquisition in many circumstances, and if, as I shall be concerned to argue in the second part of this study, some form of the social contract is the best underpinning for moral theory, and yet constraints are plausibly argued to be inherent in foundations of libertarianism, then such constraints can be accepted.

To return to the main issue, several further points should be emphasized. One is that constraints on initial acquisition cannot plausibly be made the foundation of such strongly antiliberal distributive constraints as, say, pure egalitarianism, or steeply sloped income tax schemes, and the like. The context of initial acquisition, let us bear in mind, is that there is a self-subsistent society occupying some roughly defined area, and that this area constitutes the point of departure for our Initial Acquirers. By definition, the entire panoply of resources that may exist in the previously unoccupied area has been unavailable to that entire society up until now, and it will remain so to virtually all of them in the nearish future. Our hypothetical explorer may *add* to their resources by his discoveries and labors, should he choose to return with some of them for exchange or gift. But how can his activities be thought *as such* to *subtract* from what that society already has? His new activities might pollute the air or waters back home, for instance, and then some or all of those people will indeed have a complaint. But that isn't an argument from the sheer fact of new exploration and acquisition. Surely, the only argument one could plausibly base on any such premises must appeal to opportunity costs: that is, our pioneer's appropriation of resources that others might have been able to appropriate themselves at some future time. But what is the basis of their appeal to such costs? If they want some of what might lie out there, why don't *they* go and seek them? Why should these armchair explorers be thought to have a claim in advance?

Arthur's Argument: Acquisition as Harmful

John Arthur has recently mounted an interesting argument on behalf of the claim that the acquisition of resources in the "state of nature" would *harm* those who don't get them, or who get inferior ones, and thus, on libertarian principles, would be entitled to compensation from those who got the superior ones.[10] Obviously, this is an important claim. Is it plausible to think that initial acquisition does harm others?

Reasonably proposing to define 'harm' as 'being made worse off', Arthur asks how we are to decide whether the position of others is worsened as a result of others' acquisition of hitherto unclaimed and raw natural resources. He asks, "Suppose the early arriving Boone family has laid claim to the bottom land before the Smiths arrive—weren't the Smiths, who must now farm the rocky hillside, made worse off by the Boones' acquisition of the more productive land? Clearly the Smiths would be better off had the Boones not already taken that piece of land, so don't the Smiths have a legitimate claim that the proviso that enough and as good be left was violated?"[11]

As Arthur recognizes, the answer is "Not necessarily, say Locke and Nozick. When asking whether the Smiths are made worse off, we must ask ourselves, 'Worse off than they would be . . . when?' Plainly it won't do, as he agrees, to compare the situation of the non-appropriator owning the *particular* thing which somebody else has taken. By this test the Boones have made the Smiths worse off. Neither Locke nor Nozick look at it that way, however. . . . [From Locke's perspective], the non-appropriating Smiths have no complaint because (he assumes) if the Boones didn't use the land then it would remain undeveloped . . . not only are the Smiths not *harmed* by the Boones' acquisition: their situation may actually be improved since they now can purchase the Boones' products." For "viewed from the perspective of the benefits non-appropriators receive from living in a *system* allowing for development of resources, the Smiths are better off than if the system were not there. . . . A second reason . . . is that, if we were to say an acquisition is just only if others would be no better off owning the land, oil or whatever themselves, then *no* acquisition will pass the test. No matter how much I'm benefitted by you acquiring the resources and putting it into production . . . I would be happier still if it were I who owned it. But of course that is true of every acquisition."[12] To which, of course, we should add that to talk about *making* someone *worse off* is surely, normally, to compare the condition he is in given the act in question with the status quo ante, and in the present case, the hypothesis is presumably that at the outset, neither Boone nor Smith owned anything at all, and then Boone arrived *first*. Boone's acquisition clearly doesn't affect Smith's antecedent condition at all. Smith sets off for the wilderness having no idea what he'll find when he gets there. Suppose Smith had set off in another direction and, to his astonishment, had washed up on the shores of 1987 Manhattan. Would the many millions of people there have to be said to have "harmed" Smith for getting there first?

Arthur goes on to note, "As Nozick sees it, the Smiths should compare their current situation, without the Boones' land, with one in which they lack the benefits of living in a system 'allowing appropriation and permanent property'." But as we may agree, there is a question of just how we are to interpret that. In Arthur's view, "there is an important ambiguity. . . . What, specifically, is intended by asking how the Smiths would fare outside such a system: whether the Smiths are better off as a result of living in a system of private property than in a state of nature, or whether the Smiths are better off under private property than they would be under one or more of the alternative methods society might devise to develop its resources? The former seems to be Locke's question . . . . it is fairly clear . . . that Nozick has the second question in mind. . . . So . . . with Locke and Nozick, [there] are two alternative baselines: one compares the nonappropriator's position with how he would fare in a state of nature, the other with how he would do outside of a capitalist economy. But since private appropriation of natural resources is only one alternative means of developing resources . . . Nozick's baseline and Locke's are very different."[13]

How, then, are we to select a baseline? Arthur describes five possibilities: the state of nature, a communal, or a private ownership system in which compensation was given for the nonowners or latecomers, along any of three distinct lines: egalitarian, utilitarian, and Rawlsian. Thus we are comparing our hypothetical Smiths with (1) a situation "without any system of appropriation at all"; (2) "in a society which didn't allow for *private* appropriation but relied instead on communal development of land and other resources"; (3) an otherwise private-ownership system that "would distribute proceeds of unowned resources equally", or (4) would "distribute the proceeds in such a way to maximize total welfare", or (5) would distribute them in such a way as "to maximize the expectations of the least advantaged."[14]

What situation are we going to make this comparison in respect of? Arthur proposes "the perspective of the one who would most likely be better off in a situation different from his current one. That person, W, would be the worst off member of the capitalist society." Regarding *that* member, Arthur speculates that it would be "indeterminate" whether he would be better off than in a ruleless state of nature: "Certainly unemployment, crime, drugs and despair make the lives of the poorest few in modern capitalism very unhappy indeed, so that living outside of a system of rules which provides for the orderly development of resources . . . might be an improvement. It is hard to know."[15] But for any of the others, he argues that W would surely be better off in any of them. Regarding (2), it "seems hard to imagine W's position not improving if society were to treat resources as communally owned property rather than the private acquisitions of the relatively wealthy"; as for (3), utilitarianism, "if we assume declining marginal utility of money, then we have good reason to think W would be benefitted by a rule which provides for distribution . . . according to the utilitarian principle"; and as to (4): "It is also likely that W would be better off if wealth were to be distributed so that W gets a share equal to that of every other citizen"; while in (5), of course, "W would be best off under the fifth, Rawlsian, baseline, which would distribute the income from resources so as to maximize the expectations of the least advantaged." "In sum," Arthur concludes, "for all but the state of nature baseline, it is reasonably clear that W is harmed when others appropriate resources without compensating him."[16]

That leaves the final question: which of the five baselines is the correct one? "A number of points are relevant. First, the decision should make sense in light of the fact that W is as entitled to the resources as anybody else. He wasn't born deserving a smaller share of the earth's wealth, nor is anybody else naturally entitled to a larger than average share." And "second, the baselines we select . . . must describe a society that rational persons would tend to support. . . . The rules governing distribution of the fruits of nature should be workable, and they should be rules which we feel are not unjust or unfair."[17]

Given these criteria, Arthur argues that the "state of nature" is *not* the one to use, "for it fails at least two tests. First, a society with no rules . . . is arguably no society at all—certainly it isn't a workable one. . . . Furthermore, to expect W to compare his current position with his fate in such a state of nature is unfair. It's as if a son claimed the right to all of his mother's inheritance on grounds that his getting it won't harm his sister since in a state of nature she would be even worse off than she will be without her share." And he suggests that "Equality, more than any other baseline, reflects the fact that, other things being equal, nobody naturally deserves a larger or smaller share."[18] Of course, we should also use any baseline in which W (the worst-off person, remember) is better off than the worst-off person would be in any other system, and so this might give us one of the others.

What could the libertarian say in reply? Arthur suggests this. "One other line of argument is open to the libertarian. Suppose that private ownership of the means of production were far more efficient than public ownership, and suppose further that capitalism for some reason could not survive if individuals were required to compensate others when they appropriate a natural resource for their own use. How would these putative facts affect W's demand for compensation?" In response to this Arthur offers two points. "First, W still has an important argument on his side, namely the point that a baseline should reflect the fact that nobody deserves the resources any more than he. This consideration leads naturally to equality. But whether that would carry the day against these efficiency considerations is unclear. The second point W can make is that these two assumptions are very doubtful, particularly the second. Why should it be the case that capitalism cannot survive if somebody who finds oil under his land is required to compensate others before he can appropriate it?" And he concludes that "the Lockean approach to property acquisition leads, then, to the conclusion that those who acquire natural resources in a free market, without compensating those who get nothing, harm the worst off members of society by their appropriations. . . . Thus, by the libertarians' own test . . . all private acquisitions of resources under capitalism require that compensation be paid to the least advantaged members of society"[19]

What are we to make of this intricate argument? We should not be moved, I'm afraid. Let us see why. First, there are several things more than a little suspicious about Arthur's method. Is W a paraplegic, or normally capable? If the former, then the claim that W would be as well off as the Boones by virtue of owning the better land is absurd. Nor is it plausible to say that W would benefit by a share of any resources in their raw state. Arthur says he is entitled to a share of the *value* of those resources, and indeed, of them in their *undeveloped* state—but what does that mean? There they are, in the ground. Here is W, sans technical know-how, sans a usable body to develop them himself. Plainly, the resources are of no value to W, apart from what they would fetch on a market; but they will fetch nothing unless developed. And why should those who will develop them do so only on condition that W gets a share? W certainly will be some such personage as a paraplegic, however: the worst-off person in a Nozickian capitalist society, in the absence of any charity whatever, is certainly going to be one who could not make a living under any circumstances where he was forced by circumstances to *make* a living rather than having it handed him on a silver platter. How well off such a person would be in the other systems would depend on what their attitude toward the incapable is.

Would their attitude be that we should split the *income* from the resources with the incapacitated? Should, as a matter of *justice*? Why? No matter how those resources were *owned*, the question of how to divide the income is still open, after all. A communal system might choose to reward people in proportion to their labor, as in Marx's idea about the first stage of socialism after the Revolution.[20]

A further and more fundamental question: why think that the communal and like systems *are* an "available option"? Arthur suggests two criteria for selecting the right option: "First, the decision should make sense in light of the fact that W is as entitled to the resources as anybody else. . . . Second, the baseline we select should be a reasonable one; it must describe a society that rational persons would tend to support. . . . The rules . . . should be workable, and they should be rules which we feel are not unjust or unfair."[21] We can make short work of the first one: everybody is indeed equally entitled to resources, for the simple reason that *nobody is entitled to them at all.* And regarding the second one, Arthur does not say which rational persons or under what circumstances. But if he means that *everyone* should agree to this, then the usual questions about contractarian procedure are raised. Suppose that someone insists on the "capitalist" option, and that someone else insists on a "socialist" one: we have a hung jury! What does Arthur have in mind as a way of breaking the deadlock? In my view, the way to do so is simply by Boone's leaving the meeting and going off and starting work on the land. If Smith then comes along and claims a share, Boone can reasonably ask what the *basis* of the claim could possibly be? It can't be that Smith is claiming on the basis of a system that everyone agreed was reasonable, for Boone did not.

Reasonable people will not accept a benchmark of equality, for they have no reason to. Nor have they reason to accept a utilitarian distribution; indeed, utilitarianism is simply invoking another kind of equality, as we have seen—equality of the value to *anyone* of a unit of *anyone's* utility. And they certainly have no reason to accept a policy of favoring the worst-off person.

If the other systems are not available without question-begging, then there is no need to compare the natural alternative, which is the State of Nature distribution, with them. Arthur thinks that it is "indeterminate" whether the worst-off person in a contemporary capitalist economy is better off than he would be be in a state of nature, but this claim is surely preposterous. It is completely preposterous against the Hobbesian state of nature, and it is equally preposterous, as we shall see, against a Lockean one with the new version of the proviso supplied by Gauthier, which we shall discuss in Part Two, forbidding the taking of advantage of others' persons and (therefore) their labor. A beggar on the streets of Manhattan is enormously better off than a primitive person in any state-of-nature situation short of the Garden of Eden. And if instead of making W a paraplegic, we take her to be the worst-off otherwise competent adult, there is surely no argument at all. Smith is better off with entitlement to her second-rate plot than she would be in a ruleless condition.

But Arthur, as we have seen, argues that the state of nature baseline is inappropriate for two reasons: (1) that "a society with no rules is no society at all—certainly it isn't a workable one"; (2) that "to expect W to compare his current position with his fate in such a state of nature is unfair. It's as if a son claimed the right to all of his mother's inheritance on grounds that his getting it won't harm his sister since in a state of nature she would be even worse off than she will be without her share."[22] But the first point is simply a semantic one: what we should mean here by a "society" is what Hobbes does: simply a group of humans who interact to some degree. And the reason we should consider that to be the alternative is simply that it *is* the alternative unless and until some agreement is reached. As to the second reason given, the analogy is obviously question-begging. The man's sister does have at least *a* claim on her mother's inheritance, normally, whereas our person in the state of nature has none. To make the analogy work better, let the proposal be to divide up the goods of some perfect stranger who has no interest whatever in the applicants. All *our* individual has is bodily and mental equipment and a not-quite-vacant plot of hitherto state-of-nature real estate, the best bit of which has already been occupied. The alternatives are to use force against Boone, or get to work on that second-best plot.

In short, in order to make any such alleged claims about initial acquisition the basis of an argument of the popularly accepted type against the libertarian view, appeal must be made to a fundamentally different theory from the one we are considering: some form of the theory that unowned resources are *not* really unowned, but somehow already belong to people, indeed to *everyone*, regardless of what everyone has done or what particular transactions they may have entered into. Now, we do certainly need an independent argument why we should reject such a theory. But we do not need to worry about such a theory's being somehow presupposed or entailed by the libertarian idea. It simply *isn't*. Some may find this refreshing and even exhilarating (I do); and others may find it frightening (socialists, who frighten easily). But let us at least admit that it is different.

CHAPTER 8

Property Rights Concluded

Transfer

OVERWHELMINGLY, the method by which we acquire what we come by is that of transfer from some previous right holder. That person has the right to transfer the item to us, by being its owner or an agent of the owner. Usually the transfer is conditional on our transferring something to him (usually money); this is acquisition by "exchange". The process is fundamentally similar, however, even when the transfer is one way, that is, a gift. In both cases, the essence of the matter is that the owner makes some manner of public declaration to the effect that the rights over x previously held by A are now declared by A to belong to B. The "public" may be just the two persons involved, but if the arrangement is to be upheld by further persons, it must somehow be publicly ascertainable, and of course that is a source of frequent problems and disputes. Further, we should note that transfer cannot, actually, be exclusively one way, for the recipient, B, must accept or consent to the transfer.[1] Even where x is a pure gift, B may refuse it. Nobody may force anything on anybody.

It is clear that things can go wrong. There can, in particular, be problems of communication. Suppose A misstates her intention? She didn't mean to give it to *B*, or not to *give* it to B, or she let it slip but didn't really mean it at all. And what if it was impulsive or she couldn't really afford it? It is not entirely clear that impulsiveness affects the legitimacy of the transfer, but lack of power to pay is certainly a major problem. You walk into a classy restaurant, knowing perfectly well that you can't pay the bill, dine sumptuously, and then when the reckoning arrives, cheerfully explain that you don't have a dime to your name. You have certainly violated a reasonable presumption of the establishment, as of any transaction: viz., that you can carry out your part of the bargain. Yet they didn't actually *ask* you—and you didn't actually *tell* anybody you would pay.

Details, though important details; and for the most part, we will not dwell on them here. But there is one important exception. Some will insist that transfers of property rights, proceeding as they do by the making of agreements, are not self-validating but presuppose *other principles*, especially some or other condition of equality between the parties to it. The matters mentioned thus far in this section may reasonably be accounted explications of what it is for an agreement to be genuinely voluntary. But the imposition of an equality condition would be quite another matter.

Consider, for example, a recent argument by A. M. Macleod: "It is not difficult to cite cases of agreements which are voluntary in the requisite sense, but which nevertheless yield so much more in the way of advantage for one of the parties than for the other that they must be stigmatised as unfair. Thus when the parties are unequally astute in the devising of interest-safeguarding strategies, or when they differ significantly in bargaining power, or when they have an unequal appetite (or tolerance) for hard bargaining, the agreements they conclude may satisfy both the 'voluntariness' and the 'mutual advantage' conditions—and still be unjust."[2] To be sure, Macleod's argument is addressed to a question we are not yet taking up here, that of the ultimate justice of the market. Our concern at present is the more limited one, whether the market is legitimate *if* the fundamental libertarian view is accepted; whether we should accept it for what it proposes to be, namely, the correct view of justice, we leave to the second part of this book. Nevertheless, we should appreciate the bearing of Macleod's argument on this more limited question. For it might be said that if, for example, a bargain is concluded between two agents extremely unequal in some of these respects, then it will not in fact be fully voluntary either.[3] Can *this* be so?

A distinction is needed here. The background conditions to an agreement may certainly be less than fully "voluntary" in the sense that one or both parties would like it had they been otherwise. This could be so in all sorts of ways. Few of us think we have run our lives perfectly: doubtless we regret some of our past decisions, wishing that we had chosen otherwise. And of course most of us could wish that we were better situated than we are: we'd have liked otherwise to

do things differently, leaving ourselves or those we love in better circumstances than they are. But these facts are obviously irrelevant on
the present theory. Clearly, it is not I or anyone else who limits your
liberty when you exercise it to make unwise choices; and your liberty
to do as you like is not infringed when others use their like liberty to
decide in ways that don't forward your interests as much as you'd
like. To suppose that such considerations count against the *voluntariness* of agreements is really to embrace a different theory than the
one we are considering here. This, then, is not as yet an internal criticism of the libertarian view.

A more plausible criticism would be afforded if some of the background conditions were the result of previous violations of liberty.
But whose? Suppose that the parties are A and B, and that A has
violated some right of B's in the past. It could be, then, that the current transaction takes place, as it were, under protest. Things need to
be put right before further voluntary transactions can take place. But
in such a case, there is question why the aggrieved party is willing to
conclude this further transaction at all. We are, after all, assuming that
we have a voluntary transaction here: B is not being *forced* to have
further dealings with A. It would seem that if B nevertheless proceeds, B is either setting aside the past problem, separating its influence from the present case, or else forgiving A for the previous trans-
gression. Either way, it would seem to leave the specific obligations
undertaken in the present case intact.

If those past injustices were done by others to others, however, it
is unclear what effect if any they have on the present case. Suppose
that my great-grandfather ruthlessly and unjustly despoiled your
great-grandfather of forty acres these hundred years ago. Does that
mean that when I buy two gallons of paint from your store, I may
now refuse to pay the agreed price? No. If this is something I hold
against you, then I shouldn't buy at your store, and that is that; if I
nevertheless do, there is no case for my refusal to pay up—no case for
saying that *this* transaction proceeds in violation of anyone's liberty.

A theory regarding past injustices and their relevance to the present is obviously essential, to be sure. Such a theory might, for instance, go the way of Rothbard: "historical tracings generally make
little difference. Suppose, for example, that Jones steals money from
Smith or that he acquires the money through State expropriation and
subsidy. And suppose that there is no redress: Smith and his heirs
die, and the money continues in Jones' family. In that case, the disap-
pearance of Smith and his heirs means the dissolution of claims from

the original titleholders *at that point*, on the 'homestead' principle of property right from possession of unowned property. The money therefore accrues to the Jones family as their legitimate and absolute property."[4] But whatever that theory should be, it needn't have the effect Macleod is arguing for here.

Macleod referred specifically to three possible inequalities: "when the parties are unequally astute in the devising of interest-safeguard-ing strategies, or when they differ significantly in bargaining power, or when they have an unequal appetite (or tolerance) for hard bar-gaining." Now, these are not of a piece, and it may matter which sorts of cases we are considering in this connection. In general, we surely want to say that a *bad* bargain is still a bargain. The question is wheth-er there is also a point below which it would have to be said not even to have been a valid bargain *because not really voluntary*. And this sure-ly does seem possible. It is obviously so in the case where one party misrepresents the situation to the other, assuring delivery by a certain date when he knows perfectly well that he won't be able to do that, or that this item is a genuine Van Gogh when it is a fake; and so on.

What about when party A is, say, mentally deficient and cannot really understand the transaction he is supposedly "making"? Such an individual may be incapable of making any transaction at all or of making transactions of the level of complexity of the present one, and so on. The question of how fully responsible adults are to treat those of insufficient capacity is an important and difficult one. Whatever the right answer to it, it clearly cannot be one that presupposes that those individuals are what they are not. So we shall leave those to one side for the present. (More will be said about the analogous question of children's rights in Part Three.)

We still have the case of those not "good at bargaining", or lacking much tolerance for same. Here again there is doubt that such dis-parities will upset the voluntariness of the transaction. Such persons might be easily bilked; but 'bilking' usually connotes hoodwinking, which does involve a violation of voluntariness at one level or an-other. And below that level, it seems to me, we have no option but to go along with the justice of such transactions, even though we cluck our tongues. Most of us are loathe to carry on really intense and ag-gressive bargaining, bargaining where we are aware that the persons we are dealing with have no sympathy with us, no interest in our welfare, or even a positive interest in the reverse. And we may have little talent for it. We will avoid such situations if possible, and where we can't, perhaps attempt to engage an agent more astute than we to carry on the business. But will we claim that a bargain we have struck with such a person is *thereby* invalid? I think not. Parties such as Israel and the Palestine Liberation Organization, were they ever to strike an agreement, will be quick to claim that the other party *hasn't stuck to* its bargain, but they will not claim that it was *invalid* just because the other party hated its guts, nor because they weren't as good at negotiating or had less taste for it than the other party.

Equality

The question whether justice requires equality in some further sense than is implied by the libertarian hypothesis is, of course, basic and not to be swept under the carpet. It is, however, to be tabled at present. What does matter here is just how much and what sort of equality is implied by that hypothesis. And surely the answer to this is: not very much! The parties must be sufficiently cognizant and intelligent to be able to carry on bargaining, to be sure. And they must have whatever is required for holding people morally responsible ("free will", perhaps), though whether 'equality' is a relevant concept to apply to this condition is somewhat problematic. (If I deal with B rather than C because C is, in my judgment, a "more responsible" person than B, I presume that this is a judgment about the probability that I shall get what I bargained for. But it is not a judgment relevant to the question of whether B would be at fault—whether he should be *held* responsible—if, upon dealing with him, he proved unequal to his word.) But they may be highly disparate in many other respects. Locke's considerably maligned example of the impoverished servant cheating his wealthy master is apropos here: if my master sends me out to buy a pound of bacon, I do not respect his liberty if I falsify the amount charged, pocketing the difference. He commands great resources, I few; but it does not follow from that that I am at liberty to narrow the inequality in just any way I can manage. Nor does it follow that he or anyone else has violated my liberty in the past in any way. Any such violations would need to be established independently.

Libertarianism may certainly be characterized as the view that everyone has an equal right to liberty. But here the term 'equal' clearly does not refer to a quantity of anything that may be "distributed" among a number of persons. Rather, we should say simply that everyone has the fundamental right to liberty, explained as in the preceding, and that anything that deprives him or her of this, or violates or infringes it, is an injustice. The incredibly rich may violate the liberty of the desperately poor, to be sure—but also vice versa, even if, perhaps, with more excuse in the latter case. Needless to say, it also applies independently of race, sex, and the indefinitely many other variables on account of which people have sometimes been excluded from liberty's benefit. Fundamental rights are universal and not loaded in anyone's favor, though the situations or the heritages, genetic or social, of some doubtless make it probable that they will acquire greater properties or degrees of influence or any number of other kinds of goods than other, possibly less fortunate (in those respects) persons.

Capitalist Rights Not to Be Capitalists

On one important point there is a degree of misunderstanding so pervasive that one simply has to do one's bit to ward it off: namely, the point that property rights in the view being examined here are *liberty* rights. You may, on this view, do *what you wish* with what is yours. You may wish to save assiduously, invest astutely, and increase your property as much as possible—or you may not. You may prefer the life of the ne'er-do-well, or you may prefer to spend your time helping your friends or the needy, or you may wish simply to contemplate your navel. These options are your right to choose among as you will, on the libertarian view. There is no excuse for the idea, for instance, that a libertarian society must be a "meritocracy" in any serious sense of that term.[5] In any society, some, no doubt, will be looked up to by many people, and others not; and in a society in which the rights of property are recognized there is an understandable tendency for those who have prospered greatly to be looked up to. There is also some tendency for the rich to have more political power, or at least influence, than their typical middle- or lower-income fellows. But these tendencies are just that: they have no necessary connection with the fact of substantial acquisition itself, and of course are contingent for whatever validity they have on the existence of a state—an institution viewed with much suspicion and disdain by libertarians who, like Rothbard, have anarchist tendencies.

That the connection is not *necessary* is obvious enough from the facts. There are persons of little means but great influence and even of power—not many Supreme Court justices in the United States are men of great wealth, for instance, and few among its wealthiest persons are even very much in the public eye, let alone in positions of political power.

Moreover, the wealthy in the advanced capitalist nations are often remarkably charitable people. They do not adhere to Marx's description of the "rational miser," the man who eschews everything for the sake of maximizing his capital. They spend money not only on themselves, but, often lavishly, on the public, endowing libraries, schools, hospitals, symphony orchestras, and more and more. The cynical will look for underlying pecuniary motives in their so doing, but they will have to look too deep to find anything interesting. Very charitable people have a strong desire to be charitable, and/or to be thought charitable (there are some of each kind—wealthy persons giving anonymous gifts of $6 million to some charitable cause are not out for public repute in any sense of that word interesting enough to be worth remarking.) More will be said about charity later in this book (Part Three); here we are only recognizing the fact that there is ample room for it within the scope of the libertarian theory.

Resources and Generational Considerations

The earth has finite resources, no doubt. Let us suppose that there are some finite resources that are also limited enough in extent that a very large population could press very hard on the supply of them. Productive land conceivably could be an example (though in fact it is not, at present): we can imagine there being too little of it left for everyone to have a nontrivial amount, or too little to feed all the hungry mouths there are. Does every person born come equipped with a right to some of it, that is, at least enough for her most minimal needs? Some think so, but our question for the present is whether that conclusion is inherent in the libertarian view. And the answer, it seems to me clearly, is in the negative.

We come into the world equipped with the right not to be harmed, not to have our liberty violated. But we don't come equipped with a positive right to any resource. And in a desperate circumstance, this could be taken to mean that we do not come equipped even with a "right to life". In the sense in which this is so, however, it means a *positive* right to life, that is, the right to be *helped to remain alive*, rather than merely the right not to be deprived of the life we have. In insisting that a pervasive right to liberty is fundamentally negative, not positive, we are therefore repudiating any such right as a fundamental right. There could be circumstances in which it would be essentially impossible to honor such a right. More importantly, however, there could be circumstances in which others, acting within their rights, could refuse to help even though they had the means to do so. In such circumstances, persons contemplating parenthood would need to weigh well their inclinations in this respect, for their offspring might be born into circumstances that were far from assuring them of a tolerable life, or indeed of anything but a rather short one. Hard words, some will say. But, I think, likely true, and certainly true if the general position we are considering has the support of reason. If constraining the liberty of some in order that others may prosper is contrary to justice, so is doing so in order that others may live at all.

We might take the view that those who bring children into such a world are themselves guilty of murder, or something close to it. If it is a foreseeable result of having a child in certain circumstances that it would not survive infancy, then if we nevertheless bring it into existence, we could be said to be murdering it, just as surely as you would have done so if you were to lock me in a bare room for a year without provisions.

There are subtler and less draconian issues about generational matters, but we must leave those aside for the present. Meanwhile, having sketched the libertarian theory at some length as a theory, I turn to the fundamental question of what there is to be said for it. Are there solid reasons for accepting it, or not?

PART TWO

Foundations: Is Libertarianism Rational?

CHAPTER 9

Introduction

On "Foundations"

WHY SHOULD WE ACCEPT the libertarian view? Or should we instead reject it? That is the most fundamental question to be addressed in this book, and it is time to address it now. Doing so requires that we delve into the vexed subject of the Foundations of Morals, in the sense of 'morals' in which it concerns the present subject. The subject of morality in this sense is, roughly, the normative question of general relations among people: how we are to relate to our fellows. We shall have to say something about the available options, and in particular about the options that tend actually to be taken by libertarians.

There are those among contemporary moral philosophers—probably not far from a majority, at that—who don't think there are "foundations" of morals. This is usually because they don't think there are *foundations* of anything. The idea of a "foundation" in the sense of the term in which they are against it is that of a solid, immovable set of fixtures that can support the edifice above. Less metaphorically, the foundationalist, in this much-objected-to sense, is one who looks for indubitable premises from which the general truths of the field we are concerned with can be derived, by strict deductive reasoning.

Lawrence Haworth defines foundationism as the view "that (1) warranted beliefs are possible only if they can be derived from presuppositionless first premises, and (2) at least one such premise is warranted."[1] And he objects to this as follows: "The foundationist will carry out the examination [of his beliefs] up to the point where he confronts the imagined presuppositionless first premise on which he founds his beliefs, attitudes, and actions. But if in fact that premise is, as the pragmaticist and instrumentalist hold, susceptible of the same sort of examination as his other beliefs are, he is actually misled by his philosophical position to limit the autonomy and rationality attained in his own life."[2] I am not clear why the foundationist should behave like that: surely, there is no need to put one's head in the sand just because one has reached what appears to be a presuppositionless finding. No doubt everything *can*, in some sense of 'can', be questioned—in some sense of 'questioned'! But what if the item not only seems terribly obvious, both to you and to everyone concerned but, moreover, one simply can't imagine what alternative there could be? We do not get out to check a half-dozen more times when we come across a large red STOP sign in broad daylight, even though no doubt it is logically possible that one is mistaken in thinking the object one sees to be such. At any rate, in this strict sense of the term, we will go along with the current view and not assume there are "foundations".

However, there is a more generous notion of foundations, peculiarly relevant, in my view, to moral philosophy, in which it seems to me reasonable to assume that there are likely to be some, and that if there are not, then the field under consideration is at least open to suspicion. This less stringent foundationism asks for general considerations that play a very central role in the field but is quite willing to settle for broadly empirical premises, so long as they are true or at least strongly supported by the available evidence. And it is willing to settle for something less than out-and-out deductions, where relevant. What it objects to is circular or clearly invalid reasoning, and to premises that are either virtually meaningless or, more crucially, not decidable by publicly acceptable methods of reasoning. There is, I think, particularly good reason for being concerned about such things in the field of moral philosophy.

What does a moral theory try to do, and what does it mean to say that a theory has, or supplies, "foundations" of morals? Here are four subjects that might reasonably be, and have by philosophers at various times been, identified with the idea of foundations of morals, viz.:

(1) An answer to the question "What *is* morality?", in the sense of "What does the term 'morality' (and its associated concepts, such as 'right' and 'ought') mean? Which questions are moral questions? Which phenomena are moral phenomena?" In short, analysis of the concept or concepts of morals.

(2) An answer to the question "Why do people concern themselves about morality? Why do people act in response to moral considerations?"

(3) An answer to the question "Why *should* we concern ourselves about morality? Why *should* we act in response to moral considerations?" In short, this question is "Why should I (anyone) be moral?"

(4) An answer to the question "What is/are the *fundamental principle(s)* of morality?"

All of these are legitimate questions, to be sure. But they are different, and the difference matters. The sense in which we are concerned about it is sense (3). We want a really fundamental answer to the question why one *should* embrace, accept, adopt, or pay attention to any moral requirements, principles, or concerns.

Of course, in order to do that we must know which sense of 'morality' we are concerned with, i.e., we need a suitable answer to question (1). But we should not treat the question of definition as if it were an independent project of importance in itself. For it isn't. A definition cannot be a "foundation" of anything, except in the sense of formulating more clearly just which subject we propose to talk about. The early twentieth-century preoccupation with "metaethics", the search for the correct or true meaning of the word 'good' or whatever, runs into the problem that "true" doesn't apply to "meaning." A meaning can be the same as or different from someone else's; a formulation of that meaning can be clear or obscure; and the term whose meaning it is can be useful or useless. But trying to establish which meaning of the term 'trunk'—that in which it denotes part of a tree or that in which it denotes a large lidded box for storing things—is the "right" one is plainly misdirected effort.

Won't one person's view about what "the subject of morals" is differ from another's? And won't an effort to "clarify" therefore amount to a pointless view about the Essence of Morality? There has, after all, been a great deal of disagreement down through the centuries on this matter, has there not?

Agreed: there have certainly been disputes about something in this area, but these must have been disputes about something else— something more substantial, is one way to put it—than the alleged topic of "what morality really is". Were I to take it that there must be just one "proper" definition of the terms 'ethics', or 'morals', all others being somehow ruled out of court, then this charge would be decisive and the present project would be absurd. By this time, however, we all know better than to be distressed by the failure of essentialism. We can disavow, without embarrassment, any assumption that there is just one thing signified by "the" ordinary uses of 'ethics' or 'morals'. Some linguistic reflection might help here, no doubt. If we adopt a definition that makes the subject simply unrecognizable, we will not have got off to a promising start. But what is likely to remain is that there are several distinguishable uses of these various terms, several different areas of life referred to in these different senses. What we need to do, therefore, is to decide what we want to discuss, perhaps explaining how what is said applies or fails to apply to other possibilities and certainly explaining why the one chosen is worth discussing. That is the method I shall employ here. I have identified the subject before us as concerning general, interpersonal relations. The characterization will be made considerably more precise below.

Meanwhile, it should also be noted that answers to the questions of sort (3) "Why should people have a morality?" and "Why should they be moral?" need not be entirely different from answers to questions of type (2) "Why do people have moralities?" and "Why are they moral?" Indeed, a theory on which these were totally distinct would likely be open to the charge of unrealism.

Nevertheless, we surely want to envisage the possibility of doing the right thing for the wrong reason, or for bad reasons. Philosophers are surely in the business of looking for good ones. But so are lots of people—anyone who stops to question some alleged moral requirement, for instance. We want to know whether morality, or some morality, can be supported by good reasons.[3]

The Options

At this point a textbook would whip out a considerable variety of standardly recognized moral theories, going by such names as "Kantianism", utilitarianism, natural rights theory, "self-realization", "moral realism", and various others. And many of these will indeed, if they haven't already, come in for mention at one place or another in this book. But we will not dwell on them here, by and large, except to point out that all of them have one or the other, or likely both, of two shortcomings from the present perspective. First, some of them are views on the "Foundations of Ethics" only in the fourth of my listed senses: namely, views about what the fundamental *principle(s)* of morals is (are). That certainly is an interesting and important question, and indeed, libertarianism may be viewed as a proposed answer, or partial answer, to it. But to identify and perhaps proclaim some one principle to be the sole independent principle of morals, all others deriving ultimately from it, is not, or at least not obviously, to show that that is the *right* principle. Someone might say, of some lesser principle or rule, "I agree that that one follows from the one you propose. But why should I accept the one you propose?"

Second, and closely related: virtually all of these theories, when asked to supply some good reason for accepting their proposed principle, will appeal to what philosophers call "intuition". That is, they will say one of two things: either (1) that their principle is, when you think about it, just obvious, or self-evident; or (2) that the various smaller moral principles and judgments that their principle systematizes into a unified bundle are *themselves* just obvious, and accordingly they may be used as evidence for any moral theory that supports them. (Often, indeed usually, both things are said.) This appeal to intuitions is one we should, I think, reject, if what we are looking for is a morality supported by reason.

Libertarians in general support their views by appeals to intuitions, especially intuitions about our "natural rights". This is a method that has very wide currency in contemporary philosophy; it is by no means confined to libertarians. Libertarians who base their convictions on intuition are thus in good company. This, as we shall see, is ironic, for the other members of that company have widely varying views about these matters. The burning issue thus becomes, whose intuitions are the right ones? But adoption of the intuitional method virtually precludes rational decision of that burning issue; it simply continues to burn.

My intuition about that situation is that it's not a very satisfactory one. We ought to look for better. But all this will be somewhat opaque to the reader not well versed in contemporary philosophy; and readers who are so versed will be well aware that much will depend on how I conceive the analytical details. Both, therefore, will rightly ask for some explanation.

CHAPTER 10

Intuitions in Moral Philosophy

Two Kinds of Intuitionism

WE WILL DO WELL to begin by making a distinction familiar to current philosophers, that between two kinds of intuitionism. We will refer to these respectively—with some apologies for the choice of labels—as "metaphysical" and "methodological," respectively. (Other writers have used "theoretical" instead of "metaphysical"—a rather less perspicuous choice of terminology, though by now more usual.)

Metaphysical Intuitionism

By "metaphysical" intuitionism I mean the view that there exist some sort of "ethical entities" that are denoted by such words as 'good' or 'right' or 'just' (as the case may be); and that ethical knowledge is acquired by the mind's "apprehending" or, as we may say, "spotting" one or more of those at the appropriate points. On this view, when we say that an act is Right, we mean that it has one of these properties—namely, *"That* one!" The phrase is intentional: on this view of what ethics is all about, these entities are entirely unrelated, logically, to the rest of the more familiar array of entities and characters we encounter in our ordinary experience, or even in science. Like the more exotic entities of physics, Right and Wrong, Good and Bad, and so on, evade superficial, sensory detection: we can't spot a neutrino with our naked eyes, or even with glasses, and similarly we can't spot a case of Rightness with the senses either. However, unlike the case of neutrinos, exotic technology won't help either. Building a super-Whositron for "smashing" the elementary atoms of morals won't help a whit. What we need, and fortunately have, is a sort of sixth sense, one specifically designed, or anyway suited, just for the job of spotting moral entities. Such entities are "irreducible" to any natural objects or properties.

Meanwhile, though, these exotic objects are nevertheless supposed to have something to do with practice. We *ought* to seek Good and avoid Evil, to perform acts that are Right and refrain from ones that are Wrong, and so on. If asked what this is supposed to mean, some intuitionists have given us the same story about 'ought': just as we have to spot Rightness, so we have to spot Oughtness, too.

The shortcomings of this metaphysical type of intuitionism are legion, and it is not surprising that as an option it is virtually extinct among current philosophers. (I say "virtually", because no theory I can think of is *totally* extinct among current philosophers. And a good thing, too!) Let us review the main problems.

Mysteriousness

Especially in this scientific era, the appeal to what seem mysterious entities and faculties is likely to elicit impatience, and perhaps a certain amount of irritation. To those of us who don't seem to have one of the special faculties required for detecting these strange items, this explanation isn't going to be much help. Of course, we can be dismissed as hopelessly unfit for the moral life, since we are, after all, "morally blind", according to such theorists. Needless to say, that assessment isn't going to go down really well, either.

Futility

Unfortunately, this moral blindness, in addition to being evidently incurable, goes hand in hand with another very annoying tendency on our part: namely, the tendency to act in the world, right along with all the Good folk who happily *were* blessed with the gift of Intuition. This makes us deviants a terrible nuisance in some respects, for when we persist in our wickedness, and compound the matter by questioning the very explanations given by our Betters, we sometimes get in the way. And then what? The True Believers don't have much to say to us, we being incorrigible. So does push come to shove? One would hope that we could do better than that—but how, if this view were correct?

Disagreement

Nor is this all. For, as intimated above, there is another fact that could cause a certain annoyance to the Intuitionist: namely, that even her fellows who are among the Blessed, or who claim to be so anyway, don't all behave quite as they should. For they keep having *different*, and indeed contrary, intuitions. This makes for a certain difficulty. It is as if when you see green, I, under what seem to be identical conditions, see red! And just as, when normal people seem to have different visual experiences under what seem like the same conditions, about all we can do about it is to look again, perhaps taking care that we are indeed looking in the same direction, so the Intuitionist bids us look again. Unlike what is the case with red and green, though, these moral perceptual divergences seem to happen with disconcerting frequency—depending on who you go around with, to be sure.

Society-Dependence

Which brings up another point. It is curious, if the story about morals were as the Intuitionist says, that an individual's moral "perceptions" seem to depend so much on what her mum told her when she was two, or which social circumstances she was brought up in. We don't need much training to see red, and no matter how much Mum tells you that this color over here, which the rest of us call "green", is actually red, it isn't really likely to have much effect, except maybe to get you using the color vocabulary in a very peculiar way. But those who believe that Jewishness, say, is the mark of original sin, are not just using the moral vocabulary in an unusual (and offensive) way. They are making moral judgments (in this case, abhorrent ones).

There are other problems. At the risk of belaboring the matter at greater length than it deserves, let me mention two more.

Generality

The first of them may seem, at first sight, just a philosopher's curiosity, akin to the anomalies of certain theories about the foundations of mathematics; only it isn't, and has serious ramifications. Above, I noted that the intuitionists held that moral properties were "entirely unrelated, logically, to the rest of the more familiar array of entities and characters we encounter in our ordinary experience". This feature was supposed to account for a problem known as the "naturalistic fallacy",[1] according to which it was not possible to make logically valid inferences from "factual" to "normative" propositions. However, this needed just a little bit of qualification, on further reflection. For whatever plausibility there may have been to the naturalistic fallacy idea, there was one thing that wouldn't quite do. Suppose we have two absolutely identical actions in absolutely identical sets of circumstances, performed by absolutely identical moral agents: well, could one of those acts be Right and the other Wrong? There would seem to be something very strange about that. And yet there doesn't seem anything at all odd about there being two otherwise identical billiard balls, one of which is red and the other green. Indeed, so far as ordinary observation goes, it happens every day. (As a matter of fact, the players would have a complaint, if the balls insisted on being different in other respects, too—shape or weight for instance.) There seems, in short, to be a logical dissimilarity between the supposed "properties" signified by 'good' and 'green', quite in addition to the curiously nonperceptible nature of the former. R. M. Hare insists that this logical property, "universalizability", is one that "moral judgments *share* with descriptive judgments", adding that "the differences between them in other respects are, as we shall see, sufficient to make it misleading to say that moral judgments are descriptive."[2] But his reason is lame. If x is red and y is exactly like y in all respects, then y is red. True, of course: but what if it is exactly like y only in all *other* respects? Yet the salient point about 'good', say, is—to use an example we have all got from Hare himself—that if, for instance, two pictures are exactly alike in all visible respects, then it can't be that one has the "property" of goodness and the other lacks it.

Is there an important moral to this, or is it just a curiosity? The answer is that there is indeed an important moral to this story. Roughly, what this logical point points to is that there have to be, somehow, *reasons* for claiming that some act is right or wrong or just or unjust or whatever: reasons that included, for instance, the feature that otherwise identical cases would have to come out morally identical too. As Henry Sidgwick rather ponderously but precisely put it, "it cannot be right for A to treat B in a manner in which it would be wrong for B to treat A, merely on the ground that they are two different individuals, and without there being any difference between the natures or circumstances of the two which can be stated as a reasonable ground for difference of treatment."[3]

But Sidgwick regarded that, too, as a matter of "intuition"—as an "axiom", somewhat akin to the Principle of Identity in logic. And who knows—maybe it is! In, as we say, "some sense". . . . But more about this below. Meanwhile, let's look at the other problem.

Importance

That problem is one that could have been overlooked only because the fact in question is so utterly obvious that the fact that one's theory simply doesn't account for it could be readily overlooked: after all, if it's about *morals*, it *obviously* has this feature, you know? This feature is, simply, that "moral properties" have to *matter*. The fact, if we want to call it that, that the act we are considering doing would, for instance, be horrendously wrong is not something we can just ignore or be indifferent to—or if we somehow manage to do so, others will not do so. The sense in which morals "matter" isn't like the sense in which, say, geraniums matter, as they no doubt do to some people. There are all sorts of things that matter to some people and not to others. There are even people to whom, somehow, Mahler symphonies and the last quartets of Mozart do not matter. But right and wrong are matters of universal concern—or, we think should be. Now, I think that the last quartets of Mozart ought to matter to everyone, too, and am baffled when I encounter someone to whom they evidently do not; but the fact seems to be that there are such people. Those who would claim to be indifferent to considerations of right and wrong are another matter. In particular, those who agree entirely that certain particular acts are wrong but who profess indifference to *that*, are engaging in puzzling verbal behavior. When they claimed to agree that those acts are wrong, we thought they *meant* it; and if they then quite cheerfully do them anyway, we must wonder just what they did mean, if anything.

But of course there is no reason in the world why perfectly sane, otherwise fully rational people couldn't ignore right and wrong with perfect equanimity if they are just rather peculiar "properties" that happen to be present in certain actions and not others. How interesting!—we might say, with a yawn. In a lovely passage, Patrick Nowell-Smith expresses the point thus: "Learning about 'values' or 'duties' might well be as exciting as learning about spiral nebulae or waterspouts. But what if I am not interested? Why should I *do* anything about these newly-revealed objects? Some things, I have now learnt, are right and others wrong; but why should I do what is right and eschew what is wrong?"[4] There is something basically wrong with a theory of morals that makes such questions unanswerable, as metaphysical intuitionism certainly does. Obviously, we could find "nonnatural" properties quite uninteresting just as easily as we could find spiral nebulae uninteresting.

Other analytical theories of morals in the twentieth century, impressed by the force of some of these arguments against intuitionism, went, as it were, all the way in the other direction, proposing that 'good' and 'right' and so on were fundamentally just expressions of attitudes (emotivism) or even directives (imperativism). But these theories, tying the use of ethical expressions very essentially to action, nevertheless left them unhooked from the statements of fact about people and the world, which, one would think, are all there are to give such expressions any real rationale. When we say that something is right, according to these theories, we are attempting to influence people, to *get things done*. And so we are. But what, and how are we to achieve these influences we may be attempting to exert?

Before taking up those questions, however, let us have a look at the other sort of intuitionism.

Methodological Intuitionism

In the past few decades, long after metaphysical intuitionism was relegated to the philosophical dust-bins, a presumably quite different use of "intuitions" in moral philosophy was elevated to the status of theoretical respectability—not a new one, to be sure, since philosophers have been doing it, to a greater or lesser extent, since Plato. In this version we supposedly make no assumptions about the fundamental meanings of moral terms or the sort of things they may refer to. Rather, we employ intuitions as a sort of *data* and construct a theory to "explain" them. The fact is that people have tendencies to affirm of certain things that they are right, others that they are wrong, and so on; and the moral philosopher's job is to find the principles that will account for these tendencies. Of course, this is *moral* philosophy, and so the output of our theorizing will be moral statements and not just statements about morality.

What's the difference? If I say, "so-and-so is considered very wicked among the Azanti", I make a statement *about* morality: I am making a descriptive claim about those people—about some of their beliefs, attitudes, practices. If on the other hand I say, flatly, "so-and-so is a really rotten person!", then I am not just speaking about somebody else's moral beliefs, but rather am affirming a moral statement on my own. A moral statement or claim is a statement or claim to the effect that something or other is right or wrong, good or bad, just or unjust, or whatever: it attributes some moral property or quality or status to some action, set of actions, or disposition. Descriptive statements about morality are in the general class of social scientific claims, or common-sense claims of comparable type. There are also what we might call analytical or logical claims about moral concepts, ideas, or moral language. These purport to tell us what follows from what in the realm of moral statements or expressions, but they are not intended to (and all by themselves cannot) tell us what is actually right or wrong. Moral claims are sentences that do intend to tell us just that.

Where do appeals to "moral intuitions" fit in to this classification? Clearly, the claim that somebody or other *has* a certain "moral intuition" is, on the face of it, a descriptive one; we check this claim by seeing whether the people in question do or do not exhibit the kind of behavior that we would expect of someone who believes the statement in question. But the fact that someone or other *believes* that something is the case does not, straight off anyway, show us that it *is* the case. That is true of all sorts of claims or statements, of course, and not just moral ones. But suppose that I make the moral statement myself? Suppose that I say, "Such-and-such is wrong!" I am then no longer making a claim that can be shown to be true or false by checking to see whether my behavior is consistent with the attribution to me of that belief. That would go toward establishing my sincerity or insincerity, but not the utterance's truth or falsity. For my making of that claim is an *expression* of that belief. I may be making it insincerely, or in jest or the like, but suppose that I instead am making it in full earnest. Shall I now use the fact that I have said it as some sort of *evidence* that what I have said is true? "I just *said* that watering your lawn at 3:00 A.M. is morally wrong—and I meant what I said; *therefore*, watering your lawn at 3:00 A.M. *is* morally wrong." Not much of an argument!

Now suppose that lots of people have the same tendency. Everyone agrees, for instance, that murder is wrong, and that lying is generally to be deplored. Does the fact that everyone or almost everyone thinks so *show* that murder *is* wrong and lying generally *is* to be deplored? Again, not very plausible. There are people who can be got to say, if they don't think about it too carefully, that moral statements just are expressions of generally held attitudes. But this will hardly do. Why couldn't there be a generally held attitude that, on reflection, seemed quite wrong? Suppose that some moral deviant—say, Jesus Christ in first-century Israel—comes along and says, "You have heard it said that you should hate your enemies; but I say unto you, love your enemies!" Christ presumably meant, in effect, to be claiming that loving your enemies is really the *right* thing to do, even though most people at the time didn't think so, and he knew this perfectly well. In fact, his knowledge of that fact seems to have played a significant role in his inclination to preach on the subject. Are we to say that what Christ said was just silly, even contradictory? Not very plausible, either as an account of what he meant, or as an account of what people took him to mean.

Now, consider what philosophers wish to do with their appeals to intuitions. They are discussing some controversial topic, ordinarily—nobody writes articles advocating the view that murder is wrong! But in a controversial area, we are going to have some people sincerely maintaining that something or other is right, and others that that very same thing is wrong. Abortion, for example, or capital punishment of repeat-murderers. Of what use is it to point out to people holding some view on these matters that a great many people think otherwise than they—or the same as they? Suppose some small minority thinks that a certain popular practice is quite wrong. Are they going to be impressed to hear that many people don't think so?

Disagreement, Again

It is here that this new sort of appeal to intuition gets into some of the very same problems that its less respectable metaphysical version has. When people have contrary intuitions, appeals to intuition are not likely to do much—except maybe irritate the people we're trying to persuade.

In fact, appeals to intuition can hardly constitute *reasons* for the very attitudes that those intuitions express. The best they might do is provide a rather weak sort of evidence. We might say, "Well, surely 90 percent of the people are unlikely to be wrong, are they?" Perhaps that is true. But the trouble is, it is also true that 90 percent of the people plainly *can* be wrong, about all sorts of things: why not about this, then?—Especially when the effect of their opinion is to cram something down the craws of the remaining 10 percent. . . . !

Reflective Equilibrium

Major impetus for integrating appeals to intuition into moral theory came from John Rawls's celebrated treatise, *A Theory of Justice*.[5] There he develops, and has been followed by others[6] in further developing, a method called "reflective equilibrium". The idea here is that one tries to develop a theory that is the best mix of one's considered beliefs and such theory as one can find. We go, as it were, back and forth between the moral beliefs we so strongly hold at the start and the theoretical considerations we develop from other sources—scientific, logical, semantical, common-sense, and so forth—sawing off a bit here and a bit there until we have a conceptual mix we can live with. The idea has been very influential among contemporary philosophers, who for some time now have been increasingly "anti-foundational". Philosophers once assumed that they were looking for the "foundations" of whatever area of philosophy they were dealing with. The foundations were to be bedrock, as the metaphor suggests: we find ultimate truths that we cannot doubt and then deduce everything from those, thus passing on the mantle of that initial certainty to our further results. As noted at the outset, no such view is assumed here.

But I do not need to discuss foundationism in general in order to develop my complaint about the inclusion of the *moral* views we are trying to defend in the very set of premises on the basis of which we propose to defend *them*. There are two considerations I would offer here, both to my mind decisive.

The Practicality of Morals

In the first place, we have to appreciate how *utterly* wrong was the model of moral thought and talk implied by metaphysical intuitionism. The idea that attributions of rightness and wrongness are claims that certain actions have certain occult, nonphysical, exotic *properties* is wildly, completely, and fundamentally off base. Morals is lived out in the streets of ordinary life, and it has to do with getting ordinary people to do or refrain from doing quite ordinary things. The idea that the way to get them to do this is by prattling about metaphysics is too absurd to be contemplated outside the hoary stone walls of Oxbridge. That being settled, we should now ask whether we really do any better by simply shouting at those who disagree with us. Yet addressing those who disagree is crucial. There isn't much need to preach to the converted, after all: it is the unconverted who should be worrying us—and it is precisely they who aren't going to have much patience with our preaching if preaching is all it comes to.

In short, the claim that something or other is Wrong is not as such a claim about observation at all, let alone of "observation" with a special faculty. It isn't *at all* like the claim that grass is green. It is, instead, very much more comparable to what happens in the law courts: it is an attempt to rebut a charge that, if sustained, will get you in trouble. What are relevant are considerations supporting the verdict that the agent should be let off rather than convicted. If the charge is sustained, we will think badly of him, and perhaps more—shunning him in the streets, striking him from our list of invitees, perhaps even engaging in some more full-blown sort of ostracism. Or, of course, actual punishment. Morality is not only rather like the law, it is continuous with it—to the point where the thesis of Ronald Dworkin[7] that in fact they are ultimately the same is disconcertingly plausible.

We do not get into trouble with the neighbors if we think that grass is some other color than green, though we might well get into trouble with our lawns. Morality is practical; the color of grass is practical only to those interested in it. We do not need reasons why grass is green, though quite possibly there are some. But a claim that something is right *is* a claim that there are some or other reasons for *doing* something, and moreover, something you may not otherwise have wanted to do. If no reasons are forthcoming, there is the suspicion, and very often the reality, that we have been had, taken in.

In my youth, like all good boys of Christian households, I faithfully attended church, week after week. However, unlike my more sensible friends who contrived to while away the hours (the going rate was about one phenomenological hour per physical minute) tormenting their parents, folding the church bulletins into paper airplanes, and the like, I fell into the eccentric habit of actually *listening* to the sermons, for want of anything better to do. And this eventually made me realize what a very peculiar activity the whole thing was. It was all very "edifying", in the worst sense of the term: if you accepted the premises, of course, the rest more or less followed. But never, in all of those years, was a single argument ever offered for accepting those premises, or even any effort expended at endeavoring to attach some clear meaning to them. If asked why we should accept the contents of the Holy Bible as the word of God, we were told that, after all, it *said* so right there on page one! And it was made exceedingly clear that further questions along those lines were decidedly out of order.

Nor were they at all necessary for the congregation, who seemed content to listen quite placidly to the whole ritual. A few further decades of hindsight made me appreciate that in fact 'ritual' was the right word; I mistakenly had supposed that the *other* parts of the service, with the singing and such, were the ritual. Quite wrong: the sermon was simply more ritual! Which of course meant that either one took it or one didn't—logical analysis was beside the point.

And it is hard to deny that morality can be like that. But should professional philosophers, who pride themselves on their rationality, go along with it?

Moral "Science"?

The other reason for having our doubts about reflective equilibrium as the proper model for moral theory is related to the first. Is the purpose of moral theory to explain some facts? Scientists may endeavor to explain to us why grass is green. The fact that it is so, however, is established by observation; absent observation, there would be no fact to explain. But is moral philosophy like science? Is the job of the philosopher simply to "explain" the "facts"? There is a hitch to this way of looking at it. Unlike the greenness of grass, we have various people affirming with full sincerity that this "grass" is, say, purple (still others insist that it is brown, and so on). In their view, right-thinking people can see this as clearly as you and I "see" that it is green.

In short, disagreement is not very far from being the rule rather than the exception in practical matters. People have contrary opinions. All of which might not matter—it doesn't much, after all, in the case of preferences for chocolate versus vanilla. And indeed, there is a view of morals according to which it, too, is just a matter of chocolate versus vanilla: A likes abortion, B doesn't, and that's all there is to it! Such is the theory of subjectivism (some verions of relativism have the same effect). But this, too, is all wrong.

It isn't just that the "issue" of chocolate versus vanilla is trivial. Some issues of taste are, indeed; but anyone can think of issues of taste that she would regard as not so: Ashkenazy's performance of Beethoven's "Hammerklavier" sonata versus Gilels's, for instance, is no trivial matter to the lover of piano music. To devote a major share of one's life to the task of perfecting a great interpretation of such a work makes perfectly good sense to such enthusiasts (I'm one of them). But morals isn't even like that. A terrible performance of the

"Hammerklavier" is an aesthetic outrage, a sin, an offense against everything that is true and good—but even so, the miserable cur who inflicts it upon us may not literally be molested as he slinks from the stage, nor slung into the local jail to atone for his errors. Whereas the person who picks his pocket on the way out, or waylays him in the alley afterward, or tosses a bomb into his apartment, is eligible for just such treatment. There is a difference. Morality matters *in a way* that other things do not. Awful art should be punished by not buying a ticket to the performance, or keeping it off one's walls; but that's all. The producers of awful art have the same rights as we right-thinking persons of impeccable taste.

CHAPTER 11

Morality

The Need for Clarity about Morality

MY OBJECTION to appeal to intuitions in moral theory is, in brief, that when (not merely 'if'!) intuitions conflict, we are bereft of conceptual tools for reaching reasoned agreement. Indeed, one must say that under those conditions "reasoned" agreement is impossible. Surely it would be better, at any rate, if we could have a theory that was persuasive without presupposing anything like moral intuitions.

Of course, there are intuitions and intuitions, and our theory won't be any better off if instead of appealing to *moral* intuitions it appeals to nonmoral intuitions that are equally the subject of disagreement. (Indeed, my claim that it would "surely be better" if we could get along without such appeals is itself, quite possibly, such an "intuition", of the methodological type.) I hope that this will not be a problem in what follows, but one must be aware of the possibility.

Meanwhile, I think that one reason for the popularity of what amounts to intuitionism in current writings on moral matters in the Anglo-American philosophical world is that people buy an argument that has long been much too popular: viz., that we cannot expunge all appeals to intuition in moral philosophy anyway—so why not help oneself to as many as one likes? This argument is, I believe, without merit.

The claim that we can't expunge appeals to intuition is due to a failure to distinguish between specifically *moral* intuitions and more generally evaluative and methodological intuitions. If we allow the broadest scope to the term 'intuition', then no doubt the claim that some intuitions are necessary to any philosophical argument has merit. But when we are doing moral philosophy, we really ought to confine the term 'intuition' to specifically moral intuitions, and if we do, then the reasons gone into above show that permitting such appeals *as part of our theory* virtually ensures that a major requirement of a moral theory will go unfulfilled. What we need is a credible theory of morality that does not appeal to such intuitions at all.

But why, it might reasonably be asked, should it be a "major requirement of moral theory" that it enable us to reach reasoned agreement? To answer this, we need a characterization of morality, and a characterization of the goal(s) of moral theory. I will produce a brief characterization of both here. Neither is uncontroversial, certainly, and indeed, both will involve certain decisions as to how we are to use these terms here, though neither decision, I trust, will be simply arbitrary. We start with morality.

I have claimed that morality "matters", in a way that is special, and as part of the very idea. There are two standardly recognized features of morality to which I am appealing in saying this. They are "standardly recognized" in what is, at any rate, one major *sense* of 'morality', though it is certainly the sense we are interested in for present purposes. Let us first try to identify this sense. We do so by contrasting two senses of 'morality', which we will call the "personal" and the "social" senses of the term, though those terms are very misleading in certain respects. But still, they can do the job, and are familiar in this context.

'Personal' versus 'Social' Morality

(1) By *personal* morality, here, I mean the area of decisions about how one is to run one's life, the ultimate bases on which one will make one's choices. This is an extremely wide usage, and it should be noted that it *includes* the narrower sense (2), explained below. All morality concerns what we are to do, and on what principles. But in this widest sense it includes things that may not be the subject of morality in the social sense. Should one, for instance, live a life of contemplation or action? Is pleasure the ultimate good, or are there other values to be preferred to it? I conjecture that the considerable popularity, for some time, of the emotive school of ethics may have been due to this rather indiscriminate use of the terms 'moral' or 'ethical', in which the absence of ultimately rational constraints on options has a certain

plausibility. Indeed, one might almost characterize this as the "existentialist" use of the terms 'moral' and 'ethical'.

(2) In the *social* sense of the term, however, there are, as I shall argue, some rational constraints. In the social sense, morality is quite essentially for the governance of people in general—of "society", then. This characterization involves two elements, both essential: 'governance' and 'in general'.

(*a*) The sense of 'governance', closely related to the frequent employment of such terms as 'rule' to refer to the contents of morality in this "social" sense of the term, may be captured fairly sufficiently by the idea that moral requirements can, and often do, "override" individual inclinations to act otherwise. Moral rules *overrule* us: it might, say, be highly advantageous to cheat this person, but morality says one may not. What does this mean? There has been much analytical controversy about this, but I suggest in particular two things. First, that a conscientious individual, when confronted with a choice between what morality tells her she must do and what she might otherwise like to do, will do what morality says. Somehow, we must be capable of having moral motives that are stronger than any inclinations to the contrary. And second, we may point to the social aspect. If someone proposes to do something wrong, even though it may be highly beneficial to the doer, the *rest of us* should exert ourselves to steer him back to the "straight and true" path prescribed by morality. We will not accept as a justification, nor even as an excuse, that the individual *wanted* to act otherwise. Morality constrains, in the sense that people in general will (are to) constrain, prod, push people in its direction. The reason of this is put very well by Kurt Baier: "if the point of view of morality were that of self-interest, then there could *never* be moral solutions of conflicts of interest. However, when there are conflicts of interest, we always look for a "higher" point of view . . . by 'the moral point of view' we *mean* a point of view which is a court of appeal for conflicts of interest."[1]

(*b*) The words 'in general' here must be construed quite precisely. We typically conceive morality in this sense to consist of rules—of "thou shalts" and "thou shalt nots"—with the "shalt nots" predominating. A moral rule in this sense is "general" in two senses. First, it applies to *everyone* in the society, and not to select individuals. Second, and more or less following from the first, it is about *general* conduct, that is, about the sort of things that more or less anyone can do. Anyone (which means, as always in moral philosophy, "practically anyone") can kill, steal, lie, cheat, and so on—even though there are specialized ways of doing those things that not just anyone could do, no doubt. But when A kills B by introducing a short-circuit element at a crucial place in the control unit of his technologically up-to-the-minute hydrodynamic remote-UHF-band servo-actuated thingumbob, what makes his act wrong is not the details but the fact that, in consequence, someone gets blown to bits.

There is another, and crucial, sense in which morality is general which in fact can be derived from the two aspects of overridingness and generality that have been brought out so far. This is the aspect of "enforcement". Morality is (to be) *enforced*. Not in the sense in which the Law of the Land is enforced, with specially appointed enforcers, the "moral police", but rather by what I shall call "informal" means. Verbal means are preeminent among these: we shout at miscreants, we prod and natter and nag both ourselves and others. But we each do this, as it were, on our own time. Each individual can *decide*, not only whether she herself will do x when called for by Morality, but also what if anything she will do about getting others to do or not do x.

When our moral theory concerns the latter sense, which I would take to be much more nearly the usual sense of the term 'moral', this fact, that morality is for everyone, yet informally so, has important implications for any theory of morals. First: since morality comes fundamentally from the "inside", each person being in a position to decide what to do about it—there are no high priests of morals, no Central Committee, no legislature—no moral theory has much chance of getting a grip if it can't account for the *motivation* to participate in this institution. And second: since morality is for the governance of *everyone*, and not just oneself, one cannot just pick any old principle one likes and proclaim that to be a moral principle. Nor, despite the "internal" aspect of morals, can we derive the content of morality only by looking within our own soul. There are others to worry about.

We have a habit of talking as though moral principles were simply "truths", like those of science: as though they were just "out there", to be discovered, found out. But it's not quite like that. Either you act in certain ways or you don't. No mere external truth could *make* you do that.[2] There are, certainly, "external truths" to which we *must* conform, willy-nilly: the law of gravity, for example. But the "must" here is so literal that "conform" is out of place. The gunman makes me conform, by threatening to shoot me if I do not. In some sense I *can* refuse to go along; if so, and he shoots me, I shall then literally have no choice but to die, if he's a competent shot. We "conform" to the law of gravity in the same sense that we die if shot; it simply isn't a matter of choice at all.

Moral principles and rules are just that: principles and rules *for* behavior, to which we can voluntarily conform or no. Wherein lies their normative bite, then? Whence comes the "should" about them? The answer lies in the direction of reason: we decide to go along with, or contravene, a given rule by deliberating, sizing up the reasons for one or the other, and then, it is hoped, doing what we have concluded has the strongest, the best reasons behind it.

Or, to be sure, not: that is, we might just act impulsively, or perhaps in a trance. But those are marginal cases of action in the relevant sense. We could conclude that impulsive action is just what is called for, but that could be concluded (though not at the time, of course) after much thought: it might be best, we decide, in view of this, that, and the other, to throw caution to the four winds and wade right in. That is different from simply throwing it to the four winds without any thought of whether that is a sensible thing to do. The "should-ness" of what is reasonable is not an accident, and not simply *an* additional factor pointing in favor of a given choice. That we should "follow reason" is true just because that's what reason talk is all about: what we should do and what reason tells us to do are not two different things.

And so it is important that the moral thing to do should turn out to be what we *should* do. A moral theory such as metaphysical intuitionism, which identifies what we morally ought to do with the possession or nonpossession of an incomprehensible somewhat by the acts under consideration, gives us no reason to act.

But not all reasons to act are moral. That a certain drink tastes delicious is a reason (though not of itself a sufficient one) to act, but it has no particular bearing on morality. However, the citing of a few examples is far from enough for the point I wish to press now, which is that "moral reasons" to act cannot be a separate sort of reasons from all others. When morality makes demands upon us, the question why we should go along with them, what reason there is to impose them, is *always* apt. There are no "bedrock" moral reasons: that is an illusion. To say that some act is called for by morality is to say that there are good reasons for insisting that people do that kind of thing. Those reasons are not "moral"; they are, simply, reasons. Where morality comes into it is in the administration of the requirements of reason. Reason will tell us to attempt to achieve result R, so far as it goes; but when we survey the available means, we note that getting R accomplished impinges on the reasoned actions of other people. This may complicate matters quite a lot, for they may not be interested in R. Or sometimes there may be an outright conflict of interests: others have interests that, if achieved, preclude my getting R accomplished. We then may need a rule, and where R or the conflicting ends of others are pretty frequently encountered, being aspects of the normal activities of people, then we may need a society-wide rule. Things will then look rather different.

The Compleat Deontologist?

One apparent aim of the libertarian is to provide a schedule of rights that is "hard", so that in any given case we will always be able to identify the area of permissible action, precisely bounded by the relevant set of rights. Moreover, these are to be wholly "nonteleological" in one sense of that rather obscure term. That is, they are not to be founded upon considerations of the *general* good or *general* interest. These are certainly rights *having to do with* interests, in general. They enable us, presumably, to find out which interests may be pursued in which ways. And it is certainly to be presumed that the parties concerned are acting in their interests, and acting for the purpose of promoting those interests.

Kant supposes that people do not simply act in pursuit of their interests. They have, as it were, rationally split personalities. On the one hand, they are concerned to promote their interests (which Kant, like Bentham, mistakenly if forgivably equated with maximizing their net pleasure). On the other, however, they are concerned to obey a transcendental law invoking some kind of universalizability requirement known as the Categorical Imperative, the precise nature of which is a matter of much scholarly dispute. We will assume only that it is, as Kant obviously thought, a genuinely distinct requirement from the other one. So the two aspects of reason can come into conflict, and when they do, the moral one ought to win. But as Kant depicts the situation, there are insoluble problems. For one thing, in his view "inclinations" belonged in the phenomenal world and were subject to universal causation, and so the Laws of Nature decreed that people must do what their inclinations dictate—which is incompatible with their doing what morality dictates if it ever differs, as Kant thought it often (always?) would. So he is driven to a hopeless and unintelligible doctrine of contra-causal freedom. And for another, there is no real explanation of why morality is supposed to "win"—why Categorical Imperatives are Categorical.[3]

The explanation offered here (due in considerable part to Kurt

Baier[4] and to Bernard Gert[5]), on the other hand, avoids all resort to hifalutin' transcendental machinery. (Perhaps this is a pity. As Francis Sparshott remarks in a somewhat different context, perhaps a bit of that sort of thing would add tone to this treatise!)[6] Morality overrides inclination in the sense that it is intended to settle conflicts of interest, which it could not do if it couldn't overrule one or the other or both parties. But it doesn't override "inclination" in any sense that envisages a contrast between mere "sensuous" motives and any others one could imagine. The transcendental aspirations of rival religious groups, or for that matter rival metaphysicians, can give rise to wars or other disputes that require conflict resolution just as much as any more "sensuous" motives. Indeed, quite a lot more, if history is our guide: really major fracases, such as the world wars, the Napoleonic ones, the Thirty Years' War, and so on, are invariably fought with strong ideological motivation. Some theorists, notably the Marxists, try to account for these conflicts in crasser terms—as though the Vietnam War might have been fought in the interests of profit on rubber! Since the cost of that war far and away exceeded the gross national product of Vietnam over a couple of generations, the arithmetic of this idea is somewhat mind-boggling from the start.

Conventional versus Critical Morality

And here comes another "or rather": we tend to identify morality with what is taught us in our childhoods, say, or with what the people around us will react to in certain ways. Any given society will have a number of rules that *are* enforced in the various ways mentioned above. The fact that they are thus enforced provides, and of course is intended to provide, some motivation for doing what the enforcers are trying to get us to do. But is that the end of the story? Are we to say, simply, that what is right is what people will praise and reward you for doing, or blame and punish you for not doing? It is not, and we are not. For we are capable of reflecting on these demands, and of questioning them. Suppose we think one of those demands unreasonable, and those attempting to impose it reply that reason has nothing to do with it, and we had jolly well better go along with it or they will make us wish we had! But that is not reasoning: it's bullying. And bullying is itself one of the very things that any reasonable morality will decry.

A philosophical theory of morals may, indeed, take the option of insisting that nevertheless, convention *is* all there is to it. Such an attitude is often classed with skepticism, though perhaps that isn't quite fair. For a philosopher might argue that convention *is* reasonable, indeed, perhaps that convention is literally reason itself: that the question of what is reasonable and what isn't is itself something decided by the way things are done, by the practices of one's community, and so forth.[7]

In order for this argument to be any good, the conventions in question must be very "deep". Consider, for example, the matter of racism in South Africa. Few readers will be disposed to think that just because in South Africa black people are regarded as inferior, it is therefore the case that in South Africa black people *are* inferior; that just because you will there be *told* to treat black people in certain ways, those are therefore the *right* ways to treat them. (Apologies may be due here to white South Africans, who may protest that this is not a fair statement of their practice; many of us suppose it is, and I will here assume so for the sake of the example—but with the caution that I, certainly, and you, probably, can't claim really to *know* what white South Africans think or how they actually reason on this matter.) Every philosopher I know of who is still willing, with cases such as the South African one before us as examples, to accept that what one's society tells one to do is ipso facto *the* thing to do and who nevertheless wishes to maintain that morality and indeed reason is fundamentally "conventional" must, as I say, have a very "deep" sense of 'conventional' in mind: deep enough so that what we usually think of as moral relativism doesn't follow from the claim that morality is nevertheless conventional.[8] And that sense, I believe, is too deep: it is *irrelevantly* deep for present purposes, since it essentially erases any real line between the conventional and the nonconventional.

There is, however, another sense of 'convention' in which I should not wish to deny at all that morality is conventional. The de facto rules of morality may be accounted conventional—by definition, indeed. And this in particular means that they are, at least to a degree, changeable. They are certainly changeable in *some* way, since they do change. Whether they are changeable by intention, like the law, which is made and unmade by certain intentional acts of certain people, the legislators, is quite another matter. And one would certainly have to be naïve to think that writing a tract or two is enough to do the job! It wouldn't even if everyone would read the tract, which, in a society of millions, they certainly won't.

There is thus a question of what to do, as it were, with any "philosophical" or "critical" morality we might come up with—a view of morality "de jure" rather than "de facto". But there is also an answer: one can *act* on it oneself. One can start criticizing people in the light of these possibly novel principles you have found to be more reasonable than the ones actually reinforced in your current society.

Not only *can* you do this, but there is something to be said for the suggestion that, to some extent, every thinking person does and must. It is, in fact, not entirely easy to be totally conventional, especially in a large and diverse society such as ours. For one thing, there are matters on which convention is unsettled: "society" doesn't *have* a rule on it. More precisely, it doesn't have *a* rule on it—the abortion issue, again, comes to mind. It is still possible to appeal to convention, to be sure; only it won't be the convention of society at large, but rather of some sizable segment thereof. The person in North America who wants to do "the conventionally right thing" about abortion has a problem!

One of the historic projects of philosophy is to try to find some or other rational foundations for morality, or at any rate for *some* morality, some set of overriding general guides to behavior that, even if it is not entirely reflected in current practice, has the solidest reasons for being so. Some historically popular theories, such as those proposing that there is some peculiarly close connection between morality and some or other religion, will not be examined here. The reasons for not paying them any considerable degree of attention are simple and, indeed, follow from what I have said in the foregoing. If we seek a rule for the guidance of everyone's behavior, and if only *some* accept the religion in question—as is true of all religions—then what do you say to the others? The practical answer in time past has been that you say "Boo!" and marshal your armies against the heretics who dare to question your version of the truth. One of the few appeals to "our" intuitive sense of morality that will be trotted out in this book is the intuition that this really won't do as an answer!

Meanwhile, we have the question: what *will* do as an answer? I shall shortly describe, again very briefly, what seems to be the best answer currently available. Like all answers judged to be so by philosophers, the judgment is guided by a certain sense that no other view *could* be right. This is philosophical hubris at work, no doubt: history has a way of suggesting that we have overlooked something when we make such claims. That's a risk one simply has to take.

CHAPTER 12

Contractarianism

The Idea of the "Contract" Approach to Foundations

THE THEORY WE NEED is Contractarianism. The general idea of this theory is that the principles of morality are (or should be) those principles for directing everyone's conduct which it is reasonable for everyone to accept. They are the rules that *everyone* has good reason for wanting everyone to act on, and thus to internalize in himself or herself, and thus to reinforce in the case of everyone.

In so saying, I am presenting a slanted view, so to say. As with every important philosophical theory, this one has many different versions with their own specific shades and twists, and the shades and twists are not trivial. Contractarianism can be made to seem arbitrary and silly: consider, for instance, the suggestion that long, long ago our remote ancestors made this deal, see, and from that day to this everyone has had to go along with it! Plainly, such a theory is not going to give us the rational motivation we need.

On the other hand, any ordinary contract, made in the full light of day between consenting adults, supplies motivation in just the required sense. The "required sense", as will shortly be seen, is not so simple. But few will dispute that any theory that could attain the same degree of rational "bite" as actual contracts would be doing very well indeed.

The problem is that morality is obviously not the result of a literal contract: and indeed, it cannot be, among other things for the very good reason pointed out by David Hume, namely, that "the observance of promises is itself one of the most considerable parts of justice: and we are not surely bound to keep our word because we have given our word to keep it."[1] To account for the obligation to keep promises on the basis of a general *promise* to do so seems, shall we say, unpromising. Clearly, the sense in which morality is founded upon or due to or represents an "agreement" is going to have to be less straightforward than that.

But how much less? Interest in contractarianism was virtually revived in recent times by the work of John Rawls in his celebrated and much-discussed magnum opus, *A Theory of Justice*. In the Rawlsian version the "social contract" is an idealization. It "takes place" in very remarkable circumstances: the contractors are behind, as he puts it, a "veil of ignorance", which prevents them from knowing anything about themselves in particular. They know only generalities about people but have no idea which person they themselves are (or, as we may put it, which person they themselves will "turn out to be" after, so to say, the veil is lifted). This unusual condition is imposed in order to represent what Rawls takes to be a constraint on moral principles, namely, that they must be totally impartial as between one person and another.[2]

There is a crucial question about what is intended in imposing such requirements, though. Nobody is or ever could be literally behind any such "veil"; so we would seem to have to ask what the relation is between "a person" behind the veil—where, after all, it is quite unrecognizable as a person in any ordinary sense of the word—and that "same" person on the real-life side. Namely, the question would be why the real person should pay any attention to what the idealized "person" has, from its Olympian perch, "decided". Doesn't the behind-the-veil person look uncomfortably like Plato's philosopher king, say? And if not, why not?

Actually, there are two ways of understanding the "veil of ignorance" idea: what we might call the "theoretically dispensable" and the "theoretically indispensable" versions. In the former understanding, the veil idea is only a metaphor for a real-world condition that it really is reasonable to impose—indeed, perhaps no more than the condition that our principles, whatever they are, must be impartial, in some suitable sense of that term. Thus, G. E. Pence[3] argues that the veil is redundant, since if unanimity and equal bargaining power are imposed on the social contract, we will get the same result. The question is, though: in what sense of 'impartial' may impartiality be "imposed"? For *people* are *not* impartial. But the "people" behind the veil of ignorance are—they can't help but be, for they have no selves to be partial to! In the *dispensable* version of the veil, it is only a metaphor or dramatic device reminding us that we can't have a genuine principle of justice that says some such thing as "Everything for Sam, and the rest of you clods will just have to toe Sam's line." (Replace 'Sam' with the name of any subset of persons you like—the whites, the intelligent, the courageous, the rich. . . .) In the *indispensable* version, however, not only are the principles of justice impartial but they also require *us* to be so: who gets to use this fine pair of eyes I have is quite open to discussion. My natural interest in using them myself is, after all, obviously "partial", right? And justice is impartial, right? So . . .

Clearly, we must reject this latter, strong interpretation of a "veil of ignorance" device. And since the temptation to interpret it that way is virtually irresistible, we shall avoid it by dispensing with it altogether. We will, in fact, go quite a bit further. We will insist on justifying every single one of the popularly imposed "constraints" on possible principles of morals.[4] Instead of simply building them in from the start, we will ask why we should want this, that, or the other feature to be incorporated into the principles we would want for the purpose that moral principles serve. Indeed, we will also ask what purpose that can possibly be.

After all, when we boldly proclaim, as I have done above, that the principles of justice must be impartial and therefore, for example, can't be of the all-for-Sam type, we are already wading into fairly deep theoretical waters. For as any anthropologist can tell us, there are moralities a-plenty that violate just about any requirement a philosopher might wish to put forward as intuitively self-evident. May we treat A differently from B just because A is A? They probably do in the Kingdom of Z, where dwell folk who will think you mad if you dare to raise the issue of what A has that the rest of us don't. Is morality color-blind? Not in the Land of the Ys, where being two shades lighter than the good Y burghers will get you a quick boot out the back gate, if not boiled and served up for breakfast into the bargain.

Are all these fanciful awful examples, and the many real-world counterparts of them that differ only in details, to be dismissed as not "real moralities", or "moralities" only in some secondary sense of the term? They should not be. In Y and Z and other suchlike places. everyone *does* reinforce universal conformity to the screwed-up rules of those benighted societies. Everything is in place—except that those rules don't have much appeal to a lot of us, when you get right down to it.

And for good reason. Once some deviant y or z starts thinking

about it (which is quite rare, of course), there really *would* be a problem explaining to *her* why she should be going along with the rules of
the y or z morality. If they had to justify the principles to her, or
indeed to just anyone who might be around, there would be problems. These problems are usually resolved by invoking a liberal dose
of mumbo-jumbo. The gods, after all, turn out to be extremely friendly to those of color Y, or to the great mogul A of Z, and surely it's just
obvious that if the gods are for these rules, *you* can't be against them,
right? If we aren't impressed by those devices, however, we are also
unlikely to be impressed by the rules in question.

Universality?

What the philosopher would really like is a universal "contract" in
the sense of an agreement that literally everyone would find it reasonable to accept. It is not clear that this can be done. Perhaps people are
too different, or have interests that are fundamentally, irresolvably
antagonistic. If so, it's put paid for our project. It is so because our
interests are all we have to appeal to as the basis of the "social contract".

But it should not be thought that this possibility puts paid to the
theory in question. There are at least two reasons why not. In the first
place, the truth about morality could be that it cannot be quite as
universal as all that. The insistence that it must be may be just a philosopher's prejudice, comparable to the Aristotelian idea that of
course the earth *must* be the center of the physical universe.

But second, and more hearteningly, the possible nonuniversality
we are worrying about may be nothing to worry about. There are two
ways in which this may be so. One of them incorporates what might
at first sight look like a piece of semantic trickery; the other explains,
in effect, why in fact it is not. Here they are:

(1) We may imagine that a certain principle, aimed at everyone,
has a default option: "Treat everyone with property F in way *x:* with
regard to the rest, it's a free-for-all: anything goes." Is this principle
relevantly universal, if not everyone has F? Sure it is! It tells us what
to do in every case—there are only two, namely, F and not-F—and it
tells *everyone* this. Provided we can justify the default clause, we have
our completely universal principle. In fact, as we will see, morality as
most of us understand it really is rather like that, and, as will also be
seen, the default clause is fully justifiable. Details to come; but first,
on to (2).

(2) Let us suppose that morality is a kind of club—the "morality club". Anyone can join—no problem. Those who join have certain responsibilities and certain rights, and we, the people who run this club, offer a package that we think no remotely reasonable person could really refuse; but nevertheless, some might. All we are saying is that *our* package is such that it must appeal to the widest set of people any set of principles *could* appeal to. Anyone who doesn't buy our package wouldn't buy any package compatible with living among his fellows on terms that they could possibly accept. If we can make good on this offer, then the objection that our morality is not, after all, truly universal is hollow. The respect in which it is *non*universal is not one that could form the basis for any kind of reasonable complaint about the offer. It's still a take-it-or leave-it kind of offer, but it isn't remotely comparable to the restrictiveness of the y's and the z's. It's universal in the sense of being as nearly universal as any set of restrictive rules could be. And that, we can argue, is universal *enough*.

Hobbes

All this has been quite abstract. Let us now see how it works in more nearly real-world terms. One of the contractarians' favorite real-world types is the philosopher Thomas Hobbes.[5] In the Hobbesian picture, at least as understood by me, the place to begin is a wild and unruly place known as the "state of nature". In this state—a highly artificial one, in truth, but we'll worry about that a little later—there is no morality at all. Nobody acknowledges any restrictions whatever on his or her behavior vis-à-vis others, nobody blames or praises anyone else's conduct, and it is quite literally everyone for him- or her-self. And what happens there? All sorts of horrible things, in brief. Since there are no rules at all, there are of course no rules against violence, which is freely employed whenever the person employing it thinks it will get him what he wants. Some will use violence in order to acquire other people's food or other goods, and some will use it because they think that those against whom they use it are about to use it against them—after all, everybody knows that nobody has any scruples about this, so a certain amount of paranoia would seem to be eminently rational as a working hypothesis! The condition in question amounts to a sort of general state of war, the "war of all against all", as Hobbes calls it. And the upshot of this, in the much quoted because quite unimprovable language of Hobbes, is that "there is no place for Industry; because the fruit thereof is uncertain: and conse-

quently no Culture of the Earth, no Navigation, nor use of the commodities that may be imported by Sea: no commodious Building . . .
no Arts; no Letters: no Society: and which is worst of all, continuall
feare, and danger of violent death; And the life of man, solitary,
poore, nasty, brutish, and short."[6]

What is important to the argument here is that the *cause* of this
condition is the absence of rules, rules having precisely the character
we have attributed to morality: namely, rules that can override the
individual inclinations of any person to the contrary, and rules that
are the same for all. The same, because the danger is the same and the
cure is the same. Left absolutely to their devices, so the argument
goes, people will perform actions that lead to a condition that will
make their lives immeasurably worse than if they were instead subject to restrictions: namely, restrictions on just the sort of actions that
have that effect.

It is important to appreciate just what Hobbes's argument does
and what it does not presuppose about people. It does not, to begin
with, presuppose that people are nasty or evil by nature. The term
'evil', indeed, applies only when there already is a morality, and in
the situation we are imagining, there is not (yet). Nobody in it, therefore, is evil, though some are possibly nasty. However, Hobbes does
not even suppose they are nasty. He merely supposes that they are
sufficiently self-interested that, in the absence of some sort of artificial
restraints, they will not shrink from using violence if it serves their
ends; and he is supposing that people's ends are of such a type that
violence might sometimes serve them: as when someone stands between you and what will satisfy your raging hunger, for instance.

Nor does it actually require that their interests are selfish or even
strongly self-directed, though Hobbes evidently believed that they
would normally be. But what matters is that they have *conflicting*
ends, however the conflict may be engendered. It is not required that
some people simply want to do others in; ends may engender incidental rather than essential conflict: it simply turns out that, given
certain circumstances, A wants x, B wants y, and unfortunately, if A
gets x, then B doesn't get y.

As a matter of fact, Hobbes presupposes something quite different
from the "nasty" theory. For real Nasties, what A wants is to frustrate
B, and vice versa. Anything that's good for B is ipso facto bad for A,
and vice versa. Such people have fundamental antagonisms; so long
as their interests remain of that kind, there can be no peaceful solution to their problem. But Hobbes believes that all of us are such that
peace *is* a solution to our problems, whatever they may be. He pre-

supposes that we are *not* nasty. This may be a weakness in his assumptions, in one sense: perhaps people are, after all, basically nasty. But there is, at least, a good deal of empirical evidence to the effect that most of them are not. (Some further ruminations on such subjects will be found toward the end of this book.)

The Prisoner's Dilemma

We now need to bring out a further feature about the sort of conflicts Hobbes is concerned about. From the point of view of each party to the conflict, the warlike solution may seem preferable to the peaceful one. A has some yams, but would like a few coconuts too: B has coconuts but would be happy to trade some for yams. However, A might prefer to have both the yams *and* his coconuts, which he might be able to get by force. Assuming he has no particular love for B, that outcome might look best of all from A's point of view. Not *nice*, to be sure; but niceness has nothing to do with it, so far as the sheer structure of our interests is concerned. Here you are in the hardware store, prepared to trade $5 for a frypan. But wouldn't you rather have both the frypan *and* the $5? Someone with no moral inhibitions at all and who otherwise bore no particular affection for the storekeeper would, and given the opportunity, off he'd go. And more generally, there is a problem with mutual arrangements of all sorts, since in such cases each party gives up something in return for something he wants more; yet given the opportunity, he'd presumably prefer to have both the gains from the deal and also not to have to pay the costs he has undertaken by his promise to pay.

This situation is known as Prisoner's Dilemma. This refers in the first instance to two-party cases (but any number can play). The situation is represented graphically in the accompanying diagram.

		Ms. Column			
		Cooperate		ˎ Don't	
		R	C	R	C
Mr. Row	Cooperate	2nd	2nd	4th	1st
	Don't	R	C	R	C
		1st	4th	3rd	3rd

Here the possible moves or "strategies" (or, in ordinary language, actions) that may be taken are described as "cooperating" or not doing so, and the numbers in the boxes represent the preference orderings of Row (R—left-hand number in each box) and Column (C—right-hand rumber in each box), respectively. It will be observed that their preferences have a structure that exhibits *partial conflict:* the best outcome for each is the worst outcome for the other (Row has both the $5 and the frypan and Column has neither; or vice versa), while the second-best outcome (Row has the frypan, Column the $5) is the same for each, and so is the third (Row has the $5 but no frypan, which he prefers; Column still has the frypan on her shelves and doesn't have the $5, which she'd rather have).

And it will be noted that each party may be tempted to reason as follows: "Suppose that the other individual Cooperates? Then if I Don't, I will do better, for having both the frypan and the $5 is better than having only the $5 [or the frypan, in the case of Column]. And suppose that the other Doesn't cooperate. Then obviously I shouldn't either, for having my $5 [my frypan, in the case of Column] intact is better than giving it away and getting nothing in return." This has been taken by decision theorists to mean that the *rational thing to do* for each is *not* to cooperate.

Note, too, that in situations where there is a policeman waiting at the door to nab Row if he should try to make off with the frypan without paying for it, or Column if she relieves Row of his $5 without giving him the frypan, there is no particular problem about what to do. But then their preferences would be different. The preference for having both the $5 and the frypan is only an "other things being equal" preference; it is not a "come what may" preference. And one solution to a situation that would otherwise become a Prisoner's Dilemma is precisely to alter the situation in such a way that the offending boxes no longer conflict: Row does *not* prefer having both the frypan and the $5, if he has them only for the brief period between his grabbing them and his emerging into the waiting arms of the policeman, followed by his being not only deprived of both the $5 and the frypan but involuntarily provided with a period in jail to boot. The interesting question is what to do in the case where the order of preferences really is as the boxes say, and not where it is not.

Hobbes's own view is in line with modern theorists: the rational individual will rat in such situations. And Hobbes's "solution", as we know, is the Policeman, otherwise known as the "Sovereign". Gauthier's solution is to take what many theorists regard as the heroic course of identifying rationality with the disposition to take the cooperative option. The one recommended here may perhaps be classified as intermediate between the two. Let me explain.

On the Hobbesian view, a rational agent, A, won't conclude any deals with anybody in the "state of nature". A will know that the person he deals with, B, being rational like himself, will not forego any opportunity to promote her, B's, satisfactions, including the one offered by the situation in which A puts down his money (or whatever—since there wouldn't be any money in a State of Nature) before picking up the goods. A can foresee this, so he makes no deals; if B were the party to perform first, then B similarly would make no deals, knowing that A couldn't be trusted. So, Hobbes reasons, the only security is to have someone with enough power to prevent people from reneging on their bargains, by effective threat of sufficient punishment. All we need is a government! Government will be discussed at length in Part Three. Here it will be discussed only in this specific connection, and very briefly.

The Sovereign

The Hobbesian solution may seem all well and good, perhaps. But there are two crucial shortcomings. The first is: how do we get a suitable Enforcer appointed? In our hypothetical state of nature nobody already has the kind of power needed; that power must be "handed over" by those concerned. But you don't just "hand over" power: instead, you make an agreement that gives someone the power. Terrific—but that agreement would have to be, genuinely, an *agreement*—the very sort of thing that can't be done in the state of nature on Hobbes's own reasoning!

The second is that enforcers are costly. For one thing, they cost money, or the equivalent, viz., whatever sacrifices A and B have to make in order to make it worth C's while to be Guardian. Once C somehow got the power in question, of course, there is the further point that C will surely be inclined to use it to feather his own nest—a small incidental concern, in one sense, but in another, of course, one that has been a or even *the* main problem with government, historically as well as theoretically.

The plot has thickened. The idea of setting up the Enforcer (or Sovereign, as Hobbes calls him) is to enable A and B to have the advantages of cooperation. Cooperation *dominates* noncooperation: each is better off than under mutual nonrelation (no deal) or under *general* violence (everyone trying to take the money, and maybe the life of the person supplying it as well, and running). The situation regarding violence is more complicated than that, since prima facie the one who successfully takes the money and runs is better off—she's the "winner". But a *general* regime of violence, where everyone engages in it whenever it suits, will leave everyone worse off. No one will be able to get away with it long when that is the case. (This crucial matter will loom large at various further points in this book.)

The Sovereign is costly, in two important respects: both in the sense that its maintenance will require taxes, which you and I must pay, and in the very significant sense that its existence is dangerous— it can take the money and doesn't even have to run, since it has all the guns. Suppose that A and B share the expense of maintaining the Sovereign. Then both are worse off than if they had simply cooperated in the first place, being able to rely on each other's word and thus to engage in exchanges without bearing the costs of the Sovereign. If the trouble with the State of Nature is that it is dominated by the State of Cooperation, then there is the same trouble with the Sovereign State: a state of voluntary cooperation dominates *it*. And since it is also theoretically impossible to come by a Sovereign, we seem to have a strong argument for cooperation, if it is possible.

Is Cooperation Possible? The Prisoner's Dilemma

Well, why wouldn't cooperation be possible? It matters what the answer is. In the standard view, rationality is the problem, not the solution: rational people will inevitably be unable to cooperate. For they will reason with the Defector: no matter what the other fellow does, my defecting will be better for me. But it should seem odd that rationality consists in "maximizing", that is, doing the best one can for oneself, and yet that rational persons can't cooperate *even though that would be better for both.*

Gauthier's View

Here enters David Gauthier with his intriguing new solution.[7] Gauthier insists that the rational agent, when acquainting himself with the facts of life in the form of Prisoner's Dilemma (and related problems), will see that she must modify, or perhaps reinterpret, her theory of rationality. The rational person will not Defect in the Prisoner's Dilemma game. Instead, she will adopt a *disposition to cooperate,* though not an unconditional disposition to take the cooperative option: she takes that option, *provided* those with whom she interacts are similarly inclined. This Gauthier calls "constrained maximization", as opposed to the disposition to take the money and run, which he calls "straight" maximization.[8]

The subtlety of Gauthier's view begins to be appreciated when we realize that "straight" maximization is *also* a disposition: namely, the disposition to play the defect strategy in Prisoner's Dilemma. It's not, then, the difference between dispositions and isolated acts. "Constrained" maximization is a *different* disposition: namely, the disposition to cooperate with anyone similarly disposed. The underlying argument for Gauthier's position is familiar. Commenting on the standard dominance argument for straight maximization, he points out that it presumes that "the probability of others acting co-operatively [is] independent of one's own disposition. And this is not the case."[9] If we take into account the difference between the ways in which persons of known cooperative disposition can interact as compared with persons of known uncooperative disposition, then the dominance argument works the other way around. "Only those disposed to keep their agreements are rationally acceptable as parties to agreements. Constrained maximizers are able to make beneficial agreements with their fellows that the straightforward cannot, not because the latter would be unwilling to agree, but because they would not be admitted as parties to agreement given their disposition to violation."[10] Constrained maximizers will do better than defectors, for they will do as well as defectors when interacting with defectors, since their rule is to cooperate only with fellow constrained maximizers, and they will do better than defectors when interacting with constrained maximizers, since the defector's policy is to defect when interacting with *anybody*. Gauthier's argument is that it is therefore *rational* to adopt the constrained maximization disposition, and in particular that dispositions come, as it were, logically first. "Our argument identifies practical rationality with utility-maximization at the level of dispositions to choose, and carries through the implications of that identification in assessing the rationality of particular choices"[11]—rather than the other way around, which is the standard view. This has been regarded as the problematic point in his argument. If it is indeed true that defecting maximizes in the particular case, then why would rational agents, whose rationality is defined by maximization after all, adopt a *disposition* that calls upon them *sometimes to do otherwise?*

Consider now the context of open-ended or indefinite reiteration, that is, the situation where the particular Prisoner's Dilemma game under consideration is but the first in a series that has no evident last case. Here, it is agreed by all, rational agents would do well to adopt what amounts to a policy of constrained maximization (it's called "Tit for Tat", the rule being that you play the cooperative move first and then play whatever strategy your opponent plays.)[12] In effect, such contexts enable agents to exert influence, by "rewarding" those who play ball, where playing ball is identified with cooperating, and "punishing" those who do not, by defecting. The Prisoner's Dilemma problem has thus been seen to be crucial mainly in the "one-shot" case, where no further such influences can be exerted. (There is also the question of a short finite run of games, but we won't concern ourselves here with that.)

But is it even correct to say that in a one-shot case defecting actually does *maximize?* This has been the standard view of decision theorists since time immemorial (viz., 1945, when the Prisoner's Dilemma was first formulated). To many of us, there is a ring of oddity about the claim that defectors "do better" than cooperators, even in one-shot cases. For in those cases, if they interact with persons who adopt a similar strategy, what we know is that both parties will come out worse than if both had cooperated. We *know* this, in the sense that it is fully predictable in advance of the interaction on this assumption. Shouldn't it be genuinely surprising that a strategy allegedly aimed at maximizing should be known in advance to yield a worse outcome than some other? In what sense are we "maximizing" if we settle, and settle in advance, for a strategy that we know will do worse than another possible one?

This all-but-universally accepted claim about what to do in a Prisoner's Dilemma situation has also been billed as a "paradox" (the very term 'dilemma' suggests this). There is good reason for this, as we have in effect seen. But there is perhaps a subtle further reason. For after all, one-shot Prisoner's Dilemmas are a *class* of cases. In the whole history of the universe there is not just one one-shot Prisoner's Dilemma. And the Standard View, as we may call it, is a claim about what to do in *any*, that is to say, in *all* of those. It is therefore a general strategy. But to adopt this general strategy is to adopt a *disposition*, namely, the disposition Gauthier refers to as "straight maximization". And that is precisely the disposition that is dominated by his alternative disposition, constrained maximization. The Standard View seems in effect to be committed to the thesis that the best strategy is to be disposed to the one that is known to be worse than a known alternative. Paradox, indeed.

There is a further reason why we should accept Gauthier's solution (and this is in the nature of a confession, since I was for long one of the doubters about it). The point may be put thus. Those who talk of straight maximization as being a maximizing strategy tend to use the term 'response': defecting is the best *response* to the other player's move, whatever that move may be. If the other player plays move x, *then* you should play y, since you then get, let us say, 10, which is better than the 9 you get if you play y; if the other player plays x, *then* you should play x, since the 1 you then get is better than the zero you will otherwise get. If we accept this reasoning, how are we understanding these 'ifs' and 'thens'? It is normally assumed that they are pure logical connectives with no other connotation. But is this so? In the ordinary meaning of the term 'response', a response is usually a *reaction* to something perceived to *have happened*. We cannot "respond" to something that has not yet happened: we can only formulate in advance what our *response*, in the literal sense of that term, *will* be if it *does* happen, and if we know it does. The logic of straight maximization is indeed overwhelming if what we are doing is trying to decide in advance what our responses, in this literal sense, should be if the other player makes one or the other decision. And since those are the only two decisions available, it is then concluded that our best move must be best under all possible circumstances—"all possible circumstances" in one-shot Prisoner's Dilemmas, that is! However, we *know* that those are *not* all the possible circumstances. That ought to make us think.

Now, in the classic, one-shot Prisoner's Dilemma, it is not true that our move is a response to the other person's move. We and the other player are moving simultaneously, for instance, or at any rate moving in such a way that *neither can know what the other player's move is until after we have made our own*. Real-life models of Prisoner's Dilemma may be characterized in just that way. To create any real-life Prisoner's Dilemma, we must take steps, if necessary intentionally rigging the situation, so as to ensure that this condition holds. This ensures that our move will not be literally a "response" to the other player's move. If it is a "response" at all in this literal sense of the term, then what could it be a response *to?*

It is when we contemplate this question that the force of Gauthier's position asserts itself. For it seems that the *only thing there is to respond to* here is the *disposition* of the other player. If you suppose that the other player is a constrained maximizer, then you will know that the other player is also making a judgment whether you are a constrained maximizer. Whether he plays a or b will then depend on his judgment—

which in turns depends on his best information about your judgment, which of course depends on your best information about his. (Followers of paradoxes will note the affinity here with what is known as Newcombe's Problem.)[13]

Each can know something about the other, and what each knows will be largely information about character, derived of course more or less inductively from observation of past performance in particular cases. Each can be thought of as reasoning as follows: "Is this guy going to be disposed to cooperate if he thinks that I am so disposed, or not? If he is, should I rat? But if I rat, will he have judged that I am going to do so? If so, I shall come off with less than if both of us rightly judged the other to be a cooperator and cooperated. And he does look like a cooperator, and we both know all the facts and logic about these matters. So I will cooperate." Note that if instead we reason in this way and conclude that the thing to do is defect, since the other will cooperate, then we can expect that both will reason that way; and then, of course, both will come out worse off. And both *will* reason that way if they have read and believed the literature and concluded that the thing to do in one-shot Prisoner's Dilemma situations is to defect. However, they will also know that those who have the policy of doing so will come off worse than those who have the opposite policy. This *destroys* their basis for assuming that the other player will defect in anticipation of my defecting, *or* in anticipation of my being someone who will cooperate no matter what.

None of this is designed to show that there is never any need for reinforcement of a policy of cooperation. It instead shows that any such need will be in recognition of the limited rationality of those we are dealing with. Of course, we do live in a world full of people whose rationality is imperfect—not to mention that every now and then you run into a really rotten apple! And we must also appreciate that rationality is not simply an innate faculty, supplied gratis by one's genetic makeup. We have to work at it, and more importantly, we have to train our children at it. How they respond in what appear to be Prisoner's Dilemma situations is surely going to be influenced by what we tell them, what we reward and punish them for—and especially, what example we set.

Morality, the Real World, and Prisoner's Dilemma

I use the words "what appear to be" Prisoner's Dilemma situations advisedly. Consider the case of the frypan and the $5. Abstractly, most of us could be brought to agree that we are indeed "better off" with both the $5 and the frypan. But concretely, for most of us in any real-life situation, this simply would not be a true Prisoner's Dilemma. It isn't any kind of "dilemma" at all for us: we simply pay the money and are given the goods and it doesn't occur to either of us to attempt to cheat the other. We, indeed, *would* describe that as "cheating"; moreover, we would describe behavior aimed at this as immoral, unfair, and in more colorful terminology—downright cruddy, for instance. In so doing, we are noting the armory of verbal brickbats neatly stored on the shelves of our consciences, all ready to be hurled at ourselves by ourselves should we engage in shifty dealings. They have been put there long ago, likely, by parents and others. But more interestingly, we have added to the collection ourselves in the course of life. For us, wrong behavior is a downer.

Now let's go back to the State of Nature and ask what to do. There are as yet no rules, and without them, life is miserable for everyone. What the Rational Agent will do in this situation, I suggest, is to set about rewiring herself in such a way as to be disposed to cooperate with others who are similarly disposed, if any: and we will be disposed to attempt to persuade them of the utility of doing so. And we shall set about wiring our children similarly, and hiring teachers who will reinforce that training, not only in the case of our own children but of as many others as possible.

What we will do, in fact, is whatever we can to set Morality in motion: a social institution of reinforcing behavior. And which behavior? Plainly, cooperative behavior: that is, behavior that it is advantageous from the point of view of each one of us to have everyone, including ourselves, engaging in. This is the rational thing to do in social situations for a simple reason: it doesn't cost very much by comparison with having a Sovereign (and anyway, we don't have one yet—remember? And we can't until we have enough morality to enable the Agreement to establish the Sovereign to be viable), and the advantages of general performance much outweigh the disadvantages imposed by the necessity of having to comply oneself.

Generally speaking, then, the foundation of morality is the interests of those party to it, given the facts of social life. Morality is a set of requirements that will make us all better off if they are met by everyone—and that, accordingly, are liable to the problem of defection by some who will try to take the money and run. Consider the murderer and the thief, who have been cheerfully collecting the benefits of social cooperation all along and yet at the judicious moment will take advantage of the good dispositions of those they interact with by depriving them of their lives or property without a by-your-leave.

Is life in general, for essentially everyone, enough like a Prisoner's Dilemma—in respects sufficiently like the ones we would expect morality to have something to do with—for this model to work? That the answer is in the affirmative is attested to by some of the examples already employed, as well as elementary further reflection. We may differ indefinitely in our particular interests: our views about what is ultimately valuable, our favored ways of life. But just the use of the phrase 'ways of life' already suggests an obvious answer: whatever we may think of life in general, we shall get nowhere without it. Anyone with an interest in doing anything or having anything has an interest in remaining alive, and therefore an interest in not being killed. Whatever her attitude toward other people, her interest in possibly being able to kill them when she feels like it is outweighed by her interest in remaining alive herself. And she may be quite sure that were she to put it to others: "Here, look, I'll insist on your refraining from killing me, but I reserve the right to kill you when I please", this "offer" would not get her very far. In a sheer State of Nature situation in which there was as yet no morality at all, someone making that proposal wouldn't, we may conjecture, last long.

Being Able to Complain

It is important to appreciate that in a condition in which there were no rules, there could be no *complaints*. In such a situation nothing is right or wrong, and so nobody can object to anybody's doing anything whatever, and therefore in particular to anyone's taking anyone's life. Now, if morality is an artificial construct, a rational convention, then those who have refused to make any deals acceptable to others are in the condition of rulelessness—in the Hobbesian "state of nature". Hobbes himself characterizes this condition in an unfortunate way: that everyone has a "right of nature" to do whatever he or she thinks best, no matter what it is. As we noted back in Part One, that is a useless, nonsensical employment of the term 'right' and should be dropped. Much less misleading, as we have seen, is to say that in the Hobbesian state of nature nobody has *any* rights, period. And therefore nobody has the protections inherent in a moral system, where people accept rules that limit what they may do to others. These are rules that those others have reason to accept only if they likewise extend benefits to them. And whoever has not made the deal is someone with respect to whom no bets are on, no limitations authorized; and therefore people may do whatever they wish with them. Note that the 'may' here *is* normative. The person who signs no agreements is a person such that anyone else, willing to sign an agreement of mutual advantage, *does* have a moral right to deal with that person as he may. No one may blame him for doing so. The default option, as I called it above, is the legitimate one in dealing with any who refuse to cooperate.

CHAPTER **13**

The Logic of Contractarianism

The Basic Appeal

WHY ACCEPT the contractarian view of morals? Because there is no other view that can serve the requirements: namely, of providing reasons to everyone for accepting it, no matter what their personal values or philosophy of life may be, and thus motivating this informal, yet society-wide "institution". Without resort to any obfuscating intuitions, of "self-evident rights" and the like, the contractarian view offers an intelligible account both of why it is rational to want a morality and of what, broadly speaking, the essentials of that morality must consist in: namely, those general rules that are universally advantageous to rational agents. We each need morality, first because we are *vulnerable* to the depredations of others, and second because we can all benefit from cooperation with others. So we need protection, in the form of the ability to rely on our fellows not to engage in activities harmful to us; and we need to be able to rely on those with whom we deal. We each need this regardless of what else we need or want or value.

The "Natural Law"

Many philosophers, such as Aquinas and John Locke, have held that there is a "natural law". This idea was not clarified by these philosophers, although that they had fairly explicit ideas about its content. Aquinas, for example, held that natural law (like all law) had to be for the "common good". And Locke in particular held that the natural law forbids all to refrain from injuring others in their "life,

148

health, liberty, and possessions".[1] Their lack of articulation of the concept of natural law, however, has left them short of adherents among contemporary philosophers trained in the analytic tradition. Insofar as they simply appeal to natural law without further explication or defense, they are liable to all of the charges I have laid to the door of intuitionism in all its forms.

But perhaps further reflection on the Prisoner's Dilemma and other decision-theoretic problems can assist understanding here. To say that a law is "natural", to begin with, obviously cannot mean that it is like the law of gravity, governing us independently of our wills. Were the content of Locke's natural law operative on us in that manner, there would be no need of ethics as we know it. However, this doesn't preclude a different way in which a "law" could be "natural". It could, namely, be natural in being acknowledged, recognized, or employed implicitly as a canon of interpersonal criticism of behavior, without articulation, in the normal dealings of people with each other.

Even as so characterized, it is not clear that there is a natural law. But we can inject one further element. Locke and Aquinas both insisted that the natural law was "rational", "apprehended by reason", or words to that effect. What we can forthrightly say is that there are reasons, reasons that are natural rather than being in their turn artificial constructs, favoring informal reinforcement of certain rules for interpersonal situations. Prisoner's Dilemma, concentrated on above, gives a beautiful example. Wherever the structure of preferences of the different parties is clear to both parties (and it is not always), we have a basis for a rule of precisely that kind: a natural basis for a moral rule, in fact. The claim that natural morality calls upon us to refrain from the things Locke lists, and more generally that it bids us cooperate in what would otherwise be Prisoner's Dilemmas, may be accepted if understood along the lines just explicated. We should expect any groups of persons who were clear about the options that would otherwise render the situation a Prisoner's Dilemma, and who were capable of communicating effectively with each other, to recognize as an interpersonally authoritative rule that people refrain from the "Defect" strategy, and to recognize this by verbal and other sorts of reinforcement. So understood, we may accept the idea of natural law nearly enough. What its relation to political structures may be is, of course, another question, and the main question dealt with in this book.

But it is apropos to note here that the moral factor is potentially

substantial. James Buchanan observes that "it is essential to incorpo-
rate some treatment of the role that ethical precepts play in maintaining social stability. First . . . if there is no conflict . . . there is no need
for law, as such. By the same token, however, there is no need for
ethics. . . . When conflict does emerge, however, . . . the value of
order suggests either some social contract, some system of formal law,
or some generally accepted set of ethical-moral precepts. It is important to recognize that these are alternative means of securing order.
To the extent that ethical precepts are widely shared, and influence
individual behavior, there is less need for the more formal restrictiveness of legally imposed standards."[2]

A Note on Utilitarianism

In view of its immense influence and considerable plausibility—
not to mention that this author was for long an enthusiastic adherent
of that view[3]—something should perhaps be said here about utilitarianism. The place to say it is here rather than earlier (or later), because
the foregoing considerations have been devoted to framing the idea of
morality and thus making clearer what are the terms of reference that
any substantive theory must satisfy. The utilitarian theory has it that
the general criterion of right and wrong is conduciveness to the
"greatest happiness of the greatest number", or in more up-to-date
terms, maximization of the *general* utility. There are difficulties a-plenty in understanding the import of this theory, about which we will say
a little. But there is also the question whether this is the right criterion
of right—whether there are any considerations in principle that point
in some other direction. And as will also be seen, there are indeed.

Let's start with the difficulties in understanding. These are several, to be sure, but most importantly there are two general problems.
The first and most fundamental is that the utility utilitarians ask us to
maximize is of a special type: it is (1) *cardinal* and (2) *interpersonally
comparable*. Cardinality is a matter of expressibility in terms of numbers, units. That part has its problems, to be sure: the idea that I can
plan my afternoon by choosing the activities that will give me 101
units of expected utility rather than 97 is at least foreign to ordinary
discourse. Still, these are susceptible of an at least vaguely respectable
solution at the one-person level.[4] What is far less easy is to devise a
unit meeting the second requirement, interpersonal comparability.
We need a unit that is transferable from Jones to Smith in a meaningful way, thus enabling us to say such things as that policy x will

benefit Smith enough to offset a loss to Jones and Robinson: say, 5 for Smith versus 2 each for the latter, whereas the other option gives 1 for Smith and 3 each for the others. If these numbers referred to dollars, that would afford a certain clarity—but it's not the right clarity, since as we know dollars cannot in general be equated with utility, nor is any correlation (for instance, logarithmic) more than a *very* rough guess. Indeed, to speak of "guesses" here is perhaps overly generous, since we have scarcely any idea how to proceed.

Whether we can clear this hurdle even in principle continues to be a matter of much debate. But there is another problem awaiting the utilitarian. He would like to be able to criticize existing moralities in terms of his more fundamental theory. But what if people derive a major share of their utility from the existing morality in question? What if people derive utility from x because x is required by their moral code, which they think to be the right one? This at least makes it more difficult to apply the principle of utility as a fundamental one.

This problem is a case of a more general one. Consider the cases where A gets utility from A's perception of B's utility, B being someone A loves (or hates). At a minimum, this increases the complexity of utilitarian arithmetic. And of course it raises such familiar problems as how the utilitarian is to deal with the case where a hundred people get great pleasure from seeing the hundred and first suffer considerable pain. Of course that seems unintuitive to us, at least, and I have expressed dissatisfaction with resort to intuition for fundamental purposes above. But not many theorists would live happily with the suggestion that in the case in question, the right thing to do is to torture Mr. 101 for the general entertainment.

The utilitarian is likely to respond to such cases by asking how it would be if, for instance, there was a *general practice* of torturing people for the public good. (Richard Brandt[5] is one of the more eminent names associated with this maneuver; another is John Harsanyi.[6]) A cynic might reply that it would be just about the way things are now! Then the question of how talk of general practices works into the calculus arises, and everything begins to get pretty complicated. In fact, the question begins to arise, whether utilitarianism can't account for just about anything one feels like "accounting for", once we work in enough resort to hypothetical rules, second-level utilities, and the like.[7]

Aside from these problems of interpretation, which may or may not be insurmountable, we have the more fundamental question of foundations. Why should one accept utilitarianism? If we inspect the classical arguments about this matter, we make an important discovery. Somehow, the utilitarian must say, the foundation of utilitarianism lies in the fact that pleasure (or some such) is what matters to people. But it would be too much to suppose that the pleasure of *other* people just naturally matters to people. The classical utilitarians have agreed that at least so far as our natural constitution is concerned, a hypothesis something like egoism would be nearer the truth. And besides, they want to bring in the utilitarian hypothesis as a *moral* principle, much in the manner of the analysis produced in the foregoing pages. The general utility *overrides* any given individual's utility. If it is to do so, the two can hardly be identical. Any given individual, therefore, may be expected to view the general utility as a basically alien goal. How, then, are we to account for the "oughtness" of the general utilitarian principle? The utilitarian's answer now consists of some such general principle as impartiality: one person's utility, or rather, a given amount of it, is, after all, no more worthy than a similar amount of another's. Morality constrains us to count equals equally. Utility is, by definition (or anyway, by hypothesis) all that matters to us; therefore, equal units of utility must count equally.

Well, *why* "must" they? It is here that we encounter a fundamental problem. If the claim is that it is "morally self-evident" that one person's utility should count the same as another's, then where does this self-evidence come from? If it comes merely from definition, as is essentially maintained by R. M. Hare,[8] then the question why the individual should be moral comes to the fore and has no obvious answer. If the answer is that it is self-evident that we "should" be moral, we are back where we started. And thus we realize that we now need an *intuition*—a need explicitly appreciated by Sidgwick, though not by all utilitarian writers. What's more, this is a *moral* intuition. And then all of the objections to intuitionism as a fundamental theoretical recourse come into play.

As various writers such as Rawls and Gauthier have pointed out, the attraction of utilitarianism as a moral theory stems from an extension of the theory of individual practical reason to the case of society at large, as if society were a sort of super-individual. And that is illegitimate, since society is not a sort of super-individual, but simply a whole lot of individuals, each with his or her own diverse reasons.

We could try getting from the contractual foundation to utilitarianism by arguing that individuals would agree to accept utilitarianism as the interpersonal authoritative rule for governing their interactions. But why would they do so? If we could introduce a constraint such as Rawls's Veil of Ignorance, of course, then we would indeed be on the rails to utilitarianism,[9] but this use of the veil is, as I have pointed out, illegitimate.

We need, then, to look elsewhere for the fundamental authoritative rule we seek. Before doing so, however, let us pay due respect to the undoubted attractions of the utilitarian theory. Can we really be *against* the "greatest happiness of the greatest number"? Do we not all think that a happier society is a better society? Surely we don't think that there can be a serious conflict between justice and utility when viewed in the large? We surely suppose that a just society will thereby be a happier one. True. But the snag is that the reason why the just society is happier may also be that people are happier when they perceive that their society is just! The egg of justice may grow into the chicken of happiness, rather than vice versa.[10]

Finally, let us agree on another point. Whenever we are in real-world situations closely resembling a "veil of ignorance" in some respects, then a utilitarian solution is likely to be a good one. Suppose that some system must be devised for catering to the comparable interests of a large number of people, and that those people are essentially randomly situated with respect to the sources of the benefits. It will then be true that each person maximizes her expected utility by accepting a utilitarian format. Since she doesn't know where she will be in a particular case and can essentially randomize over the various possible cases, she does best if the system maximizes the average person's payoff for the kind of situation in question. Traffic design is a good case in point. Generally speaking, everyone wants to travel everywhere and get there efficiently and safely, so minimizing *average* blockages, bottlenecks, and safety hazards will redound to the advantage of each potential motorist in the area in question. But this works because it is a limiting case, the case where individual and general utility coincide. Many cases certainly don't seem to be like that, and when they aren't, we need a different principle.

CHAPTER **14**

Contractarianism to Libertarianism?

The Project

THE SUBJECT OF the present inquiry, then, is whether we could retrieve the fundamental principles of libertarianism on a contractual rather than an intuitionistic basis. I have argued above that Rawls's view—according to which justice is indeed the set of principles that would be agreed to by rational persons for the social governance of their lives, but only what they would agree to *if* they were forced to choose under the restriction of having absolutely no idea who, as individuals, they were—amounts in fact to another appeal to intuition of the type we want to avoid. Thus Rawls's view foregoes what seems to me contractarianism's principal theoretical claim on our attention. But if we renounce the Veil, what do we put in its place?

We certainly do have a question about the appropriate way to specify the conditions of and the appropriate baseline for this "contract". But it will help appreciably to bear in mind that a moral contract is a general-purpose commitment for social life. There are all sorts of baselines all over the place, simply in the form of the status quo, more or less whatever it may be. In the absence of special reason to think otherwise (and there may, of course, be such), we should, as James Buchanan insists, reason from where we are at the moment.[1] Thinking this way, we can consider the "state of nature" as the situation we have in the absence of any special constraints with respect to the values obtaining in the situation from the point of view of each participant.

Some few of those participants got where they are by making

things worse off for people in past situations with their various base-lines. They may have disregarded values as elementary and pervasive as life and limb, for instance. For such people, we must raise the question what they think they are doing. For in that direction lies the *ultimate* baseline—the Hobbesian "state of nature" situation, the condition we would all be in if there were absolutely no recognized rules whatever. The social contract, whatever its terms, must be an improvement on that, and people proceeding in elementary disregard of persons have not gotten even that far.

But beating the state of nature at that level is, it may seem, too easy. Each rational agent wants, after all, to get the best possible deal, and not just to beat the state of nature. Exactly what the baseline should be for the *real* social contract, in which genuinely differing individuals agree to certain principles for the general social governance of their lives, is obviously not an easy problem. What will be argued here is that we will find substantial support for a libertarian or at least a near-libertarian principle as being the basic one, whatever else. There is a logic to this that the following arguments are designed to bring out. But before proceeding to them, we must consider a major challenge to the kind of theory being pressed here.

A Challenge

Arthur Ripstein has produced a brilliant and trenchant critique of the project we may seem to be doing here.[2] He argues that foundationalism in general, and Hobbesian foundationalism in particular, cannot do what it aims to do, namely, "attempt to justify political institutions without presupposing any political considerations. . . . some set of considerations is held to support a particular form of political order, without itself depending on any substantive assumptions about the legitimacy of particular forms of human interaction."[3] Ripstein's conclusion is that "The search for foundations grew out of skepticism about the sorts of political considerations we ordinarily use to show some set of institutions to be legitimate. But the very sort of skepticism that made a foundation seem necessary undermines any attempt to provide one. Nothing can both be safe from the skeptic and carry weight in justification."[4] It behooves us to have a careful look at this very powerful argument.

Ripstein shows a profound appreciation of the Hobbesian project. "A contractarian argument shows some institution to be legitimate by showing that it would be the outcome of a choice situation that preserves important features of our own situation. The specification of the choice situation acts as a *filter* to rule out certain considerations as irrelevant . . . it is able to justify not because it is a contract, but because it captures all and only those features that are important to relations between people. . . . it is not an attempt to capture or approximate some independently specifiable set of institutions; the choice situation itself entirely determines the legitimacy of institutions."[5] The justification in question tries to show that any set of political institutions is better than the state of nature and then "outlines a set of optimally mutually advantageous political institutions . . . that rational agents fresh from the state of nature would prefer above all others." Further, there is no presumption that "individuals are ontologically or chronologically prior to society. He presumed only that, given that human beings do live in society, the particular form of association must be justified to each person."[6]

Proceeding to his analysis of the Hobbesian argument, Ripstein finds that the "Hobbesian state of nature incorporates three features that make it appear to be an appropriately foundational (namely, apolitical) contractual situation." These are (1) "subjectivism about value", (2) "instrumentalism about rationality", and (3) "mutual indifference . . . together they purport to make the state of nature a politically neutral starting point."[7] Regarding (1): "If he were willing to appeal to fairness or human flourishing, his political theory would be unable to answer the fool, who cares only for his own interests." About (2), he notes that "the instrumental account of rationality . . . is secure against the two sorts of skepticism that are built into Hobbes' state of nature. It is safe against the traditional skepticism of the fool because it ensures that all action will be assessed only in terms of their advantage for the agent; the only questions of rationality are questions of efficacy in reaching the agent's ends. . . . [It is] also safe against the specifically modern skepticism that forms the background of Hobbes' project: no instrinsic values or conceptions of the human good are required in assessing arrangements for their rational acceptability. No agent is assumed to have any reason to do anything that does not stem from some desire that she or he actually has."[8] Thus "unlike political principles governing human interaction, it seems that whatever one wants, one cannot help but want to do the rational thing in pursuing it."[9]

And finally, regarding condition (3), mutual indifference, Ripstein observes that "political institutions of any size . . . will primarily govern relations between strangers. By treating agents in the state of nature as mutually indifferent, no assumptions need to be made about one's attitude towards those one interacts with. . . . In small, close-knit groups, it may be that it is more important to all concerned *not* to keep track of considerations of relative contributions and distributions, and that the very process of sharing and failing to keep track is itself a good. In such groups, ties of mutual affection might outweigh any other considerations governing the choice of a structure of interaction . . . . the parties comprising such groups do not need to be told the advantages of participation. Their mutual ties of benevolence guarantee their participation. No such assumptions can be made about interacting strangers. . . . compliance must be rational regardless of who they are interacting with."[10]

Having produced this insightful analysis of the Hobbesian project, Ripstein moves to his critique. "As reasonable as the conditions of instrumental rationality and mutual indifference may seem, I now wish to argue that they cannot serve as a politically presuppositionless foundation for any set of institutions. Contrary to the appearance I have been at pains to develop, they cannot both be safe from the skeptical challenge contained in Hobbes' subjectivist account of value *and* serve to justify particular institutions. Whatever plausibility they might have—and I cannot deny it is considerable—accrues only because they are evaluatively substantial principles. [They] can only serve to justify political institutions and only make it possible to reply to the "fool" in each of us insofar as they are conditions that we, and the imagined fool, are willing to accept. In particular, they are no more proof against the skeptical challenge implicit in the assumption of the subjectivity of value than are considerations of fairness. The Hobbesian contract, no less than its Lockean and Rawlsian offspring, can only serve to justify institutions because it incorporates political conditions we do in fact accept. . . . the Hobbesian state of nature fails to provide a privileged perspective for social choice. . . . the adoption of each depends on normative considerations."[11] Strong words! And backed by strong arguments.

"Consider first the concept of instrumental rationality. Rationality enters the Hobbesian contract as a practical principle, rather than as a political principle *per se*. It is nonetheless worth investigating the role that it plays in the argument. Two distinct concepts are run together. . . . One is trivial, and therefore safe from the skeptic, but irrelevant in replying to the fool. . . . The other plays a fundamental role in the reply to the fool, but is not safe from the political skepticism that motivates the Hobbesian project."[12]

The two are (my emphasis) (1) *"interpretive* rationality" which "involves the readiness to use available information in attempting to satisfy one's current desires. . . . one cannot help but want to get what one wants. . . . [But] because it makes systematic irrationality impossible, interpretive rationality has no part to play in explaining to the fool just how foolish he is. So long as the fool acts on some desire, he is not irrational." On the other hand, (2) "The *reflectively* rational person is willing to make immediate sacrifices for the sake of far-off gains; . . . This is the sort of rationality that Hobbes' contract requires, for the laws of nature he recommends are advantageous only in the long run." Now, "the fool who ignores the long-term costs of violating contracts is irrational by the standards of reflective rationality. . . . Yet it is a stronger condition than Hobbes is entitled to. [It] can only provide a basis for criticism of actual behavior if it is not an inescapable end of all agents. . . . But if the fool is not necessarily rational, reflective rationality may be something that the fool does not care about. . . . It is here that the modern skeptic comes home to roost: from the point of view of a big, cold, empty universe, reflective rationality is as much in need of (and by the skeptic's lights, incapable of) justification as any political principle is. . . . It is only because those of us who aspire to be reflectively rational attach paramount importance to our rationality that we are interested in the set of institutions that rational persons would agree to. Rationality is important to political justification not because it is presuppositionless, but because it is *our* presupposition."[13]

Disarmingly, Ripstein allows that "the introduction of rationality might be thought to be fairly innocuous for political justification. Perhaps it is legitimate for [Hobbes] to help himself to some unjustified practical principles, so long as he does not introduce any that are properly speaking political, that is, principles that govern the legitimate interactions of persons." But next there arises a far more crucial problem: "I now wish to suggest that the assumption of mutual indifference . . . is able to do the work it does because it rests on [a similar] ambiguity." He agrees that "in general, people cannot be assumed to take an interest in the welfare of those they interact with. . . . Sad, perhaps, but probably true . . . . But this assumption . . . does relatively little work in Hobbes' account . . . . The general absence of both fondness and antipathy toward others ensures that agreement is neither easy nor impossible; it does little to determine the nature of that agreement."

However, "Now consider a different assumption, also going by the name of "mutual indifference": individuals do not care about their conditions of interaction, except insofar as those conditions influence the satisfaction of their self-regarding desires. This assumption . . . does rather more work in Hobbes' argument. Yet as a factual claim, . . . [it] seems plainly false: the racist who would rather not reach or keep agreements with blacks or Jews regardless of the advantages that might accrue from making such agreements provides an ugly example. And the egalitarian who is unwilling to accept political institutions that designate demeaning roles, even if he could live more comfortably were others to occupy such roles, provides a cheerier example, as does the Rawlsian liberal with a prior concern for fairness. . . . They may or may not care directly for the welfare of others; but they do care for the manner in which they associate with them.

As Ripstein says, "These other-regarding concerns are importantly unlike the self-regarding desires that Hobbes focuses on. They are not the sort of ends that are readily integrated into a calculus of rationality at all, let alone that make one wish for a peaceful setting for their pursuit; the racist does not want a peaceful setting in which to go about his own business of promoting segregation. . . . We need not suppose any of the three types described above to be dogmatically unwilling to participate in any but their most favored institutions; each need only assign weight to those considerations in deciding whether any particular political institutions are worth participating in. To demonstrate to such a person the rationality of conformity to certain institutions, we must show that they satisfy those special concerns as well as can be expected given the conflicting desires of others. . . . To exclude other-regarding interests is therefore to fail to take seriously Hobbes' concern with addressing justification to agents as we actually find them. The liberal and the racist are as much in need of an answer as the rational egoist."[14]

This raises the question of why we should "exclude other-regarding concerns from the contractual situation? It might well be true that in the absence of any already formed social bonds, people would care only instrumentally about their interactions with others. If so, we could not *explain* the emergence of society from a presocial condition by presupposing any other-regarding concerns. But this fact is not enough to validate the Hobbesian enterprise. . . . Why should agreeableness to asocial creatures justify political institutions to *us*? [Ripstein assembles three possible reasons:] . . . it might be an accurate description of human motivations; it might exclude motivations that political skepticism forces us to reject; or it might be justified on political grounds."[15]

Of these, Ripstein rightly rejects (1) as implausible; but that's not all. For "if such a reduction [of apparently other-regarding concerns to self-regarding desires] could be carried off, the cost to Hobbes' project would be too high. Reducing such desires is equivalent to including them, for if they could be reduced, all desires would be purely self-regarding. The inclusion of all desires in the contractual situation is a possibility that Hobbes cannot allow. . . . unless some desires are ruled out, the resulting agreement cannot serve to justify any particular institutions or practices to the exclusion of others, for any actual set of stable institutions can pass the test of such agreement. Hypothetical agreement collapses into actual agreement, for if all agents actually are rational and mutually disinterested, any set of institutions actually is the result of choices made by mutually disinterested agents concerned to select a stable and mutually advantageous setting in which all can pursue their own welfare. . . . on the whole, what mutually disinterested rational agents *have done* is incontrovertible evidence of what they *would* do. If they have not actually convened and agreed, it can only be because their rational self-interest showed them that it was unnecessary to do so. . . . Such actualism undermines the very point of Hobbes' contract, for it leaves no grounds for choice between any existing political institutions."

And so, "Hobbes thus faces a paradox: if rationality and mutual indifference are universal, then any set of actual political institutions is justified as the outcome of a Hobbesian contract; if they are not universal, then his justification loses its foundational status, for it depends on evaluatively substantive considerations that are not intrinsic to the human condition."[16] "If Hobbes is to be a consistent subjectivist about values, then only the fact that a value is *held* can have any political significance; the racist's values are as real as the fool's. . . . Concern for fairness or for human dignity does not depend on their being intrinsically in the nature of things any more than reflective ratonality does."[17]

Ripstein goes on to propose that "If self-regarding desires enjoy any sort of privilege in justification, it is *political* privilege. Whatever justificatory power the Hobbesian state of nature has stems from the fact that it captures a plausible principle governing legitimate interactions between persons: it is illegitimate to coerce people for the sake of others' desires about what they should do. This in turn is presumably because we regard it as a good thing for people to choose their own conception of the good. This is a plausible and deeply entrenched political principle—yet one that is not justified by the contract, but presupposed by it. . . . Hypothetical consent only serves to justify social arrangement if the consenting parties have consented on reasonable grounds; prudential grounds are only reasonable if agreement is not forced by the need to reach some sort of accord with someone making unreasonable demands, whether those demands take the form of the threat of physical force, or intransigence about agreement for the sake of preconceptions about how others should live." "A liberal-individualist assumption of this sort underwrites the entire contractarian project." "The contract does not display the relation between morality and advantage, but rather the legitimacy of certain limitations on individuals going about their own business."[18]

At this point, however, it seems to me that Ripstein overstates, or slightly misstates, the case. Is it true that self-regarding desires in particular require any "privilege" in contractarian theory, and even if it does, is it right to call this "political" privilege? That the answer to the first question, at least, is in the negative is suggested by Ripstein's further consideration of some recent work of Thomas Scanlon, who suggests "that the element of truth in contractual views can be salvaged by focusing on the need to justify oneself to one's fellows in terms they cannot reasonably reject.[19] Scanlon calls this Rousseauian view "contractualism" to distinguish it from the narrower contractarianism of the Hobbesian tradition. The fundamental difference is that there is no privileged set of considerations that can be appealed to by the parties that are trying to come to an agreement. . . . No particular set of considerations is foundational, for any can be called into question if its consequences are unacceptable. Scanlon's view is directly relevant to Hobbes's project, for once we recognize that Hobbes cannot succeed as a foundationalist, his project is best viewed as contractualist in Scanlon's sense of the term; his idealizations can only be justified by the political principles we are willing to accept. . . . Political institutions are not chosen as wholes from a presocial situation; they emerge slowly and in part through our attempt to articulate the practices underlying them. In so doing, we are prepared to call some practices into question—slavery and apartheid are particulary glaring examples—but always do so in light of the considerations that we find most important. Considerations of fairness, democracy, and freedom can be raised as readily as consideration about the satisfaction of desires. So too can considerations of the sort raised by Marx about the enslaving effects of particular proposed institutions. That such considerations might not even make sense to pre-social creatures is irrelevant. If they cannot be reasonably rejected in light of the concerns of those involved, they must carry weight in political debate."[20]

Ripstein sums up as follows: "The skeptic cannot be answered by the foundationalist any better than by the nonfoundationalist. The nonfoundationalist is explicit about introducing considerations that carry the weight they do only because we cannot bring ourselves to reject them. But they are not less worthy of concern for that . . . . legitimate institutions rest on the consent of those they govern, not because the agreement of reasonable persons provides a presupposi-tionless foundation, but because it holds out the possibility that pol-itics might become a self-correcting enterprise that allows any policy or principle to be called into question, though not all at once."[21]

What are we to say to all this? Several things, in fact. First, it is of some importance to appreciate that Ripstein's use of the term "politi-cal" is somewhat general. When he argues that the agreement of rea-sonable persons does not provide a "presuppositionless foundation", we can agree in the sense that what *goes into* the particular political process that generates a particular political outcome is certainly not going to be without presuppositions, and indeed, even political ones. It does not follow, however, that liberalism is simply on all fours with Mohammedanism, Quakerism, or for that matter, Marxism, or any of the myriad other specific ideologies kicking around in a healthy mod-ern democracy. To hold that the contractualist project has "presup-positions" of the very type it proposes to supply the foundations for is very misleading.

Just what is presupposed by the contractarian procedure? Two things, in particular: (1) The individuals whose polis is in question have various values and apply reasoning on behalf of them. The as-sumption that those values are *various* is what creates a need for mor-als and/or politics. And (2) those values lie within a range, though a very wide one, such that there is the possibility of cooperation. Now, the latter assumption is not self-evident and is sometimes false. When it is, politics, in one sense, is at an end, and there is instead violence, turmoil, and war. It is the fact that that is the sort of thing that awaits a group which cannot resolve its problems by adopting internal con-straints on behavior that especially motivates those constraints; and as we have seen, it will not in fact motivate everyone to them.

But note a major point about the contractarian procedure. From its point of view, the various values of individuals or sets of them enter into the proceedings only *as* the values *of* those persons. They do not, any of them, enter as considerations having weight independently of the fact that they are the concerns and interests of those whose values they are. Now, in one sense of the term, those values are indeed "political"; they are, we might say, the very stuff of politics. It is also true that many of those values will be other-regarding values, values about the "conditions of interaction" of persons. But—and this is a very large "but"—what is the *status* of the latter? When one person is, say, a monarchist and another an anarchist, then we have two different other-directed interests confronting each other. But in that sense, it doesn't matter whether those interests are political or anything else. A cubist and a classicist would do equally well.

Yet there is a difference between the monarchist's interest qua interest, and his interest qua proponent of a political *theory*. In the latter capacity, the question about his view is whether it passes intellectual muster. Is it coherent, plausible, well grounded, and, in short, sound? If not, then it has *no weight at all* insofar as it is a candidate for political truth and, therefore, for what should hold sway as determining the form of society. And if it is, then we should all convert to monarchism. But regardless of its soundness, it can still enter the lists as *an* interest, one among others. In that capacity it can be given some weight. Indeed, if all were to agree in this respect, then presumably monarchy would issue forth. But if all do not? Then what? There would now be a question whether monarchy is the sort of government that can be legitimate if even a few object. In the absence of some kind of intellectually weighty defense of monarchy as a political institution, it is questionable that it can.

Consider Ripstein's suggestion that "Considerations of fairness, democracy, and freedom can be raised as readily as considerations about the satisfaction of desires." Is this really true? In one sense, of course: those considerations can be raised in political debates, and often are. But it is not true that they can be raised "as easily" as considerations about the satisfaction of desires. The proponent of fairness, after all, is claiming that fairness demands the satisfaction of *this* desire rather than *that* one; of democracy, that the desires of the majority should win as compared with those of the minority; of freedom, that people should be free to do as *they* desire. It is quite true that a proponent of these things could advance her interest in those things as if it were just like a desire for ice cream or Beethoven. But if she does so, think what it does to her case! Are we to do things democratically just because Jones, over there, happens to have a taste for democracy? Suppose that the case for fairness or freedom were no better than the case for Seventh-Day Adventism? Clearly, the upholders of those values do not look at them that way.

To be sure, neither, perhaps, does the Seventh-Day Adventist. Yet the absence of any publicly compelling *arguments* for his beliefs compels him to constrain his pursuit of his religious interests, whereas the case for freedom and perhaps even democracy is, in truth, a political one in the proper sense of those terms: namely, that considerations of the good order of a diverse community require that those values be observed, almost no matter what the particular character of the desires of its members may be like.

This sheds, I hope, some light on Ripstein's claim that "political considerations need to be imported into the choice situation; to forego them is to forego any justificatory force one might have hoped for." In the narrow sense of the term 'political' in which Hobbes, for instance, has a political theory, this seems to me plainly false. The genius of Hobbes lies in the fact that he shows how politics is needed even if *none* of the interests at the ground-floor level are themselves political. All they need to do is come into the kind of partial conflict that leads to the need for constraints and, perhaps, for political institutions narrowly so called.

Thus if we construe the term "political" in the suitably narrow sense that identifies *one* type of interest among many, instead of in an unacceptably broad sense in which it simply refers to any interest or tendency that impinges on one's fellows sufficiently to raise issues that might require politics or at least morality to deal with, then it remains true to say, despite the falsity of egoism, that the Hobbesian theory is "presuppositionless".

Which is not to deny—indeed, is to confirm—the possibility that the configuration of interests and powers in a given case might be such that no *political*, as distinct from, say, military, solution is possible. In the sense in which this is true, we may say that the Hobbesian idea does "presuppose" that people are such as to be able to benefit from peace and order. They may not be able to, and there is no use denying the possibility. All we can do in regard to that possibility is our best: namely, to persuade them to check again and see whether their values truly substantiate that conclusion in their case. That values must be behind these conclusions in each person's case is undeniable. The libertarian's, and in general the liberal's, case is simply that a clear-headed appraisal will confirm the wisdom of signing the social contract instead of bashing ahead as one will, and that this wisdom will be found to obtain in almost (if not quite) complete independence of what those values in particular are. For the totally imprudent or the totally fanatical, to be sure, the compellingness of politics or even of morality might be nil. For everyone else, though, the contractarian has a strong case. And just because of this substantial independence, it is a stronger case than can be made for any other political theory. Such is the contractarian's claim, at any rate. And Ripstein's arguments, though important and impressive, do not, to my mind, dislodge it.

The Road from Contractarianism to Libertarianism

In Part One we have made an effort to characterize the theory whose foundations we are now inquiring into. Admittedly it is not quite true, as many people seem inclined to think, that libertarianism is a creed whose principles are canonically engraved in marble somewhere for all to see, but still, it does seem to me—and this is one of its attractions, isn't it?—that its basic idea can be stated quite simply. A summary of the findings in Part One goes roughly as follows:

(1) Each person, A, has a determinate set of fundamental personal resources such that

(2) A has the [negative] right to use those resources in whatever way A sees fit, provided that in doing so, A does not violate the similar right of any other person, B, over the use of B's resources.

Or, more briefly yet: our sole basic duty is to refrain from utilizing the fundamental resources of others without their consent; and those resources include, at a minimum, the bodies and minds of those others.

The implications I will suppose we can draw from this are these, at least: (1) We have no *fundamental* general duty to provide others with such goods as the necessities of life, let alone some particular proportion of all the socially distributable goods there are; (2) we have in general a duty not to interfere with the operations of the "market," so long as it is truly a free market and not something else masquerading as same; (3) we should always in general prefer voluntary social arrangements to involuntary ones whenever this is definable and feasible. (4) Governments, in particular, are severely restricted in what they may properly do, and the blessings of a majority vote in favor of a given government activity is not in general a sufficient license of that activity, morally speaking.

This will do for the present. In Part Three we will go into detail. Our question is whether contractarianism would underwrite libertarianism as so characterized. It is a long way to the end of arriving at true clarity on this matter, but we must make a start. The most important thing to emphasize about the contractarian approach is that it hopes to *generate moral principles for societies out of the nonmoral values of individuals.* That is what is fundamental, and all problems of interpretation should be viewed in the light of this. Now, if our social principles are generated out of individual values, there is only one way that this can be done on our assumptions: namely, that those individual values *support* those social principles. If they do, then our individual cannot—as she can, of course, with any intuitionistic system—look in the face of what she agrees to be a moral principle, as shown by this procedure, and react with a yawn. She can't say "So what?" because the answer is that she ignores it at her own peril, as shown by her own values; and her own values are those that, by definition, she does care about. What is needed is to show that the concern we must by nature have with our own values, virtually whatever they may be, is such as to underwrite a social principle of allowing each to pursue that person's possibly very different ones—and that no other moral principles can take precedence to this one.

Values

One point to emphasize, already adverted to in Part One (Chapter 3), is that we do not assume that people attach value to "liberty as such". It is not clear what that would consist of in any case. But obviously people often willingly put themselves into situations in which they will be demonstrably restricted in various ways—taking almost any job, or getting married, will do as examples. We must not make our argument depend on the assumption that within every breast there is a little Patrick Henry waiting to burst out upon its astonished owner. Morality in general, and liberty in particular, are to be defended here as means, not as ends.

Each person, we assume, controls his or her activity in the light of a scheme of values, some few of which are perhaps explicitly held and formulated, but many of which are not. Most of these values are not as such moral values, and the ones that are, are subject, in the view taken in this essay, to critical review. Among the values that we cannot assume to be held by any particular person are the ones many of us hold dear.

A False Start: Autonomy Generalized

An important, and indeed probably the most important, case in point is provided by the concept of autonomy. Many of us think that being an autonomous person, one who leads a life of reasoned competence, is a fine thing. And Robert Nozick apparently held that any individual endowed with what he called "M-ness" (for "Meaningfulness"), which was roughly the ability to have and rationally marshal values in support of practical alternatives, would just *obviously* accord libertarian rights to all other M-beings.[22] This seems far from obvious, though. It is logically compatible with being an M-being that one regard others exclusively as means to one's own ends. If we think of the libertarian principle as prohibiting the utilization of others solely as means to one's own ends, then some non-question-begging reason must be given for accepting this prohibition. We must avoid a simplistic recourse to Moral Intuition.

Nozick's idea has an off-the-cuff air about it in *Anarchy, State, and Utopia*. But recently there has been an interesting and thorough study of much the same idea as his "M-ness," in Lawrence Haworth's *Autonomy*.[23] I have criticized the Nozickian argument[24] on the ground that it was not obvious that M-persons must value the M-ness of other M-persons. I now wish to suggest that the same line of criticism applies to Haworth's more fully worked-out version (which differs, however, in considerably more than simply being more fully worked out).

Haworth argues at length, and compellingly, that autonomy *is* a value, and a very fundamental one, for the autonomous person (or anyone?).[25] And he argues that "when representative arguments for the right to liberty are inspected for signs of . . . dependence on autonomy, two things become evident. A condition for attributing to anyone a right to liberty is that the person be capable of exercising that right autonomously. And once the idea of advancing a theological argument of the right to liberty . . . is given up, then the only way we have of making ascription of that right plausible is to acknowledge that ascribing it facilitates the individual's project of becoming autonomous."[26] And of course the conclusion will be, for instance, that "to nurture autonomy and ensure that people generally have adequate opportunity for living autonomously, it is not sufficient merely to create open options. The negative freedom that libertarians value may be taken up heteronomously as well as autonomously."[27] "The contrast between the libertarian and autonomian views," he argues, "is stark. The libertarian finds value in barely having options, regardless of what exercise of the options leads to or even of whether they are exercised. The autonomist regards the bare having of options as uninteresting or neutral, and locates the value of liberty in its indispensability for autonomous life and in its role of nurturing development of the capacity for autonomy."[28] In discussing the classical defenses of liberty, he argues for the "inevitability of the association of liberty with autonomy", namely "by tracing the ways in which typical defenses of the right to liberty invoke autonomy as the good which according a right to liberty promotes. The conclusion to which this points is that the right to liberty is not a fundamental right, if that means that people are entitled to be free regardless of the uses to which the freedom will be put and regardless of their capacity to exercise the freedom in a certain way. Just as the value of liberty, in the sense of open options, is that it creates a domain for autonomy in which one's capacity for autonomous life may both be developed and find expression, so the right to liberty is accorded in order that the individual may exist in that environment that nurtures and endorses autonomy."[29]

In analyzing the notion of rights, and especially the right to liberty, he draws "an important implication. . . . the political import of the right to liberty depends on how one limits the right." The limitation is introduced in the clause that asserts that one has a right to do as one will, "unless one's action harms or threatens harm to others (or restrains, injures or coerces them) . . . the usual interpretation of the clause has been such as to cause the right to liberty to support highly conservative and free enterprise-oriented ideologies." But, "If autonomy is the end that acknowledging the right serves, then liberty is no more important than, and cannot be accorded precedence over, other modes of treatment that are equally relevant to development and exercise of autonomy. . . . Growth of individuality requires more than liberty. It is not enough merely to be left alone. For a social environment to form a domain for autonomy, it must contain resources and circumstances that nurture critical competence and facilitate its expression. These are not automatically provided by ensuring that one confronts numerous open options."

Summing up, he says, "I have sought to establish that the value of liberty depends on the contribution which having liberty makes to people's autonomy, and that the case for a right to liberty cannot be made without taking account of this contribution. As a normative idea, liberty is subordinate to autonomy."[30]

There is a question, of course, of what kind of "subordination" is in order. Are we to marshal the force of law behind autonomy, intervening to prevent people from taking nonautonomous decisions? Presumably not. Surely, we (including Haworth, I believe) want to stick with Mill here, restricting our interventions to admonishment, advice, remonstrations, and the like. But in the end, we must allow people to act as they choose—or even as they will, contrary to their own choice, unless we have clear authorization from them to intervene.

Haworth proposes an "autonomy theory of rights", arguing that "where the utilitarian theory seems well attuned to the welfare needs of people but insensitive to their uniqueness, the libertarian theory captures this fact of uniqueness but is Scroogelike in its response to their welfare and to inequities in the distribution of the means to well-being."

"The autonomist founds the wronging criterion [needed for distinguishing acts that wrong people from those that are merely undesirable but not contrary to their rights] on the right-holder's capacity for and interest in autonomy. The general idea is that a person is wronged by ignoring or tampering with his capacity for autonomy, either by preventing or failing to nurture development of that capacity or by preventing or failing to provide opportunities for living in a way that expresses the capacity." And he suggests that "Autonomy-based rights are those modes of treatment to which the individual is entitled in order that his life and situation may have three characteristics: his domain for autonomy should be open; it should be open de facto, and not merely de jure; and he should have both the ability and the opportunity actually to live autonomously within his domain for autonomy."[31] Thus, "The right to education requires that there be technical and vocational secondary schools ? . . . the right to the enjoyment of just and favorable conditions for work requires remuneration for public holidays . . . [and so on]." Naturally, "A doctrine of autonomy-based rights cannot provide the criteria for locating the appropriate level. . . . What it can do is spell out a principle: *Every individual is entitled to modes of treatment that nurture and facilitate autonomous life.* . . . What is at issue is not whether the rights shall be acknowledged but the scale of the modes of treatment required to nurture and facilitate autonomous life."[32]

What are we to say to this? One way to put the response is to ask whether any such program of positive rights can be said to be generally respectful of autonomy. Haworth's view assumes that autonomous people attach a *value* to the autonomy of others. But why should they? He has been concerned throughout to show that autonomy *is* a value, and no doubt one who thinks so will also think that autonomous people will agree with him in that respect. But in any sense in which they *must* agree with him in it, the characterization does not show that they must attach higher value to the provision and maintenance *for others* of "conditions conducive to autonomy" than to any number of other possible situations they might value. It doesn't follow from the idea, and I don't see why it should be thought safe to assume, that all autonomous persons nevertheless do hold the value in this way. Haworth quite rightly notes that "The right to religious freedom is not thought to include a right to be given a church or other paraphernalia required in order that one might worship the God of one's choice, but only to worship that God unimpeded by others in the event one has the means of doing so."[33] Well, how is *requiring* supposedly autonomous person A to provide paraphernalia to miscellaneous other persons, B, in order to foster the growth of autonomy in them a way of respecting A's autonomy? It isn't even a way of recognizing the general value of autonomy, if by that one means the general *valuing* of autonomy (which is, after all, the only thing it *can* mean if one abandons a metaphysical view of values). For if people value things, then they *do* act so as to promote them. They make decisions about what counts more and what less, and if promotion of the autonomy of others counts more to them, then they will voluntarily foster those conditions. But if they do not? If they conclude that their energies are best directed elsewhere, then the claim that those others have the *right* that they direct them there in particular rather than to the places they judge to have higher value is, in a word, to violate their autonomy: it is to override their judgment about what they should do with their lives—the very sort of judgments that are definitive of autonomy.

It may well be, in some connections, that as Haworth says, liberty is subordinate to autonomy "as a normative idea". If I have a choice between losing my critical faculties and losing a certain social liberty, then of course I shall prefer the latter. But will I have the same sort of complaint in either case? It depends on how it is that my critical faculties are threatened. Some suppose that they are threatened by exposure to ads for Wheaties; but let us suppose instead that they are threatened by Alzheimer's disease. We do not, at the moment, know how to ward off this threat when it materializes, but let us suppose we did. And suppose then that, somehow, I can avoid the threat by coercing someone in some way, forcing them to treat my disease instead of exerting their creative autonomy by designing Wheaties ads. *I* am quite willing, perhaps, to do this, so far as my personal values are concerned. But does this method respect the other person's liberty? It would seem not. Does it respect his autonomy? Apparently it doesn't do that either. *He* may not value the preservation of my autonomy as much as I do, nor as much as he values something else (a new house, say). The case for designing our institutions on the assumption that autonomy is a sort of universal social value, capable of justly imposing many irksome requirements on their reluctant participants, does not fall straight out of the assumptions either that autonomy is highly valuable to the individual or that it is a prerequisite to any liberty worth having.

In short, if we attend seriously to the need for an argument from some theory of value to a corresponding right, then the view that autonomy is prior to and presupposed by liberty as a value still doesn't yield the conclusion that our rights extend beyond liberty rights. Not, that is, if those are understood to be fundamental rights as Haworth claims.

There is a similar problem here to the one that afflicts the moral theory of Alan Gewirth.[34] In his substantial *Reason and Morality* Gewirth hopes to show that rational agents must, on pain of contradiction, accept the familiar schedule of Western rights. These are to be extracted from a *Principle of Generic Consistency,* which says, "Act in accord with the generic rights of your recipients as well as of yourself."[35] These rights, in turn, are ones that the agent, just by virtue of *being* an agent, has to acknowledge for all, because he has to claim them himself. And this, Gewirth supposes, he must do because they are "required for his purpose-fulfilling actions".[36] But what are required for one's purpose-fulfilling actions are not rights, but only enough noninterference by others to enable one to get on with it, whatever "it" may be. What one wants, qua agent, is only the "up side" of rights, that is, noninterference (or, as the case may be, assistance) by others. It does not follow logically that one wants those enough to go to the length of being willing to accept the "down side" as well, that is, the duties entailed by wholehearted acceptance of the rights in question. That requires a calculation: viz., that the advantages *are* worth the costs—and of course that the costs are necessary: that is, that the option of simply free riding on the good will or guillibility of others is unavailable. Or it requires an evaluation, a judgment that the latter option is something one shouldn't take even if it is available. And none of these things can reasonably be claimed to be entailed *just* by being a rational agent.[37]

Another False Start: An Argument from "Survival"

Professor Ellen Paul, in considerable contrast to many of her fellow enthusiasts for private property rights, puts forth an explicit argument for them in her interesting study *Property Rights and Eminent Domain*. It will be instructive to have a brief look at it. The argument opens with the observation that people engage in purposive activity with a view to their "survival". In order to survive people must be able to move about, and so to be "free to move about", in particular to act upon the world they live in. More specifically yet, they need to be able to acquire parts of that world, for example, by eating and breathing. Do these facts lead to the necessity of recognizing moral rights on their part to doing these things? We have two alternatives: either everyone has such rights or no one does (at this fundamental level, there can't be an in-between: we are all alike in the respects stated). "The first alternative is clearly unacceptable . . . . a world bereft of morality is a world in which the survival of anyone is rendered as radically contingent, fleeting, and precarious as it could possibly be."[38] By process of elimination, then, we are left with rights for everyone.

So far, this argument won't get us the strong property rights envisaged. In regimes as horrible as you please, after all, people have moved about and kept body and soul together, despite having virtually no rights at all. And in the United States today, even though nobody has full property rights in anything, people are nevertheless managing to survive. The idea that such rights are necessary for survival, therefore, seems just empirically false—overwhelmingly disconfirmed. Note, too, that Paul's argument stems from a "need" or at least a purpose, viz., the need or purpose on the part of each person to survive. But obviously we don't get straight from needs to rights. Moreover, if we could, it is hard to see how we could claim to have headed off the socialist ideas Paul wants to ward off. No socialist is going to quarrel with the proposition that people have the right to have their needs fulfilled.

The argument then proceeds to a second "stage", designed to get us from rudimentary rights that won't ward off socialism, to sophisticated and strong property rights that will. Increase in population brings with it the need to produce, and in order to do so, we need "the erection of boundaries. Why? Production requires long-range planning, and effort. . . . If there were no mine and thine, there still might exist some production. . . . But it would remain haphazard, precarious, furtive, insecure."[39] This has, of course, been much disputed. But in any case, unless we can establish that people have the right to the particular types of security, unfurtiveness, and so on that private property entails, this argument won't generate one on its own. But if it is only rights to security of some sort or other that we get out of this, then the socialist again lurks in the wings, ready to argue that *his* State provides security and such in a degree that can't be matched by a liberal society.

Paul next proposes that, perhaps contrary to appearances, *all* value is human-created. The value of land, coal, and any other natural resource is due only to human ideas about what to do with it. If we put the formation of those ideas under the heading of "effort" or "labor," then Paul's thesis here is, I suggest, correct and important. And if we can then establish a strong property right to the fruits of one's labor, we will have what she is after: rights that are infringed or violated by such practices as eminent domain, the police power, and land taxes. But how do we get there from here? What argument will now establish that everyone has the right to use, dispose of, and enjoy all and only the particular fruits of her own labor and nobody else's, especially in the very broadened sense of the term "labor" figuring in this argument?

Now Paul returns to "survivalism". Suppose that I am not entitled to certain fruits of my labor but am entitled to some fruits of yours. What is the objection? According to Paul, this is "countersurvivalist in the extreme." The denial of such rights would, she says, be "inconsistent with the immediate end of survival because it would render the survival of each person radically contingent."[40] The former claim, though, seems clearly untrue. The claim of radical contingency is true enough, on the other hand. But then, one's survival is always contingent in any case. At any moment, lightning may strike, or one may be invaded by viruses, or whatever. For that matter, rights do not by themselves guarantee us anything: only when others *observe* those rights do we get the benefit of them, and thus we are dependent on the good will, the moral fiber if you like, of others—and this is obviously true even on the most radically libertarian account.

"What is even worse for the survival of each person", Paul goes on, "is that if he desires to act as a moral agent under this schema, his survival depends entirely upon the productive activities of others, contingencies entirely beyond his control."[41] But "entirely," in the first place, is a little unfair—possession of the vote in a democracy, for example, does give one *some* morsel of control; and in the second, more important, one is in any case thus dependent on others in any developed society, if only because of the division of labor, which renders us helpless and at the mercy of others in so many departments of life—yet as a result, our prospects of survival are in fact far better than were those of our more self-dependent ancestors.

The argument then goes to a third stage. What about all those goods that are not necessary for survival? Depending on just what one counts as "survival," after all, this would account for practically all of the retail goods we trade in these days. "To deny ownership in superfluities would entail the establishment of a moral grab bag in which all creations beyond pure necessities would fall prey to rights claims by everyone in existence except their creator. This anarchy of rights, with all individuals having a legitimate right to each superfluity . . . would lead to a war of all against all."[42] And besides, as she says, there is really no way to tell necessities from luxuries in a nonarbitrary fashion, *pace* such writers as Braybrooke.[43]

An argument of this type, attempting to deduce strong property rights from the human purpose of survival, will be spectacularly implausible if 'survival' is taken in a narrow sense. But she can hardly mean it so. Eventually, Paul has to mean by it not just staying alive in some way or other, but rather, surviving *as* a particular individual with a particular intentional track through life, with one's particular projects and purposes. This is equivalent, though, to liberty itself. Only the full right to liberty will give us survival if this is what we mean by 'survival'. But then the appearance that we are moving toward a fresh and interesting conclusion from much thinner and more obvious premises will be pretty thoroughly dispersed. Worse yet: those who do want to insist on the right to survival in the narrower usage will urge that it is precisely because survival in that sense in so important that we must cut deeply into the right to general liberty. You and I must refrain from activities which might have led to our having far nicer houses than we do, interesting vacations in places we cannot now afford, and so on and so on, because of the need of paraplegics to survive, of cigarette smokers to have their expensive cancer operations paid for by more prudent nonsmokers, and so on. If we are to have full liberty rights, we shall have to get them elsewhere than by appeals to "survival" which are bound to be either spectacularly incapable of generating those rights or else just questionbegging.

The Central Argument

Very well, then: what prospect is there that the outcome of the widest general "social contract" will be essentially the libertarian principle? The lynchpin of the argument here must be (1) the fact that contractualism is envisaged as a *voluntary* undertaking: that is, each agrees, without coercion, to whatever is accepted in the outcome of this "bargain", and (2) that the idea of libertarianism is to maximize individual freedom by accounting each person's *person* as that person's own *property*, that is, by giving each person the maximal level of rights to the disposition of that particular bit of "property" that is compatible with everyone else's having such rights. Libertarians tend to proclaim these as "absolute" rights, but it is unclear how to interpret this. Almost all of Part Three, in fact, consists in interpreting the implications of the property-rights idea.

Will this work? Do we, in other words, get from (1) to (2)? Can we get, as it were, from Hobbes to Locke? ("As it were," because there is the additional question whether Locke gets us to libertarianism. But I shall leave such questions to the scholars.) In Part Three I argue that if we accept that libertarianism does not have some of the more extravagant implications popularly attributed to it, then the prospect for getting from contractarianism to libertarianism seems to be fairly promising. My strategy is a two-stage one: first, to show that we shall "prima facie" want the libertarian principle. The argument for this follows immediately. Then second, in Part Three, to show that any alleged reasons for overriding it can either be accommodated or don't turn out to involve any overriding after all.

The Right to Liberty, Properly Grounded

We can make no appeals to what amounts to the natural sympathies of rational and/or autonomous adults. But what we may do instead is surely clear enough. The question is whether I am motivated, by virtue of my possession of almost any set of values you can imagine, to acknowledge, when I deal with others (other more or less autonomous beings, that is), any principles restricting my freedom of action in any way, and if so, which. The general form of the answer, as I have been arguing, is that we shall all adopt principles restricting the performance of actions by others that would make ourselves worse off than we would be if we didn't have that restriction. We must, by definition, favor the nonperformance of such actions, since by hypothesis we are assessing worse-offness in terms of our *own* values, whatever they may be.

A recent proposal about this by David Gauthier merits our keenest attention.[44] Suppose that we are in a Hobbesian State of Nature, and we wish to get out. The trouble with the State of Nature is that people pursue their various ends without regard to the impact of their pursuit on others' activities. All of us are busy pursuing our various ends, though, and all of us are able to do something about it when some intruder impedes our progress. But none of us is able to do a great deal more about it than anyone else, and as we redouble our efforts to secure ourselves, things go from bad to worse in the essential area of producing the various things that will satisfy our various desires. The result is horrendously inefficient.

We can't assume any degree of general benevolence on the part of those tough customers, our Fellow Persons. What principle for avoiding these awful results could find universal acceptance? The solution is to forbid just those efforts on the part of any person that, as Gauthier puts it, "worsen the situation of others." Worsen relative to what? His answer is: relative to the way things would be if the agent weren't around. "Worsening, and equally bettering, are judged by comparing what I actually do with what would have occurred, *ceteris paribus,* in my absence."[45] Borrowing a famous analogy from Nozick, suppose that people lived on separate islands, with no knowledge of each other's existence. Then it can hardly be reasonable to impute injustice to any of their activities: no one can worsen the situation of others relative to one's absence, because everyone *is* absent. Once interaction sets in, however, injustice can arise. If the As take from the Bs what the latter have produced by their own efforts, without recompense, they better their own situation *by* worsening the situation of the Bs, as compared with how it would be for the Bs if the As didn't exist. In short, they take advantage of the Bs. Gauthier argues that this Lockean Proviso provides the appropriate baseline for bargaining. We measure the gains and losses providable from future cooperation by their departures from the baseline of noninteraction or the equivalent. "Thus the proviso, in prohibiting each from bettering his situation by worsening that of others, but otherwise leaving each free to do as he pleases, not only confirms each in the use of his own powers, but in denying to others the use of those powers, affords to each the exclusive use of his own. The proviso thus converts the unlimited liberties of Hobbesian nature into exclusive rights and duties."[46]

Gauthier's interpretation amounts to a prohibition on force and fraud. It is rational to accept this prohibition because violations are *inefficient* in the well-known Paretian sense of the term: at least one party can be made better off without making the other worse off (namely, by returning to the status quo of noninteraction). Clearly, we cannot expect fully voluntary agreement to anything less, if our parties are rational agents. The interactions they prohibit, by contrast, do violate the Pareto condition, measured against the baseline of noninteraction.

But why should we accept that baseline? The State of Nature cannot be assumed to be one of noninteraction. In the Hobbesian pre-agreement condition there is plenty of interaction—indeed, the trouble is that there is too much. Now, suppose that this interaction were considerably more advantageous to some parties than others: the strong, for instance, who systematically despoil and exploit the weaker parties. Would the ones doing better voluntarily move to a situation in which their advantages were negated? In fact, the suggested answer is that they will do so, provided their situation after the agreement is better than it was before the agreement, *even if* the agreement negates their *relative* advantage over the weak. It must do so if it is to be rational, as Gauthier agrees.

The Lockean Proviso in Gauthier's interpretation leaves us free to pursue cooperative interaction, benefiting from exchanges that proceed by agreements. There can be no question that the potential gains from such interaction are immense. Are they sufficiently immense to compensate for the deprivation of predatory freedoms "enjoyed" in the amoral condition?

The Crucial Question

Our question, then, is whether parties not adhering to the Lockean Proviso are necessarily in a situation that is Pareto-inferior to that enjoyed by those who do adhere to it? Does the "social contract", along Lockean-Gauthieran lines, leave literally everyone at least as well off? Since one could hardly decide this if it appeared to be only very close in some cases, we should raise our sights from Pareto-superiority to Pareto-dominance: that is, we must argue not only that no one is worse off but that everyone is *better* off, and strikingly so.

Consider a historical case, that of the Vikings of medieval times. These hardy and ferocious warriors certainly appear to have benefited from their frequent depredations of such people as the Franks, the Goths, and the Anglo-Saxons. Should we dismiss these apparent

gains as merely apparent, illusory? We can hardly do so from the
perspective adopted here. The Vikings had a set of values that included positive relish of fighting, as well as of the plunder that such
fighting so frequently, in their case, made possible. Of course, it was
not costless. Individual Vikings often met their deaths from these
raids. Their love of a good fight as well as the expected gains from
predation were sufficient to keep them at it for some centuries. Still, it
is fascinating, under the circumstances, how readily these ferocious
people were converted to Christianity—a religion that officially
frowns upon the sort of activities the Vikings were notorious for, even
if its practitioners often managed to find remarkably little cause for
compunction in those same respects when theological push came to
military shove. And eventually the Vikings turned into the extremely
peaceable and civilized peoples we know today's Scandinavians to be.
We may surely attribute this to a sense that the predatory way of life
did not hold out much long-term promise, even for people as expert
at it as they.

Of course, one must also acknowledge the influence of such factors as the development of defensive military technology by those
they preyed upon. But then, this is part of the point. Those who propose to live as the Vikings plainly invite their victims to devote a lot of
effort to defense. Any individual's perception that prospects are better under a regime of acceptance of the Lockean constraint must come
from within, from a careful consulting of one's own values. If we
don't see it the Lockean way, however, then we must see that the rest
of the human race may take us to be issuing, as it were, a warning to
all and sundry that we are fair game for whatever they throw at us.
Eventually everyone is a member of a Spartan camp, with but little
left after the bare essentials of life. This, of course, not only makes
victory for invaders much less probable but it also greatly reduces the
spoils of such victories as we might exact. Here we have the "horrendous inefficiency" referred to above. It seems to me that the chief
obstacle to immediate and universal acceptance of the Gauthieran
constraint as the hallmark of justice lies in the area of collective actions. Hobbes's "Laws of Nature" apply in full force at the level of
individuals relating to other individuals or small groups of same. For
they assume what I shall call a general equality of vulnerability: in
Hobbes's words, "for as to strength of bodie, the weakest hath
strength enough to kill the strongest."[47] So far as social relations on
this earth are concerned, the capacity to inflict death is truly the bottom line. When A kills B, A eliminates B from the environment, leav-

ing nothing more to fear from that quarter—though also, of course, no prospect of cooperative improvement. And Hobbes's hypothesis that this capability is essentially universal is a powerful incentive in the Lockean direction.

But once people band into sizable groups, with a local esprit de corps, things may look very different. Death is indeed an evil from the point of view of almost anyone, and continued life a necessary condition for the achievement of virtually anything anyone may be trying to achieve. But when we contemplate group depredations against other groups, the situation changes substantially. It does so in at least two ways, both crucial. In the first place, the probability of death in an organized war is appreciably lower than in hand-to-hand combat. When two individuals of comparable strength fight to the death, the probability of survival for either is less than 50 percent. But when two armies fight, or when an organized band of warriors such as the Vikings fall upon a more or less defenseless community, the probability of survival generally exceeds that by a very wide margin. And in the second place, *within* one's group, there are all those emotional ties and bonds of mutual interest, which can render an individual disposed to face probable death for the sake of the advancement of the group. It is not so easy to demonstrate that groups will always do better to be peaceable. And if an individual in that group reckons his prospects of advancement against the background of group support, both logistical and emotional, then it is easy enough to see how he could reckon that going along with the group in efforts directed at predatory advancement affords the better prospect.

As against this, there are several considerations that, to my mind conclusively, tilt the balance back toward the Gauthieran-Lockean Proviso.

(1) There are groups and groups and groups; and no matter which group you are a member of, so long as it is a mere fraction of the human race, you are in a minority. The military superiority of any nation, for example, is certain to be evanescent—not, of course, mathematically certain, but merely empirically certain, having a probability of approximately 100 percent. This lesson is the more emphasized in the late twentieth century, when mere size in terms of numerousness is so thoroughly negated by superior military technology. A tiny nation equipped with a sufficiency of nuclear missiles is the equal of any nation or empire that ever was in point of power to destroy.

(2) The only terms on which predatory war is at all likely to offer a higher return than peace are those that include a positive attachment

to fighting or to perceived martial superiority, that is to say, very high value on the motive Hobbes refers to as "glory." Those who value glory above all are indeed launched on a career of stark competition. If A and B are "into" glory, then they are not in a Prisoner's Dilemma, but instead in a *zero-sum* game: A's loss is B's gain and vice versa. So the only way A can achieve the value he's after is by coming out *ahead* of B, and vice versa. Given these values, it is not logically possible for them to achieve a cooperative solution. At least one of them is therefore certain to fail. And the victor will not long be happy with his success, will seek out a new opponent or have one forced on him, and eventually he, too, will fail. This is merely empirical observation, as I say. Certain misguided supposed Nietzscheans (not, quite obviously, Nietzsche himself) and many primitive tribes may fall prey to this particular vice, but most people in most groups will soon tire of glory and begin to worry about things like comfort, security, a reliable prospect of good food in the stomach, as well as other less mundane items, such as the finer arts, interesting travel in exotic places (with good prospect of return), higher mathematics, and the rest. And if they do, then the case against war is overwhelming, especially when we take into account the next item.

(3) War is a loser, if viewed as a way of advancing one's prospects of "material" (or, if you like, "bourgeois") well-being. Those one engages, after all, will defend themselves—what else are they to do? Military conquest will therefore be costly, in dollars as well as lives; and given the economics of contemporary warfare, it will be *very* costly. There is no conceivable level of gain from military predation in contemporary circumstances that could equal the gains from peaceable trade. My example of Vietnam will serve admirably for Americans. Try the Russians in Afghanistan or the Vietnamese in Cambodia or . . . and the results will be the same. To fight a war with *those* motives is simply irrational in current circumstances. Without a very strong ideological component, no sane person would consider it.

(4) What we are doing here is investigating ideologies, with a cool eye. We are asking whether any view about the proper terms of human association will stand up against the liberal view inherent in the Lockean ideas. To prove themselves against it, those rival ideologies must show either (*a*) that the Lockean idea, with its capitalistic implications, is inherently hopeless for some reason (this was Marx's strategy); or (*b*) that some other principles offer a better prospect, reckoned in the same coin, to the rational person; or, finally, (*c*) that

some set of values inconsistent with general peace is so much to be preferred to all else as to be worth the price of war, which is extremely high and steadily mounting. (At latest estimates, the price of general out-and-out war nowadays is universal extermination.)

(*a*) My reply to the first, or Marxian, option is that it has been shown to be completely fallacious. The important point about Marx's case is that it *rests on its details* (the labor theory of value, the Marxian theory of exploitation, and a Marxian version of social class theory), every one of which is provably unsound. Marxists nowadays make their living by changing the subject, or by appealing to class prejudices from bygone times.[48] These are not intellectually useful maneuvers, have been examined and found wanting too often, and will not occupy us further in this book.

(*b*) My reply to the second is to wait and see. That is what, among other things, the third part of this book is about.

(*c*) And my reply to the third option is that you "pays your money and you takes your choice"; that is, you consult your utility function and decide. It must be borne in mind that the Hobbes-Locke offer is as follows: sign up for a social contract allowing each to be whatever she may wish to become, provided only that she respect the right of all others to do likewise, *or* be fair game in a pitched battle with what will certainly turn out to be the vast majority of your fellows.

The issue in the end is not which of these alternatives will be taken, but the reasonableness of the claim that these are the available options.

Can We Improve on the Libertarian Option?

Option (*b*) is the one that remains to investigate. The question it poses is: could I bring it about that you are at least as well off as you would otherwise have been by performing actions that violate your libertarian rights? Putting it this way is dramatic, but perhaps unfair. More precisely, the question is: could I offer you a better deal by doing the things to you that the libertarian claims you have the right that I not do?

This, too, may seem an overly restricted way of putting it. But it is not. For the alternative is whether I can benefit you by doing things to *somebody else* that are forbidden by what the libertarian claims are *his* rights. Obviously this is not an alternative which that other person is going to be happy with, on the face of it, unless he happens to be a friend of yours; but in that case, he will presumably approve of these things and so they won't violate those rights after all. So, then, let us ask whether we could improve your situation by violating the libertarian rights of someone who is *not* a friend of yours. And no doubt we often could: but can we do so with her approval? And if not, how do we justify our actions?

We are thus back to the first way of putting it: Can we conceivably argue that the individual is better off by having her Lockean rights invaded, set aside, or ignored? Clearly, this depends on a pretty precise idea of what those rights are, and although we have made some effort in this direction in Part One, the task can hardly be said to be complete. We will attempt to achieve further precision in the remainder of this book, in the context of exploring the implications of the libertarian idea and perhaps firming up the argument sketched rather broadly and abstractly here.

Here, certainly, there is an acute problem in one respect: for what if I do something to you *now* that you would object to *now* if you knew I was doing it, but which later you will come to see was just the thing for me to do, from your new point of view? I do not think that libertarianism can be reasonably construed as issuing an absolute prohibition on such actions, which would rule out all sorts of charming pranks, surprise parties, helpful therapeutic procedures, and the like. But I think they could be classified as "risky" and treated in something like Nozick's way;[49] and if they could, then of course we can make the case that rational individual A must be understood to allow actions that A would agree improve A's situation despite temporary deviations from A's (current) preferences. I tentatively conclude, in short, that we have no special problems from this quarter. (None, at any rate, that libertarianism doesn't have anyway!)

From here on in we will consider arguments against libertarianism stemming from liberal premises. Our general strategy will be to deny that those premises generate good arguments for going so far as to infringe on the libertarian rights. Either the proposed measures are objectionable and should be abandoned, because what is good about them can be got without the objectionable aspects; or they can be accommodated within the spirit of the libertarian idea. The reader, especially if of strong libertarian persuasion already, should be warned that this last may involve some "fudging". Where it does, my strategy will be to show that the fudging is legitimate on libertarian premises.

Efficiency versus Justice?

Efficiency arguments tend to be contrasted with arguments from justice. But the things said about them by people who press this contrast tend to suggest that by "efficiency" arguments, they mean arguments to the effect that the social policy, principle, institution, or procedure under investigation conduces to some supposed general social end, such as the general happiness, construed in aggregative utilitarian fashion. But I have denied the relevance of this or any other presumed social end that does not ultimately analyze into the Pareto-constrained end of maximizing the good of everyone taken individually in a way consistent with the right of each to liberty. Indeed, that right to liberty is itself derived from a Paretian argument.

It is fascinating that those who toil in the libertarian fields devote the lion's share of their efforts to persuading us that the alleged benefits of the State are illusory—that we would be better off with a cessation of all or most State activity, not only in the sense that we would no longer be subject to the imposition of tyrannical authority, but also in the various ways that defenders of the State think we are better off from having one. Here's an example: John Hospers argues against the progressive income tax not only by characterizing it as "robbery" but also by referring to its effects: "they [defenders of the progressive tax] do not see that by taxing so highly the most productive members of society, they are decreasing the wealthy man's incentive to continue to be productive."[50] Hospers is one of a small army. One simply does not find frequent instances of arguing solely from the principles as being self-evident truths, even though they are billed as such.

Are these arguments concerning effects to be *contrasted* with arguments "in principle"? That may not be an interesting question. Presumably, the intended contrast is between arguments from conceptual necessity and arguments from more or less accidental facts. But the defenders of libertarianism I have in mind do not think that the considerations leading us, as they believe, to the conclusion that the benefits of the State are illusions are just accidental. The use of force or fraud, in their view, does not just "happen" to lead to worse results but, rather, guarantees it. "Benevolent despotism", they think, is something very like a contradiction in terms. And they agree that the contemporary State thinks it is being benevolent, would dearly love to be so, and spends a good deal of your and my money trying to get us to swallow the view that it is so. The claim is that the despotism of the State is ineradicable so long as it remains a State, and systematically, necessarily, undermines its benevolence. This would seem to be argument from principle, yet with empirical ramifications. But that is the way good theories should be. We will certainly follow in this tradition in the present investigation.

The Gospel According to St. Pareto

It matters, however, how one evaluates the facts. There is no sense in saying that a normative thesis is borne out or confirmed by "the facts" unless we know how to assess the facts when they are at hand. The most significant example concerns the distinction between genuinely utilitarian arguments and arguments of the broadly contractarian type advanced above. From the point of view of the contractarian, facts matter by telling us whether everyone is getting a reasonable deal from his or her perspective. The contractarian follows the Gospel According to Pareto: among persons not guilty of any wrong, is everyone coming out better or at least as well? Or are some being benefited at the expense of others? This still does not give us an easy way of assessing the facts. But it affords rough, useful comparisons. Whenever we can assess a change as being for the better for some and no worse for anyone, we have a strong case. When we must instead tot up the gains for some against the losses for others, we have the problem of how to justify these to the losers.

I shall develop the argument from this perspective. Whether a libertarian society would completely pass muster from a genuinely utilitarian perspective is a further question, which I shall not attempt to pass on—in considerable part because, I suspect, nothing can be definitively passed on from that perspective. But if it would pass muster from the point of view of any particular individual, then that would be quite enough, I should think, for any reasonable theorist.

PART THREE

Libertarianism and Reality: What Does Libertarianism Imply about Concrete Social Policy?

CHAPTER 15

Society and the Market

The Free Market

THE DEFENSE of the market is clearly prominent on the libertarian agenda. In a sense, it is the only thing on that agenda. But it would be well to be clear about just what we are and what we are not discussing under this heading. The market, as normally understood, is characterized by a recognition of private property rights, which identify the agents whose dealings constitute the economy— they tell us whom we have to deal with if we wish to acquire this, that, or the other, or make this or that change in the configuration of goods and services. From this it follows that transfers in the ownership of goods and services will proceed by agreement of the parties involved, this being the parties whose goods and services they are. Indeed, we may agree with Marx that insofar as there are property rights, there is a market. If *everything* is owned by individuals, or its ownership is fully determinate in terms of individual ownership or ownership by voluntarily formed groups, then we have *full* market society.

To defend *some* market activity is trivial; even out-and-out communists are inclined to concede at least a bit of economic territory to the market, and in such countries as the Soviet Union, that small fraction has made an astonishingly disproportionate difference to the economic life of the country. But to defend full market society is another matter. It is not, in fact, entirely clear what it means to say that "everything" is on the market. Is the market itself on the market?

Markets could be said to be "on the market", in a loose sense of the term: namely, the political market, where purveyors of ideologies and public institutions compete for the public's vote. Also, a number of individuals can get together and agree that they will not treat certain things as being privately owned and available for exchange. This is equivalent to buying each other out, as it were, the surrendering of all individual rights to particular things to some entity such as the council of elected leaders or the entire community in town meetings, or whatever.

What about the framing rules of the market themselves? Some writers think these have a different status from anything that goes on within the market. And some contend that the market is a public institution, requiring for its maintenance a structure of laws and thus of political institutions, thereby paving the way for the claim that the market is no more "natural" than any other possible way of doing these things. Whether this is so is evidently a matter of importance. We shall see.

Market and Morals

David Gauthier entitles his largely admirable chapter on the market in *Morals by Agreement* "The Market: Freedom from Morality".[1] As John Gray quite properly points out,[2] Gauthier thereby does the market philosophy a certain disservice. His reason for doing so is understandable, however, for he defines the market he means this to apply to in terms of the abstractions of neoclassical economics. There are, by definition in this ideal market, no "externalities"—in every transaction, all costs and benefits accrue only to the parties to the transaction; all of the goods and services produced and consumed, and all of the factors of production, are the property of individuals without remainder; the technology is known and fixed; information about products and prices is complete and costless to each actor, who is also indifferent regarding the origin of the products (the consumer cares only about its utility qua product, not qua manifestation of a certain ideology, for instance); and there is perfect competition in the sense that no one producer can significantly influence prices unilaterally. In such a situation each agent simply aims to maximize her utility from her own production and exchange activities, and the result will be terrific for everybody: the Invisible Hand lives! Several very nice-sounding things are provable[3] about a market so characterized, notably, that the society thus blessed maximizes its utility—a result not to be confused, however, with what utilitarians mean by that expression.

Given this ideal market, all changes are Pareto-optimal. What is meant by "the market society maximizes its utility" is that at any particular time no one can do better than has been done without someone else's doing worse. I agree with Gauthier that the theoretical demonstration of optimality under these conditions is of real importance. But its *practical* importance is obviously a function of the degree to which these conditions are realized or realizable in the real world, and it is here that morality must enter the picture. We approximate the "ideal market" in the real world by *reinforcing* the internalizations that define it. The morality you need consists in recognition and respect for private property rights, starting with such rights in one's own person (this being the fundamental "factor of production"), and of the obligation to live up to one's agreements (not really a separate principle but a theorem derivable from the recognition of private property rights). But there is appreciable misunderstanding about certain of the "ideal market" properties when we turn to the task of real-world applications. I shall note some of these below. Then we may address, at least preliminarily, the fundamental moral question for present purposes, which is whether we ought to aim at realizing the market in this real world, insofar as feasible, or instead embrace some other set of requirements on social behavior, or restrict the market to a smaller area than would be feasible if we were to give it its head.

Two Views about Society and the Market

Jules Coleman distinguishes two views about the relation between political arrangements and the market: the "thin" and the "thick". On the thin theory, the rationality of political association is grounded entirely in the *failure* of perfect competition—if we can simply identify and then prevent those conditions making for failure, the market needs no further attention and will succeed. The thick form, on the other hand, says that political associations are needed in realizing the conditions of market success as well as in overcoming market failure: if we leave the market to its own devices, even in the absence of externalities and such, it will still fail.[4] Coleman later identifies the thick theory with the need for distributive agreements as well as productive agreements—"no agreement on distribution of gains, no gains."[5] The libertarian, clearly, advocates the thin theory. If the thick theory should prove essential, then libertarianism must be either abandoned or at least considerably modified, at least by supplementing it with further constraints.

One reasonable way would be to declare certain things to be out of bounds for the market and put in what is called the "public sector," leaving the rest for the "private sector." One way of framing our project, then, is by suggesting that the proponent of full market society is the one who holds that no such further supplementation is needed: *everything* should be on the market, except perhaps for the rules of the market itself. But we can think of near-proponents who hold that *most* of society's activities can and should be left to the market, with only modest supplementation. Thus the minimal statist's position is that the State properly protects people from force (including foreign-imposed force) and fraud, supports that activity out of taxation, and does not attempt to receive remuneration from each client in proportion to services rendered; but apart from that, it leaves all else, such as education, health, welfare, the keeping of social statistics, and the rest of it, to individuals and voluntary associations.

Defense of the market is defense of private property. But the latter usually proceeds in terms of natural rights. David Gauthier insists that "the idea of morals by agreement may mislead, if it is supposed that rights must be the product or outcome of agreement. . . . [t]he emergence of either co-operative or market interaction, demands an initial definition of the actors in terms of their factor endowments, and we have identified individual rights with these endowments. Rights provide the starting point for, and not the outcome of, agreement. They are what each person brings to the bargaining table, not what she takes from it." In short, "market and co-operative practices presuppose individual rights. These rights are morally provided in the proviso [Gauthier's version of the Lockean Proviso, discussed in Part Two]. And the rights so grounded prove to be the familiar ones of our tradition—rights to person and to property."[6]

Most libertarians would agree that the rights they insist on are natural rights: but it is doubtful that they subscribe to Gauthier's view in its total upshot. I do want to insist that the rights that frame the market must themselves be founded on a prior agreement, and that we must take up the more radical stance that holds that there is what Coleman calls "pre-market bargaining" leading to an agreement to set up the market. This, as he also points out, is equivalent to an agreement on property rights. A contractarian procedure in the spirit of Hobbes would, as John Gray has argued, "regard property rights as conventional and the allocation of initial holdings as a fundamental dictate of justice."[7] That is the view proposed in Part Two of the present work, though as there pointed out, this fundamental agreement can reasonably also be held to consist in the determination of "natural" rights. The natural endowments of which Gauthier speaks are, in our view, simply givens and not "rights"; rights to them are the up-shot of reasonable agreements. It is not clear that Gauthier means really to deny this, but if so, then here is a point on which we diverge from his account.

Jules Coleman argues strongly for the existence of all-but-insoluble problems in this project of bargaining our way into market society. Speaking of the "pre-market bargain," he argues, "it is hard to believe that individuals will reach a *meaningful* agreement, even on the savings made possible by taking advantage of economies of scale in the provision of protection. Because of what the future holds, once the property rights scheme is in place, the pre-market bargain is likely to be superseded almost immediately by strategic manipulation and rent-seeking behavior. Let me be blunt. The point of the bargain is to distribute and make possible gains associated with an efficient provision of protection. The net effect, however, of the dynamic mechanism and incentives put in place is to promote inefficiency and to undermine the terms of the original agreement."[8] Moreover, "To say that the terms of rational political association are specified as the outcome of rational bargaining is not to say that all political decisions are to be resolved by bargaining. That depends on whether, in either constitutional or post-constitutional bargains, bargainers would agree that the best way to overcome a particular market failure is by bargaining. It is perfectly plausible that rational bargainers seeking to overcome market failures owing to externalities might prefer a tax, subsidy, or liability approach to a bargaining or Coasean approach; or that bargainers in a public-goods context might agree to implement a demand-revelation mechanism, rather than try to settle on the level of provision by simple majority vote."[9] It is not entirely clear that this is "perfectly possible"; but since it is not self-evident that it is not possible, we had better say that it is, and so the question resolves itself into one of engaging in the hard analysis of particular areas to see. That, in effect, is what the rest of this book devotes itself to. Since it is a *very* large project, let me disavow any aspiration to comprehensiveness. Rather, we will look at a selection of issues. Nor will our results be unmixed, as the reader will see.

Market Morality as a Public Good

Some have been tempted to get beyond the market by reflecting on the presumed costs of having a market: who would pay them, and how would we divide up their benefits in a fair manner? Are there interventionist camels' noses sniffing their way under our market tents? Here we will pause to consider a recent foray along this line by one of the most acute among current critics.

David Braybrooke, in a stimulating review, remarks that "Readers on the Right . . . will rejoice in the political coloring given Gauthier's *Morals by Agreement* by its broad commitment to private property rights, its born-again enthusiasm for the market, and its repeated denunciation of 'free riders' and 'parasites'. . . ." But he goes on to argue that ". . . rejoicing on the Right and dismay on the Left are both mistaken. . .", that in fact Gauthier's theory cannot be used for real-world policy-making. ". . . [T]he degree of technical perfection to which Gauthier has brought social contract theory . . . has been gained at the expense of depriving the theory of any possibility of effective application. Its demands for information are fantastic—too fantastic ever to be met or even to allow the theory to be used as a guide to improvements within the reach of present social policy."[10]

Gauthieran justice consists of a set of constraints on utility-maximizing behavior. If rational agents act in a perfect market, each agent would maximize utility from private goods simply by making the best of her opportunities in the market. But we aren't ever in such perfect markets, and constraints are necessary to capture the maximum utilities at stake in those aspects of our situation that create externalities, negative and positive. We solve the problem of externalities by the production of what are known as "public goods", and the facts about people and markets result in a well-known tendency for them to be in short supply. "To obtain the goods, the agents strike a bargain, constraining them to contribute, about the combination of their contributions and their benefits." The terms of reference for Gauthier's project require that this bargain be ". . . voluntary on all sides and in all respects . . . [and] . . . Gauthier insists that the initial bargaining positions must be corrected by the 'Lockean proviso'. That proviso implies for Gauthier certain rights, for example, rights as property holders precluding victimization by others, and these rights, which must be respected both in the market and in the scheme of cooperation, have some semblance of being a source of moral constraints independent of the scheme and the bargain that leads to the scheme."[11] They do have that semblance, I agree, but I have denied that it is more than that. I have insisted that arguments are available on behalf of the Lockean rule itself, arguments persuasive to virtually all.

Still, as Braybrooke says, "Without these assumptions, Gauthier would not have much chance of reaching morally convincing results.

. . . From the aims of rational agents under other assumptions—assumptions that left predatory behavior unchecked and allowed intimidation to overshadow voluntary entry into the bargain—a convincing morality very likely could not be deduced. . . ."[12] Agreed. A morality of any recognizable sort is not to be expected in a community of utter monsters. But The Lockean rule is not an "assumption" in the same sense as the supposition that most people are neither psychopaths nor saints.

Braybrooke now maintains that Gauthier "forfeits current testability" of the kind that might perhaps be possible with Locke's own version of the theory, "as well as the possibility of there being any historical instances of societies originating in a social contract as he conceives it."[13] Two reasons are offered for this.

(1) One is that excluding private goods from the social contract and leaving pursuit of them to the market "is an untenable position. Is not the market itself—having a market—a public good? Alternatively, is it not a public good to have the constraints on force and fraud that are both empirically and logically necessary to having a market? If having them is a public good, however, the utilities obtained from them as effects of their publicness must come under the social contract for distribution according to the principles of justice that figure in the contract."[14] And here Braybrooke means Gauthier's interesting principle of minimax relative concession, which calls upon the participants in a bargain for cooperative mutual advantage to share equally in those advantages.[15]

Braybrooke raises here an important criticism that would strike to the heart were its assumptions all sound. "Can Gauthier follow [Locke's and Hume's] example and assume that the market, with effective . . . constraints against force and fraud, already exists at the ideal starting point and has only to be endorsed by the agents who . . . then turn their attention to the other public goods? . . . The constraints must have been there for the market to get started. . . . How did this happen? Hume's explanation, Gauthier has contended elsewhere, was that the constraints were in effect contracted for; agents concurred in cooperating, perceiving the mutual advantage of constraining themselves not to try to maximize utility independently. . . . Are we to have a contract for vague benefits from the constraints on force and fraud, letting the market operate without further social attention and then move on to another contract for precise benefits from the remaining public goods? This is still anomalous. . . . If government, set up by the second contract, does no more than reinforce the constraints, will this not increase the utilities received through the market?"[16]

But to all this, the libertarian has a reply that is worth serious consideration. This consists, roughly, in denying that constraints on force and fraud are public goods in a sense that would bring up the questions Braybrooke wants to bring up. Suppose that our rock-bottom State of Nature is Hobbesian. No gains either from cooperation or from individual effort are available in this awful condition. If there is only Cain and Abel, for instance, then both will end up dead in short order unless both agree to abstain from violence. Then there will be rewards for productive effort, indeed; but these include rewards which are *not* got from *cooperative* efforts in the usual sense of that word. You and I do not, in that usual sense, "cooperate" when you hoe your plot and eat your beans, and I hoe my different plot and consume my peas. The payoff from our agreement to refrain from violence does not consist in the peas and the beans, but only the *possibility* of enjoying such things, consequent upon *further* effort. If marauders threaten, we might endeavor to internalize the costs of their threats, e.g., by enslaving them for some time after subjugating them in the ensuing fracas. If we have cooperated in this defensive effort, then there will be a reasonable question about the division of the product which those slaves would produce for us. But there is not a reasonable question about the division of the benefits of the original agreement between us to refrain from further violence, for those benefits, consisting as they do merely in the possibility of each of us actually realizing the fruits of our separate labors, are abstractly equal and nondivisible. Goods arising from cooperation in the more robust sense in which, for instance, you and I might cooperatively saw up a large tree with a two-man saw are indeed goods about which a problem of fair division can arise. But there are no other problems about the division of *this* "public good", the good of nonviolence, to which a reasonable theory can address itself. And if there were, one might add, the most reasonable construal would have to be that those who foreswore the greatest gains from predation, namely the strongest and fiercest, would have to get a larger share in the fruits of civilization than the weak and mild—not quite the result Braybrooke is presumably pressing for!

Consider, in particular, the suggestion that the State's protection activities bring with them further blessings which amount to public goods needing division. In principle, however, these protective efforts ought to be internalized: that is, the *costs* of securing our various rights should be born by violators rather than by the peaceable folk whose rights they violate. Insofar as that ideal is unattainable, they can be met by ordinary contracts among ourselves, establishing the "protective agencies" beloved of anarchists. Braybrooke speaks, in short, as though protection was *inherently* a public good. But it is not. Market internalizations are possible here as elsewhere, and in this regard one gets, to a considerable degree, what one pays for.

Braybrooke also supposes that "Some people may dislike having a market: it would be a public good for them not to have one. Others may expect to get a smaller income in private goods . . . out of a market than from communal planning. Should not the maximum claims of both groups be defined on nonmarket arrangements?"[17] But there is an air of hocus-pocus about this. In my discussions of Cohen and Arthur,[18] I pointed out that it is question-begging to assume that the alternative of socialist arrangements is *available*. The reason is simple: that arrangement requires people to do various things: but either they are happy to do those things, in which case the market as conceived here has no objection to their doing them, or they are not, in which case the arrangement is not available without violating the Lockean restriction on coercion. It is not available because everyone has a veto on everything in the Social Contract. This limits our options: either we exercise the veto and resort to the State of Nature, or we do not, in which case we have only the restraints on force and fraud to go by. But this last, libertarians properly argue, simply *is* the market. That is the sense in which the market may be described as "natural". The envisaged communal arrangements, therefore, cannot be billed as nonmarket arrangements presenting a genuine alternative to market ones.

(2) Braybrooke's second objection is that if we are to employ Gauthier's Principle of Minimax Relative Concession to actual societies, we would have to have some way of calculating the maximum claims of individuals. And this requires "making fantastic demands on information, which no contracting parties and no current critics of government could ever meet." For instance, "None of us know our own utility functions even for the public goods now being produced, much less the utility functions of 24 million or 240 million fellow citizens. Nor shall we ever know."[19] And this is certainly true. But does it matter? No. The mistake, admittedly committed by Gauthier,[20] is to suppose that society as a whole—say, Canada or the U.S.A. or indeed the whole world—is itself a cooperative arrangement for mutual advantage such that a question of how to divide up the benefits of this cooperation arises. But we can simply deny this. Cooperation proceeds by agreement, and the agreements are made by individuals

who do, indeed, need to make some sort of estimate of their own advantage in order to enter rationally into the agreements they do. But there are no further cooperative agreements entailing problems about the division of the blessings of large-scale cooperation with all and sundry. At *that* level, the libertarian will properly insist, we need only the market, with its public good of peace, which makes possible the further but *private* goods in which prosperity and, in general, individual flourishing consist. The idea that there are lots and lots of strictly public goods in which this prosperity consists is a Leftist illusion, not a demonstrable fact (demonstrable empirically or otherwise). So the truth that a Gauthieran calculation for genuine society-wide cooperation would make awesome and obviously unmeetable demands on our information capacity cuts no ice against the marketeer. Gauthier's principle of fair distribution, in short, is very confined in its application. From the point of view of broad social theory, I would argue, it is essentially dispensable. Justice respects the agreements people make; if potential parties to agreements perceive proferred terms as distributively unfair, then they should not enter into those agreements.

Note that in most cases of cooperation, most parties to it enter on terms fixed by contract, and not on terms involving a division of public goods. Justice does not require that I offer some person interested in working on my project the maximin share of the surplus. It requires only that I pay him what I have agreed to pay him, and this may bear no particular proportion to my employee's maximum "claim". His *minimum* claim is fixed by his alternatives, and not by abstract considerations of distributive justice; and his maximum claim would be the entire profits of my enterprise—but I am not about to offer anything like that, nor any particular proportion of it, and on Gauthier's own view I can hardly be required to make any particular offer nor to settle on terms unacceptable to me, any more than you can be required to settle on terms unacceptable to you. My ability to entice you into working for me is a function of my ability to make you a better offer than what you can get elsewhere. The market, in short, prevails in a *far more extensive* area of life than Braybrooke or, I conjecture, Gauthier supposes; and there, I have argued, we need no help from the distributive principle, or at any rate none that would license publicly authorized coercion, which remains prohibited by the Lockean restriction.

Braybrooke goes on to draw the moral that talk of optimization of utility functions and the like should be abandoned for purposes of public policy. In its place, he sensibly suggests, we should envisage, to start with, "a social contract like Locke's, designed simply to protect property rights under some effective definition." But this is not, we may surmise, Professor Braybrooke's cup of tea. "Or", he goes on, "we must be content with a social contract on Rawls's lines . . ." , claiming that "Any advance Gauthier has achieved over Rawls in pure theory is liable to be overshadowed by Rawls's enormous advantage in relevance"[21]—proffering judicious use of Rawls' notorious Difference Principle as an example. I have elsewhere argued that Rawls's Difference Principle is bound to be either redundant or else fatal to his intentions, so the thought that it has an advantage in "relevance" should not be long entertained by the serious theorist. Nor will such notions as a "principle of precedence for matters of need over matters of preference only" be of any help. It will, instead, get us mired in the petty bureaucracy into which our lives seem increasingly destined to be sinking. If relevance is what we want, the first, or Lockean alternative, surely has it in abundance by comparison with the alternatives suggested. Property rights are a miracle of transparency and cogency by comparison with not only society-wide Minimax Relative Concession, but also with Equality, Maximin a la Rawls, invocations of the priority of need over mere preference, and the rest of that bureaucratic tribe. And the beginning of wisdom here is to see how very little there is in the area of Public Goods properly so-called. There certainly isn't enough to yield a justification for the heavy-handed and wholesale wielding of force by public agencies that is required for substantial redistributive programs.

What Is Economic?

Discussions of the "market" usually focus on what have come to be designated as "economic goods". Is there any coherent way to demarcate such a supposed subset from everything else? That depends. If we think of the province of the market as covering all exchangeable goods or services of any kind, then the least misleading answer is a simple negative. Anything that is scarce relative to demand and whose distribution or supply can be affected by exchanges can be "economized"; and that is essentially anything, including most of the usual acclaimed exceptions such as love, truth, and those best things in life that are usually claimed to be "free", such as views of the pretty blue sky above (a mainstay of the tourist trade, in fact). Decisions that certain things were not to be treated as "economic" would have to be political decisions.

But then it would have to be appreciated that many of the things we do "exchange," in the broadest sense of the term, are not exchanged for money. And many things that are in this broad sense exchanged are not explicitly exchanged for predetermined and negotiated amounts of whatever is being exchanged. When the Robinsons have the Palychniks over for dinner, they do not impose the condition that the Palychniks are to return the favor in kind. They don't *impose* this, but after the third or fourth such dinner not followed by a return invitation from the latter, the Robinsons are likely to move the Palychniks well toward the bottom of their list of invitees.

But let us for the moment focus on a rather though not terribly narrow range: viz., items of "personal consumption", and the usual sorts of "dry goods", though I am quite happy to take this to include food, housing, and a large assortment of services as well. Here utility in the narrowest sense is what is at stake: these things are means to ends, and we are generally indifferent about alternative sources and suppliers, given equal satisfaction. We do not, qua consumer, care who makes the shoes, or of what religious persuasion he or she may be; but we do care what the shoes are *like:* if somebody else makes a better one for the same price, or a similar one for less, we'll cheerfully switch sources. It is this quite thorough dissociation of a definitely identifiable, narrow range of utility values from such things as the ethnic background, religion, or ideology of the supplier that encourages the view that here we have something to gain from entering into exchange relations with anyone willing to "play", regardless of such factors, and something to lose by being unwilling to do so.

If such things and such conditions are our paradigms, then ideology and personal factors, and so on, will not be accounted as market items or "commodities". Yet freedom can prevail in those areas as well: freedom of choice for the "consumer", and freedom to supply the factor in question to such persons as desire the factor in question in whatever way it can be supplied. Many of these factors are not purchasable with money, at least in any explicit, straightforward sense. The rich cannot buy their way into the Kingdom of Heaven. True: but the rich "in spirit" can.

Capitalism and Consumerism

Capitalism has often been excoriated for assuming, presupposing, necessitating, or at least unduly encouraging "consumerism." Supposing that this attitude is to be identified with virtually exclusive devotion to the acquisition or consumption of products having the properties described in the last paragraph and normally available for purchase with money, this is a charge worth a few comments.

The first comment is that it is simply false, insofar as it is has any clear meaning. The claim that this range of consumer goods needs to be *the dominant* concern of whoever enters the market is certainly untrue. Insofar as we have such concerns, the market will work to our advantage, whether they be overwhelming or trivial in the total range of our values. However, other of our values could keep us away from the market even when it would otherwise be advantageous to utilize it. That is a fully permissible choice for the consumer and the producer in a free-market society.

To illustrate. There is a sizeable Mennonite community in my vicinity, and here you'll find people working hours and hours on handmade items whose machine-made counterparts could be bought for the equivalent of a fraction of a dollar per such hour over the counter in town. (Some of them sell these products at the local market, in fact, and fetch prices of that order.) Are they then defying the rules of capitalism in so doing? Is this activity to be recokoned immoral? Indeed not. They have differing values from the rest of us, as is their right. (Perhaps they are defying the rules of Marxism in their straightforward refusal to go for equivalents in terms of labor-hour inputs to the goods they exchange their products for?) In particular, they attach a higher utility to those productive activities than those activities have simply qua productive activities. An occupational therapist does not reckon the value of the time her patients spend engaging in inefficient productive activity at the market value of the products, if any, of that activity. But the therapist is aiming at a different product, viz., increased mental health on the part of those patients; and once this is appreciated, then we see that she will choose the set of activities for the patient that can be expected to maximize that product—that is, she does display economic behavior in the relevant sense. Now return to the Mennonite woman with her otherwise inefficient productive activity, and estimate its value to the producer in the way of (let us say) spiritual satisfaction. Then her activity, viewed in this broader way, makes perfectly good *economic* sense. (If the satisfaction in question is in turn a function of shaky or incomprehensible beliefs, that is another matter; but of course, in the opinion of the woman in question, those beliefs are neither shaky nor incomprehensible.)

My second comment concerns the attitudes of seller and buyer in these affairs: the interest of the seller in pleasing the buyer, and of the buyer in obtaining just the right thing for his needs without much worrying about matters irrelevant to those needs. This is impersonal, "non-holistic", to be sure. In attempting to get the best you can from your relations to persons on a market, you are indeed encouraged, I think, to take an analytical view of your interests. With respect to values V1, V2, . . . Vn, I see that you have something to offer; with respect to V(n + 1) . . . Vz, perhaps, you do not. But if we can leave the latter in abeyance insofar as our mutual relations are concerned, we may well come out ahead. This encourages peaceful and tolerant relations with our fellows. Concentrating instead on the aspects in which we are at odds will have the opposite effect, as when 80 million Germans lose the goods and services provided by 6 million of the most talented and productive people in their midst by savagely murdering them instead of isolating their differences under a principle of religious and commercial freedom.

However, this is not to say that there is no room for the personal and the holistic. To begin with a rather mundane, though not unimportant aspect of the issue, the consumer may prefer a store where she is assured of a friendly greeting from the salespeople, especially if they manifest a genuine interest in her satisfaction. No doubt some salespeople have a wholly contrived and assumed interest in this; but the idea that all manifestations of such interest in market contexts are like that is pointlessly cynical. The best salespeople, like the best practitioners of any other line of endeavor, are the ones who put their hearts and souls in it. Especially with regard to products that require reliable after-sales service, these are the people who will survive in the market.

More significantly, however, we should appreciate that there is a market for "holism" itself. Purveyors of a variety of religious faiths and personal philosophies abound in the free society, and those who become attached to their ideas are consumers, in the full sense of the word. That those purveyors sometimes line their own pockets to a quite remarkable degree is an interesting sideshow, but need not be taken to be of the essence. Some of those philosophies are such that ostentatious acquisition of wealth on the part of their protagonists would be evidence of insincerity—but what about Ayn Rand?! And others of them simply do not acquire, and are wholly consistent with their creeds in that respect. Those persons will account their income in terms of numbers (and "quality") of "saved souls". It seems that economic analysis can be applied meaningfully and quite straightforwardly to their activities in that direction.[22]

Information

Let us return to the subject of the "ideal market" and its model of "perfect competition". The first specification of this hypothetical market has it that there is full costless information—an axiom whose manifest unreality has been among the main sources of derision by those who decry the market as a real-world option. But they hoot too soon. It is perfectly correct to say that information is not complete and costless in the real world. But it does not follow that the market is impugned. What does follow, quite properly, is that there will *also* be a market *in information*. Those who produce information produce a useful product, and it can be bought and sold, spawning its own particular technologies and organizational problems (copyright questions, for instance). What we should recognize is that the economist's ideal market is a market for goods *of kind K* when information *about K* is complete and costless. When it is not, what should be done? Answer: put information about K on the market as well. This is precisely what advertisers of K, consumers' magazines, user groups, housewives chatting over the back fence, and many other do.

There can be information costs for acquiring this information as well. Call the information about K 'I(K)'; then information about this information will be I(I[K]), and this too will have its costs. The yellow pages directory of the phone book supplies such second-level information, at very modest cost, to the purchaser of telephone services; the people you then contact over the telephone supply you with information about the goods or services you are interested in, at a cost to you in time—a cost you might not be willing to pay, if you are very busy or hate phone conversations about such things. Ultimately, information costs will not be a further factor and at that point could be reckoned at zero, giving us our ideal market in items at the next level down.

Is there reason, now, to get information off the market? Should we lay it down that sellers of anything *must* supply all relevant information, free of charge? Certainly not. The producer of the product has an interest in imparting enough information to the consumer to induce him to buy; the consumer has an interest in full information, indeed, but it is just not true that he is *entitled* to that information, any more than he is entitled to the good or service in question in the first place. Someone must do something in order to create and supply that information, and that person is being to that degree enslaved if we require him, under threat of punishment, to supply it.

It is, in short, a mistake to think that the public ought to require producers to supply information, or require others at public expense to do so, *in order to* uphold the free market.

Perfect Competition

Next, we must discuss a much-misunderstood thesis about the market: the thesis that the existence of monopolies or oligopolies is an indication of market failure, thus possibly requiring intervention by the public in order to restore the market. To appreciate this point, we must remind ourselves of a distinction, which should be more familiar than it evidently is, between two sorts of monopoly: (1) imposed or *artificial* monopolies, where the sole provider of the services or goods is so because the government won't allow anyone else to provide them, and (2) *natural* monopolies, where some private enterprise, by virtue of superior products, more efficient operation, fortunate situation in relation to supply sources, or lassitude on the part of potential competitors, ends up with all the business, even though no one has been forcibly prevented from entering the market.

Either way, a monopolist will of course be able to influence prices by unilateral action to at least some extent, thus violating the axiom forbidding this. Just what extent is another question. The problem of identifying monopoly is a sticky one, for it involves identifying the relevant competition; and that won't be just the other makers of the *same* product or service, but rather all who offer products or services that are alternatives from the point of view of the consumer to the ones provided by the alleged monopolist. And it is, to put it mildly, unclear where one can draw this line. Thus the local Kwickie Market, two blocks from my house, has a monopoly in my neighborhood if you draw the radius rather restrictively. If you broaden it a bit, then the Kwickie is a monopoly only after 8:00 P.M. when the supermarket a bit farther away closes for the day, until 11:00 P.M., when the Kwickie also closes. After that, the variety store a bit farther yet takes over as the monopolist until 1:00 A.M., after which still another store, still farther away, becomes the reigning monopolist until 7:00 A.M.. when the Kwickie reopens. Who has a monopoly, and on what? Ontario Hydro has a monopoly on the manufacture and sale of electricity, except that you can make your own if you're willing to assemble the necessary equipment: and meanwhile, there's the gas company, with its own government franchise on the sale of its product; but the consumer is free to choose between gas and electricity for many purposes—so who is the monopolist?

At the extreme, it has to be pointed out that every time a sale is made, somebody has a "monopoly" on something: no competitor is right there at that time with that item at that price—the seller has it all to himself! And on the other hand, that the classic definition requiring many sellers no one of whom can "significantly" influence prices presupposes a certain amount of elasticity here and there. For if there are 18,000 consumers wanting, but *really* wanting, precisely 1 each, and the producer of item number 18,000 withdraws that product from the market leaving *no replacement*, then the fact that there are 17,999 other sellers does *not* mean that the price of x will be uninfluenced. Given perfect information on the part of all consumers and sellers, you can just bet it will be influenced, and there is no telling to what degree until we know more about the shape of the demand curve, and so on.

This brief excursus is designed to soften the terrain by pointing out that the whole idea of monopoly is undefinable in any rigorous way. We then go on to point out that on a free market, any monopolist is limited in her ability to influence prices by the readiness of others to enter the market. And finally, we then point out that (1) the use of one's resources for whatever purposes one will is the hallmark of liberal freedom, and (2) there are no coherent theories of "natural pricing" that make any sense, without which restrictions on monopolies scarcely make any sense either.

Given all this, we are then in a position to propose that the classical definition of "perfect competition" is useless for real-world purposes. The proper substitute for it is *perfectly free* competition, that is to say, the situation in which there are no *artificial* obstacles to entry into the market by whatever agents wish to do so, but only the incentives and disincentives of the situation facing the would-be entrepreneur in the way of market conditions, including the current pattern of justified ownership and operation of whatever other factors of production there may be. And what the advocate of market society asserts is that the optimality that is the pride and joy of economic theory is achieved by the free market in this less restrictive and more literal sense of 'free market', rather than the hopeless one of the original definition.

A Question about Factor Rent

A typical claim about monopolies of the second type is that they would be able to indulge in "over-pricing." Does this notion have any useful meaning? We might try defining the proper price of an item on a market in terms of perfect competition along the lines of the original version criticized above. Then, seeing that that will hardly do, we may want to try identifying excesses in some other way. A good example is provided by the technical notion of 'rent' in economics. Gauthier characterizes rent as follows: "The recipient of rent benefits from the scarcity of the factors she controls—a scarcity which is of course entirely accidental from her standpoint, since it depends, not on the intrinsic nature of the factors, but on the relation between them and the factors controlled by others. She receives more than is needed to induce her to bring her factors to the market; rent is by definition a return over and above the cost of supply." And he goes on to suggest that "whether the surplus represented by rent goes to the owner of the scarce factor, or is distributed in some other way, would seem to be left rationally and morally open by all that we have so far said."[23] Later, he addressed himself again to this matter, suggesting that "the terms of social co-operation, set by the principle of minimax relative concession, rule out a contract that includes factor rent. Certainly the principle does interfere with a particular liberty—specifically, the freedom to collect factor rent. But this is not part of the freedom of a solitary being; the surplus represented by rent arises only through interaction. And so it is not a necessary part of market freedom conceived as an extension of the natural freedom enjoyed by a Robinson Crusoe."[24]

The context of Gauthier's discussion was provided by his theory of rational bargaining, according to which surpluses relative to the independent efforts of those cooperating to produce them are to be divided among the cooperators in such a way as to minimize the maximum "concession" of each participant, a principle normally leading to equal distribution of the surplus after all expenses are deducted (including payoffs to match the opportunity costs of each).[25] "In a society governed by the principle of minimax relative concession, [basketball player Wilt] Chamberlain [in Nozick's famous example[26]] need forgo no more advantageous alternative if he is to play basketball. He is free to demand a remuneration sufficient to make basketball his most preferred activity, and to refuse to play should such remuneration not be forthcoming. But he is not free to pursue the maximum possible remuneration, where this would include factor rent."[27]

Whether Chamberlain gets to keep his money depends on whether it is "only the prospect of $250,000 that induces him to play another season of basketball". Were the terms of the contract he proposes to be refused, would he then prefer to retire? If so, then the payment to him covers only the cost of supply . . . for the service he provides in playing basketball," and then Gauthier agrees with Nozick—Chamberlain gets to keep the whole thing. On the other hand, if Chamberlain would play for only, say $100,000, then the other $150,000 is rent and available for redistribution in accordance with Minimax Relative Concession.[28] Socialist hearts leap for joy!

Earlier, we learned that a confiscatory tax on rent—"if it could be identified in practice"—would make no difference to the level of economic activity and represent no loss of liberty, since by definition it is the difference between what one can get and what one would actually settle for if worse came to worst. "Even a confiscatory tax, resulting in a complete redistribution of rent . . . would not and could not affect the supply of factor services, and so the production of goods. . . . [It] would not lead to any form of inefficiency." Identifying the difference, notice, requires knowledge of one's next-best alternative. Not easy to get, of course. Moreover, there is the "jackpot" factor. "Just as lottery prizes must involve substantial inequality, with a few large pay-offs, to induce widespread participation, so in many human activities substantial inequality in reward may be the condition necessary to induce widespread effort. It may be that Wayne Gretzky is receiving, not only factor rent, but also the jackpot needed to encourage all hockey players to strive to perfect themselves."[29]

Is this an opening wedge for substantial intervention in the market? I think not. To see that there must be something wrong with it, consider Gretzky's next-best alternative. What if a lesser offer than *it* would induce Gretzky to take the job if the superior Edmonton offer weren't available? And suppose that is also true of the next-but-one best? Indeed, suppose that it is true of *each* alternative down the line that Gretzky would take it at a lower wage than the one actually offered, *if* superior offers were not available. What then is happening to our rent factor? There are, in market society, no natural prices and therefore no natural wages. One takes the best offer available, and what makes it available is simply that somebody offers it. The somebody in question would undoubtedly offer less if he knew that the applicant could be got for less; but that's his business. Suppose we start taxing Gretzky at 60 percent, only to find someone phoning him up to offer $249,000, which then becomes his next-best offer. Do we now collect only the $1,000 separating his current wage from that? Or do we stick to our guns, pointing out that he'd still play at either place for $100,000?

The application of this idea would certainly be a quagmire, but

perhaps that doesn't prove it to be wrong in principle. What does that
is its apparent denial of our entitlement to make the best use we can
of our natural endowment. It seems scarcely compatible with that
entitlement to deprive people of whatever percentage of their incomes would leave them with an amount they would still be willing
to do the same thing for. —Would, if what? Would if they *had* to? that
is to say, if someone (such as the government) put a gun to their
heads and said "Here, you don't need this, so just hand it over,
please!" Yet certainly neither the government nor anyone else has a
superior claim to it.

John Harsanyi points out that when demand exceeds supply,
prices rise, giving people an incentive to increase supply and thus to
decrease the demand. "As a result equilibrium . . . will be reestab-
lished at a new *higher* level of supply, at or close to what its Pareto-
optimal level would be under the new conditions. . . . Yet, if factor
rents were taxed away, these forces in the economy would be *very
seriously impaired,* and the economy would *move away* further and further from Pareto optimality."[30] This important observation is related
to the complaint I have just been making. The entire fabric of supply
and demand is predicated on the freedom of individuals to make and
accept or reject such offers as they may. If we are going to claim that
they are not entitled to those whenever, and simply because, they
might be willing to settle for the amount they would be left with after
confiscating some portion, we do not have a nation of free participants in the economy, whatever else we have. The "freedom to collect
factor rents" is part and parcel of liberty along with the liberty to
waste one's assets, buy six pairs of shoes when one would "surely be
enough," and listen to bad performances of Mozart.

We will resume discussion of another area in which the market is
thought to break down, namely, public goods, in connection with
consideration of the State.

CHAPTER 16

The State

The State, Government, Public, Associations, Us

L IBERTARIANS ARE notoriously unhappy with the State. It will be well to begin by explaining why, and for this we must define a few terms, viz. the ones mentioned in the heading. Consider, first, "us". 'Us' refers to you and me, and the people you and I know. It is from personal association that we get most of the evidence we have for our ideas about people, and in particular the idea of the *voluntary association*. In such a configuration you are a member only if you want to be a member, and only if it wants to have you. You may want to be a member of an existing association but find yourself rejected by it. You then have the option of trying to start your own, or finding another one to the same end, and so on.

The remaining terms get us into complexities. The *public* is, simply, everybody; but of course "everybody" varies from context to context. What matters for present purposes is that there are a lot of people included in "the public", and there is only one of you or of me. What unifies this set of people? Only that we have various contacts with each other. Of course, nobody has contact with everybody. What happens is that *every* member has contact with an appreciable number of other members, there being no discrete, isolated subsets who have no contact with any others, though there will be subsets that have a lot less to do with others than with fellow members of that subset. (Aficionados of these matters will note the employment of a device like the famous Fregean definition of the natural numbers.) Is the "public" an association? Its members associate with each other, to be sure; but there is no unifying structure, because the public has no purpose, even though all of its members have purposes a-plenty. The public simply *is*. And also, it is not (especially) voluntary. You just happen to be there, rather than having joined, and though you might be able to move elsewhere, you might not (mainly because where you went would have a government that won't let you).

What about the state? Roughly, the state is a public with a government; and a government is a smallish subset of the public that has somehow acquired the power to rule, that is to say, to make people do the things it wants them to. Membership in the public is not voluntary, and being under the control of its government is not voluntary. All must "join," whether they like it or not, and the "must" really means business, for the State may enforce its commands by use of outright force. (John Hospers remarks on a bumper sticker to the effect that "The Government is Armed and Dangerous", saying that the message of those stickers is "tragically true".[1] Certainly true, anyway; whether tragically remains to be seen.) It claims, indeed, a monopoly on the use of force, in the specific sense that private uses of force must be authorized by it, whereas its own employments of force, though they too need, in the favorable cases, to be authorized, are authorized *by itself*. In the case of nondemocratic states, this leaves the unwitting victim (= "citizen") completely at the mercy of the government.

In democratic states, however, the claim will be made that the states's acts are all authorized by the free and sovereign people. This is worth a few remarks. Let us first consider the idea, as expounded by Hobbes, as it applies more generally to the State. Hobbes supposes a sort of plebiscite to establish the State followed by everyone's simultaneously handing over their power to the person who wins the election.

Of course, some wouldn't like the result. Hobbes's argument proceeds as follows. Don't these other people, it may be said, nevertheless *consent* to the outcome of the election, whatever it may be? Thus Hobbes: "A *commonwealth* is said to be *instituted*, when a *multitude* of men do agree, and *covenant, every one, with every one*, that to whatsoever *man* or *assembly of men*, shall be given by the major part, the *right* to *present* the person of them all, that is to say, to be their *representative*; everyone, as well he that *voted for it*, as he that *voted against it*, shall *authorize* all the actions and judgments, of that man, or assembly of men, in the same manner, as if they were his own, to the end, to live peaceably amongst themselves, and be protected against other men."[2] [Hobbes's emphases.]

Hobbes's argument is obviously reconstructive. Hobbes did not go around checking to see whether everyone did in fact do what he claims they did. The social contract idea requires that every *rational* person would do this, and we know she would do it because she *must*. So what Hobbes is arguing has to be that every individual necessarily has sufficient reason to authorize a smallish body of people to act for her in the manner indicated. That good reason is, as he says, to "live peaceably amongst themselves, and be protected against other men". The good reason is what grounds the whole thing. We have in the foregoing been concerned to spell out further what the fundamental normative principles of general human association are, and that is an interpretation of the reason, if any, for having government. Unlike Hobbes, we take it that this reason *limits* government even if it also empowers it (if it does at all). We take this because his argument that the State must be unlimited in its powers is fallacious and, indeed, incoherent. If peace consists in our all being able to do as we wish, then a government that won't let us do so is violating peace, and is therefore illegitimate if the sole justification for government is to preserve the peace.

For the record, and because it is important, let us observe that Hobbes's argument confuses two very different things: (1) that abstract "sovereignty," which consists in something or other's being superior to any one of us or any lesser group of us, and (2) the concrete institution, consisting of human beings, which is supposed to realize, exemplify, or instantiate these abstract properties. But in fact, what has that "abstract sovereignty", as I call it, is the fundamental laws of morality themselves, and nothing else. They are supreme because they are *defined* as being so: the whole point of talking about such laws consists in the sense that we need such things to solve certain human problems, viz., those that arise because of our mutual interrelations. But there is no shred of an excuse for confusing the "sovereignty" of those laws themselves with whatever powers any of us might invest in any concrete institution—in any actual person or group of persons. There needs to be an argument for investing any degree of authority in any such body, and the argument should not consist in a confusion. In particular, it should invest just so much authority as is requisite for the purpose at hand, and no more.

There would now be two questions. First, do people all, in the required sense, rationally want to live in peace? And second, is it necessary to have a state to get them to do this? We have discussed the first one already in Part Two. Peace in the sense of being able to depend on others' refraining from violence that would prevent one from pursuing one's own ends can reasonably be said to be something everyone has sufficient reason to want. These reasons stem simply from the having of those ends. Only in very special and, as we may say, exotic cases can someone think that war in the same sense is better than peace in that sense. (Perhaps those conditions obtained in some technologically primitive societies for some people at some times.) But the clincher in any case is that those who do not want peace, or want it only for others in relation to themselves rather than vice versa, are on their own and may in principle be dealt with by any degree of violence we like.

The second question, then, is where the "action" is; and it is immensely trickier. I have already pointed out that on Hobbesian reasoning, we ought to cooperate rather than to submit to an all-powerful sovereign, wherever feasible. Moral methods dominate political ones. But we must admit that people aren't perfect and enforcement may be called for. Furthermore, that such enforcement is legitimate may be said to be true essentially by definition (of the notion of rights).

But if enforcement is legitimate, then why should the fact that the State may enforce its laws disturb us? For several reasons.

> (1) The things that the State thinks threaten you are things you may not feel threatened by at all—you may instead feel threatened by the State's attempts to "protect" you from them.

> (2) Or they will protect you quite a lot more (or, on the other hand, less) thoroughly than you would be willing to pay for if you had the choice.

> (3) Or you will find yourself shelling out money for the protection of other people but getting precious little yourself. In fact, the people they are protecting with your money may strike you as among the ones you need protecting from rather than needing or deserving any protection themselves.

> (4) Or you may dislike the particular *methods* they use. The prospect of the Knock on the Door by uniformed men who claim to have the *authority* to cart you off may be sufficiently unwelcome that you'd prefer to try some other way of doing things.

Are these complaints *in principle?* In one way, they are not. Recognizably similar kinds of complaints, after all, may no doubt be made by all sorts of people about ordinary voluntary agencies to which they belong or which they support. Complaints, justified or no, we have always with us. But there is a difference that is affected by our principle, at least prima facie. This central complaint from the libertarian point of view is that you have no choice but to deal with this particular agency, the Government; and this not in the sense that your particular Government is the only one that happened to be around, but rather that it was the only one *allowed* to be around. Competition non grata!

This is the central libertarian complaint, but even it needs some qualifying. Drawing again from the fertile fields of the American bumper sticker, some may recall one that said "America: Love It or Leave It!" The implication at that time was that if you aren't willing to pay a whole lot of money and perhaps a son or two to enable American soldiers to go about napalming Vietnamese peasants, then you can just move to some other sniveling country, and good riddance. Now, this is the sort of thing (details apart!) that a private club can legitimately say: "If you don't like what we do here, go somewhere else and do your own thing!" But is it something a nation-state can properly say? Of course, it would sometimes be false that you "could" leave it. Try getting out of the Soviet Union if you are a citizen of that country! And it's also true that if you do leave country x, you have to go to country Y, which may well not let you in. Then what? ·

But this is still a matter of degree, though a very great one. If there were no nation-states, then it would still be true that if you are not wanted in some area where everything is already owned by others, you must find someone else who will take you on; and it is perhaps also true that those others may use guns to keep you out. But this is such a great difference in degree that it may seem a quibble to classify it as such. For there are only a couple of hundred states in the world, whereas there are several billion people; and it is most unlikely that every last one of them wouldn't want you for a neighbor (unless you are Clifford Olson, who murdered forty-three boys after molesting them—in which case it is not clear that this is a relevant counterexample).

A Note on Democracy

In what sense did "the people" authorize any particular law in a democratic state? The short answer is that in practically all cases, they didn't. But the answer is admittedly too short. The main feature of democracies to be invoked here is that the people who did make the laws are *elected*; and reasonably invoked, since that is virtually the defining feature of democracy.

A brief note on the theory of democracy is in order here. Democracy is "rule by the people," but what does this mean? It can be demonstrated that this has to mean that those who rule are *elected*. Why must it mean this? Here is a short demonstration. In saying that democracy is "rule by the people", what we must mean, put more precisely, is that democracy involves an *equal distribution of political power* among the citizens. Were it unequal, and insofar as it is unequal, we would have rule by some lesser group: those with more power would have a greater say in determining what the laws are to be. (We assume, of course, that by 'democracy' we mean a theory of *government*, which is to say, a theory to be applied to the case where there is in fact *some* political power. We could make the distribution equal in another way by simply giving everyone no such power. This would be the theory of anarchy, not democracy.)

Now, let the set of people to be governed be too numerous to assemble in one place or permit of substantial discussion (true in essentially all the interesting cases). Beyond that point, some kind of indirect or representational procedure is inevitable. So democracy amounts to a theory of voting procedures.

As to majority rule: consider any issue on which there is any disagreement. Let the issue be resolvable by a pass-or-defeat vote—itself not easy, but we take the most favorable case; plainly, any other will make matters worse. If we set the number required for passage higher than 50 percent plus one, then we give more power per person to the nays. If we set it lower, the same measure could both pass and fail, which is inconsistent. The same applies to elections of representatives. Requirement of a greater majority than 50 percent plus one will give unequal power of selection to those who would otherwise be voting for the loser.

An elected legislator will often, and is certainly in general free to, vote contrary to the known wishes of his electorate. More usually, he has little idea what those wishes are. And in any case, he is elected only by those *who voted for him*. But this is by no means all. Democracy has some inherent problems highly relevant to present concerns.

The Down Side of Democracy

The justification of democracy has usually been rather narrowly drawn. First, it is argued that we have to have a state of *some* kind; and then it is argued that if we are going to have a state of any kind, it had better be a democratic one—democracy is the least among necessary evils. The argument is certainly very persuasive, given the premise. If we are going to have such an institution, then whoever you may be, you are certainly going to want to have it on your side if possible. So you are going to want the power to select it, insofar as it is possible to have such power. Since "you" are *anyone,* however, the conclusion will have to be that this power is to be distributed equally among all those concerned: thus, democracy.

But the premise is problematic, for one thing. Perhaps we don't need a state. But much more importantly, what is established by any argument for the State is limited by that argument's premises. The argument for the State from liberal premises, if it works at all, works by showing us that having a state is better for *everybody* than not having one. If this is indeed the argument, then the same argument should show that if *a given measure* would not be better for everyone if subject to majority rule, then with respect *to that item,* we shouldn't have majority rule.

The theory of democracy is rife with exceptions to majority rule. Nobody thinks that civil rights should be subject to it, for example: whether you or I should, for no further reason at all, be flayed in the public square at noon tomorrow is not something to be determined by majority rule. Whether Jones's tax bill should be doubled next year just because a majority dislikes Jones is not an open question on any proper theory of democracy.

It should be a matter of great interest, then, that with respect to *almost every matter,* there are similar arguments against majority rule, and more especially rule by representatives who have attained their office as the result of electoral procedures. James Buchanan develops some of them: "Majority voting rules for reaching collective or group decisions will produce at least some budgetary components that are inefficient in net. . . . Some projects that will secure majority approval will yield less in total benefits than they cost. The minority will suffer net losses from these projects, and these losses will exceed the benefits secured for members of the majority."[3] Buchanan proposes a minimal efficiency constraint on collective budgetary decisions: "the estimated value of benefits from any proposal to the members of an effective majority coalition must exceed the tax costs borne by those members. Even this minimal constraint on budgetary inefficiency is not operative, however, when logrolling can take place among divergent minorities to produce effective majority coalitions on a subgroup of budgetary items. This procedure is familiarly known as 'pork barrel' legislation in the American setting."[4]

When we move to consideration of the effects of legislation by elected representatives, the situation is still worse: "The politician's bias . . . is an additional institutional aspect of the asymmetry between the spending and taxing sides of the fiscal account. Because taxes cannot readily be lowered in a differential manner, there is a public-goods barrier which inhibits independent politician initiative toward tax reduction. By contrast . . . given his degree of freedom to influence outcomes, the nonideological politician's behavior will tend to generate an exaggerated version of the nonpolitician model analyzed earlier. . . . aggregate spending will tend to be inefficiently large even if the ultimate demands of voters-taxpayers-beneficiaries could be accurately reflected in final outcomes."[5]

These results and others to similar effect are familiar fare for students of public choice theory. Their general drift is that democratic methods overwhelmingly tend to be inefficient. These inefficiencies are multiplied when the collective in question gets larger. They are, in fact, inefficiencies to scale. In huge-number cases such as a modern state, they will certainly be enormous. Indeed, they *are* enormous!

Well, what's so great about efficiency?—it might be asked. The answer is that the concept of inefficiency employed here is that someone is *needlessly worse off:* that individual can be made better off without making anyone else worse off. Just assume—what will, after all, certainly be true after even a modest number of iterations—that the losing individual is *you*. Perhaps that will add weight to the suggestion that these results should not be ignored.

Political Authority

The State claims to be an omnicompetent authority. Anything you do is something that the State must *allow* you to do: it has authority over all and sundry matters, and the citizen shall knuckle under, thank you very much. This is the theory of government under which humankind has lived for the past several thousand years. But a few moment's thought suffice to show us that it is a fraud, an outrage, a disgrace, and a travesty that no thinking person could put up with for a moment. The democratic theory of government represents an effort to modify the inherent authoritarianism of government to an extent that would give it some reasonable semblance of acceptability. But on the face of it, it doesn't help much, since it substitutes for the one or the few people asserting authority a mob of your fellow humans.

But authorities must be authorized, and in the end the only person who can "authorize" anyone to do anything to you is *you*. All the rest is a sham, varying in degrees of barefacedness.

This does not mean that nobody ever has any authority to do anything. It means, instead, that the only authority a rational person acknowledges is authority that that person has good reason to accept. And one prominent reason for accepting it would be that you gave it to someone. Example: you join organization O, which gives person P the authority to write checks in its name. A condition of remaining in the organization is that you accept a number of things, including things that imply, given various facts you also know, that P is currently the treasurer and the treasurer has signing authority on O's bank account. Or if you were a member of an organization that ran the roads and its enforcement agents stopped you for violating one of its rules, then you would have reason for accepting the authority of that individual to do so. And so on.

Authority and Coordination

In Part Two we considered at length the decision-theoretic problem known as Prisoner's Dilemma. There are other dilemmas, however, and one of them that is of first importance in the present context is the Coordination Dilemma. Here is a simple example. Assume that Ms. Column and Mr. Row would be happy to spend some time with each other and are indifferent between doing so at the beach or the park. Being at either place without the other, on the other hand, would be most unsatisfactory. So we have a new diagram.

Ms. Column

		Beach	Park
Mr. Row	Beach	great!	awful!
	Park	awful!	great!

The "dilemma" label is merited only by the fact that each one, striving to get a desirable outcome that both want, may not know which way to go. In the absence of communication, and given the facts about their preferences, there is only a 50 percent chance that they'll end up in one of the desired situations. This is due to there being too much of a good thing: if they both preferred the beach, say, then there'd be no problem.

How do we solve a problem like this? Ultimately, by two devices: (1) an arbitrary mechanism for selecting one alternative rather than another, and (2) an agreement among the parties to be guided by that particular device. For example, Ms. Column flips a coin and Mr. Row agrees to go wherever Ms. Column says. Or, to move to our political context, someone decides that all cars will keep to the right, and everyone agrees to drive on whichever side that person says. In the case of cars there are not just two people, but millions. In the absence of coordination the roads would be unusable by such vehicles as cars. Even pedestrians and bicycles may need coordination.

The central point about coordination, then, is that the outcome in which everyone acts in one way or everyone acts in another way is preferred by all to any outcome in which people act independently. The problem is only how to secure this outcome, and not about its merits once secured. Real-life situations will usually have some aspects of each, of course, and that may further complicate matters.

The moral for politics may be that we need an authority to provide coordination. Instead of everyone's looking to see what everyone else is doing, everyone simply does what the authority says to do, thus saving nuisance and effectively achieving an uncontroversially desirable result. Needless to say, we will often have situations in which this happy simplicity is not present. Then we may have to tot up the advantages of coordination against the disadvantages of the particular outcome chosen by the authority.

Are the facts about coordination any *justification* of the State? There are two points to consider. First, since everyone presumably desires the uniformity which it is the point of the authority in question to impose, it should not in principle be necessary to visit severe penalties on offenders. And if the outcome of the exercise of authority is not desired by all, then this justification can't be used. On the other hand, of course, there may be people who just like to cause trouble; and in any case, the amount of trouble that may be caused by deviating from the established rule may be very great—the rule of the road being an excellent case in point. But even criminals do not habitually drive on the wrong side of the road! Whether a state is needed to exercise the authority that may be required is what may be questioned from this point of view. Second, it may or may not be that efficiency is achieved by having a single centralized agency providing coordinative authority for all purposes. Most likely, however, it will not be. In any case, it is certainly not theoretically necessary. What matters is that effective coordination be achieved, and not who achieves it; in particular, it doesn't matter whether the authority achieving it in case x is the same as the authority achieving it in case y.

Some theorists make a good deal of the coordinative function of the State. (John Finnis comes to mind.[6]) But it is not clear how far such considerations will take us in the direction of the State. Not, I suspect, so very far.

The Right to Protection

It is important to be clear that the right to protection that follows from our fundamentally negative right to liberty is also, therefore, fundamentally negative. Thus, if by the "right to protection" is meant the *positive* right that other people protect you, then it is not automatically on the libertarian agenda. What is on it is the right that others not, in various ways, molest you. If people threaten to molest you, then there is a practical question what to do about it. This may be answered by enlisting the aid of others, who may help you for various possible reasons: out of their own free wills, because they like you, or perhaps because they have a touch of Wyatt Earpism and like a good fight so long as they are siding with the good guys, or in exchange for something, such as a monetary fee, or because they belong to your Protection Co-operative and it's their turn. But people who protect you without (and contrary to) your permission are invading your rights, as are the original molesters. And people who not only do that but who then charge you for it and force you at gunpoint to pay are combining the two violations. Yet that would seem to be precisely the situation of the State. It should now be clear that there is indeed a complaint.

Protection and Nozick's Argument for the State

Is there something special about protection that makes it peculiarly eligible for relegating to a central agency? It has generally been thought so, including by many libertarians, who favor what is called the "Nightwatchman State", whose only function is to protect the citizens from force and fraud. But is there truly good reason for this? Robert Nozick's argument for the legitimacy of the "minimal state" is an attempt to underwrite this view and is worth looking at in some detail. My examination is designed to establish two points: First, that the argument, whether or not it is successful for its intended end, clearly wouldn't establish the legitimacy of the State in its contemporary sense *even insofar as it concerns the protective function alone.* And second, that the argument is of a type that would, if it works at all, surely be able to establish the legitimacy of an equally state-like apparatus for other functions, contrary to Nozick's explicit intentions.

The argument assumes we begin with a Lockean-type anarchy: people accept our libertarian rights but don't perfectly live up to them, and some of them flout them pretty badly, giving rise to the need for protection. People form protective associations, which because of the action of various plausible market forces eventuate in its being the case that in any given area, a single agency has a monopoly of protective force. The plausible market forces in question are, notice, essential to the argument. Suppose that agency A can offer better protection at a lower price than agency B: people will gravitate toward it. But this will enable A to offer still better protection, for more people will be its clients; when co-purchasers of automobile liability insurance from the same agency run into each other, the company is able to settle with itself out of court, saving immensely on collection costs, some of the savings of which it can pass on to the consumer. This makes A's package still more attractive. And then in the nature of the case, the bigger protection firm will have more "clout" if it came to a hands-down fight with firm B, and this, too, will make it more attractive to the consumer. A natural monopoly will, then, emerge. And the result will be—what? Well, there will be a few holdouts, perhaps. But these people will have to deal with A, because almost everybody has bought into A.

There are further important complications concerning the administration of the Lockean laws, in particular concerning the reliability of procedures for convicting people of violations. These terminate, again, in cases where it's the word of A against B; but if so, it becomes a question of who can make its side of the argument stick, and the answer is, of course, A, since it is by now a de facto monopoly. This will put it in the position of being able, in effect, to forbid competition. And A will have to end up underwriting the protection of those few who will still want to hold out on their own, because it must compensate them for depriving them of viable options. "Though each person has a right to act correctly to prohibit others from violating rights . . . only the dominant protective association will be able, without sanction, to enforce correctness as it sees it. Its power makes it the arbiter of correctness . . . not . . . that might makes right. But might does make enforced prohibitions, even if no one thinks the mighty have a *special* entitlement to have realized in the world their own view of which prohibitions are correctly enforced."

"What is the explanation of how a *minimal* state arises? The dominant protective association with the monopoly element is morally required to compensate for the disadvantages it imposes upon those it prohibits from self-help activities against its clients." Voilà: the Minimal State![7]

What makes it a state? The facts that (1) it has a monopoly of force (part of the definition of a state), and (2) it caters to everyone within its area, whether they like it or not, distributing the costs of doing so among its other clients in cases of inability to pay.

Nozick doesn't add what seems to me a fairly important further item: it claims to justify its monopoly by reference to principles alleged to be authorized by its citizenry; that is, it claims legitimacy along some such lines as those enunciated by Hobbes. The states you and I know about always do this. Nozick's State doesn't and doesn't claim to, in part because the assumption is that there are some principles that are simply true, independently of anybody's decisions about anything. Perhaps it doesn't matter whether the State makes any such claim. But it would matter whether the claim would be justified if it did make it. Would it be?

(1) Now my first point: It certainly isn't a state in the sense we know about. Everyone in the state in question retains the right to withdraw from it at any time. Any subset of citizens could get together and declare independence. They could operate internally with their own set of laws, which they enforce upon each other with their own procedures—and the surrounding "State" couldn't do a thing about it. Try this in any contemporary state and see where it gets you!

To be sure, there are states and states. If the Canadian Province of Quebec were to have a referendum in which the populace voted with a resounding majority to withdraw from Canada and form a state unto itself, leaders of the rest of Canada have made it clear that they would make no effort to stop them by force and that verbal efforts would likely lead merely to negotiations about the precise terms of withdrawal. If New England attempted this with the United States of America, one supposes from the historical record that things would be rather different. So it goes. But Canada in turn would not tolerate withdrawal by, say, the Hutterite community in Alberta or the Romanian minority in some obscure part of Ontario. The point is that the Nozickian Minimal State retains a remarkable degree of anarchy. A state that admits it does not have the right to compel all of its citizens to conform to its laws in every particular is not what most of us would be inclined to recognize as a state; we are recognizably at the margin, where the question whether A is a state or not becomes essentially terminological.

(2) There is a certain amount of hocus-pocus in Nozick's argument, to be sure. We will not discuss it here, especially since others have done so.[8] But if it works at all, the argument appears to have the following general form. (*a*) Legitimate association A comes *very near* to having the sort of monopoly of legitimate powers that states *claim* to have; (*b*) various considerations about the particular commodity A deals in bring it about that the gap between A and a genuine state can be effectively closed by a procedure of compensation for the few individuals separating its clientele from the whole population.

If this is a fair characterization of the procedure, then it is difficult to see why it should be confined to the particular commodity of protection.[9] Isn't this essentially the argument of the phone companies, the electricity boards, and the gas people? Suppose we start with competing companies in area x, an area that is ideally suited for a single system of the type in question. Companies A and B start stringing up rival lines or whatever; A offers a marginally better deal, more people buy into A, the cost of installing services by B consequently rises (its customers are farther apart, A-users being frequently interspersed among them), A ends up buying out B, and the few who don't like it very much are strung along on their B contracts at B's prices and levels of service until those contracts expire, leaving the customers with a choice of A-phones or nothing—and the customer ends up just going along. Below we shall explore the prospects of universal health insurance along broadly (but not narrowly) similar lines. What is not clear is that there is all that much in the way of structural difference between the Nozickian Protective State and the municipal gas company.

People in Ontario, Canada, have little inclination to think that Ontario Hydro (the provincial electric power monopoly) is denying them a bunch of fundamental rights. This, to be sure, is in part because it isn't: anybody who wants to generate her own electricity in Ontario is welcome to go right ahead, and Hydro will be happy to buy up the excess or to supply deficiencies or provide backup or whatever, and some actually do. Some people complain because Hydro has gone into nuclear-power generation in a big (and, by the relevant standards, extremely successful) way. As things are, their complaint is essentially political, since Hydro is indeed a provincially chartered public corporation. But what if the subject were a giant American private-enterprise electric corporation such as Consolidated Edison in New York? Would the power of any small set of objectors to affect its policy be materially different? Obviously not. In New York rivals would have the right to try to establish an alternative company to compete for Con Ed's franchise, but competition for business of this kind with a company of that size is no easier—indeed, a great deal more difficult, one would think—than organizing enough voters to force Ontario Hydro to cease utilizing nuclear generation. Neither of which will happen until one of Hydro's generators goes berserk, in which case there would be hell to pay for any company utilizing them, public or private. Which is also not very dissimilar from the case with the public's protective agencies. Corruption in the police force, if uncovered, will cause a most remarkable row in any reasonably functioning democracy.

This does not leave us with no differences, but it narrows certain gaps to a quite significant degree, as will be seen further.

Law

Part of our idea of law is that it should be authoritative over everyone in the geographical area occupied by the society whose law it is. We should ask a few questions about this. (1) *Which* "geographical area"? There is no coherent principle for drawing the boundaries of nation-states in the modern sense of the term; and if we take seriously the idea that every individual has the ultimate rights and that collectives are legitimate only if they are associations rather than forced collectivities, then this purely definitional attribute of law is seen to have no interest whatever for establishing whether or not a given person should be subject to a given law. (2) And then, is geographical continuity actually necessary? If we look again at associations, what we will find is that highly discontinuous associations nevertheless have rules and regulations and succeed sufficiently in enforcing them, the primary enforcement procedure being simply ejection from the association.

This raises the question whether a society could be fully anarchic with respect to law. Could different sets of individuals intermixed in the same geographical area be subject to very different sets of "laws"? Up to a point, there is no doubt that they can, since to a degree they actually are. Different religious communities, for instance, can interlace and yet impose very different requirements on their members. Are these actually "laws", though? They certainly have some of the characteristics of law as we understand it. Those rules have generality and authority over the groups whose laws they are. Consequently, their members can use them to settle disputes by the process of weighing claims in the light of the rules in question, with appointed judges to engage in the weighing process.

What these partial sets of laws have in common is that they lack supreme authority over all, whether the individual has volunteered for coverage by them or not. That is the feature that we associate with law in the fullest sense of the term. And it is what makes the rule of law problematic if individual rights to liberty are to serve as its foundation. Given laws having that feature, we would be able to settle disputes between *any* two or more people in the society. Without them, where do we go?

The anarchist has a reply to this. Even as things now are, different areas have different systems of law, so that when an individual from area Q goes to visit in area R and runs into a problem, there is a jurisdictional problem needing solution. And it is in fact solved by having representatives from the different systems meet and reach an agreement regarding the case in question. What would prevent the same solution's being reached in a given area with rival legal systems obtaining within its bounds?[10]

Obviously there could be a practicality problem, especially if there were several such systems and not just two. Presumably there might also be a problem if some individuals belonged to no system whatever. However, there would seem to be a solution for this last problem. If individual A, subscribing to no legal system, got into trouble with an individual subscribing to System L, the administrators of L would simply apply their law to A, and that would be that. A is on her own.

But what about cases in which the respective legal systems of the differing parties could not reach an agreement? It is no good insisting that this can't happen. Nor is it any good saying that they would then "have to" reach agreement. For who would make them do so? Why *would* they "have to"? It is when we consider this possibility that the theorist is likely to resort to an idea of "natural" law. If everyone were equipped with an intuition of what is right and wrong, then a basis for agreement would always exist. Wouldn't it?

But it is fairly pointless to suppose this to be the case. And even those who think it is, like Locke, accept the possibility that there will be insoluble differences of interpretation about how that law applies to particular cases. We are then back to the original problem that drove Locke to embrace civil government as the cure for all ills. But as we have seen, any government inherently faces the problem of legitimacy from the point of view of nonconsenting individuals, and we would seem to be off and running again.

A possible solution to this kind of problem may go as follows. When individuals from rival systems run into a problem of the kind we have envisaged, and efforts to reach agreement by representatives of the respective systems fail, the parties would have two options. Either (1) they would consent to a procedure of binding arbitration, or (2) it would be "settled" by force. If it is objected that force doesn't settle anything, the reply is that that is perfectly true. All it does is to leave just one party in the field. If that isn't satisfactory, then the case for preferring binding arbitration is evidently made. And if it isn't satisfactory, then that is testimony to the truth of our guiding assumption here, that the State needs justification and that it will not be easy to supply it.

Enforcement and the Problem of Punishment

If we need to enforce laws, how do we do so? One of the most vexed areas of moral philosophy has been the theory of punishment, and we can hardly undertake a full-fledged study of the subject here. Nevertheless, there is an interesting, distinctively libertarian suggestion that is worth serious thought.

To begin, we should distinguish between "enforcement" in the narrow sense of that term, in which it is virtually equated with "punishment" and "reinforcement." Enforcement is part of a larger system that we may call "reinforcement," and reinforcement, I have urged, has a central, or perhaps even *the* central role in morality. For an act to be obligatory or wrong is for it to be the case that its performance or nonperformance should be universally reinforced, positively or negatively. Positive reinforcement is reward—the carrot; negative is punishment—the stick. But the "stick" begins at home and consists overwhelmingly of verbal reinforcement, accompanied by appropriate gestures and such.

The role of this level of reinforcement, basic to theory in my view, cannot be overemphasized in the larger context of criminal law. Studies have confirmed what common sense and Aristotle have both told us for a couple of millennia: if a child is properly brought up, it will have the disposition to cooperate and to obey reasonable rules.[11] And if it is not, then it very likely won't. This is so to the degree that one might wonder why we do not hold parents responsible for the crimes of their children, especially those committed in their teens. Some of libertarian persuasion will complain that this is a denial of human responsibility and basic freedom. But it is nothing of the sort. It would, on the contrary, be to hold responsible those who plainly *are* responsible for actions that violate *our* rightful liberty. The irresponsibility of children is a reflection of bad, and especially of inconsistent, upbringing by their parents. This is a correctible syndrome on the part of the parents. Needless to say, it would also be extremely and genuinely desirable for the children: faced with the choice between the kind of life generally available to the cooperative and law-abiding citizen and that led by the criminal, few will find the latter more attractive. But the basis for public concern about erring parents is not the well-being of their children, as such; it is the well-being of those who will be victims of the future criminal activities of the adults whom those children will ere long become.

Meanwhile, however, we must of course deal with those who do violate reasonably imposed requirements. Even at this level, it is clear that education is a nontrivial factor. One must wonder whether criminals genuinely believe that their crimes constitute rationally objectionable behavior, and if they do, why they continue to engage in it. The desirability, perhaps even the necessity, of effective verbal reinforcement at the adult level seems difficult in principle to deny. But we can't expect much in the way of results if this part of the job of dealing with criminal behavior is left to the likes of clerics. Criticizing rationally objectionable behavior in the light of nonrational theological doctrines is unpromising when those who engage in the behavior are rational adults rather than impressionable children.

Punishment: The Options

Still, this leaves us with the need for further responses to criminal behavior. There are three theories in the field at present, two of which are theories of punishment properly so called, and the third of which, though it can reasonably be so classified, is strictly a theory calling for a fundamentally different mode of responding to criminal acts. These are, respectively, those calling for retribution, deterrence/protection, and restitution or compensation. I offer a few remarks about the first two, and a little more about the third.

An important point to be borne in mind throughout this discussion: Although for the sake of efficient exposition I use the term 'crime' to denote the set of actions we are concerned with here, it must be clearly understood that I am not using it in the sense of actions that are forbidden by the de facto criminal law of whatever community the acts in question take place in. Instead, we assume throughout that the acts forbidden are *reasonably* forbidden. The view that crime in the de facto sense ought to be punished is simply unacceptable. Bad· laws should be eliminated, not enforced, and it is only slightly overly dramatic to suggest that those against whom they are enforced are the victims, those who enforce them the criminals.

Keeping this in mind, let's turn to the remarks in question, taking the three theories in order: retribution, deterrence/protection, and restitution.

Retribution

So understood, our theories are in fact a mixed bag. The "retributionist" aims to visit the criminal with an amount of negative utility roughly equal to that which the criminal inflicted on his victim. This is what punishment, on his view, should attempt to bring about. But pressed for an account of the rationale of this behavior, the retributionist characteristically has little to offer. Either she produces an intuitionist response of some sort, saying that *lex talionis* is a basic principle of human nature or some such thing; or she produces reasons that amount to shifting over to the deterrence/protection theory.

The difference between retribution and deterrence as theories of punishment can hardly be a difference about the basic purpose of having the system at all. That the purpose of having a punishment system in general is to protect the public is, in fact, too obvious to be a fit subject of discussion, and defenders of retribution do not, as they cannot, deny it. The thought that visiting pain upon people who have visited pain upon others is a kind of interesting entertainment, a charming spectacle, or a source of existentialist drama, and in one of *those* ways "valuable in and of itself", is abhorrent to any retributionist. The question for retributionism has to be what the point of visiting this pain upon criminals might be, insofar as this pain is inflicted *independently* of what he agrees to be the point of having the criminal law system at all. And this, as I have suggested above, is really not easy to answer. It may indeed, and presumably often does, make the victims of criminal activity *feel better*. But it would be difficult for a retributionist to admit that this was the justification of retribution.

The Deterrence/Protection Theory

There is a great deal of confusion about the deterrence/protection view. The deterrence/protection theory has it that punishment is part of a broader social system whose purpose is to minimize crime—or rather, and much more precisely, to minimize the *social costs of criminal behavior*. Were there no such costs, there would be nothing to deter and nothing to exact retribution for. But, as the restitutionist will point out, if the costs were completely compensated, there would again be no obvious need for either deterrence or retribution.

This minimization of social costs has two aspects to it—not, as seems to be all but universally misunderstood, just one. No sane theory could hold that any procedure whatsoever would be completely justified if it could be shown to be reasonable to expect that it would reduce the overall probability of *criminal* behavior. What matters is costs, and although criminal behavior is a prominent source of such costs, it is obviously not the only one. Another obvious and major source of costs arises from the enforcement of the law, and from the infliction of punishment itself. When punishments strike us as "excessive", the sense is that we lose more than we gain by reacting to the particular crimes thus punished in the particular way that that punishment constitutes. All dealings with criminal behavior are to at least some degree costly, and it is obvious that the cost may be too high. When it is, a theory of punishment proposing to justify punishment by virtue of its expected reduction in criminal behavior must, in consistency, call for a reduction in the noncriminal activities that entail those excessive costs.

Now, the punishment system is one particular way of attempting to control criminal behavior. It is a very specialized way in fact, and cannot be appropriately employed in many cases of what we may term broadly criminal conduct, such as that in which the criminal activities are due to insanity. A punishment system, in fact, is an exercise in the *rational* control of behavior. Recognizing the facts of Prisoner's Dilemma, we propose to prevent criminal conduct by altering the values in the game-theoretic situation facing the would-be criminal. We attempt to attach disutilities to the outcomes in what would otherwise be the single-defect boxes by punishing the agent sufficiently to make the crime in question unattractive to him.

The proposal to do this generates further perplexities, to be sure. Nozick observes that " 'the penalty for a crime should be the minimal one necessary to deter commission of it' provides *no* guidance until we're told *how much* commission of it is to be deterred. If all commission is to be deterred, so that the crime is eliminated, the penalty will be set unacceptably high. If only one instance of the crime is to be deterred, so that there is merely less of the crime than there would be with no penalty at all, the penalty will be unacceptably low. . . . Where in between is the goal and penalty to be set?"[12] Plainly, at a minimum, it must just more than offset the gain from the proposed crime. Determination of the maximum would be set by several considerations, a main one being the concern that we not induce people to ignore the difference between lesser and greater crimes, and another the increase in risk for all when high penalties are used, owing to the probability of convicting the innocent. Whether these completely answer the criticism, however, can't be determined here.

What matters is that this procedure absolutely presupposes capability of rational behavior on the part of the criminal. Nor is that all. It also absolutely presupposes that the penalties in question must, in order for the system to function as intended, be *publicly* attached to the acts in question. The would-be criminal, A, cannot be deterred by the threat of punishment P for crime C unless A knows ahead of time that C will bring P. A further point. C is only one crime among many others. Being concerned with crime because we are concerned with the disutility it brings, we must therefore be concerned to deter criminal activity in proportion to its expected disvalue to us. We must therefore attach greater penalties to greater crimes, since otherwise the criminal's motivation to refrain from lesser crimes will only be equal to, or perhaps greater than, his motivation to refrain from greater ones. But by definition, we are more interested in the nonperformance of greater ones than lesser ones, other things being equal.

It has not been sufficiently noticed that the result of this approach to crime and punishment is that we must attempt to bring it about that (1) nonrational persons are not to be punished, but require a different kind of response ("treatment")—to assimilate punishment to treatment has to be self-defeating; (2) the punishment must be proportionate to the crime; and (3) *all and only* guilty persons should be punished (or if not outrightly punished, at least apprehended, arraigned, and warned, as with a lighter punishment or suspended sentence for the first offense).

Why (3)? If we ask, what is the point of punishing any particular criminal, A, within the framework of deterrence/protection, the answer has to be threefold: (*a*) it renders A's repetition of the crime impossible during the period of punishment (if, as typically, it is by incarceration); (*b*) it decreases, we hope, the probability of A's repetition when his punishment is concluded, by graphically bringing home to him what he's in for if he does repeat; and (*c*) it adds evidence, for the benefit of prospective criminals, to the hypothesis that crime does not pay, that is to say, that if they commit C, then there is a sufficient probability of P, which by hypothesis is sufficient so that if that probability were 1.0, it would deter the rational prospective criminal from committing the crime.

The amount of misunderstanding generated on this last point in the philosophical profession is truly depressing. Indeed, the standard textbook objection to the deterrence/protection system, found in virtually every discussion of this theory in the literature, is that it would justify punishment of the innocent, namely, in those cases where punishing person B would bring it about that less crime is committed by persons who take the punishment of B as evidence that they too will be punished. The problem here is simple: the objection depends absolutely on *misperception*. And if B is innocent, then there are two obvious problems: first, the point of the system is to avoid costs on law-abiding persons. (We could say, simply, to avoid costs on *persons*; but it is part of the logic of the deterrence-protection system that once a person has inflicted such a cost on someone else, that makes him eligible for having costs inflicted on him. The net effect is, therefore, that the point of the system is to avoid costs on law-abiding persons.) But if people are going to be punished whether or not they are guilty, why should they bother to abide by the law? To the rational person, law-abidingness is not a good in itself. It is a means, to the general end of living a better life. That B, in this case, has been done a signal injustice is entailed by the framing presupposition of a deterrence system.

And second: given that B is innocent, it follows that someone else, A, has in fact done the crime and that A, far from being deterred, has now been given a new incentive to continue criminal activity, since the public's action in willingly punishing innocent B despite the fact of B's innocence shows A that the system doesn't work—that A *can* commit crimes with impunity. And thus, of course, the public has not been protected—which was the whole point of the punishment system in the first place, according to this theory. Punishing the innocent and not punishing the guilty are by definition the two ways in which a deterrence-protection-based punishment system *fails*.

Restitution

Another view, so different as to amount to a different idea altogether about how to respond to crime, proposes that we simply junk the idea of punishment, as such. Crime, after all, consists in inflicting disutilies on someone or other. From the point of view of that person (the "victim"), this suggests a quite especially appropriate mode of response: make the criminal compensate the victim. How much? The property theory supplies the relevant basis for an answer. The criminal, C, has taken something that belongs to the victim, V, and this had a certain value, to V. Thus there is a measure of cost: the difference between the value of V's life to V had things gone on as usual and its value, reduced by the criminal act, given the occurrence of the criminal act, x. So the criminal *owes* the victim enough restitution, R, to restore V's life to the level V would have otherwise enjoyed.[13]

In simple cases the effect is easy enough to determine. Suppose that C has deprived V of some material good, M. Obviously C owes V the return of M. This component of the restitution, then, we may call Rm. In the process of identifying C, V incurs various costs of apprehension and detection—paying detectives and lawyers, for instance. C, of course, has caused these costs as well by his criminal act, and so these too must be added to his "bill": this component is Ra. And so too must V's inability to enjoy M during the period before it is restored to him. It, too, has an estimable cost, compensation for lost use-time of the material good M: Ru. The total bill, then, is $Ra + Rm + Ru = R$.

The idealized level of *full* compensation, as it is called, in the unlikely event that it could always be met, would seem to have the fascinating feature that if it could be perfectly administered, it would render criminal activity a nonproblem. In the first place, since it is all but impossible that R would be exceeded by the criminal's gain in performing the act x in the first place, the full-compensation system would probably also function as a full-deterrence system. It is unlikely that there would be any criminal activity. And in the second place, the occurrence of crime would become literally a matter of indifference to the victim, since, by hypothesis, full compensation would leave the victim precisely as well off as if the crime had never occurred!

Some defenders of retribution mistakenly assimilate it to compensation. But this is an unlikely assimilation as a general hypothesis, for the psychic satisfaction to A of seeing the man who crashed A's new

Lotus sitting behind bars for a year is unlikely to be equal to her satisfactions of driving and admiring it during the period of disruption. So long as the victim is left otherwise uncompensated, indeed, it would seem that she has a justifiable complaint against any punishment system. For the benefits of punishment from her point of view are generally likely to be next to nil. She is still without whatever it was that the criminal took from her, and what she is offered in exchange is not only virtually irrelevant but also, when you think of it, of such a kind as to reflect adversely on her *taste*: do we really want to be the kind of people who derive as much satisfaction from the sight of others being punished as we would have from the use and enjoyment of whatever they have taken from us? But that is what a punishment system encourages.

Obviously, the problem is that there will be many criminal acts which it is impossible to compensate for. The classic instance is murder, where compensation to the victim herself is out of the question, and compensation to the others concerned likely to be problematic in the extreme. What parents will be equally happy with several million dollars as they would have been with their son or daughter unmurdered? Or those that entail loss of bodily or mental powers (same question, with the examples of total loss of memory, or of both legs, and the like). And there is the further point that in the more important cases compensation will be impossible because the criminal simply won't command the necessary resources. Life enslavement to the victim or her family, in the form of, say, 80 percent of the criminal's future income for life, might be considered. And here, interestingly enough, we have an example that will likely strike the upholder of the more usual punishment system as a case of gross injustice. (A smashes your Lamborghini, or burns up your Rembrandt, the interest on the equivalent monetary value of which would exceed A's maximum earnings in any given year.) Nevertheless, it is hard to deny that the deterrent value of required compensation, were the requirement highly likely to be fulfilled, would probably be quite enormous.

The fact that compensation would often not be forthcoming either because of inability to catch the offender or inability to pay if caught would motivate us to take out "crime insurance", which in turn would motivate the insurance company to catch such criminals as it profitably could. Criminals would have plenty to fear from these highly motivated companies, who of course would acquire from their clients the right to such compensation as they could exact, at least up to the level of full restitution. It would be interesting to know whether the net effect would be more satisfactory than the current system, but when you consider the all-but-total failure of the punishment system actually employed in, say, the United States and Canada, it is difficult to believe that it wouldn't be a major improvement.[14]

Everyone agrees that we have very far to go in the way of improving our system of responding to crime. It is a sobering thought that getting rid of one of the most spectacularly cost-ineffective systems in the history of mankind short of war is perhaps even less likely to be seriously considered than is abolition of war.

CHAPTER 17

Redistribution

Redistribution and the State

THE MOST TYPICAL libertarian complaint is that the State forces you to do things simply for others, for example, to pay for things to supply others' needs. It is, indeed, this in particular that gets the libertarian his reputation for befriending the ungenerous. Libertarianism, as Lawrence Haworth puts it, "captures this fact of [individuals'] uniqueness but is Scroogelike in its response to their welfare and to inequities in the distribution of the means to well-being."[1] The trouble is, as we have seen, that the only way of the State's being less "Scroogelike" about such things seems to violate some people's autonomy. If we assume that property rights are genuine implications of the liberty principle, then taxation is a prima facie violation of it, and so is the meddling insistence on providing unwanted services.

Such is the libertarian argument. But note carefully the words 'prima facie' in the last sentence. It is not a small matter. Taxes are collected without asking us as individuals whether we wish to pay them. But we are all members of various voluntary organizations that collect fees, dues, and the like from us on occasions when we'd rather not pay them. We pay up because we have subscribed and because they are worth it to us—especially so, in the case of the electric company, because life without their extremely useful product would be too inconvenient and uncomfortable to be worth the sacrifice of it for the sake of mere Principle.

Well, suppose someone claims that the State *is* worth it to us? Peter Singer, in discussing Nozick's argument for the limited state, observes that "Nozick does not say that a state is a good thing and we are all better off with a state than we would be without one. This obvious procedure for dealing with the anarchist would be foreign to Nozick's entire approach and would set a precedent subversive of his aim in the second part" (in which Nozick argues that no further State is justified).[2]

Singer has in mind evaluating the State in utilitarian terms. But these need not be the only terms of evaluation. Suppose instead we assess the State in terms of the values of each person who would be participating in it, and the claim is made that every one of them would find it better. That such an argument is "foreign to the libertarian's entire approach" is also, apparently, what is usually thought, at least since Nozick's work brought libertarianism to the forefront of discussion in Anglo-American philosophical circles; and it may well be what Nozick thinks, too. But it is not what we can think if we are defending libertarianism on a contractarian basis. If a rational agent prefers x to y, then other things being equal, he will choose x. If the only way he can get x is by sacrificing something, he must decide whether the something is worth sacrificing in exchange for x. If he concludes that it is, then he will sacrifice it, and cheerfully. But this is not a *utilitarian* argument. We agree with Nozick that there is an in-principle objection to utilitarianism. A rational agent will not make sacrifices simply for the good of others; she will do so only if she makes the good of others her own good, of it she sees the good of others as in turn promoting what she agrees to be good, for instance, her own good. And we are agreeing, indeed insisting, that it is not necessarily true of the rational agent that she will accept either of those things.

The Hobbesian claim is that the State makes us all better off than we would be without it. But as we have seen, his argument virtually implies that we would all be still better off without the State, *if* we could do without it. In principle, that is to say, it may seem that any benefit the State can give us is one that could, in principle, be got by voluntary efforts on the part of individuals not acting under any kind of compulsion other than the usual self-imposed discipline required for virtually any cooperative endeavor in life. A successful defense of the State as an institution will have to show that there are benefits for all which can plausibly be got only by having a nonvoluntary, coercive agency to assure them. And to be true to our libertarian premises, it will have to show that this benefit, for the worst-off beneficiary, exceeds the cost implied *by its being nonvoluntary.* Under this condition, however, we will accept that the involuntariness *has been justified* from this person's point of view.

In this we depart from the libertarian tradition—perhaps. 'Perhaps', because it is not entirely clear what this tradition is, or what its foundation is supposed to be. But we do the best we can for it, in my view, by attributing the sort of contractarian foundations proposed in Part Two. And on those foundations, the fact that something would be a good deal from the point of view of the individual concerned, in relation to other available deals, is all there is to rationally justify anything. There is no point in talking about justification if that won't do it. And it is the sort of justification that many critics in effect urge for the State. It behooves us to take a closer look.

A Tale of Two Scrooges

Let us return to the charge of "Scroogism". One who thinks that redistributionism is not in principle objectionable, in fact simply not objectionable in any way, will still argue that we are being Scrooge-like. The rest of us, however, should pause to reflect on the fact that there were two Scrooges: Scrooge *before* and Scrooge *after* being exposed to the Ghost of Christmas with his vivid depictions of the sufferings Scrooge could be relieving. Neither of these Scrooges was compelled by the State to be the way he was, and such compulsion had nothing to do with his change of heart. In a world of strong property rights, there will no doubt be lots of Scrooges. But which sort— Befores or Afters—will they be, and why? Perhaps there are as many preconversion Scrooges as there are in the world in part *because* of the State, not *despite* it; and perhaps there would be far more postconversion Scrooges were it not for the State. When the State helps itself to 50 percent of your income, after all, it provides you with two very good reasons for being less than terrifically charitable: (1) you no longer have all that much left to be charitable with, and (2) the government has been braying in your ears ever since you were born how much good *it* is doing with your money—so why should you do any more?

The reason you should do more, however, is that all governments, everywhere, are to greater or lesser degrees incompetent. At least prima facie, no government can spend a dollar of your money more effectively than you, because you know what to do with it and it does not. And in the cases where it would take many people to make a given project work, it is again prima facie plausible to suppose that the set of people interested in that project are the ones who should supply the money and the direction of it, rather than others who are neither interested in it nor competent to direct it. But belief in an omnicompetent agency to do all things with the money of all people, taken from them by force or threat of force (though on a "fair" basis, of course) is akin to belief in fairy godmothers and Superman. But No, Virginia, the world contains no fairy godmothers and no Superman, alas. There are just ordinary folk like you and me—pumpkins and Clark Kents. So the question whether we should do it or instead "let" the government do it is a question whether one set of pumpkins should do it or another set—the difference being that the other set will do it by forcibly depriving us of our money first, then letting us apply in sextuplicate for permission to offer advice about where it should go, and then doing it badly if at all.

The right way to get a thing done, on the other hand, is for the people interested in doing it to get together (to whatever degree such togetherness may be appropriate) and *do it*. And the only reason why modern governments in the more decent places in the world are tolerable at all is because they approximate to some degree the model of free men and women working in concert or individually to get things done that they want done.

The question before us, then, is whether there is any reason—any excuse, one might better say—for supposing that we shall do these things better by having a government than by going without one.

Public Goods Arguments

The modern theory of government has one major crutch among theorists. It is a special application of the problem of Prisoner's Dilemma and is widely thought to yield an overwhelming argument for the State. Clearly, we must have a careful look.

Public goods are one form of 'externality'. Suppose there is an exchange between A and B; each transfers something to the other in return for something he prefers to what he had before. But in the process someone else, C, ends up better or worse off, and does so without having the power to prevent it, where it's worse off, or without A's or B's having the power to prevent it, where it's better off. This is an effect on someone's welfare that is "external to" the transaction. Where there are externalities, obviously, there are problems in the real world, despite the neat proofs of welfare economists about the virtuous effects of free markets.

A good is "public" when it goes to others besides those who have produced it, without agreement by the producers; these recipients receive the good without having to pay. Suppose I have a friend, Bill, and I arrange to celebrate his birthday by having an airplane fly over his house trailing a huge sign saying "Happy Birthday, Bill!" But everyone else in the neighborhood will be able to see this sign, too. For some that will be good and for others, bad; but those for whom it is good will be able to get it for free, while those for whom it is bad will be able to do little about it, other than try not to look at the thing as it goes by. Simpler examples: you mow your lawn with a gasoline-powered mower; I, next door, get to listen to the racket for an hour, unless I leave or close all the windows tight, depriving me of the fresh spring air. Or: I am watching the parade, and you, upwind, are smoking a cigar. I have my choice between leaving my favored location or choking half to death. These last are public "bads"; their removal would be a public good (so far as this portion of the "public" is concerned, anyway).

Given complete freedom, everyone gets to do whatever he or she pleases. If so, we have problems. Consider any public good that costs anything to supply. Those who supply the goods will not be able to retrieve their costs. Either they provide them for others free of charge or they don't provide them for themselves. Public goods, given complete freedom, tend to be undersupplied. Public bads, supposing they are by-products of remunerative activities—pollution from manufacturing is the favored example—tend to be oversupplied. What, then, is to be done? And in particular, do we have an argument here for state intervention?

Why is this an instance of Prisoner's Dilemma? Because those who collect the goods without paying for them are in the position of those in the Prisoner's Dilemma who take the "default" option: I get the goods and keep my $5, you not only don't get the money but you lose the goods as well. The polluter collects the profits from sales while others pay for the pollution in the form of lost years of life due to lung cancer, or of the monetary costs of cures if they are available, or of clean-up or preventive methods: for instance, in the case of air pollution due to tobacco smoke there might be dry-cleaning bills. smoke filters, "No Smoking" signs, and any extra costs of enforcement that might be required to keep people from engaging in the polluting activity; and so on.

Thus we have the familiar four possible outcomes for each "player": (1) A "wins": he collects the profits *and* pays no costs of pollution, whereas B pays the costs and collects no profits; (2) A's second-best: net profits from gross sales less costs of cleaning up or preventing the pollution, and the same for B; (3) third best: profits greatly diminished by having to bear costs of the *other* fellow's pollution while B bears the costs of A's [among those costs may be, for example, an earlier death for each while they're at it); (4) worst of all: A bears all the costs *and* the reduced profits while B collects the profits and pays no costs of pollution. The cooperative solution, (2), is where each bears the costs of keeping his or her act clean.

The main culprit in public goods cases is the "free rider", the person who collects the benefits made possible by someone else's effort without paying for them himself. But we should distinguish immediately between two cases of free ridership: the one who is welcomed aboard the bus, and the one who is not. It is the latter that concerns us, for if producers wish to be generous, that is certainly their right.

"Tails" on the coin that has the free rider culprit as "heads" is the Assurance Problem. Suppose you are one of the suppliers of one of these goods, and you look out upon the sea of free riders: do you contribute? On the one hand, you may reason, if enough other people contribute, then I won't need to—I'll join the free rider club and save my money. On the other hand, if not enough people contribute, then there won't be enough to supply the good, and my contribution will be wasted. Of course, there is the logical possibility that precisely the right number will contribute and that I'll be precisely the last necessary person. In that happy event, of course, the situation will be just the same as the usual one with nonpublic goods: I get my refrigerator if and only if I pay the market price for it: pay, fridge; no pay, no fridge. Contribute x to the opera, and there's opera; no contribution, no opera.

But of course, it is *immensely* unlikely, in large-scale cases, that you will be in that position, or indeed that anyone will or could know himself to be in it even if he is. And then Prisoner's Dilemma looms in full force. Everyone reasons that either enough others will contribute so I won't need to, or not enough others will and mine will be wasted. Thus, no public goods.[3]

The case is put by James Buchanan not only on behalf of what we may call, following his terminology, the "protective state", but more importantly still on behalf of the more substantial State of recent times, the "productive state":

"[G]overnment . . . operates in a dual capacity. There is a part of government whose action is different, in principle, from that of rule-keeping or enforcement. . . . what we may call the "productive state" is the constitutional process through which citizens accomplish jointly desired objectives, a means of facilitating complex exchanges *among* separate citizens, each of whom enters the contractual or exchange process with rights assigned in the more fundamental legal structure. In this role, government is *internal* to the community. . . .

"In this role or capacity, the state is not 'protecting' defined individual rights. Government is a *productive process*, one that ideally enables the community of persons to increase their overall levels of economic well-being, to shift toward the efficiency frontier. Only through governmental-collective processes can individuals secure the net benefits of goods and services that are characterized by extreme jointness efficiencies and by extreme nonexcludability, goods and services that would tend to be provided suboptimally or not at all in the absence of collective-governmental action."[4]

Should we be impressed? In some ways, certainly. But we should look carefully at the claim that this is necessarily an argument for *government* in particular. Note the phrase "collective-governmental" in the last sentence. The implication is that they are so closely connected as to amount to the same thing. But this is not so; they should not be assimilated. A voluntary association is a collectivity, but a voluntary one; it is not a state. Its powers are limited strictly to matters pertaining to its own members, and so far as it goes, that is all to the good if we accept the general thesis that legitimate power must derive from those over whom it is exercised. But it doesn't follow that they have no or very little power. To the extent that membership in a given association is valuable, the threat of expulsion or lesser loss of privileges is a substantial one.

Moreover, as we saw, it is possible for the informal machinery of morality to have some influence. As we also saw, Buchanan himself noted this and agreed that it is important. "When conflict does emerge, . . . the value of order suggests either some social contract, some system of formal law, *or* some generally accepted set of ethical-moral precepts. It is important to recognize that these are alternative means of securing order. To the extent that ethical precepts are widely shared, and influence individual behavior, there is less need for the more formal restrictiveness of legally imposed standards."[5] It is an open question how much power those standards do have, but it is obvious that they *can* have a great deal.

Next, we must bear in mind an important point about the real-world free market. The idea of the free market is to "internalize" ex-

ternalities. They are not internalized all by themselves. A social network of moral and possibly legal reinforcement is needed for virtually
any market. Polluters are liable for the damages they inflict on others
with their polluting activity; free riders who impose a cost on those
who provide the free ride (the "unwelcome" class, that is) are thieves.
In other words, it is wrong to say, what is so often said as to be a
virtual truism, that public goods problems are endemic *to the market*. If
they are to be so regarded, they are such in the same sense that liars,
frauds, cheats, swindlers, thieves, extortionists, and other immoral
persons are so. But this "truism," which is true enough, tends to be
confused with a quite different proposition that is anything but
truistic, being just the opposite—a "falsism," if you like. That is the
claim that the market system *approves* of such activities or has no protections against them. Simple moral integrity is, of course, the fundamental and major "protection." But it is not the only possible one.
Considerable reinforcement can occur within the framework of the
market. People can, as Nozick pointed out, hire other people to help
reinforce agreements when those agreements need reinforcing.

Some of the problems in question are much more difficult to deal
with than others, to be sure. Take pollution, for instance. The libertarian points out that pollution is a violation of individual rights,
namely, of those whose lungs or other property ends up deteriorated
because of the pollution. In principle, therefore, tort action is an available option: find the guys who did it, and sue them! But if your stand
of fir trees is dying from acid rain, which of the immense number of
polluters whose activities may have contributed do you sue? This is
tough not only because of the enormous difficulty of identifying the
appropriate culprit but also because of the need for verifying the
causes, which take an enormous amount of scientific research.

On the other hand, if the Chamber Music Society is going to turn a
loss unless it gets contributions from the membership, how much
should *you* contribute in particular? In the latter case, the answer is
relatively easy. You size up the need, you divide by the number of
known members likely to contribute, and you then consult the intensity of your affection for chamber music in relation to the size of your
wallet. You contribute that amount, and you wait and see what happens. If the management has to pass the hat again, you repeat the
process. Everyone can "free ride," of course—once. Then there will
be no chamber music concerts next year and your problem will be
solved by elimination. You choose!

Meanwhile, if it does survive and you were one of the ones who contributed, you get both the satisfaction of having the concerts and the satisfaction of knowing that you were one of those who enabled it to do so. A community of dummies won't be able to manage this level of sophisticated generosity. But a community of intelligent people can and does. (The example here is taken from real life, by the way.) The story is repeated all over the affluent parts of the world, and the decision-theoretic claim that "rational" people won't be able to manage it is an absurdity and an insult.

There is a further method worth mentioning. Suppose you wish to get a certain kind of public good going, and you know that it is unlikely that it can be commercially workable on ordinary terms. On the other hand, you suspect that many people will subscribe or donate, provided that they think enough others will go along so that their money won't be wasted. How do you proceed? You collect pledges to contribute, convertible to cash on the condition that enough pledges are collected to do the job; if they aren't, the costs of collecting the pledges are all you're out. The person doing this, or her backers, is gambling: she thinks the chances of success are enough to justify the effort, and if things don't work out, too bad. The point is that no contributor of a pledge can then reason in the manner described by the Assurance Problem. She isn't going to lose anything if not enough is collected, and if enough is, then hers is going to be put to good use, because they'll stop collecting when they get enough. (Of course, no fund-raiser will ever admit to getting "enough". Instead, he will find a useful way to expand the project and throw in a dandy reception for all contributors with the leftover proceeds.)

The size of the problems facing a modern state may make it seem as though any informal, nongovernmental solutions of the kind mentioned here are sure to be ineffective or unavailable. One reason this is so widely thought is that the question is begged: these are indeed problems "facing a modern state"—*of course* the state has to do something about them, for that's whose problems they are! (This attitude is a national disease in Canada; Americans are not far behind.) But it's not true. Some of the state's problems are indeed problems we wouldn't have if it weren't for the state, to be sure. But otherwise, the problems in question are problems facing us, facing people as members of large societies. It is part of the inherent dynamic of government that it just loves to take on our problems. And having unlimited terms of reference, it of course gets what it wants. But we have to realize that state action is only one solution among others, and the fact that state action is virtually certain to be inefficient, often extraordinarily inefficient, is surely an excellent reason for considering the alternatives.

A Note on the "Minimal State"

Nozick argued that the only justifiable function of the State was protection of individual rights, specifically from individual violations requiring protection by the use of force. This was the "Night-Watchman State" of nineteenth-century liberalism. Earlier, we saw that the character of his argument for the Minimal State would not, if it works for its main intended purpose of refuting anarchism, suffice to show that no more than the minimal state is justified. If Nozick's argument is in fact a species of public-goods argument, as seems plausible, then it is worth mentioning that such arguments simply can't be counted on to justify no more than the Minimal State. They might, in the end, justify less—anarchism will win! But if they justify the State at all, they will likely justify more.

Chris Morris has well argued for this conclusion in a recent paper.[6] He asks, "Why is it that the state should enforce voluntary agreements among people?" correctly replying that "Hobbesians . . . will justify state enforcement of contract only insofar as it produces benefits for all . . ." and then observing: "It turns out that enforcement of contract, as well as prevention of fraud, have collective benefits and are (impure) public goods. . . . However, regulations concerning product safety, product standards, and the like may also be rationalized thereby. And so may be conditions on enforceable contract. . . . The state may be justified in imposing conditions on the agreements it is willing to enforce."[7]

If one is to object to the State in its further, welfare-state activities and the like, then, Morris suggests, "Hobbesian defenders of the minimal state may now wish to argue that the inefficiency of state provision of public goods, our apparent inability to control states, and their tendency to redistribute to the wrong groups (e.g., the powerful and the wealthy) may suffice to condemn the welfare state as well as the liberal minimal state. . . . It may be that the state is so inefficient in *all* its functions that anarchy is yet preferable, the disadvantages of the Hobbesian state of nature notwithstanding. Supporters of the minimal state should certainly not suppose that the state is more efficient at providing the services they favor (e.g., defense, police protection) than others (e.g., welfare services, regulation of industry). Casual acquaintance with the U.S. Department of Defense does not leave an impression of particular efficiency."[8]

The arguments do not prove, of course, that a further state is justified nor that even the minimal state is unjustified. But they do suggest that we would have to be fairly selective in our account of what could or could not be done by a state if our argument is, as ours is, ultimately Hobbesian. The points about efficiency, however, are suggestive. What they suggest is that the State might well do a lot less.

A Tale of Three Rules about Mutual Aid

Once upon a time there were three ordinary blokes. B1, the first of the three, had read the New Testament and went about endeavoring to do unto others as he would have had them do unto him. B1 had some hard times. For one thing, there were a fair number of others who didn't want to be done unto as B1 would like to have had done to him, and this caused a certain amount of embarrassment. And then there were annoying people who took B1 for a merry ride, for B1's beneficence was unconditional. He shelled out unto seventy times seven, and then, of course, he went broke. B1 died rather young in the poorhouse, and he did not enjoy eternal life, for it turns out that there was none.

B3, on the other hand, was a realist, which as usual with people who think of themselves that way meant that B3 was pretty much of a cynic. *His* rule was to do unto others as they do unto you. If they were nasty to B3, B3 was superb at being equally so right back at them. B3 had read his Axelrod but had forgotten about the first part: start by being nice, and *then* do what they do. The people B3 encountered in life had the same view of things as he did, and had also forgotten the same bits. Things didn't go very well for B3 either. He lived a bit longer than B1 but not much, for of course nobody would lend a helping hand to B3, knowing they could count on his nonassistance at all times. He died one nice day for lack of a ride to the hospital.

B2 lived by the Silver Rule, which says: "Go out of your way a bit to be helpful, and don't stop at just once or twice, because it might take a while for the others to get the idea—but don't make a fetish of it either. Eventually they'll come around, and when everybody is into the habit of helping when it'll do a lot of good for the other fellow and won't cost a lot, then we'll all be better off in the end." And they were, and he was. And B2 lived a long and useful life, died in pretty good financial condition, and was much admired and respected by his fellows, and for good reason.

The Silver Rule is where Prudence crosses paths with Morality. B2 does good unto others but expects a return on his investment. Not that he has his eye always fixed on the dollar signs in the distance when he gives a dollar to a beggar or spends a bit of extra time drawing a nice clear map to show a stranger how to get to the public library. But B2 has his limits. When the ne'er-do-well comes around for the sixth time with palm outstretched, B2 rises to a certain eloquence in telling him where to get off.

Is there a *positive right* to the assistance of one's fellows? A tricky question, and if regarded as a question about our *fundamental* rights, then best answered in the negative. On the other hand, though, the totally unhelpful person needs a couple of earfuls. He's out to lunch! In the world we live in, no one can reasonably expect to get along totally without the assistance of others, over and beyond what he or she may have contracted for in his or her market dealings. We cannot literally take out an insurance policy on life in general, because nobody would know how to make it out or administer it. But we can do the next best thing, which is to invest, in good B2 fashion, in good works. To be generally disposed to assist one's fellows when they are in need is virtuous, not in a merely conventional sense but rationally: that is, it is a disposition that it is rational to positively reinforce in others and in oneself. The rule is that the amount of help the others can be reasonably expected to derive from your efforts at assistance is well in excess of the amount of trouble it costs you to render it. Measuring the "well in excess" variable is a matter of Aristotelian intuition, and here we need make no objection to the concept. With any luck, it won't matter if you err this way or that a good deal of the time.

The probability that you will some day benefit from the assistance of the very person you have helped, if that person is a total stranger, is not high. But the probability that you could very well benefit from the assistance of *some* stranger in the not-too-distant future is very high indeed, unless you are a true recluse. If people generally are like that, then the probability that the next stranger will be helpful rather than the reverse is high. In such a regime you will have made a good investment. Rational people will live by the Silver Rule. They will adopt a disposition that has the same structure as that on which they renounced the use of force for the attainment of their private ends. Everyone will reasonably expect everyone to be tolerably helpful. As rules go, this one can't easily be improved upon. The totally helpful person is virtually certain to turn into an intolerably meddlesome person, and the totally unhelpful person will richly deserve the cold shoulders of his fellows.

A Note on Symphony Orchestras

In many countries governments have a penchant for supporting the arts at public expense. Underwriting this disposition with libertarian principles is a good deal more difficult. It is true that many voters will also vote in favor of such support, but here the majorities are a lot smaller than in the case of the Ontario Hospitalization Insurance Program; and one can be forgiven for wondering whether their hearts are in it, or whether there is perhaps a larger bamboozlement factor to worry about. It is more difficult not to sympathize in this area with such libertarians as John Hospers, who says "what they are advocating [state support of the opera] is nothing more nor less than legalized plunder."[9] And considering the nature of tastes in this area, there is the further thought that it looks very much as though a public support scheme would bring it about that the poor are subsidizing the well-to-do, rather than vice versa. Whatever there is to be said for subsidies in the other direction, it's very difficult indeed to see what there is to be said for them in this one!

No doubt some, especially the artists involved, will put it down to education: let's improve public taste by forcibly depriving them of enough of their incomes so that a little of it can be returned to them in the form of subsidized opera tickets. Neat, huh?

CHAPTER 18

Insurance Arguments and the Welfare State

ENDS SUCH AS the universal attainment of a certain level of education, a universal minimum level of income regardless of desert, the extension of same into old age, a rather high level of medical attention, and equality of opportunity in employment are regarded by many as requirements of *justice*. It is difficult to see how any of these could be so regarded if justice is a matter of *fundamental human rights*, no matter how generated and especially if generated by a social contract theory.

It makes more sense, and is much more nearly in accordance with what people say, to try to generate these things out of *insurance arguments*. Such arguments do not involve any claim to rights. Their premise is simply that the things in question are sufficiently important from the point of view of any person that she would do well to take out insurance against the prospect of being without them.

Do we, it is then asked, really want to throw ourselves entirely upon the tender mercies of the free market for these essentials, without protection against the exigencies of life? These in particular include unexpected high health costs, job loss not due to culpable incompetence, inability to make a living due to such things as desertion by spouses on whom one was dependent, being suddenly left with family in one's sole care, or just plain unemployability due to the current situation of the job market. As to education, it has to be realized that this is a benefit for others as much as for the child, who is thereby far better equipped to make its way in life when he or she becomes an adult. The insurance here is almost as much insurance for the others who need to rely on people's being able to read and write and operate with tolerable intellectual efficiency in the commerce of daily life as for the parent, who might otherwise be unable to secure that level of competence in her children.

We asked whether our typical rational adult would take out insurance against these things. If she would, then the further move to State involvement leans on premises about efficiency and certainty. If the State guarantees the benefits, there is no worry about the insurance company's going broke or making an unfortunate mistake in your case, and the like. And if everyone is covered automatically, economics of scale are realized. The resulting insurance will be cheaper and better, then, if it is universal. But if the benefits are worth it to everyone, then those accepting them without paying for them would be free riders of the culpable variety. Thus, the insurance may be financed out of taxation.

The Libertarian Reply

But here the libertarian has an answer that is, it seems to me, at least abstractly very compelling indeed. The answer takes two parts. First, it points out that the alternatives of "throwing oneself on the tender mercies of the market" and having sufficient insurance against these things are not exclusive alternatives and never have been: one can *both* throw oneself on the market *and* protect oneself against the exigencies in question, namely, by taking out free-market-generated insurance against whatever exigencies you are inclined to feel the need of protection from.

Second, there will be the question of whether the private market can supply "enough" protection, especially for those who "can't afford" it. The reply to these important challenges would go as follows:

(1) Compulsory protection may not be "enough" either: certainly we will be able to find, for any level you care to name, some individual who wants more; and it is difficult to see how any premises that allow scope for freedom could claim to identify a "correct" amount for all and sundry.

(2) The cost of this protection in a compulsory scheme is thrown on all whether they wish to pay that much or not; yet surely no contractarian argument could yield a principle that could be foreseen to require some people to pay for things they don't want, whether they like it or not and independently of any perceived value *to them*.

(3) Nobody advocates such measures independently of democratic procedures. The proponent of compulsory social insurance always insists that the scheme would be popular with the voters and would be illegitimate if it were not so. Let us suppose that it is highly popular, then. But then, if the value of such insurance is as great and if it is

as popular as the argument requires, it would *also* be possible to form a private insurance scheme with essentially the same schedule of costs and benefits, but which extended only to all those who were interested in sharing in those benefits at those costs. So why would we have to go all the way to the compulsory scheme, which is bound to have serious problems with those who really aren't interested, with inequities in administration of various kinds, and so on?

A fairly interesting approximation in the real world would be afforded by comparing the American Blue Cross/Blue Shield schemes, which are noncompulsory (at the government level, but not, of course, in many areas of private or public employment) with the Canadian system, which if not out-and-out socialist, is substantially equivalent to socialism in its effects. As John Kenneth Galbraith remarked of the American versus the Soviet industrial system,[1] a visitor from Mars would be forgiven for not seeing all that much difference between their respective health systems. The visitor in question, however, when he heard about individual differences and such, might quite possibly prefer the American version. Yet the resident of Canada prefers the Canadian system, which is also envied by many Americans. The example bears closer consideration.

The point about this last argument is that it shows that some necessary conditions of the acceptability and workability of the compulsory scheme under consideration are such that a noncompulsory scheme *must* be possible offering the same advantages but without the disadvantage of being compulsory. And so it merely remains to point out that one who was contracting for general social arrangements could not be understood to consent to arrangements requiring us to pay costs for *unnecessary* benefits.

This last argument is, then, a dominance argument. It says that from the contractarian point of view, libertarian systems dominate their alternatives. The fulcrum of such arguments is that rational persons can't be in favor of outcomes that, by definition, they are not in favor of. It's pretty difficult to knock that principle, I should think. And so it seems that, at least abstractly, the argument goes through pretty smoothly.

Insurance and Charity

Notice that the argument I have put into the mouth of the advocate of compulsory social insurance is *not* an appeal to current intuition at any level. Now, many people do think that another aspect of the welfare state, viz., its catering to the down-and-out independently of ability to pay, is itself a reflection of concern for justice. Libertarianism, including the contractarian-generated version of libertarianism being explored here, certainly rejects this particular "intuition." In principle, on this view, concern for the down-and-out is a matter of charity, not justice.

But we now have another interesting factor to consider: how *popular* is charity for these particular ends? At first sight, this may seem an irrelevant question. Justice is not decided by popularity polls, after all. If even one single person is being made the victim of highway robbery in order to help the poor, then injustice is done and we ought not even contemplate a system involving it. Right? Well, not so fast!

Let us suppose that practically all persons are as altruistic as they claim to be. If so, it's hard to see why a voluntary scheme wouldn't also provide the benefits for the very poor that compulsory schemes currently (are alleged to) provide. And if, on the other hand, they are not that altruistic, then it's puzzling that majorities always vote for schemes with such features—unless, as I suspect, they think that they themselves are getting some free insurance out of it. We will deal with that possibility in a moment.

One more piece in this particular puzzle may also be mentioned at this point. Thomas Nagel, the title of whose well-known review of Nozick, "Libertarianism Without Foundations," formed part of the motivation for this book, observes that "Nozick would reply that such ends can be achieved by voluntary donations rather than by compulsion, and that people who are well-off and who deplore the existence of poverty should donate significant portions of their assets to help those who are unfortunate. But this is not more plausible coming from Nozick than it was coming from Barry Goldwater. Most people are not generous when asked to give voluntarily, and it is unreasonable to ask that they should be. Admittedly there are cases in which a person should do something although it would not be right to force him to do it. But here I believe the reverse is true. Sometimes it is proper to force people to do something even though it is not true that they should do it without being forced. It is acceptable to compel people to contribute to the support of the indigent by automatic taxation, but unreasonable to insist that in the absence of such a system they ought to contribute voluntarily. The latter is an excessively demanding moral position because it requires voluntary decisions that are quite difficult to make. Most people will tolerate a universal system of compulsory taxation without feeling entitled to complain, whereas they would feel justified in refusing an appeal that they contribute the same amount voluntarily. This is partly due to lack of assurance that others would do likewise and fear of relative disadvantage; but it is also a sensible rejection of excessive demands on the will, which can be more irksome than automatic demands on the purse."[2]

This interesting argument deserves specific comment here and has considerable relevance to the issue before us. But we should factor out two strands in it. (1) The first is a claim about human psychology, pure and simple: people find voluntary giving irksome when they would not particularly mind automatic deductions for the same purpose. (2) The second is the application of this to moral argument. The claim is that it is *unreasonable* to impose this "irksome demand on the will" as compared with simply imposing a tax.

The psychological claim is intriguing, true, and important. The moral argument is shabby, corrosive, and so outlandish that it could be offered only by people who already believed in the antecedent justice of taxation for these purposes and are so enamored of the State—as is almost everyone nowadays, after forty years of the welfare state—that their moral imaginations have been reduced to pudding.

Everyone who has been involved in the performing arts knows of the superior advantages of subscriptions over single tickets. You sell a subscription once, whereas you have to sell the single tickets each time a performance comes up. The amount of effort involved for the seller is scarcely any different. The psychological principle involved is one that can be utilized by all sorts of sellers, good and evil alike. But it also suggests a simple answer to Nagel's argument at the level it *seems* to be pitched: those who are so upset about the poor that they are inclined to vote for a scheme that would deprive them compulsorily of 25 percent of their incomes for the rest of their lives have but to sign up with Charity, Incorporated, whose friendly bankers will be delighted to see to it that that amount is painlessly and automatically deducted from their accounts every month.

The writer, in fact, subscribes to a scheme for feeding the poor with precisely that feature (though in considerably lesser amounts!) Every month I have admirably made my modest contribution to this worthy cause. When I show up at the Day of Judgment, it will be noted that I have contributed a quite remarkable amount for the poor, which I will blushingly acknowledge—while noting mentally that in many of those years I had forgotten all about it! The Supreme Justices, however, will properly award me my due share of positive psychic reinforcement for this beneficence, which it really is, after all, just as much as if each month I had reached for my checkbook and contributed the same amount. The hungry have been equally well served by the automatic system (better, actually, because the Canada Trust never forgets!), and I have saved myself a great deal of nuisance. If Nagel's *argument* depended on this by now elementary administrative point, his problem is simply that he hasn't learned about late twentieth-century technology; I commend him to the Canada Trust Company, and we are done with the argument!

As for the moral argument, however, that's another matter entirely. The thought that the amount of nuisance involved in giving a voluntary donation for a worthy cause is so great as to justify resorting to armed robbery instead, if that is what it is, is surely too bizarre to be entertained seriously for two seconds. If feeding the poor *is* a matter of charity, then this factor has no weight at all; its moral considerability is absolute zilch. If taxation is the equivalent of armed robbery, then its use for what ought to be charity is a violation of justice and that is that.

Taxation is not usually *thought* to be the equivalent of armed robbery, and it is one of the virtues of Nozick's book that it has made us face up to the question what the difference is. Neither Nagel nor anyone else really thinks that armed robbery is quite all right so long as the ends for which the proceeds are used are good enough. ("Stick 'em up!" "Huh?—Oh, right, he's collecting for Harvard Graduate School again—where'd my wallet go, honey? . . .") You *have to* have a good argument here, once the question has been raised. The natural thought that anything the State does must be okay, especially if it is a democratic state, will not do, and once it is seen that it won't, then this Nagelian argument has to be put firmly to rest.

As we saw, Nagel noted that the phenomenon he discusses "is partly due to lack of assurance that others would do likewise and fear of relative disadvantage." Agreed. But this fear is either justified or unjustified; and it is justified only if the others have a *duty* to contribute, which is the very point in question here. It cannot be argued that they have a duty in order to make it easier for you to pay! Something further is needed. So let us see what the prospects are in some other direction.

By way of introducing this "other direction", let me take off the table a point mentioned earlier: "It's puzzling", I suggested, "that majorities always vote for government-fostered health-care schemes with such features—unless, as I suggest, they think that they themselves are getting some free insurance out of it." Is it possible that they are right in so thinking?

Their main reason, to be sure, is just a fuddle-headed mistake. The fact that A does not pay at the door each time he enters the doctor's office or the hospital certainly doesn't mean that A doesn't pay for what he's getting. If it's tax-financed, he may be paying a lot more than if he had simply paid at the office each visit. But it's surely worth asking whether he might be paying appreciably less.

Overwhelming Majorities and Administrative Overhead

An interesting and, in context, important question. But it should be appreciated that this looks very much like a question with empirical ramifications. Let us distinguish between two aspects of the issue, one of which is not empirical, being a conceptual issue of moral or political principle, and the other of which at least seems to be.

The conceptual aspect is as follows. Let us suppose that some institutional arrangement is extremely popular. A majority on the order of 95 percent, for instance, would vote for continuation of the institution approximately as it presently exists, as compared with reverting to private initiatives, at least as they have been perceived (with some evidence) to have been. Such is the case, quite likely, with the Ontario Hospital Insurance Program (OHIP) vis-à-vis the set of voters in Ontario. Suppose also that of the remaining 5 percent, nearly all would in fact purchase insurance at approximately the prices that they are in fact paying in taxes for the OHIP scheme. It would then be in principle possible, though to be sure difficult in practice, to enable the few remaining persons to opt out of the program and be relieved of a proportionate share of their taxes. That would seem to satisfy the requirement of unanimity satisfactorily enough, at least so far as results are concerned. (Some of those 5 percent might be die-hard libertarians. But this fact, obviously, can have no moral significance in itself.)

Now, the plot thickens. Doctrinaire libertarians urge that governments can't do anything right, because bureaucrats, with no personal stake in efficiency, will expand their empires without expanding services to the public, etc., etc. And in ample numbers of cases, what they say is true. But we do not live by doctrine alone; all such beliefs are subject to counterexample. And here's an interesting one, at least apparently: the administrative costs of OHIP are reported to average about 4 percent of gross, whereas the administrative costs in American private insurance companies average about 15 percent. Admittedly, the American system is a hodge-podge mixture of public and private, managing to combine the disadvantages of each in remarkable degree, contributing to the world's most expensive medical system for far less than the world's best public health. And there is the question whom to blame: are the failings due to the free-enterprise component, enabling doctors to charge what they please? Or are they due to the public components, enabling those same doctors to charge much more than they would if they faced a genuinely competitive medical system? Or the tangle of options and paucity of clear information to the consumer, thus contributing to the enormous overhead? There is evidence to support each view.

Whatever the case, it is not easy to blame Canadian voters for preferring their publicly run system. One can't blame people for continuing the public system with their votes when they note that if they must suddenly go to the hospital for some terrible disease, they'll at least emerge with no personal financial burdens, no matter how expensive their treatment; whereas their counterpart patient across the aisle, who came from Illinois with the same malady, will emerge with a bill for $158,000 to worry about.[3]

If it came to that, this same voter would *not* vote in a system requiring her to shell out another 40 percent of her income to support hospitals in Pakistan or Novosibirsk, even though the people in those places have much the same array of medical needs that we do. Not for the voter—except in the rhetoric of political sermons—the doctrine that there are universal human rights against the affluent, of which, to her surprise, the typical Ontario voter turns out to be one. But this voter is definitely impressed by a good buy in insurance, and if OHIP provides it, who, as I say, can blame her for keeping it going?

It is a characteristic of government-run insurance that it extends its benefits to those who can't afford the premiums as well as to those who can. The destitute and the undeserving are indiscriminately admitted to hospitals in Ontario, along with the well-to-do and the hardworking middle classes. The more affluent among them probably have extra insurance enabling them to get single beds or at least double rooms rather than wards, to be sure (this gives the student newspapers, obligatorily socialist in their political leanings, something to complain about); but so far as the services of expensive doctors, x-ray technicians, and senior nurses are concerned, the poor get much the same service as the rich.

Well, who pays for it all, and how much? It would be very hard to answer that, in fact, but it is much more than just a reasonable conjecture that most people pay for pretty much what they get. To be sure, it is characteristic of modern tax systems in advanced countries that it is virtually impossible to determine who pays what. For example, the high income taxes of high-salaried professional people are undoubtedly among the factors that prompt them to earn those high incomes. And who pays the fees of which those incomes consist? Those who buy their services, some of whom are further professionals. But then, they in turn earn their money from still others, and adjust *their* fee schedules in the light of what they know they will pay in taxes.[4] Then there are all of those who earn salaries in the public sector—around half of all the incomes in the United States are now in that sector, and more than half in Canada. But *their* high salaries are paid for out of taxation, and who pays that? Yes, indeed: the factory hands and the carpenters and so on. So it is not easy to answer the question of who is paying what, and whether A is paying A's share or more or less. One has to make a simplifying assumption, even though it is certain to be false in detail: viz., that each person's income is about what it should be, and that the tax system is not distorting it beyond recognition. Then one can determine the total cost of the system, and one can divide this figure by the total population being served. This gives us a figure that we can compare with the person's actual tax outlay. And the results are pretty impressive relative to the costs, by comparison with the partially free-enterprise model south of the Canadian border. If we likewise check this out against the figures about income distribution, we get a figure that one would be able to ask an Ontario voter whether she would be willing to pay if she had her choice. Most, I conjecture, would do so, especially if asked to choose between the three alternatives: (1) that amount, with OHIP-level benefits; (2) American-style Blue Cross, with its level of benefits; and (3) go it alone, sans insurance.

The existence of the latter option, at least in principle, is important. James Buchanan, discussing the problems raised by the use of unanimity rules in large public-goods contexts, points out that "if those persons who do not choose to join in collective arrangements under which all cost-sharing decisions are to be made unanimously . . . can be excluded from any enjoyment of the subsequent benefits of public-goods provision, Pareto optimality or efficiency will tend to be attained voluntarily even in the pure public-goods cases."[5] This would not be terribly difficult to do for a scheme like OHIP, and in fact an opt-out scheme would be quite practical. If we suppose that almost nobody would opt out, then it is reasonable to argue that the whole scheme fits the requirements of liberty.

Consider now the difference between the 4 percent administrative overhead in Ontario and the 15 percent overhead in, say, California. You can serve a lot of patients with that kind of money. So let's put that 11 percent down to the costs of servicing the destitute. Is this, then, unfair to the working classes? (Let us include in those the professionals and the managerial classes, and in short virtually everyone who has income sufficient to live on.)

Well, it certainly *would* be, were it not for two further factors. (1) In the first place, it is unclear that the system could be run as efficiently if it had to discriminate against the poor. After all, a lot of that 11 percent extra administrative cost in the American system is spent on the wages of those who are busy booting out the poor from the hospital gates, or doing all the paper work involved in making sure that only A *pays for* the services performed for A (justice, remember?). Perhaps, then, a good deal of the cost of servicing the poor is absorbed in the saving made possible by servicing them without bothering to try making them pay for it!

(2) And in the second place, there is the rather important fact that most Canadians don't *mind* seeing the health of the poor taken care of and are perfectly willing to have a small extra charge added to their health bills if that's what's done with the money. Of course, my conjecture that they don't mind *is* conjecture, but it is not without empirical support. I literally don't know *anyone* who begrudges this portion of the tax bill, for starters. Moreover, a couple of decades of acquaintance with the contents of Canadian newspapers adds a fair amount of support to this hypothesis. True, most Canadians evidently think that the poor have a *right* to health care at public expense. This, on the view urged in this book, is a mistake. But on the other hand, on that same view people are entitled to think what they like, and that is what they do think. Besides, there is plenty of evidence that Canadians are a fairly generous lot of people, like affluent people in most places on this earth—especially if those places have occasional stints of −40° weather to remind them of the inadequacy of the isolated human individual in the face of nature.

But Canadians are not unique, though they may be a little more generous than most. When the television sets bring us graphic evidence of starvation in distant places, not only Canadians but also Americans, Englishmen, Frenchwomen, Germans, and Scandinavians reach for their checkbooks, and in short order the problem is not where to find the food but how to get it through the so-called "socialist" bureaucracies in those faraway places so that the starving can actually be fed. It is not plausible to think that this level of generous sentiment is due to the pernicious influence of socialist philosophers.

Let us suppose, then, that we add together the force of these two considerations: the administrative efficiency of catering to those who can't pay right along with those who can, and the charity factor. Now, suppose that these factors between them bring it about that virtually every person treated is treated by someone whose services are paid for by someone willing to pay the insurance costs of a system that intentionally treats that person, whether it be the sick person himself or someone else. What case is there, then, for the thesis that a gross violation of rights is going on?

One can imagine it otherwise. For instance, if most Canadians were Scroogelike in their attitudes toward the poor, and if the administrative costs of a publicly run system were at least as high or higher than would be encountered in a private-enterprise insurance system, then such a case could be mounted, and the public system would run into heavy weather at the hands of thinkers such as myself. But as things evidently are, I see little reason for libertarian complaint.

In 1986 there was a brief doctors' strike in Ontario, ostensibly occasioned by the Liberal government's withdrawal from them of the privilege of "over-billing", the practice of charging the patient a bit more than the official public schedule of fees allows and billing for the difference. (It was said by many doctors, however, that the strike was occasioned even more by various frustrations of medical practitioners, some real and others no doubt imagined, who felt increasingly under the thumb of the system's administrators.) The majority of those doctors didn't practice over-billing anyway, in fact, and participated in the partial strike only out of sympathy. And most of them felt relieved when they went back to work with the issue not resolved in their favor (except that in 1987—what do you know?—the government not only brought the fees almost into line with what the over-billing doctors had previously gotten, but also issued retroactive bonuses to doctors, compensating them for lost revenue during the strike.) Interestingly, almost none of them took the option of fleeing to the United States, with its substantially higher medical incomes; yet this was an option that really was available to virtually any of them who wanted it. Thus the "Love it or Leave it" slogan, in their case, would have been literally applicable, had anyone chosen to put it that way. Almost no one did, and apparently the medical profession on the whole elected the first alternative.

Given these facts, should we stick with the doctrinaire view of some libertarians that the system is grossly violating all sorts of people's rights? Or should we accept that the system, when all things are considered, respects at least *almost* everyone's rights? And then we'll note that it would be all but impossible to determine whose rights, if anyone's, are genuinely being cut into, which makes it a bit difficult to compensate those who are put out. Even the private insurance companies are pretty happy, for they in fact are handling a large portion of the requisite administration, as well as making a goodly sum on the insurance business in extra services (the single-bed hospital rooms, and so on) permitted by the OHIP system. Surely, something can be chalked up to the credit of a system of politics that seems to have managed to find something in it for everybody, at least in this case. In short, it seems clear that a great many people are manifestly happier with that medical system, and nobody is demonstrably worse off. Pareto seems to be alive and reasonably well in Ontario, for the time being.

None of which is to deny that there is room for improvement. Here are some examples, all of which make good sense from the libertarian point of view. Those who (voluntarily) live manifestly less health-hazardous lives should surely pay less for their insurance: nonsmokers, for example, might well get a tax break, along with those who receive frequent checkups for early detection of things that will be much more expensive to deal with (and with much higher probability of success) than if detected too late. Most people should probably have a sizable deductible portion which they pay for on their own, independently of the insurance component; it could vary with income, from perhaps a hundred dollars a year for low-income earners to a couple of thousand for people in the highest brackets. This would discourage excessive use of the system for trivial ailments and probably bring down the tax bill by a more than equal amount. And methods should be found for motivating efficiency in hospitals. Treatment in the home and use of motel rooms instead of hospital beds for many ailments, for example, could be encouraged. A great deal of emphasis should be put on prevention rather than cure in the many areas where there are pretty well-confirmed hypotheses about how to head off a given malady. And there should be some motivation for encouraging people to think *very* hard on the subject of whether they really want to have been paying all their lives for fantastically expensive methods of prolonging those lives for a few painful weeks or months at the end. (Example: give the patient his choice between that treatment or donating the equivalent to a charity of his choice—or 50 percent of it to his children.) Many of these features would, one would think, be more easily found in private insurance schemes, and schemes with such features are to be found in the United States more readily than in Canada. Perhaps OHIP should mimic the better features of the private system more extensively than it presently does.

This is not intended to be a treatise on health care. It is, instead, intended to mention a number of relevant considerations bearing on the issue of public versus private health-insurance and health-care systems. The sum of these considerations has, in my judgment, the moral that a doctrinaire rejection of public systems in favor of private ones is not *automatically* forthcoming even if one shares libertarian sympathies. Facts really do matter!

A Defense of Charity

Charity, in my view, is an important and useful category in morals, and, moreover, a reasonably clear one. But we have an important criticism of this claim in a recent article by Allen Buchanan. Buchanan considers several ideas about how to distinguish the two. One, to which libertarians would be sympathetic, would stem from the claim that justice concerns only negative duties. But, says he, "Anyone who seeks enlightenment on where to draw the line between justice and charity . . . is unlikely to find much solace in [this] claim, since [it] is as controversial and in need of justification as the very judgments about charity and justice it is supposed to support and explain."[6] In particular, he points out that if one's objection to positive rights is that they involve "unacceptably frequent and severe disruptions of individuals' activities as rational planners or to intrusions that are intuitively unjust", one could reply that although *some* schemes would do this, others would not. For instance, "a right to easy rescue—by a person who can do so without unreasonable cost or risk to herself, cannot be dismissed as either intuitively unjust or as unacceptably disruptive. . . . And . . . the problem of drawing a line between reasonable and unreasonable risks or costs here seems no more difficult than that of applying a 'reasonableness standard' in other areas of the law. . . . For example, self-defense."[7] As the reader is aware, we can accept that example, at least.

But, he goes on, "There is an even more basic reason for rejecting the attempt. . . . The libertarian can be put on the defensive by one simple but powerful observation about what is at the heart of morality: morality is fundamentally (though not exclusively) concerned with avoiding states of affairs that are harmful for individuals. Such states of affairs, clearly, can be avoided not simply by refraining from harming but also by preventing harm. . . . The burden of argument, then, lies initially on the libertarian to show that even though the harmful state may be the same, there is a right not to be harmed by another but never a right to be aided in such a way as to prevent harm."[8] Again, we can accept most, if not quite all, of this. (In particular, the libertarian will be inclined to attribute the wrongness of harm to its violation of liberty, or to interpret "harm" as such violation. But this doesn't matter particularly for the present discussion.) He continues, "In addition, at least part of what makes harmful states a matter of moral concern, namely, a regard for the well-being of individuals, must make beneficial states morally important as well. But if this is so, then strong arguments will be needed to deny that if there are rights to be aided so as to avoid harm, there are also at least some modest rights to be benefited. None of this *proves* that there are positive rights, of course, but it does bring home the initial strangeness of the view that there are only negative rights and makes it clear that the libertarian needs powerful arguments to support his position."[9] Buchanan then proposes a strong counterattack: "I shall show that . . . the thesis that duties of charity need not be enforced must be rejected. . . . The thesis that only those duties having correlative rights may be enforced is a very sweeping yet too rarely questioned claim about the sole condition under which coercion is morally justified."[10] Obviously, this would be something to worry about indeed, if Buchanan can make it out. Can he?

His principal arguments concern our old friend, collective goods: "Perhaps the most serious challenge to it rests on the recognition that enforcement is sometimes necessary to secure contributions to *collective goods*, that in some cases, at least where the collective good in question is extremely important, such enforcement seems morally justified, and that its being justified does not appear to depend upon any assumption that the individuals in question have a moral right to the good in question. . . . It is true, of course, that collective goods problems can in some cases be overcome without recourse to enforcement. . . . Nonetheless, enforcement of a duty to contribute is sometimes the only effective means for securing some collective goods. Hence, unless one is willing to advance the very sweeping and implausible thesis that the need to achieve important collective goods *never* provides an adequate justification for enforcement of duties for which there are no correlative rights, one must conclude that it is false that only rights principles may be enforced."[11]

Not only is the justifiability of the use of coercion to secure public goods widely recognized, he claims, but "the force of such justification does not appear to rest either implicitly or explicitly upon the assumption that there is a right to the good in question. . . . Indeed, it is rather odd—perhaps somewhat hysterical—to say that by not contributing each noncontributor has thereby *violated the rights* of each potential beneficiary of a collective good, including himself."[12] Indeed, "whether or not a share of it is *owed* to each individual and regardless of whether those who fail to contribute could rightly be said to have *wronged* all potential partakers of the good, some collective goods are of sufficient importance that enforcement seems justifiable if that is what it takes to secure them."[13]

Here follow the usual arguments, superbly articulated by Buchanan[14] as to why enforcement might sometimes be needed: how there might otherwise be "free riders", who collect the benefits without contributing, and how indeed even the benevolent might not come through: "since altruism is generally limited, the *scope* of duties to aid which we can expect people to fulfill voluntarily is probably considerably narrower than that of duties they would discharge if those duties were enforced,"[15] and "even if an individual does not himself wish to take a free ride on the contributions of others to a system of aid to the needy, he still may be unwilling to render aid to the needy. . . . He may be unwilling to contribute without assurance that others will do so. . . . (a) He may conclude that it is better to expend his "beneficence budget" on an act of independent charity toward some particular person in need rather than risk contributing to a collective charity in which the threshold of contributions needed for success is not reached. (b) His commitment to being charitable may be limited by a requirement of fairness or reciprocity. . . . collective action to create and maintain systems of aid may falter even if some individuals are significantly altruistic."[16] My negative assessment of this as an argument for enforcement has already been presented.

Buchanan then attributes to this author the following argument: "Everyone has a moral right against coercion. . . . The only thing morally weighty enough to justify infringement of this right against coercion would be another moral right. Therefore, if enforced contribution is ever morally justified, then its justification presupposes that individuals have a moral right to the good in question."[17] And he criticizes this view, which I remain sympathetic to, by pointing out that the right against coercion is either *rigorous* (nonoverridable) or not. If it is held to be the former, then the question is begged "against the nonlibertarian who maintains that in some cases duties to aid may be enforced so long as costs are not excessive and are distributed fairly. For the nonlibertarian can simply point out that his moral intuition is that a virtually unlimited moral right against coercion is simply too unlimited a right to be plausible. . . . he does not find intuitively plausible the much stronger claim that there is a moral right against coercion if this latter claim entails that the only thing morally weighty enough to justify coercion is a moral right."[18] I have also expressed dissatisfaction with appeals to intuition, but let us not worry about that here. What, then, do I have to say about this?

First off, it must be admitted that the "issue" of whether it can be justified to coerce anyone on behalf of anything other than a right of some person strikes me as essentially a verbal one. If we *define* justice as that which is enforceable, and define rights as what is required by justice, or alternatively and equivalently as what are enforceable, then of course if someone claims that we are justified in using force to get people to do x, then that person is claiming that those people have a duty of justice to do x; and if x consists in, and has as its rationale, the securing to someone else of good G, then this, it seems to me, is as much as to say that those who get G have a (positive) *right*, and moreover a right against that very group of persons, to G. To deny this would be to use these terms in a somewhat different—and to me, at least, unclear—sense. Can we unravel this semantic difference to arrive at the substantive issue?

Obviously, it must be possible. We cannot make anything important rest on a choice of language. On my reading of the matter, then, what Buchanan is saying is that we may often coerce—force or intentionally restrict—the otherwise legitimate liberty of A in order to get certain benefits for B. I would still be inclined to describe this as a claim that B has a positive right against A, whereas Buchanan might not. Very well. But anyway, the question is whether he is right about this quite basic moral issue.

Now, it is a striking point about his arguments that if this is the claim, then he is not. For he appeals to public goods arguments. But these are arguments that everyone, *including* A, will benefit if a lot of people, *including* A, are forced to contribute. Thus it is not a pure case of requiring A to do something that will benefit B. So the questions now arise, (1) whether A *wants* the benefit in question, and (2) whether A wants it sufficiently much that A is *willing* to be coerced, if necessary, in order to provide it. If this latter condition is met, then of course the libertarian can cheerfully accept it. Take the case where I get you to wake me up by throwing cold water on me if I am not out of bed by 7:00. No violation of rights here, despite the use of coercion—merely a very wet face on the part of the author in the event of nonperformance.

But I submit that cases of charity are not like this. Agreeing with Buchanan, I would want to say that cases of charity are ones in which the recipients do *not* have the right to the aid being considered, and also where the donors are not eligible for aid of the type in question, or at any rate do not suppose so, and are in fact quite unlikely ever to be. It would not, therefore, be to their advantage to sign up for contributing aid as part of an insurance pact. Let us now simply add that, furthermore, they are not willing to have people in general be coerced into providing the aid in question. They would be willing, for instance, to sign a paper authorizing deduction of money from their bank account for the indefinite future, until further notice, in order to make the contributions; but that is a self-authorized case of "coercion", if we can call it the latter in any sense.

And so the question remains: is Buchanan claiming that *these* cases, which I would insist are the only genuine cases of out-and-out charity, are eligible for coercion? And if he does, how can he deny that he is in effect maintaining a right on the part of those aided to the aid in question?

I agree with Buchanan that "the libertarian must discharge two difficult tasks." "First, he must clearly specify *which* basic moral rights would be violated by all attempts to enforce any duties to contribute to important collective goods or to enforce duties of beneficence. . . . Second, he must provide a coherent and plausible *justification* for the claim that these moral rights do exist."[19] I suggest that the right in question is simply the basic right of liberty—though I deny, as we have seen, that *all* enforcements of collective goods violate that right. And I have provided an argument, at any rate, for the basic rights claim in question (in Part Two). So I now wish to put the ball in the other court: is Buchanan going to maintain that there is a basic right to force some people to do things simply for others, with no direct or indirect self-authorization of the use of force in question? And is it, in fact, even unintuitive, let alone implausible, to maintain that there is no such right?

Libertarians have quite rightly pointed out that a very strong system of positive rights such as those insisted upon by socialists (one much stronger than that Buchanan argues for) suffers from what they and most people—I hope!—would see to be the defect that they make charity *impossible*. If, whenever some cause is worthy enough to prompt generous people to acts of charity, the State instead descends on them, gun in hand, to collect before they are even asked, then charity no longer exists. Tibor Machan, for instance, argues, "In morality it is not generally possible that any act of compassion, kindness, generosity, honesty, decency, and so forth be undertaken unfreely, under coercion. Rather, moral conduct must be undertaken as a matter of conscience and free choice; otherwise the act loses its moral worth. A society that forces its citizens, under threat of punishment, to help the less fortunate is less, not more, compassionate."[20] Generalizing this to *all* "moral conduct" won't do, if this were meant to include any enforcement of what morality tells us to do. But there is a narrower sense in which it will do, for to act from moral motives is not to act from threat of force, to be sure. But I have attempted to establish the reason for confining enforcement to negative rights. In my and Machan's way of talking, an "enforceable duty of charity" is a contradiction in terms; and the enforcement of the acts in which, as we normally think, such charity consists, is morally unacceptable.

Buchanan goes on to discuss the option of suggesting that while there is no *ex ante* right to charity, yet once an institutionalized system is set up, within which benefits of the type in question are enforced, then we may indeed say that its recipients have the right to it. This would preserve the intuition that we may enforce the supplying of benefits only for those with a right to them. But, he says, though this maneuver is "*consistent* with the thesis that duties of justice are perfect and those of charity are imperfect, there is a sense in which it also *trivializes* that thesis. For what those arguments show . . . is that the distinction between perfect and imperfect duties is in no way a fundamental distinction in ethical theory, but, rather, a shifting one which changes as our institutions change or as we move from one type of society to another."[21] I would agree with this assessment, if that is the particular option taken. But I don't think we should take it. In my view, we must show *first* that the proposed recipients *do* have a right to the things in question *before* we set up the institutions in question. Either that, or we must show that the system in question amounts to a very large-scale equivalent-to-voluntary system. Take my example of the Ontario Hospitalization Insurance Program (OHIP). This, I suggested, is basically, as its title would suggest, an insurance scheme, and only secondarily a charitable scheme; but in both aspects it is enthusiastically endorsed by the overwhelming number of those who involuntarily contribute, with effective compensation for the few who would have preferred not to contribute at that level. Suppose that that description is, near enough, accurate (I don't deny that it may not be, but if it is possibly so, then that is enough for present purposes). Then the rights that indigent Ontarians have against the system are legal rights rather than fundamental moral rights; but they are legal rights that have been properly, voluntarily authorized by those who contribute to their maintenance. Officials within OHIP who then failed to give adequate service to some persons legally entitled to it might well be acting immorally; but the wrongness of their behavior is now dereliction of their duties of office rather than failure to perform moral duties of charity.

Duties of Charity

Should we speak of "duties of charity" at all? What would an "unenforceable duty" be? The suggested answer to this is along the lines laid down by J. S. Mill: that such a duty would indeed be enforceable, but only by such means as verbal admonition, withdrawal of certain kinds of civil benefits such as one's affable company, and, of course, that familiar liberal recourse, the "pains of conscience" of those who share the feeling that they ought to be doing that kind of thing.[22] Mill's view is pertinent here. Regarding shortcomings in such things as charity and other items of moral interest but not strict requirements of justice, he says, "These are good reasons for remonstrating with him, or reasoning with him, or persuading him, or entreating him, but not for compelling him, or visiting him with any evil in case he do otherwise." In an extremely interesting discussion of Mill's doctrine, Peter Dalton points out that Mill suffered exceedingly from remonstrances of this sort from his erstwhile friends because of his notorious connection with Harriet Taylor; yet they were acting consistently with Mill's doctrine.[23]

Finally, Buchanan advances an interesting theoretical claim about the implications for charity of the general type of position that I am advancing in this book: "nothing in the description of [Rawls's] original position either reflects or seems capable of generating a distinction between principles of justice and principles of charity. The same seems true not only of Rawls' theory but of hypothetical contractarian theories generally, including, most recently, David Gauthier's."[24]

But I suggest that there is a perfectly good answer to this. I have argued that contractarianism would underwrite the libertarian idea as the basic moral principle governing the use of force, and that we might, in line with this, in some circumstances utilize broad-based insurance arguments for certain social institutions providing welfare benefits rather than only protections against the use of force. Let us now turn to the subject of *nonenforceable moral duties* in the sense I have just described. Can we "generate" these? I believe we can. Consider, first, what would make a nonenforceable duty nevertheless a *moral* duty on our view. The answer would have to be that there is a universal *basis* for it. In the case of charity in the specifically moral sense, the basis for this would be that we are rendering aid of a kind that any human might conceivably need, aid of a kind that we can sympathize with the need of and, if we ever did need it ourselves, would be glad to have supplied to us. Next we have the arguments, which I take to have been already provided, why we may not use force against anyone to procure the benefits in question. Finally, we can now define a second-level sort of "enforcement": viz., the duty to approve of those who do contribute to the causes in question, even if one doesn't do so oneself. While the duty to be charitable is itself "supererogatory", the duty to approve, as well as the negative duty to refrain from impeding, those who engage in such activity is not quite so supererogatory. It behooves us, as reasonable members of society, to be so disposed. We shall, in fact, make charity a *virtue*, in a quite understandable sense of that hoary term: those who manifest the disposition in question are doing something that we should approve and support, namely, by offering such things as praise and congratulations to those who do them. This is that department of morality in which the carrot rather than the stick is to be employed.

There can be such an institution as a moral virtue in a society only if there is substantial agreement on what is for people's good, of course. In one sense, to be sure, there is much less than universal agreement on such things. However, let us now recollect the Gospel According to Pareto: if everyone in S1 is at least as well off, according to her own lights, as she would be in S2, and at least one person is better off in S1, then the rationally moral agent positively *prefers* S1 to S2—rather than just being indifferent between them. That agent needn't put himself to any appreciable amount of trouble to bring about S1 rather than S2. But he should put himself to that tiny amount of trouble that consists in manifesting approval of those who do bring it about. If people generally have the disposition to favor S1 over S2, regardless of just what particular view of the good the persons better off in the one than the other may be employing, then there is again reasonable prospect of eventually benefiting from membership in the society in which this disposition is cultivated. Those who disagree totally with that concept of what is good, of course, are not required to join in. But those who are otherwise indifferent to it should do so. It is, after all, no skin off anyone's back if charity in this sense is practiced—not even the backs of those who do not share or strongly disavow their concept of the good. (The Jew in the ditch is grateful for the aid of the Good Samaritan, his erstwhile disdainee. There is a lesson for us all in this story, is there not?)

In the case of charity as ordinarily conceived, of course, there is usually all-but-universal agreement about the preferability of the states being promoted. Health, life, pleasure, and opportunity to exercise one's faculties and talents, for example, are goods in virtually anybody's view of the good. That those who trouble themselves to enable others to have more of these than they otherwise would are deserving of our good opinion would seem to most people to be close enough to self-evident to leave it at that; but in case they aren't, we cheerfully propose our contractarian argument on behalf of this conclusion.

The "Social Minimum"

A great many contemporary philosophers and thinkers about our society are of the view that it is a function of justice to provide for everyone in the society an ensured minimum, a cushion or floor, whatever happens. This manifests itself in the form of welfare payments to those unable to work, unemployment insurance for those able to work but unable to find jobs, compulsory pension schemes, and so forth. The minimum wage may also be thought of as a part of this package.

Support for such schemes ranges from appeals to high principle to an assortment of "pragmatic" considerations. The details cannot detain us at length here. For example, the substantial rates of officially recognized unemployment in the past couple of decades in the "capitalist" countries, a maddening problem for politicians and civil servants, is too often pointed to as evidence of the failure of market society to bring about that level of well-being for all that is promised by its apostles, and a justification for unemployment compensation schemes is then attached to this. Some such justifications involve misunderstanding of the "promises" in question. The libertarian, of course, does not promise a rose garden. He claims, instead, that if nobody is artificially forced either to work or to provide others with work, there will be work for all who want it, and that those who do not don't obviously merit payment for their leisure. They do not promise that everyone will be happy with the particular work they are able to get. Such promises are reserved for the socialists to make to their gullible followers.

There is ongoing controversy among economists about the proper diagnosis of unemployment in more or less flourishing modern societies. Libertarians argue, persuasively to my mind, that unemployment is essentially incomprehensible in a genuinely market society, and that the high incidences of unemployment mentioned are due to distortions, largely or entirely the fault of public policy rather than of market forces as such. Evidence in favor of this general view seems to me not far from overwhelming, but it is certainly an issue, and dogmatism is not appropriate. Proponents of the libertarian view can point to many facts. Notable among them is that unemployment is characteristically a problem of people not being able to get "suitable" work, rather than of not being able to get work at all. Thus we have the phenomenon of imported labor in many areas despite high unemployment rates, for instance, and of people's cheerfully announcing that they will remain on unemployment as long as possible and then resume working when their eligibility runs out. And one can point to the distorting effects of union-inspired wage settlements, increasing the costs of goods and artificially restricting employment opportunities.

There can be basic issues underlying this. Many egalitarians and socialists of various stripes will contend that there is a fundamental duty of equality or something of the sort underlying programs of the kind we are now considering. This is ill-conceived in at least two ways. I have discussed equality as an abstract goal of justice in Part Two, and elsewhere.[25] Attempts to appeal to intuitive self-evidence fall strikingly short of universal persuasiveness, and it has the substantial further demerit of being without evident reason. The closest proponents seem to be able to come to an out-and-out argument is the desperate maneuver of proposing to extract from the purely negative premise that no one has *more* claim to this, that, or all resources than anyone else, in the abstract, to the strongly positive claim that all are entitled to some substantial equal amount, or even to an equal portion of all that there is. This is utter non sequitur, of course, and once the fact that this particular emperor is quite devoid of raiment becomes as well known as it ought to be by now, the paucity of further argument will likewise, one hopes, become apparent along with the need for it.

Moreover, this arbitrary premise, that all are somehow entitled to an equal share of whatever there is, if brought in to support a program of a "social minimum," amounts to a case of philosophical overkill. A minimum for all by no means amounts to equality, even if it is an equal minimum—for all those who have to make do with that minimum—and if one is going to shy short of the full bit (which carries with it its own dire problems of definition and, I suspect, of coherence as well[26]), then where is one to stop? The only plausible view to be sought in this direction is somehow to arrive at a theory of basic human needs, and then urge people to see to it that the needs in question are satisfied. You can get somewhere with this: a minimum nutritional complement can be vaguely identified for each person, though it will have to be suitably relativized to the recipient's size and several other factors, and enough shelter and clothing to prevent freezing or severe discomfort, and so on. Where you will get, of course, will not be an equal share nor an equal amount, since at every possible level of analysis needs will differ substantially.

Apart from these problems, a further point looms before us: a society that sets out to define these minima will find itself establishing a materially different set from other societies, notably, the poorer ones. Those on welfare in Canada or California make two or three times the income of a quite non-desperate Mexican. How is it that these people manage to make do with so much less than the "minimum", one wants to know? The minimum somehow, but invariably, managed to end up being a minimum fraction of prevailing GNP, something Mother Nature, who is presumably responsible for the setting of need thresholds, has presumably not heard about.

It would seem that the "minimum" is not simply the minimum for human life, but more nearly the minimum *that their fellows are willing to see the persons in question get on with*. Naturally, we tend to see them through the filter of our perception of what *we* would possibly be able to get by with. Not surprisingly, this turns out to be quite a lot. (I have noted a tendency among my academic colleagues to set the minimum somewhere around the current university level for supporting senior graduate students; equalitarians tend to set the upper limit at about the top of the full professor rank. Precise figures will vary according to the scales current at the institutions of the theorist.)

Few will dissent from the general proposition that poverty, along with disease, is an unhappy thing and that it would be nice if there were none of it, or at least less than whatever there is. Almost everyone, on the other hand, dissents at least in practice from the view that the poverty of every poor person in the world is her own responsibility. And there is not much doubt that the present system tends to be self-perpetuating at least, and likely self-accelerating as well. One wonders how much of the problem would disappear if the particular kinds of efforts to eradicate it made by governments were to disappear as well. A reasonable guess (but it is a guess, not based on precise, currently available figures) is that if 100 percent of the taxes meant for this purpose were eliminated, the decrease in the problem would be at least 50 percent; for this would not only free up that money for private investment that creates new jobs but also might usefully redirect the talents of the numerous well-educated and capable people now administering the funds in question. And it would be interesting to know how much of the remaining problem would succumb to the efforts of charitable people with good ideas about how to do something for those in need. Here, for example, is a newspaper[27] showing a photo of former President of the United States Jimmy Carter nailing a piece of siding to the wall of a house, one of fourteen being put up by himself and several hundred other volunteers for the use of low-income persons, who themselves will put "hundreds of hours" into similar work on both their own houses and those of further poor people. None of this was done with tax money, and the large organization that occasioned the effort is determined that there will be much, much more. In Mennonite communities one sees barns being erected by a large crew of volunteers from the area around. Aren't these better models for helping the poor, if that is what we wish to do, than the current efforts of governments?

As with the case of health insurance, there is the question to what degree expenditures on the "social minimum" are genuine insurance efforts and how much may be attributed to state assumption of charity. Again, we may surmise that measures of this kind are extremely popular with the electorate. But in the case of health insurance, at any rate, there is little reason to think that the size of the problem is in any appreciable degree a function of state efforts to solve it, and of government monetary and fiscal policies; whereas those factors are surely substantial when it comes to poverty.

CHAPTER 19

The Problem of Children

The Problem

ACCORDING TO the libertarian, our rights are fundamentally only negative. This in itself creates an embarrassment, measured against most people's moral beliefs; for a very young child or infant is not going to get very far in this world if left to fend for himself with nothing but negative rights to rely on. Consider an infant left on a doorstep by its distressed parent. If the householders act on their rights and do nothing, there will soon be a dead infant there. Or should we say that a parent who leaves an infant exposed to the elements, without food or shelter, has killed it? If so, the line between negative and positive rights becomes blurred. The idea of negative rights for adults is that they have capabilities to do something about their situations. Left to themselves, competent adults will cope. Not so young children, however.

Most of us suppose that parents, especially, have duties toward their children, and further that people in general have duties of care toward those comparatively helpless humans, duties that go much beyond mere refraining from abuse and misuse—though children are frequently enough abused and misused as well. The sight of a helpless waif standing on a street corner, lost and (so far as it can see) parentless, is enough to move most of us to action, and perhaps also to tears. Among our strongest duties, surely, are our duties to help distressed kids, and indeed to be willing to go to a considerable amount of trouble to do so. It would, as I say, be an embarrassment to the theory were it unable to underwrite these feelings.

Nor is that all. The very expressions 'abused' and 'misused' sug-

gest that children do indeed have rights, at very least the same negative ones enjoyed by you and me. But if our derivation of rights is
contractarian rather intuitional, then we have a problem even on this
front. For infants are not rational creatures eligible for participation in
the "social contract". The rational persons of contractarian theory
need to be fairly competent adults, and not only rational but possessed of considerable personal *powers*. It was, indeed, these powers
and the rational control exerted over them by their owners that made
for the problems that Hobbesian contracts are designed to solve. But
infants are not, or at least not in the same way, part of the problem,
nor can they be part of *that* solution. The contractarian, evidently, will
have to say that infants and young children (at least) do not *have* fundamental rights. (And the same, even more so, for animals, of
course.[1]) Either our theory is going to look wildly contrary to what
most people think, or we are going to have to give this area a careful
rethinking. In fact, I think we will find that things are not so bad as
they may seem.

Nonfundamental Rights

We must begin by observing that in contractarian theory we create
rights, by granting them to people (on condition that they recipro-
cate, of course). To give another a certain right is, as Hobbes put it, to
"lay down" our own liberties with regard to the matters in question.
If I give you the right to cut corners across my yard, that means that I
intentionally refrain from attempting to chase you off or punish you
for doing so, and let you know that I do thus refrain.

If that is the genesis of rights, then clearly any creature can acquire
rights, at least against (and from) particular people. Most of us, for
example, will be disposed to grant rights, not only of nonabuse but of
care, to infants and many animals. If I treat my cat badly on a given
occasion, I complain to myself, on behalf of the cat. The question
must be whether we can expect to generate any *general* rights for children (I leave the case of animals out of the present work). How do we
get, or can we get, the result that people in general, at least members
of our "society", have the kind of duties mentioned?

Children's Rights

Two facts about children stand out in any consideration of the
bearing of morality on them. The first concerns what we may call the
"emotional factor". The main aspect of this is that those who have

children—most people, at least so far—are connected to their own children with emotional ties. These motivations, for typical people, are very strong indeed. Hell may have no fury like a woman scorned, but that woman takes a clear back seat to a woman whose children are seriously threatened. But it is also true that, although to a lesser degree, most of us are emotionally interested in the well-being of children generally. My waif on the streets in the previous example can be anyone's child, and most of us will nevertheless be moved by it. It is, of course, a part of the de facto morality of our culture that people will at least be ready to cluck their tongues at a parent who might get his child into such a situation and ready to offer at least some slight show of sympathy with its plight. But there is surely a considerable basis of natural sentiment for this—as indeed there must be for any really strong and stable moral attitude.

When we insist that we have duties of a strongish kind toward children, most of us, then, are preaching to the converted. Still, this leaves some who have little or none of this natural sentiment, or in whom it has been eroded or perverted. What of those who would abuse their children, for instance? (There are, uncomfortably, many such.) For that matter, what about infanticide?

The second factor of fundamental importance is that infants and young children are not denizens of a separate species of organism from the rest of us. They grow up into adults, recognizably like ourselves. A great deal of the fascination that most of us experience in dealing with children (when they aren't being a nuisance, at any rate!) is due to the ways in which they are recognizably immature adults and adults-in-training—aping our ways with charmingly mixed success, showing the same sort of emotional dispositions, in far less inhibited form, and manifesting curiosities and childish insights mixed with whimsy that tell us much about ourselves, both about what we are and what we might have been.

But these quasi-aesthetic reflections are, of course, just a part of it. The fact is that the children of today, being the adults of tomorrow, are also the producers of tomorrow and the supporters of the aged, and the utilizers of our wisdom, the bearers of the burdens of our errors, and so on. In short, they are the human world of tomorrow, and thus the repositories of much that we hold valuable. —Much, that is, that most of us (practically all of us) hold valuable. So again we have the question whether numbers matter here; and if our foregoing reflections on the welfare state were on the right track, then we may suspect that the answer will again be in the affirmative.

Abortion and Infanticide

The primary and fundamental locus of rights, on the view we are exploring, is in the competent and rational adult. It is their concerns, whatever they may be, plus considerations of social interaction, that generate the general right to liberty that is our fundamental right. Prominent on the list of what is thus protected is our own bodies: to do as we think best with them and our associated faculties, and not have our persons subordinated to the views of others, is essential. If we view the question of abortion from this perspective, then, where must we emerge? Plainly, a human organism before birth is not, as it stands (or rather, snuggles), in a position to claim any rights. The female body in which that fetus lies is the exclusive property of the woman whose body it is. If it is her decision to terminate a pregnancy, then, very little can count against her, except for explicit and clearly made commitments on her part toward other relevant adults, such as her husband. (And even those must be *very* strongly made to reverse this elementary freedom.) Abortion is a plain right of the female person, and there is no scope for "fetal rights" to counteract this liberty.

But is the case the same with her children, once born? I think not. Once detached from the body of its mother, it is no longer true that whatever is done to the fetus is ipso facto done to her. There is now, typically, a sort of emotional umbilical cord replacing the physical one that has been cut, and it will often be much stronger than that physical one. The question before us, however, is: what if it isn't? Suppose that some parent develops a negative disposition with respect to her or his biological offspring, of such an intensity as to incline that parent to terminate the life of the infant?

Few of us will look with equanimity on such a development, to be sure. But we do well to recollect that infanticide has been a recognized social practice in many human societies, not only in much earlier times but in a few societies even now. Infanticide as a method of population control has been frequent, and as a sort of rough eugenic practice perhaps even more so. The Greeks and the Vikings, to cite two, would inspect newborns and, if they found any to be defective, expose them on hillsides. (That this was the usual method of disposing of them is interesting in itself, as it suggest a recognition of the distinction between killing and letting-die, which would be relevant only if they supposed that even newborn infants had something approximating negative rights.) At any rate, the point is that whatever one's instinctive reaction to the contemplation of infanticide may be, it is not a reflection of a universal human feeling, even in the sense of one that has been typical in every culture and society.

This suggests that the circumstances of those societies have something to do with it. And that seems to me to be as it should be. In a society of very limited resources, where life is harsh, people cannot afford to devote those resources to the sickly or lame; in a society where the food supply is just equal to the population as is, expansion of population is everyone's enemy. It is not reasonable to grant strong positive rights to life to all and sundry newborns in such circumstances.

But if we move to an affluent society such as the one nearly any reader will be a member of, things may be different. How different they are in respect of granting rights depends very strongly on one question in particular: are we to suppose that infants are the *property* of their parents? If they are, then it will be difficult to justify social imposition of sharp restrictions on what may be done with them. If they are not, however, the situation is different.

In so raising the issue, of course, I imply that whether or not x is the "property" of someone is decidable independently of law, custom, or rule. But that is misleading. The rules of property are, we think, supportable by reason, and those reasons are in turn independent of such rules. A good reason for regarding x as A's property is that A found it, made it, or acquired it from someone else whose property it was. But all of these are subject to restriction from third-party effects. And in the case of children, there is the complication that ere long they have minds of their own, and by virtue of that will come to have the sort of independent rights that persons have. The interests that the rest of us have in that child will be much modified by the interest that the child herself has. By then, the child will not be anyone's property except her own.

So what is the nature of the property right which it is reasonable to concede to parents before the child becomes sufficiently mature to be an independent holder of rights? In view of humans' enormous potential for third-party effects, there is certainly a large public-interest factor in the construction of these rights. We can reasonably restrict what parents may do in the light of this potential.

There is an additional factor that is more crucially relevant to the question of infanticide in particular. Most of us, I have suggested, regard children with affection and interest. It pains *us* to see children badly treated and also to see them killed. To those who value their children so little as to be inclined to kill them, we are in a position to say that we will take them off their hands, if that is what they wish. The parent can spare himself the burden of raising the unwanted child and save us the pain of seeing a child killed by the simple expedient of letting us have it.

Are these considerations sufficient to justify the threat of force by way of enforcing this rule? Probably not. The hurt we feel upon seeing an infant killed is not injury to our bodies, but to our emotions. For someone to flout our wishes in this regard is more like offense to our opinions than to misusing or taking advantage of us. And the hurt to the infant does not justify restrictive action, as it would if it were a rational agent. "Hurt" is misleading, actually. And for real hurts, we have a different reason to intervene: for if the child is to become an adult, then the hurts done to it now can affect its future well-being as well as its present condition. The public interest in our fellows' welfare is sufficient to justify requiring parents to take proper and nonabusive care of their children.[2]

In no other area of moral philosophy, though, is the contractarian-libertarian line at quite such discomfort in relation to ordinary opinion. It is an emotional matter in part, and that is always something to be wary of; for our emotions may not be shared by those whose actions we would like to control in the light of them. At the same time, the pressure of intense feelings can be virtually irresistible. And for those who would be moved to adopt an intuitionist view at this point, there are the questions we have posed for intuitionisms generally in Part Two to worry about. But it seems to me that the case for a public-interest handling of this matter is strong; perhaps, on reflection, it is also sufficient.

CHAPTER **20**

Freedom and Information

Education: Should We Sell the Schools?

Is EDUCATION a public good? Do the standard arguments apply here? Few will doubt that education is a good, speaking abstractly. But when reaching for our pocketbooks, 'abstractly' is rather lame. The many who don't doubt that education is a good might have second thoughts if asked to pay as they go or, more likely, as their children go. The rational agent, obviously, will make an estimate of the marginal value of more education and decide whether his budget can stand it. And the typical citizen who sends her children to the public school would no doubt be horrified at the suggestion that she pay as she goes.

But that attitude is naïve. Ms. average citizen is certainly paying for her children's education. She probably even knows it. What she doesn't know is just *how much* she's paying, since she may not even see the bill, and in any case, whatever bills she does see are unlikely to tell her the whole truth. For instance, if she owns her house, then she will likely have a property tax bill, and this is likely to tell her what portion of it goes for education. What she doesn't know is how much of all the other innumerable taxes she pays also goes for education, nor of course how much goes for the education of her children. And it would be very difficult or indeed, most likely, impossible even in principle to find this out. The question just how much she pays for education is probably unanswerable.

What isn't unanswerable, however, is how much the education of her children on the average *costs*—costs whoever pays it, that is. And if our parent is an average parent, then she can take it that she's pay-

275

ing about that much, assuming she has the normal number of children (1.9!). So one interesting thing to do would be to see how much she or someone is on average paying, as compared with what current private schools charge. Most parents would be intrigued to hear that education in the public schools tends to cost *more* per pupil than all but rather posh private schools—probably 50 percent more. And does Ms. Average Parent think that her children are getting a *better* education at the public schools? Not likely. It's much more likely that she would be delighted to have them go to a private school, but she can't afford it!

In addition to getting, in all likelihood, a better education at a private school, she would also, in all likelihood, have a great deal more *control* over her children's education in a private school. In the first place, the class her child was in would probably be significantly smaller. Second, she would probably have much readier access to the powers that be in the private school. And third, since she doesn't *have* to send her children there, the school lies under a general threat of withdrawal. If she doesn't like the way things are going there, she can take her business elsewhere. This is the basic safeguard of the voluntary exchange system, of course—and it would be interesting to know what effect it would have on the school system.

What warrant might there be for intervening so thoroughly into the market for an important good like this? That there *is* a market for it is beyond question. The continued existence of private schools amidst such powerful disincentives is sufficient testimony to that. But a further point beyond question, mentioned here because it is so widely questioned, is that *very* few people (in the affluent countries) would do without education on grounds of cost if there were no "public" schools at all. Let us suppose, as there is every reason to believe, that the cost per pupil for better education (for the moment, let the criteria of betterness be those of the person concerned) would be appreciably less. This means that if there were a totally privatized school system, the average person would be paying *less* for schooling, over his or her lifetime, than at present. How many of the perhaps 85 percent of the population of parents who would be able to afford such costs would voluntarily refrain from educating their children in that case?

But the question on most people's minds will be: what about those who *can't* pay? This question resolves into two. (1) The first is: what is the nature of this criticism? Is it being claimed that there is a *positive right* to education, that is to say, that everyone else has the duty to pay for your children's education whether they want to or not? (And maybe whether those children's parents want them to have it or not?) That is the assumption of tax-supported education; clearly, it raises a fundamental point and needs discussion. We shall return to that in a moment.

(2) The other is whether in fact there would be children going un-educated under a wholly privatized regime. (Or rather, not going to school—not quite the same thing!) Let's attack this one first, by way of adding perspective. I shall first assume that a very small fraction of the populace would in fact be seriously unable to finance their children's education. My suggested figure of 15 percent[1] is probably a little high, if anything, but suppose we work with it. This means that if all children were to be educated, an extra 15 percent, roughly, of budget would have to be found for supporting them. Since the saving as against having a public school system would likely be a good deal more than this, it is not unreasonable to suppose that the money can be found. And who would pay it? Several obvious groups come to mind. (1) First, persons sincerely desiring that these children get an education and willing to help fund scholarship support for them; (2) firms and enterprises that might be able to utilize their services, and who could not do so if they were uneducated; (3) people who fear the consequences of children who go without education. (4) To which we can add, the schools themselves, who would like to have some subsi-dized children aboard, as many private schools do even now. And of course the teachers in those schools, who are likely to be people with a certain passion for educating people and a vision of the value of their wares. These educators are likely to be quite persuasive in their pitches for money for this purpose. These schools would appeal for funds, or could increase tuition to those who do pay, for the purpose of accommodating such cases.

Many will nevertheless feel that subsidization of the poor for this purpose would be inadequate. They will likely feel that those who do not contribute for this purpose are free riding on those who do. Are they right? To accuse of "free riding" is, of course, to assume that we are talking about a public good, in the technical sense discussed near the outset of this part. Is it so?

They have a point in one important respect. It is advantageous to each of us—especially the educated among us—that other people be reasonably well educated. We probably believe that others are less of a threat to the public safety if they are well educated (the incidence of murder among Ph.D.s is strikingly smaller than in the general populace!), or less of a threat to something less tangible—the public "tone", perhaps we can call it. Others are easier to talk to and to deal with in many respects requiring communication if they are reasonably well educated. (Except, of course, for the familiar impossibility of discourse between extremely specialized academics, or between any two married persons, especially if they have Ph.D.s.) And so on. And it is definitely not easy to internalize this. The uncouth and the dangerous are not likely to confine the ill effects of these unsavory properties to those who failed to contribute to the worthy cause of educating them.

It is probably at least in part this kind of reasoning that has led thinkers otherwise persuaded of the propriety of private education to propose schemes for funding the education of the poor at public expense in one way or another, without going to the extreme of adopting public schooling in its current form. But certainly there are other considerations that have moved them.

(1) Some will maintain that any scheme of the kind characterized above would have the result that education for the poor is "separate and unequal". If this is a matter to worry about, however, it plainly presupposes that everyone is entitled by right to equal educational opportunities, and that constitutes disagreement on a matter of fundamental principle with the libertarian view. Separateness and inequality are not in principle objectionable on that view.

(2) These same advocates have a problem that will certainly lead to a further disagreement on a matter of perhaps even more fundamental principle. The problem is simple: the world has about five billion people nowadays, of whom only a tiny fraction inhabit even so populous a country as the United States. What, then, about all the others? Is the advocate of universal equal opportunity in education committed to advocating that the American taxpayer fund education for the children of every poor person in the world—all four billion of them? Not likely! Instead, he will have to maintain that a certain minimum standard of education should be maintained by the people of each country in accordance with the means of that country. This solution, then, requires that the doctrine be relativized to nations, thus presupposing a substantial degree of nationalism in the doctrine. The right in question cannot be seriously maintained as a "human right"; rather, it is a "human right" against the other humans in the *country* the human in question happens to live in.

The "liberal" view, as it has come to be called in recent years, is, in short, a Statist view. This would raise the question of how the liberal justifies the State—which may seem a rather large issue to be raising at just this point. Of course it is, but the issue is raised here in a connection that doesn't require an entire treatise to deal with. For there would seem to be only two options. Either the "liberal" in question justifies the State as an agency *necessary to carry out the proposed slate of human rights*, or he takes it that the State is a kind of "existential" entity, a given unto itself—"My station and its Duties" (Bradley)—"Our country, right or wrong!" (Stephen Decatur)—"My mother, drunk or sober!" (a former professor of mine). And here this kind of liberal is in a dilemma. If he takes the first horn, he has no explanation of why the duty to the poor stops at the boundaries of his State. If the rights come first and the State is wholly subordinate to them, then the fact that one's *State* can do just only so much is in principle irrelevant: everyone who can afford it should be sending money off to educate the Sudanese, the Tamils, the Peruvian Indians, and so on—all four billion of them!

But if, on the other hand, the State is crucial and prior, then the liberal is a conservative and should admit it. (This is the view of Roger Scruton, who thinks, with much plausibility in my opinion, that liberals are just inconsistent.[2]) But if he is a conservative, then he is hard put to argue against other states with a different view about how their societies should look. Not *the* State, but *my* State makes it true that we have to provide equal educational opportunities for *our* children. Very well: but then, *your* State could take the line that education beyond what is necessary to read the Bible is evil, self-defeating, and useless.

In a libertarian society those who think that everyone should have a Ph.D., or whatever, are welcome to form a philanthropic association for the purpose of promoting this laudable end. And the fundamentalists are free to blinker as many children as they can get their hands on the parents of. And so on.

This last matter brings up another profound issue. If we allow people real freedom in education, won't they bring up their children in all sorts of absurd or outrageous doctines—at very least, pump them full of ideas quite alien to modern life? (Or perhaps, empty them out of *other* ideas essential to it?) And at worst, what about totally antihumane and antisocial ideas (Nazism, Ku Klux Klan, etc.)?

There are really two issues here, not just one, and we must be careful to appreciate the difference. (1) On the one hand, there is the worry that people will be free to teach their children the *wrong* things; (2) and on the other hand, there is what we might call Balkanization. Vietnamese immigrants will get educated in Vietnamese (language and history both), Mexicans in Spanish, Ukrainians in Ukrainian, and by the time they finish school, they will be unable to talk with anybody but their ex-schoolmates. In larger terms, we shall have a society without unity.

Let's deal with the Balkanization issue first. The objection seems to assume, for one thing, that people don't care about fitting in with the larger society that has taken them on. But that is hardly plausible and certainly contrary to what we know of most groups moving into such societies as those of Canada and the United States. They have come there for a better life, and this better life is available only to those who can interact efficiently with the people already there—people who are not about to learn some other language in order to deal with the newcomers.

In its political aspect, in which the worry is about lack of social unity and such, there is the question whether this is a real worry. In part this hinges on the interesting issue of the *psychology* of Statism, that is, the tendency to ascribe value to one's nation or state, perhaps to "identify" with it, and so on. Precisely why one should do this with anything so mundane as a government is hard to say; most who have these feelings at any very intense level most likely do not identify with government so much as with their fellow x-ians.

But they can still do this anyway, can't they? Patriots can root for their team in international sports competitions, for example. In the crowd at a hockey game one will find rooting for the Canadian team all sorts of people—people of Ukrainian, English, German, Vietnamese, Italian, and any number of other ethnic extractions. One tends to assimilate the customs and the language of those one lives among—without any need for making it illegal not to do so. (And wouldn't the sincerity of those who affected such assimilation, if they were legally required to, be in doubt?)

In any case, there is still the right to be different, if that is what one insists on. And that gets us back to the original problem. Rights come from within. We have the right to be different, *and* the right to exert various influences on those around us to bend to our ways. When a large percentage of the inhabitants are exerting similar influences on behalf of similar ways of doing things, the likelihood is that newcomers will bend in their direction much more than the majority will bend in the direction of the newcomers. And so we end up with *a* society. Anarchistic forces are all one needs, as well as all that are justified. And they have the advantage that you end up with a real society, instead of a society that is artificially fostered by the Canada Council!

This brings us to the other issue: won't full freedom of education lead to the teaching of error, absurdity, or even intellectual depravity? (Not that public schools have been wholly without this problem anyway.)

Obviously, the simple answer to this has to be "Yes." And yet there is a reasonable concern that those so taught will also end up being coerced, or without an appreciation of the rights of others in the community. Let us see.

The Orwin Thesis

Clifford Orwin, in an interesting attack entitled "Nozick's Liberal Utopia", has suggested that the Nozickian defense of "the environment in which people are free to do their own thing" "exemplifies . . . liberalism's penchant for fostering sameness by talking up diversity". Orwin's claim is that in attempting to foster the framework for a vast variety of utopias, "even liberal/libertarian society necessarily constitutes such a community, not just a neutral 'framework' for them." The good life as conceived by essentially anyone, Orwin points out, "is a life fostered in the only way we know how, viz., by gestation within a community whose ideal of the good life it is. But libertarianism tells us that the widest community must be one that fosters *no* particular view of the good life, instead creating only a social framework, the libertarian rights, within which subcommunities could flourish, each promoting its own particular vision." But in view of the outermost structure being libertarian, "the devotion of the members to each community must be strictly voluntary, unblemished by ignorance of the alternatives or of their basic libertarian right rather than fight. Of this right, then, the community itself must advise them."[3] And in so doing, alas, "it compels them to assert what every self-sufficient community must deny, that acting as one pleases comes before devotion to the community."[4] And so, each community must "therefore in the decisive respect simply replicate the 'framework'. They become so many special interest chapters of one and the same Libertarian Legion. . . . So many communities each respecting the same rights as fundamental: what are these but so many versions of the same community?"[5]

This is a powerful challenge to liberal thought of all kinds, and not only to libertarianism in particular. At its maximum, the Orwinian complaint spells the death-knell of liberalism: for what it says is that the liberal idea is impossible, that every true community is conservative, necessarily and inescapably. And he goes on to suggest that if we ask what the libertarian way of life that would inevitably be fostered by a libertarian society consists in, the answer is inevitably going to be, simply—money making! "In it, as to an appreciable extent in contemporary America, the business of the society will be business, and those with great wealth will be the local Gods."[6]

Relief from the Orwinian dilemma is at hand, however, when we contemplate the half-truth in this last affirmation. In America, look at the amazing array of ideals that have managed to flourish. And if money making is so important, why is it that the typical American would be totally unable to name a single one of the fifty wealthiest men in the country, unless by chance one of them had recently happened to do something outlandish enough to get him a place in the news? Why do so many shun it quite deliberately, and why are so many others relatively indifferent to prospects of greater monetary reward? On the other hand, athletic stars and movie stars are known far and wide—but not, certainly, because of their wealth, though it is in many cases considerable.

There is a major problem inherent in the theory regarding the "freedom of exit requirements" for its subcommunities. Children can certainly be steeped very thoroughly in some religious faith at home, then sent to schools within the same faith; and the author is well aware how insulated from contrary doctrine this kind of upbringing can be. Where does the libertarian put his foot down, one wonders?

Yet there are also firm adherants of many faiths and doctrines who are well versed in the teachings of rival bodies of belief. It would be false to say that communities can survive intact only if they are totally closed off from others, or that general knowledge of a requirement that those wanting to leave the faith may do so of their own free will is incompatible with continued wholehearted practice of that faith. Or nearly "wholehearted," since the libertarian view would certainly disallow attempts to proselytize by threat of force. Or to take another example, the exalted spiritual message of the late quartets of Beethoven can be appreciated by people who accept that they have no right to require others to listen, and who know that there are those who find no value in them at all. The musical community nevertheless manages to thrive even in the midst of musical barbarism and cacaphony.

"Primitive societies" are likely to be another matter. Natives in their dugout canoes sporting Sony Walkmans are an anomaly of our age, along with aborigines in painted faces and blue jeans. Respecting the requirement that our interaction with natives not be carried on by force is easy enough (now; it was not so for those who settled this continent). But refraining from contact, however voluntary, that can be expected to alter radically the character of life in the primitive community requires a great deal more understanding and restraint. Do we insist on an inevitably corrosive contact with these peoples? Or should we attempt to keep strictly off, watching their babies die of dysentery from unsanitary water supplies and mass famines when primitive technology can't cope with prolonged droughts? On the libertarian view, it seems to me, these options are available. There is no compulsion, missionary-style, to intervene for their own "good." But what actually to do in any particular case must be very difficult to decide.

Knowledge

Thus far we have been discussing *education*, rather than *knowledge*. Education is training, considerably if not exclusively intellectual training, but training nevertheless. Teaching people to read and write is imparting useful skills without which they will get on with much difficulty in a society where the transaction, at least one side of which involves the conveying of technologically somewhat advanced equipment or services, is ubiquitous. Even the smatterings of history and literature, mathematics and science may up to some point be marshaled under the same heading. Eventually, however, we cross over from education, which promotes the workability of the technologically advanced society, into knowledge, which may or may not have any such object. The universities, which are the primary seats of this kind of activity, are indeed educational institutions while they're at it; but a major part of the teaching even of undergraduates is aimed at imparting intellectual skills whose main use will be, as we say, to add to the sum of human knowledge.

You can never tell when abstract knowledge will turn out to be useful, especially if we employ that very broad sense of the term in which the discovery of the basic technology of nuclear weapons counts as "useful." But does this justify the transplantation of intellectual activity into the *public* sector? Is it plausible to say that new light on the structure of fourteenth-century Italian love poems, or on nonlinear differential equations of the third order, are developments that benefit everyone, from the coal miner to the physiotherapist to the real-estate developer? Do we have the right to force all of these people to support such research, any more than to supply persons of more taste than means with a steady diet of high-quality operatic productions? Not obviously!

Who should pay the cost of basic research, and why? Discussions of the subject of proper government support levels for this kind of thing often take on a somewhat hysterical tone: "we must have more support or we shall fall behind the ____s!" (Fill in the blank with the name of some other nation—preferably Oriental.) But how odd to classify research in theoretical physics or cultural history along with the Olympic games! On second thought, though, perhaps we should say that that is precisely where it belongs, in the sense that the case for genuinely public support of either seems equally weak.

If instead we simply let the chips for such things fall where they may, leaving financial support of these arcane endeavors up to whoever shares enthusiasm for advancing human knowledge, it is hard to say whether research would be funded more or less generously than it now is, but at least it would be funded by the right people. By contrast, what we have now is the spectacle of political leaders engaging in a rather fraudulent effort to persuade the *hoi polloi* that those activities are so much for their benefit, unbeknownst to them of course, that we must require their involuntary support.

Freedom of Speech and the Ideological Marketplace

From what has been said above, it is clear enough that the libertarian will favor that free competition for the minds and hearts of people that has rightly been the pride of liberals since liberalism's inception. And there are indeed interesting questions here. But we should note the general character of these questions: they are, namely, of interest in the *public domain*. If we take the extreme property-rights view of social organization, however, there would be no such domain. Whoever owned the property on which a given exchange of speeches took place would establish the rules of what may or may not be said there, and when. Is this an adequate solution? It is if one accepts the argument that the public domain should be empty. Most will not do so; and insofar as one doesn't, then the problem will remain. Some things said, in some places and in some ways, will infringe on the liberty of others; some will not. Some will be defensible along the line taken by J. S. Mill, that they tend in some way to promote human knowledge; but some will not.

But there are different things to distinguish here, not all of which need be supported in the same way. There are:

(1) "Academic" freedom: the particular kind of freedom rightly treasured in universities and like institutions: freedom to pursue one's research and present it to one's interested colleagues, with a view to ultimately advancing human knowledge. We can perhaps group artistic freedom, which is roughly the right-hemisphere counterpart of scientific and humanistic research, along with the pursuit of knowledge.

(2) Freedom to proselytize, as practiced by Christians, Mohammedans, Moonies, Nazis, and what-have-you.

(3) Freedom to chatter, as exemplified by cronies on park benches, friends at dinner, and guests at cocktail parties.

If we consider the pure cases represented by those who simply seek knowledge, it is plausible to claim that such activities have no particular externalities and are on that ground to be defended. The very claim that they have none, however, is loaded. For some religious groups will no doubt claim that some kinds of knowledge, at very least, are evil, and furthermore that more than just so much knowledge is evil, too. And again, there is the obvious possibility that some of the knowledge produced will have practical applications, for better or worse. The discovery of nuclear energy is a spectacular case in point, but a great deal of the progress of science over the past few hundred years is likewise rife with implications for practice by various and sundry persons and states.

Once one decides that one's goal is truth, however, there seems little doubt that we have to buy the J. S. Mill–type arguments for freedom of inquiry, and of speech insofar as it is viewed in the context of inquiry. But there is a problem insufficiently noted in this connection: namely, that the goal of *freedom*, per se, and that of *efficient inquiry*, per se, are distinct and capable of conflicting. Consider, as a case in point, the controversies in some parts of North America of late concerning the teaching of "creationism" in the public schools. The groups promoting this doctrine urged, in the name of free speech, a right of equal time for its teaching along with the scientific establishment's preferred view, evolutionism. Did they have a point? That depends on the aegis under which this right is pressed. The creationists, of course, pressed their claim under the heading of the pursuit of knowledge. Their real purpose was obviously to proselytize. But the only one of these categories under which they would have had a plausible case is that of the nattering cronies and the cocktail chatterers. Let us consider.

Though I have distinguished above between education and the

pursuit of knowledge, there is nevertheless a clear link between them: in educating people, what we teach them is advanced on the assumption that it is true—that what we are passing on to students is indeed knowledge. And if we advance it as being in the public domain, then we must employ publicly usable methods of evaluating beliefs, rather than the esoteric or idiosyncratic ones of cults and religious creeds. It is the public confirmability and disconfirmability of propositions in the realm of science, the use of evidence and standards of reasoning available to all, with repeatability under controlled conditions an essential component of the methods employed, that enables us to have any excuse at all for "public" schools whose function is to educate rather than to indoctrinate.

Once what we presume to teach is subject to the disciplines of scientific method, however, the idea that all hypotheses deserve an equal hearing is simple nonsense. With regard to any given object of knowledge, after all, there are an unlimited number of possible hypotheses. Equal time for each of these—all but a very few of which are not worth consideration even for the amount of time necessary to put them in the scientific trash heap—is plainly out of the question. The teacher faces the students for just so many hours per day, and her object is to maximize her students' knowledge and intellectual skills. Spending some of this valuable time examining silly ideas is admirable as an exercise, but only as such. From the scientific point of view, of course, creationism *is* a silly idea: "Here, let's explain a whole bunch of phenomena by positing a Deity who created the whole lot"—end of "explanation"! That the hypothesis in question is scientifically meaningless doesn't bother the creationists in the least; nor should it, if their view is advanced under the heading of proselytizing. But if science and understanding is our goal, then the idea that it deserves equal time with the evolutionary hypothesis is simply preposterous.

Note my generous use of such nonneutral terms as "preposterous" and "silly" in the preceding discussion. This is intentional. To teach is to make judgments, judgments of the intellectual merits of alternative ideas. We cannot *teach* without making such judgments, and to make them is to select and reject. The constraint of getting something done in a finite amount of time entails that we must reject a great deal, and reject it efficiently at that. An infinitude of possibilities will not even come in for mention, and the justification of not mentioning them is that they don't deserve consideration. In the judgment of the scientific community, creationism is to be classed with the latter, and the only intellectual justification for considering it would be under the heading, not of freedom of speech in respect of advancing human knowledge but, rather, of the sociology of religion or perhaps of exposure to a variety of religious points of view.

What about freedom to proselytize, though? Here there may also be advanced an idea of "equal time": let's get exposed to all the different religious ideas, for instance, so that we can choose intelligently. But now we have an analogous problem to what we had with the goal of promoting human knowledge: there is an infinitude of possible creeds, and if the idea was to give them equal time, then the amount each would get is zero! Obviously, what those who advocate "equal time" here have in mind is choice from the much more limited number of creeds actually adhered to by considerable numbers of humans. (Without such a further restriction to *popular* creeds, we would still have an unmanageable number to consider.) Strictly from the point of view of "choosing intelligently", however, it is hard to see why we should confine ourselves to popular ones.

But that is where the other mistake comes in. To talk of choosing intelligently here is to treat religion as if it were science and therefore subject to the same intellectual constraints, by virtue of having the same purpose, that of increasing our understanding of the world around us. But what if this isn't the purpose? What if, instead, religions are more like ways of life? Then they come under the rubric of indoctrination rather than promotion of knowledge. And now it makes lots of sense to discriminate sharply between one's own doctrines and those of everyone else. The confirmed adherant of a given religion looks at other people's religions out of scientific curiosity, or respect, or out of a laudable effort to promote good relations with those other people—but *not* because he thinks the other doctrine might be so attractive as to consider switching allegiance to it. The very willingness to do so would suggest less than the recommended degree of religious enthusiasm. Again, "equal time" is a nonstarter.

Religions, or many of them, do proselytize, however, and in a mixed community or an open community, there is obviously an important issue about which proselytizing activities are to be permitted and which not. The methods of the Moslems in the seventh century, which are said to have consisted of giving the proposed convert his choice between accepting Allah or having his head cut off, are clearly not acceptable from the libertarian point of view. On the other hand, the distribution of tracts that can be easily thrown into wastebaskets by the uninterested seems prima facie unobjectionable, although there will be a problem with those who regard it as sinful even to cast eyes on such stuff. Here we would have a problem analogous to that of pornography. The shops of purveyors can hardly even be identifiable by prospective customers without offending some people. What to do?

Evidently the rule must be something like this. The relevant variables are: (1) how easy is it for a member of the public to avoid the relevant stimulus if it is offensive to that member, (2) probability of such offensiveness; and (3) degree to which it monopolizes public resources in getting its message across. To a degree (1) and (3) interact: if the doctrine or performance in question completely monopolizes the public resource available, as when its radio program utilizes the only usable frequency, all others having been jammed by the station's jamming equipment, then even if it is easy for the citizen to avoid it (by simply turning the radio off), its practice is objectionable on grounds of fairness. If the message offends no one, as is nearly the case with a few exceptionally bland billboards, then it doesn't matter as much if it's not so easy to avoid. And so on. The problem here is one of optimization, and clearly no universally satisfactory solution is possible.

Finally, we have the Right to Chatter. Now, *here* we have the ultimate test of doctrines of free speech. If we thought that the right to speak was defensible only by virtue of the potential for contributing to human knowledge, then very short shrift would be given to most ordinary conversations, which have no such aim—unless we wish to count gossip and other humdrum verbal activities as specimens of such endeavors. But we shouldn't. Over the back fence, Mr. A and Mr. B pass the time of day by keeping the immediate air full of agreeable sounds engendered by the other party. Here at last we have a footing for a very rough doctrine of equal time: unless A prefers that B do all the talking, in which case there is no problem, B will recognize that A's voice should be the prevailing sound from time to time instead of exclusively B's, and vice versa. To be a conversational lion in such contexts is impolite and has little to do with the intellectual, cultural, or any other sort of merits of what is said, down to some point at which the listener will simply leave the scene. Had the creationists advanced their rights under *this* heading, there would be no problem. But of course it would have been very far from meeting their interests. What they wanted, for one thing, was a captive audience rather than a free back-fence forum, all participants at which are voluntarily in attendance. And for another, they think of their point of view as serious stuff.

Perhaps the primary context of free speech from the point of view of democratic political theory belongs in a different category from any of the ones demarcated: namely, speech concerning public policy and its correlative type, speech pressing the merits of rival candidates for political office. Such activity is practical, and unlike much practical speech, it has a quite special potential for impact on all: for who gets into office determines what the government does, and governments have power to affect the lives of all. It matters to everyone, therefore, what goes on in this sphere. We can't seriously claim that in principle it doesn't matter who gets into office—Nazis? Flat-Earthers? the Red Legion? the Khmer Rouge?—so long as they get a majority. The practice of democracy requires enough savvy on the part of the populace to appreciate that those who propose the abolition of democracy in favor of some utterly tyrannical regime can be tolerated at the hustings only if they have no serious chance of attaining to power. But if they do have such a chance, then what? A massive educational campaign by those in power, which is bound to be taken for propaganda, may in any case be beyond their means. One can sympathize with those who would exclude such parties from participation, despite the contradiction of democratic principle that appears to entail.

It is interesting to speculate on the character of political life in a fully libertarian society—since, after all, it seems that there wouldn't *be any*, as we are currently accustomed to it. The kind of objectives currently pursued by political means would instead be commercial or philanthropic endeavors. One would see advertisements for the sort of projects that are currently the subjects of political speeches, insofar as there would be any such projects. The projects would go through when the consent of everyone affected had been obtained, and otherwise not. When the organizers were fairly close to the requisite unanimity, they would no doubt increase the intensity of their appeals and/or the attractiveness of their financial offers to the holdouts. How much does this differ from politics as we know it? Not quite unrecognizably, perhaps. But the sense of drama, of *issues* urgently needing to be resolved, would evidently be missing. For the most part, I think that would be a positive change from the status quo. But for many people, of course, not entirely. People are political animals.

We must not forget, however, that voluntary associations have their political aspects. Organizations have officers, functionaries of various kinds, and there are "departmental politics" (in universities, for example), "office politics" in businesses, and ample scope for organizational politics. It is not to be supposed that political life would be nonexistent simply because all associations were voluntary.

Pornography, Hate Literature, and the Like

Pornography and hate literature deserve special attention in any discussion of freedom of speech because of the special issues they raise. Pornography, of course, is usually objected to by those who object to it on the ground that it is "obscene," which seems to mean, roughly, that it depicts, more or less favorably, sexual activities of which they disapprove on what they would claim to be moral grounds. Is this a relevant ground for restriction? Here we must be careful. Plainly the claim that some activity *is* immoral is relevant—how could it not be? (Many liberals talk as though it is not relevant; but they, I suspect, are using 'moral' in the confusingly over-general sense, in which it refers to ways of life—"lifestyles", for instance—which we have set aside in Part Two.) The question is whether these activities can plausibly be claimed to be immoral in the public sense that we have been employing throughout; and the answer has to be, so far as it goes, in the negative. Far from clearly harming noncon-senting parties on the face of it, as do murder, arson, theft, and so on, the viewing of pornography is engaged in only by consenting parties. That's not the end of it, of course, and we will consider the crucial matter of third-party effects further below. Meanwhile, the other question is whether the fact that people *consider* it immoral is a proper ground of restriction. And that is another matter altogether; here the answer must surely be in the negative, again as far as it goes, for the good and very basic reasons inherent in our viewpoint. These have been well expressed by Ronald Dworkin in his well-known essay "Is There a Right to Pornography?"[7] There he proposes, as the specific right relevant to such matters, the right of "moral independence": "not to suffer disadvantage in the distribution of social goods and opportunities, including disadvantage in the liberties permitted to them by the criminal law, just on the ground that their officials or fellow-citizens think that their opinions about the right way to lead their own lives are ignoble or wrong."[8] And if there were no worries of the type we shall be considering below, that would simply be an end of the matter. But there are such worries, and so it isn't.

Note, before proceeding further, that this right is itself relevant only in *public spaces*.[9] Obviously, the fact that person A disapproves of activity x is an entirely sufficient reason why people may be forbidden to do x on A's property—just as the fact that she disapproves of those people doing anything else on her property is such a reason, regardless of whether what they are doing on it is intrinsically something she disapproves of or not. The problem about public spaces is always that nobody owns them: like the "state of nature," the public spaces are "commons." And thus the problem of rational allocation of these spaces is formidable. But it is not, as some libertarian writers apparently think, hopeless (or: not always hopeless). For example, whenever an activity can be carried on in a public space whose only negative effect on anyone else is that it denies other persons the use of that particular space at that particular time, it must be permitted on all occasions when the Lockean Proviso is met, that is to say, that others are not thereby deprived of space to perform that or other activities. As they sometimes are, of course—the case of rock concerts being a singularly good one. It is entirely right that some procedure of licensing or the like is imposed for the carrying on of activities such as that.

Another good example of activities that would require a bit of scheduling would be displays of public nudity or other activities that are likely to offend those who might be exposed to them in public spaces. Semi-privatization is then required. For example, an area of otherwise public beach could be set aside for the nudists, and it be let known to all others that if they go there, they can expect to see people in the nude. What won't do is a flat forbidding of such activities in all public spaces. This would be a deprivation of the right of liberty, in the circumstances. It would be a treating of public space as if it were the property of a *subset* of the public, such as the city fathers or the current government or the bureaucrats put in charge.

But the problem with pornography and hate literature—which could well be regarded as different species of the same genus, for that matter—is different. We may agree that some speech activities may plausibily be singled out as requiring special protection, for example, the dissemination of weird political ideas at London's famed Hyde Park Corner. Thus Dworkin again: "In the case of free political speech, we might well concede . . . that each person has an important interest in developing his own independent political convictions, because that is an essential part of his personality . . . also . . . that political activity in a community is made more vigorous by variety, even by the entry, that is, of wholly despicable points of view. These are decent arguments why individuals and the community as a whole are at least in certain respects better off when the Nazi has spoken his piece." But in the case of pornography in particular, Dworkin's next comment is very much to the point: "the parallel arguments in the case of most pornography seem silly, and very few of those who defend peoples' right to read pornography in private would actually claim that the community or any individual is better off with more pornography rather than less."[10] Here, of course, there is a problem of when a doctrine ceases to be a "political viewpoint", if a "despicable one", and degenerates into simple slander or libel; this is especially a problem regarding hate literature. Like every need to make distinctions that matter, this generates administrative problems that can be formidable in particular cases.

Nevertheless, there remains a different and much more formidable type of problem regarding such things. Pornography is widely objected to not on the ground that it is obscene, as such, but rather that it is *demeaning*, especially to women. Some instances (quite a lot, I gather) of pornography portray outright cruelty or torture of women and/or children, sexual acts that are not only disgusting but also of a type likely or certain to be harmful to those engaging in them, and so on; and in context, these acts are portrayed with what amounts to approval, so that the literature or pictures in question can reasonably be regarded as virtually advocating activities of those kinds. This is Problem Number One: when a certain kind of activity *is* clearly immoral, in the narrow and politically relevant sense of 'immoral' we are employing here, then what about *advocacy* of such acts?

Suppose that Jones writes a letter to Smith urging Smith to murder Robinson. Is the letter's content a matter of indifference, to be protected by a principle of free speech? What if Smith then goes out and does as he is urged to do, and what if he does so *in consequence of* Jones's advocacy. Is Jones innocent and Smith guilty? Surely not, or at least not just like that. Depending on details, it might even be that Jones is the primary culprit. It seems reasonable to say that Jones murdered Robinson, in the same sense as that in which Khufu "built" the pyramids—viz., by telling a whole bunch of other people to do it in circumstances in which they were disposed to follow his directions. But, somewhere near the other end of the spectrum we have the Marxist who advocates violent revolution against the "capitalist oppressors", or the anarcho-syndicalist who proposes random terrorism as a method of protest against the institution of government.

Plainly, a theory is needed here. And it is impossible to doubt seriously that empirical support for the theory in question is required. There are circumstances in which the political advocate of violence is by his advocacy essentially committing violence himself and chargeable as such. There are others in which it would be outrageous to suppress what he has to say on any such grounds. Consider the case of Karl Marx, whose writings are in some respects pretty heady stuff, and whom many followers have taken to have established the case for violent revolution on behalf of socialism, with (mostly depressing) familiar results. But do we have a case for suppressing the works of Marx? No more, surely, than King George III had a case for suppressing the works of Tom Paine and Benjamin Franklin.

In the case of pornography the analogous problem is whether people are sometimes stimulated to perform such acts as rape on the basis of their reading of it. In the case of TV and the movies, there is the question whether people, especially immature ones, go forth and commit murder or whatever by virtue of their exposure to it. For that matter, isn't there a question whether the American public as a whole has a lot of the bellicose tendencies it seems to have because of exposure to the same sources?

Obviously there are real *conceptual* difficulties here, and they cannot be dismissed with an airy wave of the liberal hand—or, of course, any other hand. Those who propose extreme restrictions against pornography on the ground that it *might* induce people to rape have the same problem as those who propose extreme freedom for pornographers on grounds of high principle. Advocates of the latter whose daughters are then raped by someone who turned out to be a confirming instance of the hypothesis that pornography can trigger such behavior are likely to be discomfited, at the least. But advocates of the former whose daughters are raped by extremely repressed persons who might instead have benignly satisfied themselves with movies of people doing the same thing would also have occasion to wonder about the wisdom of their views. Here is an area where it is very difficult indeed to get at the facts, and to assess the significance of them when we do have them. For one thing is very clear: if there is any sort of plausibly causal connection between exposure to pornography and the incidence of rape, it is certainly slim, statistically speaking.

Thus, the researcher would first have to solve some knotty methodological questions: How would one even quantify this? Number of "exposures" against number of rapes? Or number of exposures against number of rapes by persons who figured in the exposures in question? What would count as "one" exposure—does a five-second examination by a casual peruser in the porn shop count the same as a four-hour session by an avid consumer? But however one does it, we are certain to get the result that some extremely small *percentage* of those who read pornography commit rape.

This then leaves us with the question of whether that provides a basis for restriction. And here we come up against another issue, this time one that has *not* much concerned the censor boards and the assorted tribal elders who have busied themselves in these matters. If we deprive 1,000 people of the liberty to do something that they very much want to do in order to prevent 1 person from committing some undoubtedly evil act, don't we *owe something* to the 999 who remain entirely innocent of such acts? If we stop 500 motorists to see whether they have been drinking, don't we owe something to the 450 who have not, and who have been considerably and unjustifiably inconvenienced? (And what about the 47 of the remaining 50 who, though they have indeed been drinking a bit, are nevertheless entirely capable of getting where they are going with no more than the normal probability of causing an accident on the way?)

The general principle here would seem to be something like this. If an activity is inherently legitimate from the public point of view, then to prohibit it on the ground that *some* instances of it lead to serious harm is not a plausible way to proceed. But if we do proceed that way, then the public ought to be aware of what it is getting into: in particular, it ought to be *liable* for the provably unnecessary among those restrictions. Were it not for the attitude that the law can do just any old thing it pleases, so long as elected officials somewhere back up the line were responsible for the law in question, the bland facility with which censor boards and the like are permitted to operate as they do would be materially inhibited.

A few things, it seems to me, emerge with at least some clarity from this very murky area. One is that we simply cannot deny the relevance of the claim that inherently legitimate activity x nevertheless produces, as a side effect, an increase in the incidence of plainly illegitimate activity y. Another is that when we proposed to put restrictions on activity x on the basis of such a supposed connection, then we need (1) hard evidence that there really is such a connection, (2) good reason for thinking that other ways of preventing y are unavailable, ineffective, or too expensive or difficult, (3) some clear and perspicuous criterion for concluding that a statistical correlation of size n rather than some greater number is sufficient to justify restriction of x on this basis, and finally (4) a scheme of real compensation to those who are wrongly restricted by the restrictions in question. This is a pretty difficult bill to fill and is almost never in fact met by governments in the current dispensation. And it is not necessary to be a "die-hard libertarian" to think that there is a real case for substantial change in the way we do many of these things.

A Libertarian Postscript

To take a case in point of quite extraordinary interest, consider the case of drugs—marijuana, cocaine, and the rest. The American way with these substances has been to outlaw them, and the case for doing so is sometimes put forward on the sort of grounds we have been considering above—for example, that they induce criminal behavior. But evidence for the proposition that they do so is rather scant except in one important respect: the fact that it is illegal generates a vast amount of crime, one that simply bears no proportion to the crime supposedly prevented by making the drugs illegal in the first place. Walter Block has succinctly put the point: "When a commodity is outlawed, in addition to all the usual costs of growing, harvesting, curing, transporting, merchandising, etc., the costs of evading the law and paying for the punishments meted out when the evasion fails, must be added [Block goes on to detail several more] . . . . But for these many extra costs imposed by the prohibition of heroin, the price would not differ in any significant way from the price of other crops (wheat, tobacco, soya beans, etc.)".[11] Thus these products, which would be trivially cheap were they left to the market, become astronomically expensive—Block estimated the annual cost of a heroin habit at $35,000 when he wrote; today it is no doubt at least twice that. But in order to meet these costs, the addict, who no doubt has been fired from her job by this time whether or not her addiction caused any real inability to perform it, is forced to turn to theft. However, stolen goods do not sell easily, as dealing in them is likewise (and in this case, properly) illegal. Thus the criminal must steal property worth several times what she will get for it to sustain her habit. One heroin addict, then, requires a career of grand larceny to sustain her habit. Needless to say, this results in an astronomical amount of theft. It has been estimated that over 90 percent of the theft in New York City—a place where it is difficult to find any dweller whose house or flat has *not* been raided in the last year or two—is committed by addicts. The public will take this as further evidence of the evils of drugs—but it is an evil engendered almost *entirely* by the fact that it is illegal, simply on the economic face of it alone. It is likely that, at most, a fairly trivial proportion of America's serious crimes would have occurred but for that nation's addiction to illegalization for whatever it doesn't approve of. The claim that this crime is "due to" drugs is, thus, simply question-begging. And, of course, the public, which is often caught in the cross-fire, is the very reverse of protected by such legislation.

Pornography in the United States and Canada is not entirely illegal as yet, though the restrictions under which business in it is carried on have already promoted substantial connections with gangsters in the trade. But the comparison is important. If we are to argue that x should be prohibited because it leads to y, we had better check to see whether y isn't due even more to the prohibition of x than to x itself.

CHAPTER 21

The Public and Its Spaces

"Public Property"

PUBLIC PROPERTY is property of the public, obviously. Only what does that mean? With private property held by just one owner, the answer is easy. With private property held by a number of people, various arrangements are possible, but ordinarily those arrangements have been made, and if they have not, we can expect trouble when the joint owners diverge regarding the use to which it is to be put. In the case of public property, however, ownership being totally "collective", these problems are legion. It might be thought that public ownership gives unlimited "access" (as in the socialist's "access to the means of production"). But obviously a given thing cannot be *completely* available to all, or indeed to more than one. Rules will have to be framed so as to assure a fair shake for all potential users, say, or something of the sort. The point is that with public ownership, we must resort to politics to decide who is going to do what with it and when—with all the difficulties that entails.

Libertarians often maintain that the very idea of public property is nonsensical. Morris and Linda Tannehill, for example, in their near-classic libertarian work *The Market for Liberty,* argue thus: "Ownership necessarily involves the right of use and disposal as the owner sees fit, barring coercion against others. Since the king was an individual, he could actually exercise control over royal properties. . . . But the 'public' is not an individual . . . [it] has no mind or will or desires of its own. It cannot make decisions, and so it cannot decide how to use or dispose of a piece of property. 'Public property' is, in fact, a fiction."[1] Thus do the Tannehills give very short shrift indeed to democratic processes of any type whatever. One wonders what their view would be about such things as clubhouses or corporate property. They are right, of course, in noting that the idea of property involves the idea of use and control, but they are entirely wrong to think that such control con't be exercised by any collectivities. Their objection must really be to the involuntariness of the public collectivity in particular. And this is objectionable, indeed. But the objection needs to be shown to be decisive, and the philosophical objection cited above is much too thin to be so. Possibly there is even more objection to private ownership?

Ellen Frankel Paul attributes to Locke the view that "the right to acquire, possess, and enjoy property is the fundamental liberty upon which all other inherent rights of life and liberty depend"; and she avers that "average Americans, landowners or not, would probably endorse some variant of [the] Lockean principles as their own. They would entertain the conviction that when they owned a portion of this earth, they thereby possessed the right, absolutely, to exclude all others from encroaching upon it, so that they could use it, enjoy it, or dispose of it as they alone choose."[2] That is not easy to believe. Would ordinary Americans vote so resoundingly and so consistently for the astonishing network of land-use restrictions they encounter everywhere if they truly believed what Paul ascribes to them? People grumble when they encounter the heavy hand of the bureaucrat, indeed, but they do not deny the right of the bureaucrat to lift the said hand. They don't deny it—but perhaps they should. Let us see, though, whether anything can be said for public property.

Grotius, Ellen Paul points out, "derived the power of Eminent Domain from the presumption that those who consented to join civil society, by affixing their names to the social contract, thereby intended that private claims should give way to those of 'public utility'. Precisely why such a presumption should be inherent in the social contract, Grotius did not say. That a polity might be conceivable that lacked the power to dispossess private owners did not occur to Grotius and his contemporaries."[3]

We probably can conceive of this. But it doesn't follow automatically that what we thus conceive is so. For one can also understand how such a provision *might* be appended to the "social contract". That contract, after all, stems originally from a public goods argument: the need to control the horrendous negative externalities of the Natural State. The reasoning for extending the basic prohibitions on violence that are definitory of the civilized condition to prohibitions on unlimited rights of private property might go something like this. Every person benefits, indeed, from having rights of private property. However, if there is cases in which public access to those items is overwhelmingly more beneficial to great numbers of people than restricted private uses, then it may be that the antecedent probability that anyone, including the private citizen currently enjoying the uses in question, will have a greatly positive marginal benefit from exercise of eminent domain, times the value of the benefit in question, exceeds the product of the probability that he would throughout his life enjoy greater private benefit in the absence of any such right, times the value of that benefit. If so, it would be in everyone's interest to disallow complete privatization of the items in question.

Streets and roads may be decent examples. We would like to be able to get from A to B, where these are widely separated, without frequent stops to obtain permission of the sundry owners of the segments of the road going from one to the other. The probability that such unimpeded progress would be a benefit is essentially 1.0; and the value of being able to do this is surely greater than the value of being the owner of any segment, with its entailed right to exclude all others, given that other segments are likewise owned by persons with power to exclude. It may be argued that it would be in the mutual interest of the set of owners to extend access to potential users on very easily met terms. For example, instead of installing toll booths every few blocks, the owners of a 1,000-mile stretch might all agree to coordinate on just one toll's being paid for whatever stretch the motorist wished to travel on. And then the owners of all the other roads might enter into a reciprocal agreement so that all toll booths are dismantled and the motorist pays for right of access when she purchases her vehicle's fuel. (This would look very like a tax on gasoline, in fact.) And the set of all owners of streets and roads, being everyone, would collect the income from their ownership simply in the unlimited use of those facilities. But if this is roughly the picture of how things would go, then how does it differ, details apart, from what we actually have? Only, one surmises, in the fact that those large, geographically demarcated collectivities known as national states insist on installing toll booths along their borders. The frustrations of having such coerced stopping places are familiar to every traveler and to every importer or exporter of goods. When privatization is proposed as an alternative, there looms before us the vision of what amount to national borders every couple of hundred yards, or every few miles at the most, and the mind correspondingly boggles. Under the circumstances, the argument that publicization of roads is an illegitimate incursion of a natural right to private ownership wears very thin very quickly.

The Tannehills surmise that "Total property ownership would also lower crime rates. . . . A private corporation which owned streets would make a point of keeping its streets free of drunks, hoodlums, and any other such annoying menaces, hiring private guards to do so if necessary. . . . A criminal, forbidden to use any city street because all the street corporations knew of his bad reputation, would have a hard time even getting anywhere to commit a crime."[4] Presumably, they wrote this in the midst of New York City as people by the millions went to and fro in the fabulous melee for which that city is justly famed. One wonders what their conception of administrative realities must have been to suppose that each and every individual wanting to use a particular stretch of street could be checked out for security upon each entry. Once the numbers mount up in the thousands, though, one surmises that either the whole thing will get remarkably unmanageable, or we are back to admitting total strangers with evil intentions. Doing altogether without "the public" may be conceivable, but just barely; and insofar as it is conceivable, it certainly looks astronomically impractical.

Paul goes on to remind us[5] of Locke's argument that the right of eminent domain could hardly be transferred to the government, because it is something we did not have to begin with. She does not, however, review Hobbes's argument that, since there are absolutely no restrictions on what we may do in the State of Nature, there is no problem at all about our handing over that particular power along with all the rest of our powers to the proposed Sovereign. (As I have observed earlier, Hobbes obfuscates the situation by referring to these powers as 'rights'. Thus Hobbes may be misleadingly represented as contradicting Locke on this point, affirming that we had such a right where Locke denies it.) Indeed, on Hobbes's own view, there is no way to resist the wholesale relegation of all power over property to the Sovereign, to whom "is annexed . . . the whole power of prescribing the Rules, whereby every man may know, what Goods he may enjoy, and what Actions he may doe, without being molested by any of his fellow Subjects: and this is it men call Propriety. For before constitution of Sovereign Power . . . all men had right to all things; which necessarily causeth Warre: and therefore this Proprietie, being necessary to Peace, and depending on Soveraign Power, is the Act of that Power, in order to the publique peace."[6]

The question is whether there is a basis either for choosing or for finding a middle way between these two apparently extreme positions. The plausible answer is that we should distinguish distinct cases, insisting on total private ownership wherever our interest in being able to exclude vastly outweighs our interest in general access—plausible examples being the parts of our bodies, say—but likewise calling for public access where its benefits greatly outweigh those of having the power to exclude, the plausible case being roads. This still leaves us with an array of less obvious cases in between, such as houses and fields. We certainly want the right to exclude from *entry* to our houses, but what about the right to block sunlight to one's neighbors, or to present upon their surfaces absolutely any configurations of visible colors and shapes to the passersby? And even the right of entry could be limited, as in the case where an occupant is on very good presumption suspected of murder. If we disavow intuitionistic appeals to natural rights and opt instead for contractarian arguments, as I have insisted we should in Part Two of this book, then the attempt to defend absolute private property in all things runs into very heavy weather.

"As a simple thought experiment if nothing more," Ellen Paul argues, "one can easily conceive of a government, functional and powerful enough, bereft of the right to take property, and shorn of at least a goodly portion of the police power as currently conceived."[7] This comes pretty close to being so, if we take "property" to refer to takable, "solid" objects. But Paul has emphasized that our right to property stems from our right to our labor, and this is expressed in the case of most of us not directly in the form of property but in the form of income, available for expenditure on solid property but also on services of various kinds. And government without the power to commandeer some of our income, if not some of our real estate, surely is scarcely conceivable. A "government" run by voluntary contributions or by sales of its services is not a government.

Nevertheless, the property tax in particular is liable to serious objections. It has the effect, as the Tannehills rightly observe, of making the supposed owner of land and houses, for instance, effectively a renter of those premises. "When a man is required to 'rent' his own property from the government by paying property taxes on it, he is being forbidden to fully exercise his right of ownership. Although he owns the property, he is forced into the position of a lessee, with the government the landlord. The proof of this is that if he fails to pay the taxes the government will take his property away from him (even though it is his property and not the government's)."[8] Here is a distressing and by no means atypical example of what may happen. Along the Atlantic Coast of the American states of Georgia and South Carolina are dozens of small islands inhabited, until recently, largely by the descendants of slaves—people who have owned small plots of land, usually as family inheritances, stretching back to the American Civil War when many plantation owners' estates were broken up and divided among their former slaves. These people's present situation constitutes a classic example of violation of property rights in our time. To start with, oyster fishing and canning, their principal source of income after the boll weevil destroyed the cotton industry, was scuttled by industrial pollution from the Savannah River manufacturers and residents. Then, in the last couple of decades, middle-class white Americans descended on the islands, turning them into playgrounds. Development proceeded apace, and "as development causes land to become more valuable, taxes rise. Consequently, the occupants of heir's land are sometimes obliged to sell it in order to pay taxes."[9] The inhabitants may well have no wish to sell their land even though, in consequence of the development, it would now fetch a high price. But they can't afford to stay on it, even though the increment in tax value had nothing to do with their own activities, which were economically marginal. Property taxes can be paid by the rich, but not by those with virtually no money income with which to pay them. Taxation of land and other property erodes property rights, with evils that are likely to fall most heavily upon the poor—as usual, one might add.

Ellen Paul supplies many horror stories about land-use regulations. She cites, for example, a study concluding that local land-use regulations contributed 18 to 28 percent to the cost of housing; further regulations led to a situation in which "only higher-priced homes held out the promise of a reasonable profit."[10] The result was an astonishing increase in the cost of housing. Of course, this increase makes it impossible for the poor to afford their own housing, so the public now turns around and subsidizes housing for the poor, every step of which turns more and more of our lives over to the bureaucrats. The right to unlimited draws on the time of ordinary citizens by officials, to unlimited harrassment, has become a mainstay of modern life; a similar right to waylay their property is inherent in property-tax and land-use regulatory schemes. In arguing, as I do below, for some adjustment of property rights in many contexts, we should keep this in mind. Libertarians do well to devise methods by which these considerations can be accommodated without such specters as are too often presented by well-meaning governmental committees.

Zoning Laws

An intriguingly large number of people, academics among them, are all ready to point to the United States in particular as a hotbed of private property rights run amok. It should come as something of a shock to these people to realize that there are *hardly any cases* of genuine, full-blooded, no-holds-barred property rights in that vast and populous bastion of free enterprise. Closer investigation reveals that every square foot of real estate in that country, as in most others, is hemmed in with zoning restrictions, property taxes, and the ever-present specter of expropriation by Eminent Domain, to name what are no doubt only some of the most obvious respects in which "owners" of real estate fall short of unlimited liberty to do as they please, as our definition in Part One has it, with what was somewhat naïvely thought to be theirs.

This gives rise to an interesting immediate issue: when someone buys up a piece of real estate, for instance, in full knowledge that it is subject to all those interventions from several levels of government, should we say that since she acquired it knowingly, the restrictions aren't in violation of her right to voluntary activity? Or should we say that since the restrictions aren't justified, the proper comparison ought to be with how things could be if they were the way they should be? If indeed things should be much different, then we might say that her activity of acquiring these assets is not fully voluntary, since she would still more have preferred to have full ownership if she could get it, and the only reason she couldn't get it is that some government(s) wouldn't *let* her have that option.

Since on the above reasonable construction of the issue, this question depends on the prior question of whether the restrictions are in violation of her rights, we are not quite ready to blow the trumpets of freedom in the direction of city councils, zoning committees, and planning commissions. Let us first see whether there is anything to be said in their favor.

To start with what could reasonably be considered the most fundamental case of all, consider property rights in land for residential purposes. Here, then, is a nice lot, about a quarter of an acre in extent, just right for that affordable dream house that at last seems to be within sight. What determines the price of the lot? All sorts of things, of course, among them being the demand for residential land in the neighborhood. However, this last is not one of the things that determine the *utility* of the lot to the consumer, and it is its utility in comparison with alternatives, after all, that determines demand. Our question, then, is: what characteristics of the lot give it its utility and thus determine, given the prevailing level of demand for such things, the price you are willing to pay?

At this point we bring you the latest in a series of no-news bulletins: it might interest the reader to know that there is probably an all-but-identical piece of land, square foot for square foot, in the middle of a modest wood in the southwest corner of some remote county in Arkansas, which you can get for a song. Were some magician to root up precisely the same amount of that land from its current location and whisk it sight unseen to your prospective lot in Xburg, Ohio (the very town you want to dwell in), plunking it down on the spot you have your heart set on owning, and whisking your lot, as is, off to Arkansas, neither you nor your eagle-eyed real-estate agent would ever know the difference. But the price of your lot, interestingly enough, will not depart with the magic carpet, nor will the trivial price of the Arkansas lot be transported to your chosen place. Now, why is this?

In considerable part, of course, it's because of what is known as "location". The nice thing about this lot is that the neighbors have nice lots too, and the whole area is convenient to shopping centers and schools and your place of work, and . . . and so on. So what have you bought, yours to do as you want with, when you buy your lot? In fact, you have bought all those convenient distances to all those *other* pieces of property, and the sight of the nice lots which your new neighbors will live on or already do, and similar items too numerous to mention. But of course you couldn't do this if your neighbors literally had the right to do *whatever* they pleased with those lots. What if one of them wants to build an exceedingly ugly fence 75 feet high around his entire lot, right up to the lot line? This would quickly render your lot only slightly more desirable than the ugliest vacant lot in the ugliest town in Pennsylvania—on which few would want to live even if they could, and which is in any case zoned (*sic*) for industrial use. Or what if the Satan's Choice Motorcycle Club should acquire the lot next door, with a view to setting up a clubhouse? On the other side, of course, someone will install a discothèque.

Each of us humans, at any particular time, comes in a quite well-defined physical package with a fairly definite set of equipment: arms (two), legs (two), and so on. Standardly included is a fair amount of sophisticated perceptual and information-processing hardware, with remarkably varied software to match (or, as the case may be, to mismatch). These latter items put us in touch with our environments in many ways. We are immersed in such media as air, sights, smells, and sounds, and among the latter are a great many that assault us via interpretation supplied by the aforementioned software. The software, however, does not come on little discs that we can conveniently eject when we retire at night, leaving us to sleep peacefully amid frightful dins, noxious odors, blizzards, and what-have-you. Total and absolute ownership of a plot 50 feet wide and 150 feet deep isn't going to get us too far if the plot itself is subject to all of these vicissitudes. It will help, to be sure, but the degree to which it helps is immensely affected by the dispositions of those who own the rest of the neighborhood.

What to do, then?

As it turns out, acquiring real estate in one of Hobbes's or Locke's States of Nature is in many ways a snap compared to acquiring it in Xburg, Ohio. You don't have to worry much about the neighbors in the former places (apart from the possibility that they're headhunters; this is infrequent in Xburg, but the incidence of paranoia is about the same and of various more modish syndromes, quite a bit higher). But you assuredly will worry about the neighbors in Xburg, and why not? After all, you'll be seeing them and their houses and the yards in front of and behind those houses (pink flamingos and all) for a long, long time. What is needed is to negotiate an agreement with them. However, they have already moved into the area and their agreements with each other have got there ahead of you. It's part of what you buy when you move in. As time goes on, the agreement may change a bit, and you will have your share of influence on this. But unless you are affluent enough to buy up the whole area, or quite incredibly charismatic, your influence will fall well short of 100 percent.

Moreover, the whole neighborhood isn't safe, either. Imagine that an airport moves in along its boundary, with 747s taking off and landing all day and much of the night. Or a huge factory, ejecting large volumes of noxious chemicals into the air, or storing hazardous substances in places where they might now and again take a notion to leak or explode. Are we to suppose that all anyone has to do to install either of those items, or any number of others with comparable effects on you, is buy up the requisite number of acres? ("You have 2,297 acres available? Terrific, I'll take it—my airport will just fit!") I trust not.

Nor should we think that the libertarian idea implies this. Among the better reasons that there is scarcely a square foot of North America for sale with absolutely no restrictions on what may be done with it is that neither its previous owners nor the neighbors are damned fools. Those of your activities that inevitably strike my eyes, ears, or nose are not exclusively your business if we take seriously the idea of self-ownership. We are not separate islands in that sense. What we are is separate *centers* of experience, but with more or less overlapping peripheries. And the "more or less" varies, from near zero in the case of Robinson Crusoe to around 99.7 percent in the case of a large family living in a one-room apartment in Moscow. For all these cases the correct model is the social contract from an initial position of complete self-ownership; but for almost all of them those contracts will be complex documents incorporating dozens or hundreds of liens, short-term leases, provisions for borrowing, zoning regulations and adjustments on same, and what-you-will. The newcomer to any of these humanly active scenarios is not striding forth into the State of Nature. The status quo antecedent to his arrival is shot through with understandings and arrangements that he will have to respect, and rightly so.

Does the libertarian idea have a useful impact in these areas? The drift of my argument thus far is that it is not going to issue in a markedly different outcome from what most of us already have. Zoning committees and the like should, on this view, be constituted from the group up (if you'll forgive the figure). The largest input should come from the people already in the zone in question, with accommodation for advice from areas farther away. Thus if some resident, A, wishes to utilize his space for activity Z, an activity not officially recognized in the existing laws, the main criterion for whether A should be permitted to do Z is whether the existing set of neighbors are bothered in any way by Z's going on there. Does it make too much noise? Does it discolor the neighbor's grass? Does it choke the neighborhood streets with unwanted cars? If nobody objects, it should be essentially a foregone conclusion that A is permitted to do Z, though remoter effects might possibly be detected. But these are the very things that do count with most real-life zoning committees. The people on them are neither fools nor ogres—normally. Whether there is any infallible method for making sure that they are neither is another matter; but until one comes along, the libertarian is unlikely to have a very weighty complaint. Once his native preoccupation of invoking the "rights of property" is put in perspective, it's all over but the details; and they are not likely to be capable of being settled in the pages of books on philosophy.

Rules, Regulations, and Bureaucrats

In all communities familiar to this writer and, probably, the reader, there are codes of rules requiring that buildings of various kinds comply with various requirements. A typical example: in my community you can't build a bathroom with two sinks unless there are also two separate drain pipes leading all the way to the main sewer pipes of the house. The obvious economy of splicing the two sinks into one just below counter level is forbidden. Any code one is likely to encounter is sure to contain examples equally bizarre.

Here is another example. A somewhat eccentric professor owns a house with a large room in which he and some friends decided to put on a series of chamber music concerts. After some years of doing so, in perfect safety, the local newspaper announced that the room in question had never been investigated for compliance with the local fire regulations. Sure enough, within a couple of days, along come the local fire inspectors and announce that various alterations in the building would be necessary if the concerts were to continue. Cost of the alterations, several thousand dollars. Increase in fire safety: zero, in the owner's estimation and that of most people who attended the concerts. Sample requirements: put a lit "Exit" sign over the main exit door, which was of course clearly visible from every point in this small room and which led directly to the outdoors; install smoke detectors all over the building, electronically connected with each other, so as to give ample warning to the concertgoers who presumably could not be trusted to notice that the house was on fire otherwise.

Regulations of this general sort are one of the standard burdens of life for builders and buyers of buildings everywhere. And regulations by the hundred infect every other aspect of modern life. Many of them strike the individuals affected as arbitrary and pointless, whereas others seem perfectly reasonable. As things are, however, there is little point in arguing with the authorities, because of the very fact they *have* authority. The citizen is left with the helpless feeling that the laws are made, not for the benefit of the public but for the benefit of building contractors, say, or of persons with axes to grind; or that they

aren't made for anyone's benefit, but simply in order to give scope for
the egos of the administrators of the regulations—or indeed, to justify their existence, usually at rather good salaries, thank you very
much.

Obviously there is a public interest in safety, for example. And in
some cases the regulations will pertain to peace and quiet, or health,
or olfactory tolerability. How can these interests be catered to without
the various tyrannies, small and large, that are the by-products of
virtually every regulation ever made? And, of course, their concomitant inefficiences, which have such side effects as increasing the costs
of dwellings and other amenities to levels that may well be regarded
as insupportable by many potential purchasers.

What is the proper solution, given the general right of freedom?
The business of telling the individual how much safety she must
have, how much health, how much comfort, and so on and so on
without seeming end, is certainly a prima facie violation of the right to
liberty. If I am trying to decide whether to buy a building, I will make
a judgment about its level of safety, will I not? And if I judge it to be
too low for the price, I won't buy at that price.

Very well: but do we extend this also to the people who routinely
enter my shop every day for casual business? Shouldn't there at least
be public regulation of safety (in particular) because of that? After all,
we can hardly expect the customer to inspect every store entered to
see whether it seems safe enough.

Though that sounds impractical, of course it isn't all that impractical even as it stands. Suppose the customer will be in the store for,
say, five minutes. What is going to happen in five minutes that could
possibly deter a reasonable customer, barring revolutionists with Mo-
lotov cocktails?

But in any case, there are other ways. For example, safety is a
commodity of such general desirability that there is ample opportunity for the entrepreneur to step in. Armed with no authority whatever, Safety, Inc., can devise a set of standards, offer to inspect premises and issue ratings that would be prominently posted (Safety, Inc.,
will impose a suitable charge for companies that take down the signs,
and take them to court if they alter them materially, and so on.) The
customer would see at a glance that this place was "A", "B", "C", etc.
and act accordingly.

Another part of the "accordingly" will concern the matter of liability. Should I be able to sue a company with unsafe premises if I in
consequence break a leg there? But what if there is a clear sign saying

that the customer should use caution and must proceed at his own risk? (And what if *that* sign isn't posted clearly enough?) All of these matters can be taken care of in good anarchist fashion, with suitable negotiations, and with no need for Authorities with enforcement powers except possibly for the last-ditch need to enforce properly made agreements in the event of violation.

It is reasonable to expect that all parties will be better off in consequence: the business owner, who can run with lower costs, and customers who benefits from those costs at (perhaps) a slight increase in risk—or who will pay more for reduced risk elsewhere—and so on down and up the line. And instead of a tax-supported bureaucracy with the power to impose arbitrary requirements, there will be Safety, Inc., and insurance inspectors, and so on. Unlike what was the case with my example of OHIP, there is not a likely prospect of savings from having these things handled by a central bureaucracy. Instead, there is a certain prospect of massive annoyance and high costs to the citizenry, as well as out-of-line administrative costs relative to such real benefits as result.

Sell the Streets?

Let x and y be distinct points on the surface of the earth. Then for any given individual A there will be a set of pairs, {x,y} such that A would like to be able to get from x to y, preferably efficiently, comfortably, and in one piece. In all likelihood A would ideally like to be able to get from *any* point to *any* other: all pairs {x,y} would be values of A's want-to-go function. And in many cases the shortest route from x to y will cross someone's property.

Questions: Suppose that y is owned by B, and that B would be delighted to have A come for a visit, or to do business, or whatever. Suppose that A owns x. Are we to understand the rights of acquisition of property to be such that it might be *impossible* for A to go from x to y? Or is there always a right of any A who owns x to get from x to y, so long as y is owned by some B who is willing to have a visit by A? If all property in between is wholly owned, then this right is not logically assured, since all of the intervening owners might forbid A's access through their territory. Or one or a few parties might buy up a complete ring of territory around A's house, leaving him bereft of through routes.

Apostles of public ownership may claim that public ownership guarantees 'access'. See, for instance, the many socialist writers who talk as though a problem of capitalism that would be solved by socialism is "lack of access to the means of production". Those writers should try entering a factory district in the outskirts of Novgorod in the Soviet Union, where the present author was once arrested for trying to find the main road; any actual resident of the Soviet Union who did not work at one of those "publicly owned" factories would have fared at least as badly. And regarding the problem under discussion here, it might be noted that for the offending set of routes {x,y} violating our above condition of access, the great majority of closed routes go through States who prevent the access in question, and the great majority of those States claim to be socialist! Simply declaring that there is a right of ownership lodged in some nebulous collective will not assure the access in question, or come anywhere near to doing so. Indeed, as we have seen in Part Two, simply *declaring* a right whenever one feels like it is also of no use. We need to know the "why" of the matter.

Let us call the condition that A owns x, B owns y, and B is willing to have A at y, "condition F." We shall designate the routes from x to y by the letter R (with subscripts as necessary). Supposing that A is neither criminal nor psychopathic, and that freedom to get from x to y for any pair {x,y} meeting our condition F is worth something to A, then accordingly there will be an interest on the part of others to provide A with some route R. Some entrepreneur, E, will be able to charge A and his fellow travelers, and to charge more in proportion to the efficiency, comfort, security, and visual attractiveness of R. The entrepreneur would make offers to those owners C, whose permission is necessary if R is to be available. Consider Mr. C Natural, a holdout who will not provide the required 10 feet along the edge of his property that would enable R to go through, even though all others along R will do so at a reasonable price. Or Ms. C. Sharp, who holds out so as to be in a position to charge a great deal more than anyone else, knowing that her permission is now crucial. E, anticipating this, may have lined up another set of owners along a less efficient route, R', thus placing an upper limit on C#'s feasible selling price.

All these maneuvers will help, but we may raise another question. If all property holders retained total rights in this regard, it might be feasible to threaten C Sharp with encirclement, ringing her with neighbors unwilling to grant passage and thus preventing her from going *anywhere*. We may imagine that C Sharp would not be too keen on that outcome. The fact that people could be threatened with this if they were unwilling to cede passage, or indeed for any number of other reasons such as that the neighbors just don't like them very much, makes it very plausible that part of the environmental social contract will be a clause requiring everyone to be willing to make some concession if need be so as to make every place on earth meeting condition F accessible to all those interested in going there.

This is meant as a moral argument, but it seems to me conclusive for its purpose. Note that it allows cases where sets of contiguous owners can keep all others away from their property on an associated basis. Savvy aborigines, for example, might well, in retrospect, have wanted to keep intruding white people out of what is now the Northern Territory of Australia, had they known what was to come. The right to private property is certainly the right to keep people off *your* property. (In the case of aborigines, who we may think of as owning large areas collectively rather than individually, there will be the usual problems of collective ownership in the event that there is any disagreement among the members of the tribe about who should be allowed where or what should be done with which parts of the territory in question. But our theory simply says that this is their problem. Those who think that collective ownership is a solution rather than a mare's nest of intractable problems will do well to ponder the mechanics of tribal decision making in such cases.)

The argument here is simply for a mildly enforceable obligation to permit such adjustments as are necessary to enable every noncriminal nonpsychopath to go anywhere on earth so long as those at her destination are willing to receive her. Now, the term "every noncriminal nonpsychopath" takes in a lot of human territory, as it were.

Some of these humans do not like some of the others very much, for reasons ranging from understandable to despicable. Let us, then, take the latter as our guide: the Ws hate the guts of the Zs, for no reason whatever. In the immortal words of a former dean at Harvard upon turning down some department's candidate for a full professorship, they "just don't like the cut of his jib." Suppose that the Zs wish to travel to the kingdom of the As for purposes entirely agreeable to the latter and that the only tolerably efficient routes lie through the land of W. What is reasonable here?

If the Zs don't care about going anywhere, they will be in a fairly good moral position to tell the Ws to go around. But suppose they, like most of us, do want to go places, and that some of the tolerably efficient routes lie through the land of W. Then we have a basis for a deal. Even if none of the desired destinations of the Zs require routes going through W, we may still have such a basis. For it may be that the Ws trade with the As, who trade with the Cs, who trade with the Ds, and so on, in a chain leading all the way to Z-land. The interests of all intervening parties may lead to a suggestion to the Zs that perhaps they'd better open the road to the Ws, under the circumstances.

Moreover, individual Zs may well have maverick interests in associating with Ws or at least having a look at the W-countryside. Our theory tells us that Z-land is violating their rights if they permit them no scope for these activities as separate individuals. The bottom-up view of these matters promoted by our individualistic outlook tells us that the prospects for general rights of access become stronger and stronger as the range of possibilities becomes greater. Here, as elsewhere, tribalism goes on the defensive.

Within a given territory the standard method of accommodating this interest in getting from x to y is to put it all in the hands of the Dominant Protective Agency, otherwise known as the State. The standard method of accommodating all interests in everything is to do this. On the face of it, this is not a very sensible idea. Why should the police know more about highways, real estate zoning, education, health, fisheries, vital statistics, welfare problems, professional sports, and so on and so on?

It is, of course, a caricature to say that the standard system is to put the police in charge of all these things. But it is close enough to the truth to be described as a caricature rather than a total fabrication. For to create a *single* agency, one endowed with a monopoly of force, to do all these very different things is to make machismo our guide in all matters foreign and domestic. The guys with the guns make the decisions. Insofar as this is what goes on, is it not too outrageous to bear examination?

There are at least two alternative models to consider. Highways could be literally owned by entrepreneurs—the "Sell the Streets" model. Alternatively, highways could be owned and operated by user-cooperatives. Both models make a good deal of sense, and a great deal more sense than putting them in the hands of the police. And both would, I believe, converge toward accommodation of our hypothetical right of access to every destination owned by willing visitees on the part of every willing nonviolent visitor—and do so, as I have suggested, more effectively than leaving the transportation system of each different state in the hands of the government of that state.

Those who think that either such system must lead to an uncoordinated hodge-podge might ask themselves why it is that roads going up to international boundaries (except, again, in the odd Marxist state) invariably continue right on across to matching routes on the other side, despite the fact that the road system on the other side is the exclusive property of another sovereign state. Somehow, even sovereign states manage to act, much of the time, like rational individuals or associations of same. Similarly, if there are two road systems in adjacent territories and numerous drivers interested in traveling smoothly through both, the owners or operators of those systems would be interested in accommodating these interests.

The idea of private ownership of roads is intriguing, but most people will no doubt blanch at the thought. This may be because they simply haven't tried such thoughts. But more likely, the idea is regarded as vaguely ludicrous. Why, though? An interesting question indeed. There is a certain aura about such pieces of public property as roads, parks, forests, and so on, that is very difficult to shake. That, and the usual fallacies ("if it's public, then we all have the right to use it", as if that made any clear sense, or again that it doesn't cost the user anything). But the case for public ownership is harder to make once the fallacies are eliminated and the aura disappears.

On Discrimination in Hiring

Few beliefs about justice are so passionately held nowadays as the belief that it is unjust to *discriminate*, for example, on grounds of race, sex, religion, or national origin. At the public level this belief manifests itself especially in the areas of employment and housing. But there is a severe problem in this view, a problem that you don't need to be a libertarian in order to appreciate. Libertarianism certainly exacerbates it, however. The case is of such interest that we will examine it in slightly more than cursory fashion here. For convenience, and because so much of the "action" is in this area, we will mostly talk about discrimination in employment.

First we must ask, what constitutes (unjust) discrimination? Whenever we make a choice, we make a "discrimination": we choose x rather than y for some reason having to do with what x has that y doesn't have, or vice versa: we prefer x's properties to y's properties. When people say that discrimination is unjust, they clearly can't be speaking as generally as that. A closer analysis is obviously required.

First, discrimination in the relevant sense is by some agent, A, and "against" another person, the "discriminatee," whom we shall designate as person B. Moreover, A's discriminating against B consists, especially in our favored context, hiring, in preferring some other person to B; we'll call this other person C. The act A does in doing something to B that constitutes discrimination against B we shall call x. In addition, there must be some property or set of properties of B and of C on account of which A prefers C to B. Let us call the *respect* in which A prefers C to B the "discriminandum" (e.g., color). We will refer, for convenience, to the particular value of this discriminandum, the property B has that makes A prefer C to B, as 'F-ness'. Thus we have, in any case of discrimination, A doing x to B rather than C, which is a case of A's *preferring* C to B, because B is F and C isn't. The term 'preferring' here is important: it implies that A either singles out C for a benefit of some kind that A might instead have rendered to B, or singles out B for some kind of harm that A does not in turn inflict on C. In general, then, let us say that the discriminatory act, x, consists in treating B in a manner that is *less desirable than* the treatment given to C instead.

Preferring how or for what, though? That is to say, which actions done by A to B constitute discrimination? Here we should make a crucial distinction. Much of what has been called "discrimination" has in fact consisted in denying the discriminatee some basic right, such as the right to life, as in lynching of black people in the American South in the early part of this century, gassing of Jews by Nazis, and so on. The libertarian holds that everyone has strong rights over her person, things that can't be done to her either under any circumstances or at least unless they are legitimate methods of punishment for some wrong she has committed. These acts are wrong no matter to whom they are done, and, except for the special case of punishment, wrong no matter why. Much discrimination has been of that kind: the blacks or Jews in the examples mentioned were killed without justification of the required kind. The important distinction to be made here, then, is this: what they did to those people was certainly *motivated* by discrimination, but what made it *wrong* was not that it was so motivated—rather, it was what they actually did to them, viz., violate their fundamental rights.

However, the claim that discrimination *as such* is *unjust* must be the claim that there are things we can do to people that are made wrong *by the fact that they are* discriminatory, rather than by the fact that they consist in doing something to them that would have been wrong *anyway*. What we want to know, then, is when is it the case that *A's doing x to B rather than to C on account of C's having property F is* wrong? Here we are taking our examples from the context of employment, so x will be a job. And the usual values of F, the properties people have been concerned about in this context, are such things as race, sex, religion, nationality, and the like. But what determines this class of properties F such that to hire or not hire on account of F or lack of it is wrong?

The usual philosophers' answer to this question has been that x is discriminatory when the properties F are "morally irrelevant." What is this supposed to mean, though? One possibility is that moral irrelevance is a matter of being such that it ought not to be taken into account. But we don't have much of an explanation of discrimination if we are told that discriminating against someone means doing something to him for a reason that we ought not to take into account. We want to know which things it is wrong to take into account, and why it is wrong to do so.

Another interesting suggestion would be that the set of discriminanda for this purpose consists of properties that *should not figure in basic moral principles.* Clearly, the fundamental principles of morality won't tell us that people who are black or women or Polish or whatever are to be treated in some ways, and others in different ways, no explanation given. But if that's what is meant, then proponents of this view are in for a bit of a shock. For those who are concerned about discrimination in hiring want to say that there are certain reasons for which you ought to hire, and not others; and on the basis of *these* properties, you *are* to discriminate. Especially prominent on this list (perhaps unique) is "competence" at the job in question. Yet it is as obvious as anything can be that the *basic* principles of morality should not, for example, be loaded in favor of competent as opposed to incompetent stenographers. Competence is morally irrelevant, if anything is.

Another suggestion, and in the case of hiring the only really plausible one, is that F consists of properties other than those that are "relevant" *to the job.* A's hiring B rather than C for a stenographer's job because B is prettier than C, even though C is a better stenographer, is a typical example.

This bring us to the basic problem here. We are talking about employment by private businesses, not just public institutions. But if a business is really private, that means that it is the property of its owners. They can do as they wish with it. There is a good reason why the owners of business must be presumed to be able to "do as they wish with it": nobody has to go into business at all! If the free-market idea is our guide, all business activity is voluntary—nobody has to partake in it. Thus nobody has an obligation to hire anybody, either in general or in particular. But if nobody has to hire anybody, then how is it that it is obligatory for businessperson A to hire individual B rather than individual C—no matter *what* the reason for preferring B to C? No matter how much B or C needs the job, this particular employer had no obligation to make any job available at all, to anyone at all. If he doesn't go into business at all, people are no worse off than they were before; so he isn't *harming* them by not starting the business. Thus the job is, from the point of view of the employee, in effect a benefit. Not to get it is, then, not to have received a benefit; but it is not to have incurred a harm. C *hasn't* been harmed by not getting the job rather than B. (Someone, for some dark reason, has failed to make me Prime Minister. Have they "harmed" me thereby?)

Lest there be misunderstanding on this point, let us agree that, often, people will be badly off if they don't get a certain job: they need some job, and this particular one is available and would do. They will, of course, be worse off if they don't get it than if they do. True. But they will not be worse off *than they were prior to A's nonhiring of them.* A does not *make* them worse off; she merely fails to benefit them in a way that she otherwise could. Note, too, that *whoever* doesn't get the job will be in a similar situation. That person will be better off having the job than not having it—else why would he have applied? And a further point in this connection: the factor of the unhappiness of the losers doesn't obviously favor the competent. If anything, perhaps the reverse: competent people are more likely to be able to get employment elsewhere, or to employ themselves.

In fact, why don't we say that hiring for competence—a "morally irrelevant" characteristic, after all—constitutes discrimination against the competent, and especially wrongful discrimination because they are more likely to suffer as a result?

Further conundrums loom as we reflect further. What constitutes a "job"? This is important for the following reason. If we are to try to spell out the ideas of "discrimination" in terms of "morally irrelevant", and in turn to make relevance turn on the job to be done, with its appropriate criteria of competence, then the concept of wrongful discrimination would seem to be determined by the type of job it is— by the *job description*, as we shall call it (meaning, not just what is put in the advertisements, but rather the set of objectives that the holder of that job is, as such, to be pursuing). The idea is that it is wrong to hire persons for reasons other than those related to performance on the job—meaning, then, the job *as described*. But who describes the job? That is to say, whose job is it?

If the job is in the "private sector" of the economy, it would seem that this description is determined by the *owners* of the firm, normally through their higher-level employees, the managers. Is there any limit to the way in which they can *frame* a job description? For example, can they say "Wanted: Secretary/mistress: Successful applicants will be chosen on the basis of probable performance in the office and in bed. Here's a picture of your boss-to-be: . . . ."? Or "Wanted: black stenographer"? Or what about "Professor of Logic—definite advantage if applicant is black"?

On one view of the matter, they could do this. In the case of the mistress/secretary, they likely wouldn't get a very good response to their ads, though (and perhaps the ones who did reply would be rejected as "unsuitable"—insufficiently sexually attractive, say). And then we may say that those who apply to ads that *didn't* include the extra bit about bed performance and then are turned down for reasons actually having to do with that have indeed been unjustly treated, for the job has been *misrepresented*. They have been wasting their time applying, for the job they thought they were applying for isn't the one they were being "looked over" for! (Suppose the job description said: "secretary/coffeemaker: in addition to usual secretarial skills, successful applicant is to make and serve coffee to senior staff, etc." The inclusion of this not unusual supplement to a secretarial ad would, I think, solve a lot of problems, for many people would apply for such a job. Would those who would apply have a legitimate complaint? Is there fixed somewhere in the heavens an Essence of Secretary that clearly specifies that secretaries are *not* to make coffee for those whose secretaries they are?)

Similarly, if the claim about injustice is based on this consideration, then employers who want to discriminate on the basis of race, for instance, could also do so so long as their ads were properly worded. But the Ontario Civil Rights Commission would not allow this, and neither would the current version of the Canadian Charter of Rights and Freedoms, nor the current interpretation of the U.S. Constitution by American judges. Should these documents forbid such things?

There is a difficulty in doing so, since sometimes the forbidden values of F *will* be relevant to the job. For a chorus line or a model for women's underwear, the employer does want a woman; for other purposes, a black person may be just what is needed (cf. the Black

Muslim Church of America); and so on. On what grounds does the
government decide whether this kind of distinction is "discrimination" or not? What if the Catholic Church discriminates against wom-
en for the priesthood? (There was recently a to-do in the papers concerning a girl who wanted to function as an acolyte, this being
contrary to Catholic tradition. Did she have a case?) How about when
the Black Muslim Church discriminates against white persons? Or the
Equadorian Friendship Society discriminates against non-Ecuadorian
applicants for janitorial or secretarial positions; or . . . . These are all
jobs that *could* be done by women, or whites, or non-Equadorians,
and so on.

Discrimination, Inefficiency, and the Market

Usually, employers want to make as much money as possible. For
those who do, it is heartening to note that discrimination in employment is usually cost-ineffective. Why so? Because discrimination
in employment is supposed to consist essentially in selecting people
on a basis other than competence. Discrimination in employment,
then, must consist in hiring the less competent when you could get
more competent people for the same money, and this must, by definition, be inefficient. Suppose that women will do the job for 60 percent
of the pay but are just as good as men at it. Then a rational employer
would hire nothing but women at that job, and the competition, if it
insisted on hiring men, would incur unnecessary costs! Of course, the
typical way of responding to this situation, by governments and by
the women's liberation movement currently, is to make wage differ-
entials *illegal*, thus removing this incentive for increasing employment in the discriminated-against segment of the populace. And just
incidentally, in prohibiting the free market in a respect that is clearly
essential to its quite properly much-touted success: it disallows rational shopping, in this case shopping for employees.

There are, to be sure, some interesting exceptions. Usually employers want to make as much money as possible, but sometimes not;
so even the fact that discrimination in employment is usually cost-
ineffective won't keep everyone from practicing it. Among the interesting exceptions are those already noted above: such "firms" as
churches, social clubs, ethnic organizations, and the like. Consider a
church: if it insists on hiring persons sharing the religion that church
is devoted to as janitors, secretaries, and so on—let alone pastors—is
it not discriminating on the basis of religion? And what about legisla-

tion designed to put tariffs against foreign products: why isn't that, in effect, discriminating on the basis of nationality?

The Public Sector

The foregoing remarks have all applied to the "private" sector. The case is, to be sure, quite different when we look at the "public" sector. This is the set of organizations that operate under the aegis of government: bureaus, public corporations, and the like. Acting for and on behalf of the public, they have a set of terms of reference that private firms do not have. The public, after all, consists of *everyone*—not just men, or women, or whites, or whatever. If the business of a given organization is to serve the public, then it cannot prefer some arbitrary subset of members of it to some other arbitrary subset. And since it is to offer the best service it can, it must hire on the basis of competence. However, there is another and potentially conflicting criterion: insofar as these jobs are a benefit (and why else do political parties regard them as "plums"?), it ought to be distributed on a basis of equality to the public. So we have the general premise that is needed for showing why discrimination in *these* jobs is wrong. But this is a premise that is conspicuously lacking in the private sector. It is of the essence in that sector that freedom, as much as possible, should reign. And of course the very existence of the public sector is problematic from the point of view we are considering.

What basis is there, then, for the sort of antidiscrimination laws we tend to have nowadays? I think this is a great unsolved problem in contemporary "liberalism"—a case where the received view has not been called into question sufficiently. However, one can suggest a few things. For instance, one purpose might be to prevent community disharmony—the F-bearers might get very mad and start throwing things, causing riots and suchlike. To prevent this might seem a worthwhile public aim. It is also, of course, to knuckle under to threats, for if my analysis is right, those who would be throwing things have no case.

A more drastic "solution" is to insist that *everything* belongs in the public sector—hiring by private persons is just as public as hiring in the public sector normally so called. This is the way taken by socialists and the like, and apparently by many a contemporary "liberal." In my opinion, there is a severe problem of coherence in the application of nondiscrimination at the kind of level it would presumably have to have in socialism—but we can't pause to discuss this here. Suffice it to say that what may be at stake here is the very idea of private business. Of course, so much of private business is affected by public legislation today that we might also just reckon nondiscrimination regulations as the price one must pay to do business under today's governments. But notice that it is a price that businesses are not given any choice about, normally.

It might be objected that these private businesses are producing things for the public, and thus that public criteria of hiring ought to be applied. There is something in this, to be sure. But not that laws ought to be passed forcing private employers to hire some people rather than others (and of course substituting the State's judgment for the employer's judgment concerning who would make a good employee). For if buyers don't like the practices of a certain company, they can refuse to buy those products, and they can try to get other people to do likewise. The boycott is potentially a powerful weapon and has had considerable effect in many places in the past few decades. But notice that in general, one would expect these to be unnecessary. For if the business in question is competing with other businesses, as all are in the private sector, and if, as we have pointed out, discrimination is inherently inefficient, then all the public has to do to help stamp out discrimination is what they've always done: buy the cheapest product of the desired quality that they can find.

Reflection on discrimination opens major Pandora's boxes in the house of (what passes for) contemporary liberalism. At one time, liberalism was identified with being *liberal:* that is to say, of allowing people to act on their own judgment and in the light of their own convictions about what to do, so long as they infringed no other person's similar right. Somehow this has evolved into the present incoherent hodge-podge of promoting opportunities for allegedly oppressed group K at the expense of the public, of group M at the expense of businesses and therefore of their customers and therefore of the public, and of groups N, O, P, Q, and so on, all at the expense of this same public—which by this time, of course, includes the members of K, M, N, O, P, and tomorrow, when groups R and S get their pieces of the action, of Q as well. And who gains? Bureaucrats and politicians, who not only get very secure jobs at very good salaries but also have the satisfaction of dispensing virtue and "justice" to the community. —Such is the libertarian comment on recent politics in the Western democracies. The reader will have to decide who has the stronger case. But it does seem to me that the libertarian has the *clearer* case, and has it on principles once thought strong.

CHAPTER 22

Defense and International Relations

Libertarianism and War

JOHN HOSPERS WRITES, "The greater the hold of government upon the life of the individual citizen, the greater the risk of war." With this we may certainly agree, not only in principle and in theory but in the hindsight of history. Hospers goes on to claim that "war is typically started by totalitarian (statist) nations against free (or at least freer) nations."[1] The empirical claim has been upheld by Michael Doyle, who compiled a historical survey of wars for the purpose of testing Kant's hypothesis that the way to perpetual peace is by liberalization. His striking finding is that *even though liberal states have become involved in numerous wars with nonliberal states, constitutionally secure liberal states have yet to engage in war with one another.*[2] Doyle's criterion of liberalism is commonsensical, having mainly to do with the presence of representative government established and altered by election procedures. The likelihood of war given libertarianism, one can reasonably suppose, would be yet lower.

One could, of course, *define* 'war' in such a way that wars between libertarian societies, supposing that such societies would lack governments in the ordinary sense of the word, would be impossible. That would trivialize the thesis, which we should not do, of course: certainly very large organized groups of armed people can have the sort of conflicts most people would want to call 'wars'. Nevertheless, it remains a reasonable hypothesis that the sort of large-scale conflicts we have had over the centuries have been possible only because some few people were in a position to command large numbers of men prepared to do their bidding, and to support their activities with taxation. If the funds had to be raised entirely by voluntary means, war, especially in modern times, would be a rarity indeed.

There was an ill-considered theory, at one time, that wars were due to "capitalism". As a hypothesis about the origin of the most sizable recent conflicts among nations, that view has little to recommend it, most especially because war is an inherently expensive way of getting something, whereas if it is a thing that is inherently capable of being transferred, then it is certainly going to be cheaper simply to buy it. This most especially includes human labor, by far the most likely service to be the object of beady-eyed capitalists abroad, but also resources of any other kind one can think of. Nations already at war may find it essential to appropriate such things as oil by force, but for erstwhile peaceable nations the idea is largely too absurd to contemplate.

Nevertheless, people would want to know how defense would be possible on libertarian premises, supposing a society was threatened by external aggression. Such defense is, after all, virtually the supreme example of a positive externality, as economists call it. If you defend a given area, then you defend the occupants of that area, whether they have paid for it or not, and whether they wanted to be defended or not. Is this, then, perhaps one instance in which the case for forcing payment is established? Perhaps it is. But if it is, note the reason: if those defended would otherwise be dead or enslaved, then it is difficult for them to argue that your activity has made them worse off than they would be if they were instead forced to assist in the defense. On the other hand, the libertarian will be duly appalled at the lengths to which states will go, as when pacifists are "beaten, half-starved, left naked in dark, damp cells. The sixty-nine who died were not murdered in the usual sense, just mistreated to death"[3]— and this in one of the most civilized countries in the world at the time (England during World War I). Treatment in plenty of other countries and at earlier times has ranged downward from there.

The problem is that they might not view the result of conquest by the particular enemy in question as "slavery", and a great problem that is. A lesser problem is constituted by the cases of those who don't approve the particular tactics or strategy by means of which their defenders propose to defend them. The well-known advantages of totalitarianism over unruly democracy then assert themselves. In a major defense effort the need for effective coordination is extreme and is unlikely to be met by a situation of extreme liberty. There is, alas, no help for this. If this be weakness, then it will have to be faced and accepted as part of the "price" of liberty.

Nevertheless, it is not as though people can do nothing. The American colonies faced a similar situation and somehow managed. And in any case, in the modern world the arguments for surrendering the necessary amount of refractory autonomy to a single leader would be plain enough to most people. Men have not been found lacking to join military forces despite the absence of literal compulsion to do so, and given appreciable reality to the threat that might be facing a free society, it is not to be doubted that calls for enlistment would find ready response. The devices of the market need not be utterly abandoned here, either. One can imagine the organizers of rival "protection agencies" staging mock battles with each other, which would give potential customers an idea of who provides the better bargain in defense. The advantages of size and superior performance would likely leave all but very capable rivals out of the picture. It is an intriguing question whether effective defense is possible in the absence of central authority, and these few points obviously do not settle the matter.

As I have elsewhere pointed out, "Those who would make war have the upper hand, for there is no way to resist without going along."[4] Thomas Powers puts it thus: "When war comes, it leaves little room for choice—one either fights back or submits to the dreams and whims of the victor."[5] Some admire the pacifist, who would resist by suppressing the impulse to fight back under any provocation; but against a determined enemy pacifism is a self-exterminating policy. In any case, there is no room for the view that pacifism is a duty of justice; that we have the *right* to defend ourselves is too fundamental a principle to be denied coherently.[6] The problem is how we are to observe the strictures of right in wartime, especially when the most potent weapons are also the most indiscriminate in reach. There is no easy solution to this problem, and the only real solution, one supposes, is universal peace. Whether "real" is the right word to use here is also questionable, to be sure; but there is real hope, as this is written, that recognition of the limitless evil of nuclear war will compel us to general peace, as it perhaps has already done for some decades.

Foreign Policy toward Nonliberal States

The difficulties of defense pose one set of interesting problems. Another that deserves mention is what we may do regarding highly illiberal states. Should we be trying to help overthrow evil regimes? Or do we have to stand by while their citizens get robbed, tortured, and pushed around?

When there are governments, whose actions are viewed as representing and signifying very much more than just the actions of individuals, motivated by their particular views of what is to be done, an individual is scarcely *able* to act on his or her own. It is very much to the credit of the American government, for example, that as this is written it does not prevent private American citizens from assisting, on their own initiative, the people of Nicaragua in various peaceable ways even while their government supports an insurgent military force whose scruples about the treatment (or perhaps discernment) of noncombatants leave a great deal to be desired. Though it may seem a cop-out, it is surely *very* difficult to render philosophical advice to states in their mutual relations in this respect. By and large, however, a governmental policy of minimizing bloodshed, especially the blood of innocent persons, whether they be citizens of one's own or the other country, is surely to be generally commended. This is not only because shedding blood invites and invariably leads to retaliation, but also out of a sense of realism about what can be accomplished.

The suggested policy, bland though it may sound, in its suggestion goes against a major grain of libertarian thought in one respect. On the view pressed by Nozick, for example, that rights are rigid, incapable of being legitimately violated even for the sake of preventing wholesale further violations by others, it is hard to see how effective forcible intervention against tyranny could *ever* be justified. For there is hardly any possibility of (for example) fomenting a revolution that does not endanger the lives of innocents.

Proponents of the hard libertarian line on this matter may invoke the doctrine of Double Effect, holding that although there is an absolute prohibition on intentional killing of innocents, the same cannot be said of policies that are merely risky, involving such killing or other harm as a perhaps foreseeable side effect. I have complained about this doctrine elsewhere,[7] pointing out that if people have the right not to be killed, it is the right not to be *killed*, rather than the right not to be "intentionally" killed, in any narrow sense of that term. It is generally wrong to take lives in the hope that it will prevent others from being taken, in particular if the situation has the structure of a bribe or deal to persons who, by their very willingness to put other people's lives at risk in pursuing their ends, show themselves to be untrustworthy. But it is hard to lay this down as a totally rigid policy, just as it is hard to lay down a policy of doing nothing that will endanger innocent lives. People will rationally take great risks for freedom, including the risk of losing one's life from efforts to undo tyranny that go awry. But we bank on this at very great risk; the efforts in question need to be extremely well planned if they are to be justified.

The Nonrevolutionist's Evolutionist Handbook

Many have mounted revolutions in the name of liberty, and the claim has varied in plausibility from one case to another. Revolution-aries aim to seize the reins of power. This makes it a little difficult to mount a "libertarian revolution", since the object of this would be as nearly as possible the complete absence of power, properly speak-ing—certainly of *political* power, at any rate. This object is rather short of "reins" to seize. A further point is that there is some question how a libertarian "regime" would proceed: by having the elected officials busy themselves eliminating their positions, one presumes. Not to be expected, if history is our guide!

In another context James Buchanan makes a wise point that can well be commended to the would-be revolutionist. He frames an ex-ample of someone who inherits a capital asset, a building constructed in 1900, yielding an income stream of ten units per year which, if capitalized, indicates the capital value of the asset to be one hundred. Assume it can't be sold in its current use, and that the scrap value is twenty units. There may be alternative opportunities for investment where a hundred units yield 15 percent, but the building can't be converted to this alternative. Hence, it remains rational for him to keep rather than scrap it. This analogy, Buchanan suggests, "is quite helpful when we consider law and the calculus of an individual con-cerning his optimally preferred level of legal restrictiveness. An indi-vidual might prefer that the legal structure . . . take somewhat differ-ing form. . . . But he inherits the legal order as it is, not something else. And he cannot 'sell' this order to third parties. His choice set reduces to [these] alternatives. . . . He can scrap the structure and start anew, but in so doing, . . . a large share of the income flow from the asset will be destroyed, a flow that may not be fully restored until new investments mature over time. . . . Or, he can hold on to the structure as it now exists, despite his recognition that alternative structures would be more desirable. . . . Straightforward economic analysis suggests that large thresholds may exist as between these choice alternatives. . . . The erosion of constitutional-legal order should be recognized for what it is—the destruction of social capital, with all of the consequences therefrom."[8] Similarly: the revolutionary is destroying the social capital of the order he seeks to replace, and there is usually a very high likelihood that the new investment will not pay off soon, and a considerable likelihood that it will never pay off at all, when the cost in human lives and disruption is considered. Other methods are to be greatly preferred.

Reflections on Libertarianism

What Has Not Been Proven

THE TIME HAS ARRIVED for some final reflections and assessments. Where do we stand? What will attract about this doctrine, and what not? In these concluding reflections I will not advance further *arguments* for the libertarian view. Instead, we will consider more precisely what has been established, in some reasonably strong sense of 'establish', and what has not. And then the question is, how much falls between the cracks?

What do the efforts of Part Two show? The foundations we have considered there are anti-intuitional, in the sense pertinent to this area of inquiry. The appeal is to one's pre- or nonmoral values, virtually whatever they may be. Assessing rationality by the standard of maximizing valued states of affairs, they attempt to establish, via contractarian reasoning, that the libertarian idea is a *rational* doctrine: that it is rational for anyone who is a member of a group to attempt to bring about general reinforcement of the libertarian principle, and also that the prospects of internalized, self-imposed reinforcement are excellent.

Excellent, yes: but not perfect. There are at least two serious problems at this level. In the first place, there is the qualification "virtually" in the aforementioned characterization. Some values of some persons are going to lie beyond the reach of the civilizing doctrine we are examining. Two sorts in particular come to mind: (1) fanatics and (2) psychopaths. Regarding the first: some religious beliefs, for example, will be highly resistant to tolerance and accommodation at any level. Nor need the belief be religious in any narrow sense: certain

types of Nietzscheans, preaching an ideal of superiority that entails
the legitimacy of subjugating the rest to the allegedly superior persons in question, will likewise qualify. And second, persons of extremely nonprudential cast of mind will likewise not be convinced.
Those who live for the moment and care not what the future will
bring are beyond the reach of arguments such as ours. Both kinds of
people are, in a sense, at war with the rest of us—not merely with
rival fanatics and psychopaths, but with that vast majority of normal
folk to whom, it is hoped, the sorts of arguments advanced make
eminent sense. From the broader point of view, the psychopaths are
not usually much to worry about, but fanatics are quite another
matter.

This is especially true because of the second principal limitation,
as I see it, of the arguments advanced: if enough agreement among
enough people can be reached, through proselytization and the like,
then a sizable group of fanatics could come to feel able to hold out
against the rest of humanity. The external danger from such groups is
not likely, in the near future, to be great. Relations with them are
likely to be uncomfortable, to be sure, and there is always the danger
of exotic new weapons by means of which they may decide to threat-
en the human race into some kind of submission. However, the internal danger to possibly deviant members of the societies dominated by
such sectarian ways is extreme. Prospects for extension of the freedoms we have been defending, freedoms that most readers will likely
hold dear (with the probable exception of the views advanced about
private property in the narrow sense of the term "property"), are essentially nil in such societies. Proponents of freedom for all have their
work cut out for them in dealing with such groups.

Not that we need concede the full rationality of such sectarian
groupings, however. For they found their fanaticism on doctrine, and
the familiar species of such doctrines are not intellectually compelling. They do not have the status of science, which is compelling to
anyone with an interest in knowing how things are. From the point of
view of an outsider, religious doctrines (which are my paradigms)
have the status of poetry at best, and of gibberish at worst; the insider
is likely unwilling or unable to distinguish poetry from fact. For her,
they are *truths*, and not just unprovable items of faith. Being (in her
view) true, and not just one person's strongly held beliefs among others, it must follow that all others are in error, and likely culpable error;
at any rate, it follows that the rest need not be allowed to stand in the
way of the march of truth in the world. And so the car-bombs are

wheeled out with abandon. Prospects for reasonable relations with such people, based on mutual acknowledgment of human rights, are not good.

But I do not regard this as a *weakness* in the principles examined in this book.

The Lure of Nationalism

The most prominent arguments for the State considered in Part Three have been arguments of the "collective goods" or "public goods" type. As arguments for the State, as such, these have by and large been found wanting. If the typical modern state were put to trial against such arguments, it would not survive the test in recognizable condition. It would be shorn to a ghost of its former self.

But those ready to watch with glee as the State withers away before our very eyes had better bring very comfortable chairs and ample provisions, for they have a very long wait ahead of them. It is clear that the State has an attraction to large numbers of people that exceeds the reach of any such arguments. Part of the attraction, to be sure, lies in misguided perceptions and fallacious reasoning: the State is not providing a free ride—it is, on the contrary, a very expensive and uneconomic as well as involuntary investment—and its claims to be literally indispensable are without rational foundation. But these things are probably only a significant fraction of the support enjoyed by any State that hasn't fallen well below the extremely modest standards of competence that apply in this area. Clearly, most people regard their nation as something more like a very large family, a group to whom they have ties of affection and loyalty, of faith, hope, and love, the locus of courage and ready self-sacrifice. They indeed regard the State as "higher" than themselves. No examination of the day-to-day operations of mere governments, as they set about on their dreary business of imposing taxes, framing further unnecessary restrictions on the lives of their citizens, and so on, will bear out the idea that the State is "high". To get insight into these matters, one must instead stand in the shadows of their magnificent capitol buildings, watch (from a suitable distance) their displays of military might, and get a feel for the history of their people.

But that's not all. There is also the gun, and the badge of authority. To some extent, I am sure, these are different. But there is the uncomfortable feeling that the State is looked up to in part because of its power to force people to do its bidding. The State as slavemaster is not extinct. And the habit of asking whether the State has any *right* to hold its citizens subject—the term subjects was once standardly used to denote citizens—is still confined largely to philosophers, of either the professional or the cracker-barrel type. It is, of course, a habit essential to freedom, and one that professors of philosophy endeavor to inculcate into their bright-eyed students; but it is still fairly rare, and not very deep.

So we have the question whether the spiritual satisfactions of the nation can be separated from the tawdrier aspects of the State without irreplaceable loss. Of course the satisfactions in question are by no means universal, but merely very widespread. But just as one who leaves a religious doctrine in whose embraces he was reared is apt to look upon its adherents with a certain affection and its doctrines with a sort of nostalgia, so, too, we would doubtless feel that we had lost something rather nice were we to arrive at the era of genuine state-lessness.

Still, it is hard to see why the Canadian National Hockey team can't continue to be a reality even if the Parliament buildings become, as in some respects they already are, merely further places of business. There is, indeed, some basis for hope that people will find the Canada-Russia hockey competitions not only a lot safer (for the spectators, anyway) but also really more *interesting* than World War III.

Privatization, Trivialization, and the Eternal Yuppie

The other side of the same coin is to be found in some criticisms from the high of brow among us, who look out upon the very civil society in which a great many of us live out our lives in the parts of the world most favored by freedom—and (very stylishly) retch. For no doubt the view in Suburbia is the view of the future of Liberal Mankind, with its substantial, mid-to-high-tech houses, not noted for architectural distinction but very long on creature comfort, each with its hard-working professional couple, its 1.8 children with their shining, well-scrubbed faces, their shelves of personal computer games, their eternal trips to the ballet lesson, the hockey team practice, and so on and on. In the other direction, they will see McDonald's Hamburgers, Shell Oil stations, and further rows of glitzy, high-convenience shopping facilities. For many thoughtful onlookers the view will inspire the question whether this, indeed, is what all the patriots' blood was spilled for, all the philosophers' ink, all the politicking.

And they will wonder, in view of it all, whether life is worth living. This question, of course, is not often asked by those living the lives we speak of here. Is this because they are too busy with their trivial pursuits to ask the question, or because they find the answer self-evidently in the affirmative? And if the latter, is it testimony to the enduring value of lives of that kind, or is it due to narrowness of vision, a failure to face the question straight on?

There are all sorts of reasons to stare down the intellectuals in question, not the least of which is that those who ask it also enjoy getting from A to B in an excellent modern automobile, comfortable, safe, comparatively reliable, and efficient, enjoy the culinary arts practiced by their hosts with the help of modern technology and organization, know that they can make their way by modern airplanes to less civilized areas of the globe in half a day's travel, and in general shirk not from availing themselves of the "material" advantages of contemporary life.

Nor is that all. This same sophisticated critic can also view superb operatic performances on her TV set, or can even make her way to the opera house itself, if she can spare the time from looking down her nose at the triviality of modern life. She can hear performances of the late quartets of Beethoven that would have left Beethoven himself, could he have but heard them, astonished in admiration. And so on. Free-wheeling, crude, trivial, and bourgeoisified America has meanwhile quietly assembled an absolute majority of the entire world's supply of symphony orchestras, including most of its best ones. It's a familiar lesson that must not be overlooked: if you let a thousand flowers go, a lot of them will look to any given observer like weeds, but a few others, if you look carefully, will turn out to be orchids.

There is a recrudescence of a sort of tribalism in current political philosophy, elevating the bonds of commitment to a philosophical status that they can't, in my judgment, bear for that purpose; but the effort is instructive and thought-provoking even if misguided. In a world in which religious wars are still raging, and indeed are the only ones seriously probable in the near future, we can hardly miss the lesson, that tribal blood is still thicker, in many quarters, than liberal water. But sober reflection may lead us to think that perhaps suburbia, if one must take one's choice, is the way to go. After all, the very freedom that makes suburbia possible is also an invitation to those who dwell there to make it interesting, even deeply satisfying, while we're at it. And also, of course, to abandon it for your favorite commune or a shack in the woods of Maine, British Columbia, or even the Yukon. We are not, after all, *fated* to remain in suburbia!

The Secular Problem of Evil

Thinkers interested in theology have long pondered the Problem of Evil: how could a supposedly perfectly good, which presumably means benevolent, God who is also omnicompetent and omnipotent allow the world we live in to be the way it is, with its ample quota of disasters, famines, plagues, and worst of all, wars—especially wars in which far too many of the good guys meet awful deaths? Fortunately, we needn't concern ourselves with that problem here. My concern is with what we may call the secular version of the problem. Imagine a world truly at peace, where everyone invariably respects everyone's rights, where the evils of violence are completely absent and in consequence all lives flourish as they may within that framework. Is this a prospect to gladden the heart? No doubt in the main it is. But the human soul has a quarter in which the reaction to this prospect is boredom, not to say insanity. Could any of us *stand* it for long in Paradise? What has passed for greatness among humans over the past several millenia has included a disproportionate share of military and political accomplishments involving massive use of force. The Alexanders, Caesars, Napoleons, and likewise the Abe Lincolns and Woodrow Wilsons of this world have in common that their unshakable convictions about how things should go have been pursued at the expense of millions upon millions of lives taken by violence. Well, suppose all that absent, and that all pursuits of the human race had been exclusively peaceable. Suppose, in short, that the nice guys *had* finished first. Morally admirable, no doubt: but can we really deny that it would have been altogether less *interesting*? Do we not, in our generally peaceful communities, watch movies about war and conflict? Aren't the pages of newspapers filled with reports of automobile accidents, murders, rapes, disasters? Isn't that what *sells*?

If this is indeed a problem, as I find it difficult not to feel it to be, then it is one for which the libertarian certainly has no solution. It is one that *has* no solution, for that matter: for the problem, in a nutshell, is that evil is one of our goods. The best we can do, in the real world, is to create conflicts of lesser dimensions, among persons willing to engage in them—the conflicts of games and sports will do as examples; or we can move to the world of the imagination, to make movies or write books and symphonies exploring the spiritual aspects of these things, making them vivid without the need of real-world violence. These, so far as I can see, are the best we can do. Let us hope they will be sufficient.

Advice to Libertarian Political Parties

What would the budding convert to libertarianism, anxious to spread the blessings of liberty, do in our State-dominated age? One obvious major avenue is to do the same as everyone else with a cause: go into politics. This is bound to be less comfortable when, as was observed above, this particular breed of politician's main aim must be to depoliticize as much as possible. It is an interesting question where he would start—and, of course, how far he would get. (Such candidates have not gotten very far yet: to my knowledge, a libertarian candidate for any office of major consequence has yet to be elected in North America.)

The biggest problem will be interrelatedness. Will the candidate propose to disassemble the welfare state? He will have problems, unless he can come up with credible proposals to get broadly similar results accomplished by nongovernmental means. This is where the "action" must be: hard work on the design of effective voluntary institutions. After all, the libertarian's fundamental argument, if this study has been on the right track, is that anything worth doing that the Statist can do can be done better by individuals and voluntary associations acting on their own. Here, then, is the challenge: to put up or shut up.

But going into formal politics is not necessary. It is possible for the private citizen to get somewhere without actually occupying elective office. She can go into the insurance business and try to improve on what the State has to offer; he can stimulate interest in a police review board of concerned citizens; and in any number of ways, the considerable degree of freedom we enjoy in these luckier parts of the world can be taken advantage of.

Some will speak of reversing the rising tide of State activity before it is too late, as though some kind of specific catastrophe looms before us otherwise. But that is hysteria. The impending disasters represent extreme and consequently improbable extrapolations from existing policies and institutional trends. One deals with these by finding alternatives whose superiority will be increasingly evident at the margin. Nothing is done in a moment, life has a way of going on, and the need is for specific and workable solutions, not for grand gestures or sweeping rhetoric.

Does It Matter?

The libertarian advances a two-pronged thesis: first, that practically everything done by modern governments violates someone or
others' rights; and second, that likewise practically everything they
do is inefficient. A main claim of this study has been that these concerns are not all that different, in the end. Rights are founded on
considerations of efficiency, if of a fundamental kind. A large part of
the violation of rights asserted has to do with the collection of taxes,
that is to say, the rights violated are property rights in the sense of
rights to payments for whatever services one sells to make one's living. Few—though some—violations in contemporary democracies
consist of outright, overt uses of force against the citizen. The Knock
at the Door, as suggested at the outset, is subtler than that, and the
particular form in which the modern state exerts itself against us both
relatively civilized and relatively benign by historical standards.

Turn, then, to the contemporary citizen and let us ask how much
she *minds* all this violation. The answer will of course vary a certain
amount, but the fact is that most citizens will not readily be persuaded that all sorts of awful things are happening to them every day
of their lives. Not from this source, anyway.

Actually, we should be able to come up with a sort of measure, or
bill, in principle. Here's the amount of taxes paid; here's what you're
getting for it; here's what you might pay on a reasonable private supplying of the same thing; here, then, is the amount you would save by
turning most or all government functions to private hands. Would the
amount be very great? It would be very difficult to say, and certainly
most of the speeches of libertarian politicians would consist in offering and backing up figures of this kind. Nevertheless, the point is that
we could presumably come up with some sort of moderately plausible
figures, which in most cases would probably not be tremendously
large. Then there would be the fact that these taxes were involuntary.
The citizen was deprived of a certain liberty in their determination.
As we have seen, one would have to convince the citizen that this was
so, since she might very well feel that in having the vote she had such
a liberty. But she would likely concede that there was indeed a difference of this kind, at any rate. The question is, how much would all
this, in the end, *matter* to her? The compulsory nature of the taxes is a
point, but a small point in view of the fact that most of the services in
question are, she would claim, necessary or important, so even if it
might be a little better if she had more say in them, it would be at best
a matter of degree. And then, you know, there's the fact that when

the State does them, they are *done* and one doesn't have to think about it. And in the case of national defense, it would be a very uphill battle to show the citizen that we could get along without State supply of that service.

All in all, then, the case is that the libertarian's proposals are, well, *interesting*, but not all that terribly important. They don't have the level of importance that, say, a proposal to go full-blown socialist would have. There, the citizen can see, there is much to lose and little to gain. But turning to the libertarian, he will feel that there may perhaps be a bit to gain, maybe, but on the other hand, we're not much, if really any, worse off with the present dispensation.

The libertarian's reply to such attitudes will have to consist, first, in attaching a monetary value to the claimed losses that will mean something. What if the typical citizen isn't just a little worse off but a *lot* worse off than if few or no services were compulsorily collectivized? And as to the value of particular liberties, we can identify cases where people are losing a lot, rather than just a little, in respects that don't admit of ready monetary quantification. What about those whose sons are spending years in jail for dealing in drugs, for example? What about all the little things you just aren't allowed to do? Most of us live reasonably comfortable lives where things go reasonably well, and we don't get in much trouble with the law. But for a great many people, things do not go so well, and they do get in such trouble. Is the law, on the whole, doing them down? Those things would have to be looked into, in detail, and possibly the results could be made to matter to many. It remains to be seen.

What doesn't remain to be seen is the general observation that a sense of crisis is not really justified. But that is in good part because we have many liberties now, and the public sectors of our societies, by and large, are doing things that few people think ought not, in one way or another, to be done. The libertarian's battle is an uphill one: his enemies are apathy, affection for the State, and lack of rallying cries. It will be interesting to see whether proponents of this viewpoint will be able to make appreciable headway against these obstacles.

Concluding Note

For the libertarian, the lives of individual people are the trees, and the danger of political life is to be so busy looking at the forest that one fails to notice those trees of which, after all, it ultimately consists. But people are not in fact trees, and one cannot go thinning out a few over here so as to improve the look of that lot over there. Many and sometimes all trees will do better if we have an occasional look at the forest, to be sure. The necessity to do so is increasingly frequent in modern times. Nevertheless, those who undertake to be forest rangers do so at the behest of and for the sake of particular maples, spruces, and the rest of it. One does not assure responsiveness to this by securing one's office via a majority vote of the rest of the trees. One might even recall that forests flourished from time immemorial with no caretakers at all! Fundamentally, trees take care of themselves. People are even better equipped for this, being rational animals. Turning them loose and wishing them good luck may be the best prescription for any number of ills.

Notes, Bibliography, and Index

NOTES

PART ONE

Preface

1. Robert Nozick, *Anarchy, State, and Utopia* (New York: Basic Books, 1974).

2. *Dialogue* 16, no. 2 (1977): 298–327; but work on it began over Christmas, 1974.

3. Jan Narveson, *Morality and Utility* (Baltimore, Md.: Johns Hopkins University Press, 1967).

4. David Gauthier, *Morals by Agreement* (New York: Oxford University Press, 1986).

Chapter 1

1. Ronald Dworkin, "Liberalism," in Stuart Hampshire, ed., *Public and Private Morality* (Cambridge: Cambridge University Press, 1978), p. 127.

2. David Gauthier, *Morals by Agreement* (New York: Oxford University Press, 1986), p. 341.

3. Thomas Nagel, "Moral Conflict and Political Legitimacy," *Philosophy and Public Affairs* 16, no. 3 (Summer 1987): 215–240.

Chapter 2

1. Alan Gewirth, *Reason and Morality* (Chicago: University of Chicago Press, 1979), makes this a defining feature of the rational agent, and the foundation of a right of liberty. I have criticized his procedure for attempting to derive this right in "Gewirth's Reason and Morality—A Study in the Hazards of Universalizability in Ethics," *Dialogue* 19, no. 4 (December 1980): 651–674. (Further discussion will be found in Chapter 14.)

2. Lawrence Haworth, *Autonomy* (New Haven: Yale University Press, 1986).

3. Ibid., summarized from p. 42.

4. Ibid., p. 45.

5. Ibid., p. 46.

6. Jan Narveson, *Morality and Utility* (Baltimore: Johns Hopkins University Press, 1967), esp. pp. 71–79.

Chapter 3

1. Wright Neely, "Freedom and Desire," *Philosophical Review* 83, no. 1 (January 1974): 32–54.

2. Aristotle, *Nichomachean Ethics*, I.1.

3. John Gray, "On Negative and Positive Liberty," in Z. Pelczynski and J. Gray, *Conceptions of Liberty in Political Philosophy* (London: Athlone Press, 1984), p. 322.

4. Ibid., p. 337.

5. Ibid., p. 396.

6. Isaiah Berlin, "Two Concepts of Liberty" (pamphlet; Oxford: Oxford University Press, 1958); revised version in *Four Essays on Liberty* (Oxford University Press, 1969).

Chapter 4

1. This point is due to Robert Nozick, *Anarchy, State, and Utopia* (New York: Basic Books, 1974), pp. 28–29.

2. Ibid., p. 206.

3. For a very interesting discussion of J. S. Mill's view on what we are permitted to do by the principle of liberty, see Peter Dalton, "Liberty, Autonomy, Toleration," *Philosophical Papers* (Capetown, South Africa) 15, nos. 2–3 (1986): 185–196. I return to the point in Part Three, Chapter 19.

4. Richard Taylor, *Freedom, Anarchy, and the Law* (Buffalo: Prometheus, 1982).

Chapter 5

1. M. T. Dalgarno, "Analysing Hobbes' Contract," *Proceedings of the Aristotelian Society* 76 (1976): 209–226.

2. John Stuart Mill, *Utilitarianism* (London: J. M. Dent, Everyman Library, 1968), p. 45.

3. Thomas Hobbes, *Leviathan* (New York: Dutton, Everyman, 1950), p. 107.

4. Ronald Dworkin has enunciated this doctrine in various places. One is in his "Is There a Right to Pornography?" *Oxford Journal of Legal Studies* 177 (1981): 177–212: "Rights . . . are best understood as trumps over some back-

ground justification for political decisions that states a goal for the community as a whole. If someone has a right to moral independence, this means that it is for some reason wrong for officials to act in violation of that right, even if they (correctly) believe that the community as a whole would be better off if they did" (p. 200).

5. The example is Elisabeth Anscombe's. See her well-known article "Modern Moral Philosophy," *Philosophy* 33 (1958): 1–19.

6. The famous example is due to a discussion by Immanuel Kant, "On a Supposed Right to Lie From Benevolent Motives" in T. K. Abbot, trans. and ed., *Kant's Critique of Practical Reason and Other Writings on the Theory of Ethics* (London: Longmans, Green, 1954), pp. 361–365.

7. Hillel Steiner, "How Free: Computing Personal Liberty," in A. Philips Griffiths, ed., *Of Liberty*, Royal Institute of Philosophy Lecture Series 15 (Cambridge: Cambridge University Press, 1983), pp. 73–90.

8. Robert Nozick, *Anarchy, State, and Utopia* (New York: Basic Books, 1974), esp. pp. 29–32.

9. Ibid., p. 32.

10. Ibid., p. 30.

11. Charles Fried, *Right and Wrong* (Cambridge: Harvard University Press, 1978), p. 12.

12. Ibid., p. 12.

13. Judith Jarvis Thomson, "Some Ruminations on Rights," reprinted in Jeffrey Paul, *Reading Nozick* (Totowa, N.J.: Rowman and Littlefield, 1981), pp. 130–147.

14. Jan Narveson, "Utilitarianism and Formalism," *Australasian Journal of Philosophy* 43, no. 1 (1965): 58–71.

15. Gilbert Harman, "On Moral Relativism Defended," *Philosophical Review* 84, no. 1 (January, 1975): 3–22. See also Harman's *The Nature of Morality* (New York: Oxford University Press, 1977), esp. chs. 8–9.

16. The reader may wish to compare my discussion in Jan Narveson, "Positive/Negative: Why Bother?" in Eric Mack, ed., *Positive and Negative Duties*, Tulane Studies in Philosophy (New Orleans, 1985), pp. 51–66.

17. Kai Nielsen, *Equality and Liberty* (Totowa, N.J.: Rowman & Allenheld, 1983), p. 304. My review of this work is found in *International Philosophical Quarterly* 26, no. 2 (June 1986): 192–194.

18. Nielsen, *Equality and Liberty*, p. 310.

19. Ibid., p. 311.

Chapter 6

1. Kai Nielsen, *Equality and Liberty* (Totowa, N.J.: Rowman & Allenheld, 1983), p. 267.

2. Ibid., p. 253.

3. Ibid., p. 252.

4. Narveson, "A Puzzle About Economic Justice in Rawls' Theory," *Social Theory and Practice* 4, no. 1 (1976): esp. 2–7.

5. Robert Nozick, *Anarchy, State, and Utopia* (New York: Basic Books, 1974), ch. 6 ("Distributive Justice"—also reprinted separately in *Philosophy and Public Affairs* 3, no. 1 [Fall 1973]).

6. The idea that property ownership is actually a complex "bundle" of rights is now widely accepted. One of its main originators is A. M. Honoré; see, for example, "Property, Title, and Redistribution" from *Equality and Freedom: Past, Present and Future*, ed. by Carl Wellman, ARSP Archives for Philosophy of Law and Social Philosophy: Beiheft Neue Folge nr. 10 (Wiesbaden: Steiner-Verlag, 1977), pp. 107–115.

7. Murray Rothbard, *Power and Market* (Menlo Park, Calif.: Institute for Humane Studies, 1970), p. 76.

8. In connection with freedom of speech, see Narveson, "Rights and Utilitarianism," in W. E. Cooper, K. Nielsen, and S. C. Patten, eds., *New Essays on John Stuart Mill and Utilitarianism, Canadian Journal of Philosophy* Supplementary Vol. 5 (1979): 148; for the general thesis, see "Human Rights: Which, If Any, Are There?" in J. R. Pennock and J. W. Chapman, eds., *Human Rights*, NOMOS XXIII (New York: New York University Press, 1981), pp. 175–198.

9. G. A. Cohen, "Self-Ownership, World-Ownership, and Equality," in F. Lucash, ed., *Justice and Equality, Here and Now* (Ithaca, N.Y.: Cornell University Press, 1986), p. 109.

10. Ibid., p. 111.

11. Ibid., p. 113–114.

12. Ibid., p. 112.

13. Nozick, *Anarchy, State and Utopia*, p. 178.

14. Cohen, "Self-Ownership," p. 131.

15. Ibid., pp. 132–133.

16. Ibid., p. 135.

17. G. A. Cohen, "Self-Ownership, World-Ownership, and Equality" Part II, *Social Philosophy and Policy* 3, no. 2 (Spring 1986): 77–96.

18. Ibid., p. 80.

19. Ibid., p. 85.

20. Ibid.

21. Allan Gibbard, "What's Morally Special about Free Exchange?" *Social Philosophy & Policy* 2, no. 2 (Spring 1985): 20–28.

22. Ibid., p. 21 (my emphasis).

23. Ibid., p. 22.

24. Ibid., p. 23.

25. Ibid., p. 24.

26. Ibid., p. 25.

27. Ibid.

Chapter 7

1. See G. A. Cohen, *Karl Marx's Theory of History* (Princeton: Princeton University Press, 1978).

2. G. A. Cohen, "The Labour Theory of Value and the Concept of Exploitation," *Philosophy and Public Affairs* 8, no. 4 (Summer 1979): 338–360.

3. Robert Nozick, *Anarchy, State, and Utopia* (New York: Basic Books, 1974), p. 163.

4. Onora O'Neill, "Robert Nozick's Entitlements," *Theoria* 19 (1976): 468–481.

5. O'Neill's note here refers to Nozick, *Anarchy, State, and Utopia*, pp. 280–282.

6. O'Neill, "Nozick's Entitlements," p. 471.

7. Ibid., p. 469.

8. Ibid., p. 476; cf. also Nozick, *Anarchy, State, and Utopia*, pp. 174–159.

9. Nozick delightfully discusses the difficulties in Locke's formulations: *Anarchy, State, and Utopia*, pp. 174–175.

10. John Arthur, "Resource Acquisition and Harm," *Canadian Journal of Philosophy* 17, no. 2 (June 1987): 337–347.

11. Ibid., p. 338.

12. Ibid., p. 339.

13. Ibid., p. 340.

14. Ibid., pp. 340–341.

15. Ibid., p. 342.

16. Ibid., pp. 341–343.

17. Ibid., p. 344.

18. Ibid., p. 345.

19. Ibid., p. 346.

20. Karl Marx, "Critique of the Gotha Program" in Robert C. Tucker, ed., *The Marx-Engels Reader* (New York: Norton, 1978), pp. 529–530. Note that Marx explicitly insists on deducting from the common product a share for those unable to work, but he says nothing at all about how we are justified in requiring those shares of the able. And when the chief complaint has been that they are "unpaid" labor, it's a little difficult to see how that is going to be justified!

21. Arthur, "Resource Acquisition," p. 344.

22. Ibid., p. 344.

Chapter 8

1. Randy Barnett, "A Consent Theory of Contract," *Columbia Law Review* 86, no. 2 (March, 1986): 269–321.

2. A. M. Macleod, "Justice and the Market: Rejoinder to Cragg and Mack", *Canadian Journal of Philosophy* 13, no. 4 (December 1983): 583.

3. David Braybrooke, "Justice and Injustice in Business" in Tom Regan, ed., *Just Business* (New York: Random House, 1984), pp. 167–201. See esp. p. 174, where he argues that persons having extraordinary wealth are "in a position to restrict other people's freedom and exercise power over them, in any of a number of ways, from hiring henchmen to beat them up to influencing politicians to disregard their claims."

4. Murray Rothbard, *Power & Market* (Menlo Park, Calif.: Institute for Humane Studies, 1970), p. 99.

5. Kai Nielsen, *Equality and Liberty* (Totowa, N.J.: Rowman & Allenheld, 1983), discusses this idea at some length, giving no apparent credit to its utter disconnection from the libertarian theory even though he takes it to be the archetypal defense of property.

PART TWO

Chapter 9

1. Lawrence Haworth, *Autonomy* (New Haven, Conn.: Yale University Press, 1986), p. 41.

2. Ibid.

3. Parts of this section derive from my "Remarks on the Foundations of Morality", a paper delivered at the Canadian Philosophical Association meeting, Guelph, Ontario, June 1986.

Chapter 10

1. There have been shelves written on the subject of the naturalistic fallacy. The term stems from G. E. Moore, *Principia Ethica*, ch. 1 (Cambridge: Cambridge University Press, 1903, and many later editions). Among the many critical articles on the subject, George Nakhnikian's "On the Naturalistic Fallacy" in H-N. Castañeda and G. Nakhnikian, *Morality and the Language of Conduct* (Detroit: Wayne State University Press, 1963), would likely be useful to the reader not already immersed in the subject. So too would W. D. Hudson, *The Is-Ought Question* (London: Macmillan, 1969), which has a number of important essays relevant to the subject. Readers will not want for other sources.

2. R. M. Hare, *Freedom and Reason* (Oxford: Oxford University Press, 1963), p. 10.

3. Henry Sidgwick, *The Methods of Ethics*, 7th ed. (London: Macmillan, 1961), p. 379.

4. Patrick Nowell-Smith, *Ethics* (Harmondsworth, Eng.: Penguin Books, 1955), p. 41.

5. John Rawls, *A Theory of Justice* (Cambridge: Harvard University Press, 1971).

6. For example, by Norman Daniels, in "Wide Reflective Equilibrium and Theory Acceptance in Ethics," *Journal of Philosophy* 76, no. 5 (May 1979): 256–282.

7. Ronald Dworkin, *Taking Rights Seriously* (Cambridge: Harvard University Press, 1977), esp. chs. 4–6.

Chapter 11

1. K. E. M. Baier, *The Moral Point of View* (Ithaca, N.Y.: Cornell University Press, 1958), p. 190.

2. We owe this point to David Hume in modern times. The classic source in his *Treatise of Human Nature*, Bk. III, Pt. I, Sec. 1.

3. Kant's views are found in his two major ethical writings, *Foundations of the Metaphysics of Morals* and *The Metaphysics of Morals;* these are available in Library of Liberal Arts editions (Indianapolis: Bobbs-Merrill). *The Foundations* and the Preface to the *Metaphysics of Morals* (provided in each of its halves in the Bobbs-Merrill edition) supply the main sources.

4. Baier, *The Moral Point of View*, esp. chs. 7 and 8.

5. Bernard Gert, *The Moral Rules* (New York: Harper & Row, 1966), esp. chs. 1–4 and 11.

6. F. E. Sparshott, *An Enquiry into Goodness* (Toronto and Chicago: University of Toronto Press and University of Chicago Press, 1958), p. 247. This much under-appreciated book should be known to every moral philosopher, not only for its interesting analysis, but for its inimitable style.

7. Such a view seems to have been advanced by Richard Norman, *Reasons for Action* (Oxford, U.K.: Basil Blackwell, 1971), esp. ch. 3.

8. Ibid., ch. 5, for instance. Current advocates of ethical relativism include Gilbert Harman and David Wong. See the former's *The Nature of Morality* (New York: Oxford University Press, 1977) and the latter's *Moral Relativity* (Berkeley: University of California Press, 1984). My critical notice of the latter, which details the problem of conflict inherent in this kind of view, is found in *Canadian Journal of Philosophy* 17, no. 1 (March 1987): 235–257.

Chapter 12

1. David Hume, *Inquiry Concerning the Principles of Morals*, Appendix III (Indianapolis: Bobbs-Merrill, Liberal Arts Press, 1957), p. 122.

2. John Rawls, *A Theory of Justice* (Cambridge: Harvard University Press, 1971), sec. 24; more generally, ch. 3.

3. G. E. Pence, "Fair Contracts and Beautiful Intuitions" in Kai Nielsen and Roger Shiner, eds., *New Essays on Contract Theory, Canadian Journal of Philosophy* Supplementary Vol. 3 (1977): 137–152, esp. sec. iv, "The Veil of Ignorance," pp. 148ff.

4. Rawls has an interesting list: see *A Theory of Justice*, ch. 23, "The Formal Constraints of the Concept of Right."

5. See in particular his *Leviathan* (London, 1651); one modern edition is in the Everyman Library (New York: Dutton, 1950).

6. Ibid., p. 104.

7. David Gauthier, *Morals by Agreement* (New York: Oxford University Press, 1986).

8. Ibid., ch. 6.

9. Ibid., p. 172.

10. Ibid., p. 173.

11. Ibid., p. 187.

12. Robert Axelrod, *The Evolution of Cooperation* (New York: Basic Books, 1984), esp. chs. 1 and 2.

13. It seems that our "players" are both *predictors* in a position not so very far from that of the predictor in Newcombe's problem. David Lewis has argued that Prisoner's Dilemma *is* a Newcombe's problem (*Philosophy and Public Affairs*, Fall 1973). There is plausibility to this view, inasmuch as the Newcombe decision maker is in the curious position of "responding" to a presumably past fact, yet one that looks very much as though it is a function of his present choice.

Chapter 13

1. John Locke, *Second Treatise on Civil Government* (1690), ch. II.

2. James Buchanan, *The Limits of Liberty* (Chicago: University of Chicago Press, 1975), p. 117.

3. Jan Narveson, *Morality and Utility* (Baltimore, Md.: Johns Hopkins University Press, 1967).

4. See David Gauthier, *Morals by Agreement* (New York: Oxford University Press, 1986), esp. pp. 42–46.

5. R. B. Brandt, such papers as "Some Merits of One Form of Rule-Utilitarianism", in S. Gorovitz, ed., *Utilitarianism, with Critical Essays* (Indianapolis: Bobbs-Merrill, 1971), pp. 324–344.

6. John Harsanyi, "Rule Utilitarianism, Equality, and Justice," *Social Philosophy and Policy* 2, no. 2 (Spring 1985): 115–127.

7. I develop these problems in a presently unpublished paper, "Two Views of Utilitarianism," read at the Canadian Philosophical Association meeting, Montreal, May 1985.

8. R. M. Hare, *Moral Thinking* (New York: Oxford University Press, 1977).

9. I have argued that Rawls is one of those thus "railroaded," despite his evident intentions. Cf. Narveson, "Rawls and Utilitarianism" in H. Miller and W. Williams, eds., *The Limits of Utilitarianism* (Minneapolis: University of Minnesota Press, 1982), pp. 128–143.

10. This question is explored at some length in my "Rights and Utilitarianism" in W. E. Cooper, K. Nielsen, and S. C. Patten, eds., *New Essays on John*

Stuart Mill and Utilitarianism, Canadian Journal of Philosophy Supplementary Vol. 5 (1979): 137–160.

Chapter 14

1. James Buchanan, *The Limits of Liberty* (Chicago: University of Chicago Press, 1975), ch. 1.
2. Arthur Ripstein, "Foundationalism in Political Theory," *Philosophy and Public Affairs* 16, no. 2 (Spring 1987): 115–137.
3. Ibid., p. 115.
4. Ibid., p. 133.
5. Ibid., p. 118.
6. Ibid., p. 120.
7. Ibid., p. 123.
8. Ibid., p. 124.
9. Ibid., pp. 124–125.
10. Ibid., pp. 125–126.
11. Ibid., p. 127.
12. Ibid., p. 127.
13. Ibid., pp. 128–129.
14. Ibid., pp. 129–130.
15. Ibid., p. 131.
16. Ibid., pp. 131–132.
17. Ibid., p. 133.
18. Ibid., pp. 133–134.
19. The reference here is to Thomas Scanlon, "Utilitarianism and Contractualism" in A. Sen and B. Williams, eds., *Utilitarianism and Beyond* (Cambridge: Cambridge University Press, 1982).
20. Ripstein, "Foundationalism," p. 135.
21. Ibid., pp. 136–137.
22. Robert Nozick, *Anarchy, State, and Utopia* (New York: Basic Books, 1974), pp. 48–51.
23. Lawrence Haworth, *Autonomy* (New Haven, Conn.: Yale University Press, 1986).
24. Jan Narveson, critical notice of *Anarchy, State, and Utopia, Dialogue* 21, no. 2 (1977): 298–327.
25. Haworth, *Autonomy,* esp. pp. 125–127.
26. Ibid., p. 7.
27. Ibid., p. 6.
28. Ibid., p. 131.
29. Ibid., pp. 167–168.
30. Ibid., p. 169.
31. Ibid., p. 213.
32. Ibid., p. 216.
33. Ibid., p. 215.

34. Alan Gewirth, *Reason and Morality* (Chicago: University of Chicago Press, 1978).

35. Ibid., p. 135.

36. Ibid., p. 96.

37. My objections are detailed in a critical notice, "Gewirth's Reason and Morality—A Study in the Hazards of Universalizability in Ethics," *Dialogue* 19, no. 4 (December 1980), 651–674.

38. Ellen Frankel Paul, *Property Rights and Eminent Domain* (New Brunswick, N.J.: Transaction Books, 1987), p. 226. Paul goes on to suggest that "Such an amoral universe is also logically absurd. Survivalism necessitates morality and rights, for without them purposive activity, aiming at the survival of the agent, is rendered as precarious and uncertain of fulfillment as possible" (p. 226). But this is really the first argument all over again—no new point of "logic" is invoked here.

39. Ibid., p. 230.

40. Ibid., p. 232.

41. Ibid., p. 233.

42. Ibid., p. 234.

43. See David Braybrooke, *Meeting Needs* (Princeton, N.J.: Princeton University Press, 1987); but see also Alex Michalos' critique of same, *Dialogue* (forthcoming, 1988).

44. David Gauthier, *Morals by Agreement* (New York: Oxford University Press, 1986), ch. 7.

45. Ibid., p. 204.

46. Ibid., p. 209.

47. Hobbes, *Leviathan*, ch. 13.

48. My "Marxism: Hollow at the Core," *Free Inquiry*, Spring 1983, pp. 29–35, presents my summary of the case regarding Marx's classic arguments. See also Mark Blaug, *A Methodological Appraisal of Marxian Economics*, De Vries Lectures (Amsterdam: Elsevier-North Holland Press, 1980); Jon Elster, *Making Sense of Marx* (Cambridge: Cambridge University Press, 1985), which has been greeted with highly mixed feelings by those who had hoped the title meant that there was sense to be made of him; Richard Miller's *Analyzing Marx* (Princeton: Princeton University Press, 1984) will serve as an example of the lengths to which a sympathizer must go in attempting to retrieve a theory.

49. Nozick, *Anarchy, State, and Utopia*, ch. 4.

50. John Hospers, *Libertarianism* (Los Angeles: Nash, 1971), p. 208.

PART THREE

Chapter 15

1. David Gauthier, *Morals by Agreement* (New York: Oxford University Press, 1986), ch. 3.

2. John Gray, "Contractarian Method, Private Property, and the Market

Economy," forthcoming in J. R. Pennock and J. W. Chapman, eds., *NOMOS* 31 (New York: New York University Press, 1988).

3. Amartya Sen, "The Moral Standing of the Market," in J. Paul, F. Miller, and E. Paul, eds., *Ethics and Economics* (Oxford: Blackwell, 1985), pp. 1–19.

4. Jules Coleman, "Market Contractarianism and the Unanimity Rule," in ibid., pp. 69–70.

5. Ibid., p. 85.

6. Gauthier, *Morals by Agreement*, p. 222.

7. Gray, "Contractarian Method," p. 39.

8. Coleman, "Market Contractarianism," p. 97.

9. Ibid., p. 101.

10. David Braybrooke, "Social Contract Theory's Fanciest Flight", *Ethics* 97, no. 4 (July 1987): 751.

11. Ibid., p. 752.

12. Ibid., pp. 755–756.

13. Ibid., p. 757.

14. Ibid., p. 757.

15. Gauthier, *Morals by Agreement*, ch. 5.

16. Braybrooke, "Social Contract Theory's Fanciest Flight", p. 758.

17. Ibid., p. 759.

18. This volume, pages 72–73 and pages 91–93.

19. Braybrooke, "Social Contract Theory's Fanciest Flight", p. 760.

20. Gauthier, *Morals by Agreement*, p. 274: "Society may be viewed as a single co-operative enterprise."

21. Braybrooke, "Social Contract Theory's Fanciest Flight", p. 762.

22. Gary Becker, in *The Economic Approach to Human Behavior* (Chicago: University of Chicago Press, 1976), attempts to show how a wide variety of ordinary behavior not ordinarily thought of as "economic" can be explained using economic concepts and principles. Alexander Rosenberg discusses, along Beckerian lines, "Prospects for the Elimination of Tastes from Economics and Ethics" in Paul, Miller, and Paul, *Ethics and Economics*, pp. 48–68.

23. Gauthier, *Morals by Agreement*, p. 98.

24. Ibid., p. 276.

25. Gauthier's minimax relative concession principle is developed in ibid., ch. 5. A criticism of his argument for this interesting principle is advanced in my "Contractarian Starting Points", delivered at the University of Western Ontario Conference on Contractarianism, and forthcoming in the proceedings of that event, ed. Peter Vallentyne (Stanford, Calif.: Stanford University Press, 1989). Detailed discussion of this intriguing but controversial principle seems out of place in the present inquiry.

26. Robert Nozick, *Anarchy, State, and Utopia* (New York: Basic Books, 1974), pp. 160–161.

27. Gauthier, *Morals by Agreement*, p. 276.

28. Ibid., p. 276.

29. Ibid., p. 274.

30. John Harsanyi, review of *Morals by Agreement*, forthcoming in *Economics and Philosophy*. I am indebted to Professor Harsanyi for supplying an advance copy of this review. My own review of *Morals by Agreement* is found in *Canadian Philosophical Reviews* 7, no. 6 (July 1987).

Chapter 16

1. John Hospers, *Libertarianism* (Los Angeles: Nash, 1971), p. 17.

2. Thomas Hobbes, *Leviathan*, ch. 18.

3. James Buchanan, *The Limits of Liberty* (Chicago: University of Chicago Press, 1975), p. 154.

4. Ibid., p. 155.

5. Ibid., p. 158.

6. John Finnis, *Natural Law and Natural Rights* (Oxford, Clarendon Press, 1980).

7. Robert Nozick, *Anarchy, state, and Utopia* (New York: Basic Books, 1974), pp. 118–119. The argument in fact occupies the opening five chapters and is exceedingly intricate.

8. Cf. the careful detective work on this argument in Robert Holmes's "Nozick on Anarchism" in Jeffrey Paul, *Reading Nozick* (Totawa, N.J.: Rowman and Littlefield, 1981), pp. 57–67.

9. Henry Shue advanced a criticism in "The Bogus Distinction—'Negative' and 'Positive' Rights," in Norman E. Bowie, *Making Ethical Decisions* (New York: McGraw-Hill, 1985), pp. 223–231, which is relevant here. I reject, of course, the thesis that the distinction is bogus. But it is essential to bear in mind that people do not have a fundamental right to protection any more than to any other service people could supply. There has to be an argument why the State should do no more if it does anything at all.

10. David Suits speculates interestingly on this in "On Locke's Argument for Government," *Journal of Libertarian Studies* 1, no. 3 (1977): 195–203.

11. James Q. Wilson, "Raising Kids," *Atlantic Monthly*, October 1983, pp. 45–56.

12. Nozick, *Anarchy, State, and Utopia*, p. 61.

13. Ibid., ch. 4, esp. pp. 78–84.

14. An important thinker along these lines is Randy Barnett. See his "Restitution—A New Paradigm of Criminal Justice," *Ethics* 87, no. 4 (July 1977): 279–301.

Chapter 17

1. Lawrence Haworth, *Autonomy* (New Haven, Conn.: Yale University Press, 1987), p. 212.

2. Peter Singer, "The Right to Be Rich or Poor," in Jeffrey Paul, ed. *Reading Nozick* (Totowa, N.J.: Rowman & Littlefield, 1981), p. 39.

3. See Jules Coleman for the argument that public goods problems are Prisoner's Dilemmas. See Allan Buchanan, *Justice, Efficiency, and the Market* (Totowa, N.J.: Rowman & Allenheld, 1984), for outstandingly clear expositions of this and related matters.

4. James Buchanan, *The Limits of Liberty* (Chicago: University of Chicago Press, 1975), p. 97.

5. Ibid., p. 117.

6. Chris Morris, "A Hobbesian Welfare State?" (forthcoming in *Dialogue*). I am indebted to the author for an advance copy of this interesting and important paper.

7. Ibid., pp. 19–20.

8. Ibid., p. 31.

9. John Hospers, *Libertarianism* (Los Angeles: Nash, 1971), p. 79.

Chapter 18

1. J. K. Galbraith, *The New Industrial State* (Boston: Houghton Mifflin, 1967). The thesis is enunciated on pp. 389–392 in particular, but the whole book is an argument for it.

2. Thomas Nagel, "Libertarianism without Foundations" reprinted in Jeffrey Paul, ed., *Reading Nozick* (Totowa, N.J.: Rowman & Littlefield, 1981), pp. 191–205. Quotation is on p. 200. Originally in the *Yale Law Journal* 85: 136ff.

3. Toronto *Star*, July 4, 1987.

4. I am indebted to my colleague Rolf George for impressing this point on me. I have no doubt that in his opinion, it has not, however, made a sufficient impression as yet.

5. James Buchanan, *The Limits of Liberty* (Chicago: University of Chicago Press, 1975), p. 39.

6. Allen Buchanan, "Justice and Charity," *Ethics* 97, no. 3 (April 1987): 559.

7. Ibid., pp. 560–561.

8. Ibid., p. 561.

9. Ibid., pp. 561–562.

10. Ibid., p. 562.

11. Ibid., p. 563.

12. Ibid.

13. Ibid., p. 564.

14. See also his admirable book, *Ethics, Efficiency, and the Market* (Totowa, N.J.: Rowman & Allenheld, 1985) for further analyses of these matters.

15. Buchanan, "Justice and Charity," p. 565.

16. Ibid., pp. 565–566.

17. Ibid., p. 566.

18. Ibid., p. 567.

19. Ibid., p. 568.

20. Tibor Machan, "Should Business Be Regulated?" in Tom Regan, ed., *Just Business* (New York: Random House, 1984), p. 217.

21. Buchanan, "Justice and Charity," pp. 570–571.

22. J. S. Mill, *An Essay on Liberty* (London: J. M. Dent, Everyman Library, 1968), p. 73.

23. See Peter Dalton, "Liberty, Autonomy, Toleration," *Philosophical Papers* (Capetown, South Africa) 15, nos. 2–3 (1986): 185–196.

24. Buchanan, "Justice and Charity," p. 575.

25. Jan Narveson, "Equality vs. Liberty: Advantage, Liberty," *Philosophy and Social Policy* 2, no. 1 (Autumn 1984).

26. Ronald Dworkin, "What is Equality? Part I," *Philosophy and Public Affairs* 10, no. 3 (Summer 1981).

27. Toronto *Star*, August 3, 1987.

Chapter 19

1. I review some of the options in "Animal Rights Revisited," in Harlan Miller and William H. Williams, eds., *Ethics and Animals* (Clifton, N.J.: Humana Press, 1983), pp. 45–60.

2. See also my "Abortion and Infanticide," *Bowling Green Studies in Applied Philosophy* (Bowling Green, Ohio: Department of Philosophy, Bowling Green State University, 1986), pp. 76–89.

Chapter 20

1. It consists of those remaining after subtracting the 85% who, I supposed above, would be able to do so—since they do so now, without realizing it. My guess is that the figure is high for Canada; interestingly, many Americans, with the specter of the slums before them, find it easy to believe that the figure is considerably higher in their considerably wealthier country.

2. See Roger Scruton, *The Meaning of Conservatism* (New York: Pelican Books, 1980).

3. Clifford Orwin, "Nozick's Liberal Utopia," unpublished paper delivered at Canadian Political Science Association meeting, Guelph, Ontario, June 1985), pp. 2, 7.

4. Ibid., p. 8.

5. Ibid., p. 9.

6. Ibid., p. 11.

7. Ronald Dworkin, "Is There a Right to Pornography?" *Oxford Journal of Legal Studies* 177 (1981): 177–212.

8. Ibid., p. 194.

9. Recall the passage from Murray Rothbard in Part One, Chapter 6.

10. Dworkin, "Is There a Right to Pornography?" p. 193.

11. Walter Block, *Defending the Undefendable* (New York: Fleet Press, 1976), p. 40.

Chapter 21

1. Morris and Linda Tannehill, *The Market for Liberty* (New York: Laissez Faire Books, 1984), p. 60.

2. Ellen Frankel Paul, *Property Rights and Eminent Domain* (New Brunswick, N.J.: Transaction Books, 1987), p. 3.

3. Ibid., p. 75.

4. Tannehill and Tannehill, *The Market for Liberty*, p. 61.

5. Paul, *Property Rights*, p. 76.

6. Hobbes, *Leviathan*, ch. 18.

7. Paul, *Property Rights*, p. 247.

8. Tannehill and Tannehill, *The Market for Liberty*, p. 54.

9. Charles L. Blockson, "Sea Change in the Sea Islands," *National Geographic* 172, no. 6 (December 1987): 740.

10. Paul, *Property Rights*, p. 53. The study is by Kenneth Rosen and Lawrence Katz, "The Effect of Land Use Controls on Housing Prices," Working Paper 80-13, University of California, Berkeley, Center for Real Estate and Urban Economics, 1981.

Chapter 22

1. John Hospers, *Libertarianism* (Los Angeles: Nash, 1971), pp. 411–412.

2. Michael Doyle, "Kant, Liberal Legacies, and Foreign Affairs" (in two parts), *Philosophy and Public Affairs* 12, nos. 3,4 (Summer, Fall 1983), p. 213 (italics in original).

3. Thomas Powers, "The Gentle Heroes" (review of Caroline Moorehead's *Troublesome People: The Warriors of Pacifism*, *Atlantic Monthly*, August 1987, p. 78.

4. Jan Narveson, "At Arms' Length: Violence and War" in Tom Regan, ed., *Matters of Life and Death*, 2nd ed. (New York: Random House, 1986), pp. 125–174. See p. 172 for quotation.

5. Powers, "The Gentle Heroes," p. 79.

6. Narveson, "At Arms' Length," pp. 137–142; Powers, "The Gentle Heroes," p. 78.

7. Jan Narveson, "At Arms' Length," pp. 157–159.

8. James Buchanan, *The Limits of Liberty* (Chicago: University of Chicago Press, 1975), p. 129.

BIBLIOGRAPHY

Anscombe, Elisabeth. "Modern Moral Philosophy." *Philosophy* 33 (1958): 1–19.

Arthur, John. "Resource Acquisition and Harm." *Canadian Journal of Philosophy* 17, no. 2 (June 1987): 337–347.

Axelrod, Robert. *The Evolution of Cooperation.* New York: Basic Books, 1984.

Baier, K. E. M. *The Moral Point of View.* Ithaca, N.Y.: Cornell University Press, 1958.

Barnett, Randy. "Restitution—A New Paradigm of Criminal Justice." *Ethics* 87, no. 4 (July 1977): 279–301.

———. "A Consent Theory of Contract." *Columbia Law Review* 86, no. 2 (March 1986): 269–321.

Becker, Gary. *The Economic Approach to Human Behavior.* Chicago: University of Chicago Press, 1976.

Berlin, Isaiah. "Two Concepts of Liberty" (revised version). In *Four Essays on Liberty.* Oxford: Oxford University Press, 1969. (Orig. ed., Oxford University Press, 1958.)

Blaug, Mark. *A Methodological Appraisal of Marxian Economics.* De Vries Lectures. Amsterdam: Elsevier-North Holland Press, 1980.

Block, Walter. *Defending the Undefendable.* New York: Fleet Press, 1976.

Blockson, Charles L. "Sea Change in the Sea Islands." *National Geographic* 172, no. 6 (December 1987): 735–763.

Brandt, R. B. "Some Merits of One Form of Rule-Utilitarianism." In S. Gorovitz, ed., *Utilitarianism, with Critical Essays.* Indianapolis: Bobbs-Merrill, 1971. Pp. 324–344.

Braybrooke, David. "Justice and Injustice in Business." In Tom Regan, ed., *Just Business.* New York: Random House, 1984. Pp. 167–201.

———. "Social Contract Theory's Fanciest Flight." *Ethics* 97, no. 4 (July 1987).

———. *Meeting Needs.* Princeton, N.J.: Princeton University Press, 1987.

Buchanan, Allen. *Ethics, Efficiency, and the Market.* Totowa, N.J.: Rowman & Allenheld, 1984.

———. "Justice and Charity." *Ethics* 97, no. 3 (April 1987): 558–575.

Buchanan, James. *The Limits of Liberty.* Chicago: University of Chicago Press, 1975.

Cohen, G. A. *Karl Marx's Theory of History.* Princeton: Princeton University Press, 1978.

———. "The Labour Theory of Value and the Concept of Exploitation." *Philosophy and Public Affairs* 8, no. 4 (Summer 1979): 338–360.

———. "Self-Ownership, World-Ownership, and Equality." In F. Lucash, ed., *Justice and Equality, Here and Now.* Ithaca, N.Y.: Cornell University Press, 1986.

———. "Self-Ownership, World-Ownership, and Equality," Part II. *Social Philosophy and Policy* 3, no. 2 (Spring 1986): 77–96.

Coleman, Jules. "Market Contractarianism and the Unanimity Rule." In Paul, Jeffrie, Red D. Miller and Ellen Frankel Paul. *Ethics and Economics.* London: Blackwell, 1985. Pp. 69–114.

Dalgarno, M. T. "Analysing Hobbes' Contract." *Proceedings of the Aristotelian Society* 76 (1976), pp. 209–226.

Dalton, Peter. "Liberty, Autonomy, Toleration." *Philosophical Papers* (Capetown, South Africa) 15, no. 2–3 (1986): 185–196.

Daniels, Norman. "Wide Reflective Equilibrium and Theory Acceptance in Ethics." *Journal of Philosophy* 76, no. 5 (May 1979): 256–282.

Doyle, Michael. "Kant, Liberal Legacies, and Foreign Affairs." (in two parts) *Philosophy and Public Affairs* 12, nos. 3, 4 (Summer and Fall 1983).

Dworkin, Ronald. *Taking Rights Seriously.* Cambridge, Mass.: Harvard University Press, 1977.

———. "Liberalism." In Stuart Hampshire, ed., *Public and Private Morality.* Cambridge: Cambridge University Press, 1978. Pp. 113–143.

———. "Is There a Right to Pornography?" *Oxford Journal of Legal Studies* 177 (1981): 177–212.

———. "What Is Equality? Part I." *Philosophy and Public Affairs* 10, no. 3 (Summer 1981): 185–246.

Elster, Jon. *Making Sense of Marx.* Cambridge: Cambridge University Press, 1985.

Finnis, John. *Natural Law and Natural Rights.* Oxford: Clarendon Press, 1980.

Fried, Charles. *Right and Wrong.* Cambridge: Harvard University Press, 1978.

Galbraith, J. K. *The New Industrial State.* Boston: Houghton Mifflin, 1967.

Gauthier, David. *Morals by Agreement.* New York: Oxford University Press, 1986.

Gert, Bernard. *The Moral Rules.* New York: Harper & Row, 1966.

Gewirth, Alan. *Reason and Morality.* Chicago: University of Chicago Press, 1978.

Gibbard, Allan. "What's Morally Special about Free Exchange?" *Social Philosophy & Policy* 2, no. 2 (Spring 1985): 20–28. Also published as *Ethics & Economics* (Basil Blackwell, for Social Philosophy and Policy Center, Bowling Green State University, Bowling Green, Ohio, 1985).

Gray, John. "On Negative and Positive Liberty." In Z. Pelczynski and J. Gray, *Conceptions of Liberty in Political Philosophy.* London: Athlone Press, 1984. P. 322.

———. "Contractarian Method, Private Property, and the Market Economy." forthcoming in *NOMOS* 31, ed. by J. Roland Pennock and John W. Chapman (New York: New York University Press, 1988).

Hare, R. M. *Freedom and Reason.* Oxford: Oxford University Press, 1963.

———. *Moral Thinking.* Oxford, 1977.

Harsanyi, John. "Rule Utilitarianism, Equality, and Justice." *Social Philosophy and Policy* 2, no. 2 (Spring 1985): 115–127.

———. Review of *Morals by Agreement,* forthcoming in *Economics and Philosophy.* (I am indebted to the author for supplying an advance copy of this review.)

Harman, Gilbert. "On Moral Relativism Defended." *Philosophical Review* 84, no. 1 (January 1975): 3–22.

———. *The Nature of Morality.* New York: Oxford University Press, 1977.

Haworth, Lawrence. *Autonomy.* New Haven, Conn.: Yale University Press, 1986.

Hobbes, Thomas. *Leviathan* (Everyman Library edition). New York: Dutton, 1950.

Holmes, Robert. "Nozick on Anarchism." In Jeffrey Paul, *Reading Nozick.* Totawa, N.J.: Rowman and Littlefield, 1981. Pp. 57–67.

Honoré, A. M. "Property, Title, and Redistribution." In *Equality and Freedom: Past, Present and Future,* ed. by Carl Wellman. ARSP Archives for Philosophy of Law and Social Philosophy: Beiheft Neue Folge nr. 10. Wiesbaden: Steiner-Verlag, 1977. Pp. 107–115.

Hospers, John. *Libertarianism.* Los Angeles: Nash, 1971.

Hudson, W. D. *The Is-Ought Question.* London: Macmillan, 1969.

Hume, David. *A Treatise of Human Nature,* ed. by L. A. Selby-Bigge. Oxford: Clarendon Press, 1957.

———. *Inquiry Concerning the Principles of Morals.* Indianapolis: Bobbs-Merrill, Liberal Arts Press 1957.

Kant, Immanuel. *Foundations of the Metaphysics of Morals.* Indianapolis: Bobbs-Merrill, Library of Liberal Arts, 1959.

———. *The Metaphysics of Morals.* Indianapolis: Bobbs-Merrill, Library of Liberal Arts, 1964–1965. (Its two parts are published separately as *The Metaphysical Elements of Justice* [1965] and *The Metaphysical Principles of Virtue* [1964], respectively translated and edited by John Ladd and James Ellington.)

———. "On a Supposed Right to Lie From Benevolent Motives." In T. K. Abbot, trans. and ed., *Kant's Critique of Practical Reason and Other Writings on the Theory of Ethics.* London: Longmans, Green, 1954. Pp. 361–365.

Katz, Lawrence, and Kenneth Rosen. "The Effect of Land Use Controls on Housing Prices." Working Paper 80-13. Berkeley: University of California, Center for Real Estate and Urban Economics, 1981.

Lewis, David. "Prisoner's Dilemma Is a Newcombe's Problem." *Philosophy and Public Affairs* 8, no.3 (Fall 1973): 235–240.

Locke, John. *Second Treatise on Civil Government.* In Ernest Barker, ed., *Social Contract.* Oxford: Oxford University Press, 1960. Pp. 3–147.

Lucash, F., ed. *Justice and Equality, Here and Now.* Ithaca, N.Y.: Cornell University Press, 1986.

Machan, Tibor. "Should Business Be Regulated?" In Tom Regan, ed., *Just Business.* New York: Random House, 1984. Pp. 202–234.

Macleod, A. M. "Justice and the Market," *Canadian Journal of Philosophy* 13, no. 4 (December 1983): 551–563. Also, "Justice and the Market: Rejoinder to Cragg and Mack," ibid., 575–584.

Marx, Karl. "Critique of the Gotha Program." In Robert C. Tucker, ed., *The Marx-Engels Reader.* New York: Norton, 1978. Pp. 529–530.

Michalos, Alex. Critical notice of David Braybrooke, *Meeting Needs,* forthcoming in *Dialogue* (1988).

Mill, John Stuart. *An Essay on Liberty.* London: J. M. Dent, Everyman Library, 1968.

———. *Utilitarianism.* London: J. M. Dent, Everyman Library, 1968.

Miller, Richard. *Analyzing Marx.* Princeton: Princeton University Press, 1984.

Moore, G. E. *Principia Ethica.* Cambridge: Cambridge University Press, 1903.

Morris, Chris. "A Hobbesian Welfare State?" (forthcoming in *Dialogue*).

Nagel, Thomas. "Libertarianism without Foundations." Reprinted in Jeffrey Paul, ed., *Reading Nozick.* Totowa, N.J.: Rowman & Littlefield, 1981. Pp. 191–205. (Originally in *Yale Law Journal* 85. 136 ff.)

———. "Moral Conflict and Political Legitimacy." In *Philosophy and Public Affairs* 16, no. 3 (Summer 1987): 215–240.

Nakhnikian, George. "On the Naturalistic Fallacy." In H-N. Castañeda and G. Nakhnikian, *Morality and the Language of Conduct.* Detroit: Wayne State University Press, 1963.

Narveson, Jan. "Utilitarianism and Formalism." *Australasian Journal of Philosophy* 43, no. 1 (1965): 58–71.

———. *Morality and Utility.* Baltimore, Md.: Johns Hopkins University Press, 1967.

———. Critical notice of Nozick's *Anarchy, State, and Utopia. Dialogue* (1977): 298–327.

———. "A Puzzle About Economic Justice in Rawls' Theory." *Social Theory and Practice* 4, no. 1 (1976): 1–27.

———. "Rights and Utilitarianism." In W. E. Cooper, K. Nielsen, and S. C. Patten, eds., *New Essays on John Stuart Mill and Utilitarianism. Canadian Journal of Philosophy,* supplementary vol. 5 (1979): 137–160.

———. "Gewirth's Reason and Morality—A Study in the Hazards of Universalizability in Ethics." *Dialogue* 19, no. 4 (December 1980): 651–674.

———. "Human Rights: Which, If any, Are There?" In J. R. Pennock and J. W. Chapman, eds., *Human Rights.* NOMOS XXIII. New York: New York University Press, 1981. Pp. 175–198.

―――. "Rawls and Utilitarianism." In H. Miller and W. Williams, eds., *The Limits of Utilitarianism.* Minneapolis: University of Minnesota Press, 1982. Pp. 128–143.

―――. "On Dworkinian Equality." *Social Philosophy & Policy* 1, no. 1 (Autumn 1983): 1–23.

―――. "Animal Rights Revisited." In Harlan B. Miller and William H. Williams, eds., *Ethics and Animals.* Clifton, N.J.: Humana Press, 1983. Pp. 45–60.

―――. "Marxism: Hollow at the Core." *Free Inquiry* (Spring 1983): 29–35.

―――. "Equality vs. Liberty: Advantage, Liberty." *Philosophy and Social Policy* 2, no. 1 (Autumn 1984): 33–60.

―――. "Positive/Negative: Why Bother?" In Eric Mack, ed., *Positive and Negative Duties. Tulane Studies in Philosophy* (1985): 51–66.

―――. "Two Views of Utilitarianism." Paper delivered at the Canadian Philosophical Association meeting, Montreal, May 1985.

―――. "Abortion and Infanticide." *Bowling Green Studies in Applied Philosophy.* Bowling Green, Ohio: Department of Philosophy, Bowling Green State University, 1986. Pp. 76–89.

―――. "At Arms' Length: Violence and War." In Tom Regan, ed., *Matters of Life and Death,* 2nd ed. New York: Random House, 1986.

―――. Review of Kai Neilsen, *Equality and Liberty. International Philosophical Quarterly* 26, no. 2 (June 1986): 192–194.

―――. "Remarks on the Foundations of Morality." Paper delivered at the Canadian Philosophical Association meeting, Guelph, Ontario, June 1986. (A French translation is pending from the University of Quebec at Montreal.)

―――. Critical notice of David Wong, *Moral Relativity. Canadian Journal of Philosophy* 17, no. 1 (March 1987): 235–257.

―――. "Contractarian Starting Points." Paper delivered at the University of Western Ontario Conference on Contractarianism, London, Ontario, April 25, 1987. (Proceedings forthcoming: Peter Vallentyne, ed., *Contractarianism and Rational Choice: Essays on Gauthier* [Stanford, Calif.: Stanford University Press, 1989].)

―――. Review of *Morals by Agreement. Canadian Philosophical Reviews* 7, no. 6 (July 1987): 269–271.

Neely, Wright. "Freedom and Desire." *Philosophical Review* 83, no. 1 (January 1974): 32–54.

Nielsen, Kai. *Equality and Liberty.* Totowa, N.J.: Rowman & Allenheld, 1983.

Norman, Richard. *Reasons for Action.* Oxford, U.K.: Basil Blackwell, 1971.

Nowell-Smith, Patrick. *Ethics.* Harmondsworth, U.K: Penguin Books, 1955.

Nozick, Robert. "Distributive Justice." *Philosophy and Public Affairs* 3, no. 1 (Fall 1973): 45–126.

―――. *Anarchy, State, and Utopia.* New York: Basic Books, 1974.

O'Neill, Onora. "Robert Nozick's Entitlements." *Theoria* 19, (1976): 468–481.

Orwin, Clifford. "Nozick's Liberal Utopia." Paper delivered at Canadian Polit-
    ical Science Association meeting, Guelph, Ontario, June 1985.
Paul, Ellen Frankel. *Property Rights and Eminent Domain*. New Brunswick, N.J.:
    Transaction Books, 1987.
Pence, G. E. "Fair Contracts and Beautiful Intuitions." In Kai Nielsen and
    Roger Shiner, eds., *New Essays on Contract Theory. Canadian Journal of Phi-
    losophy* Supplementary Volume 3 (1977): 137–152.
Powers, Thomas. "The Gentle Heroes" (review of Caroline Moorehead, *Trou-
    blesome People: The Warriors of Pacifism*). *Atlantic Monthly*, (August 1987):
    78–79, 137–142.
Rawls, John. *A Theory of Justice*. Cambridge: Harvard University Press, 1971.
Ripstein, Arthur. "Foundationalism in Political Theory." *Philosophy and Public
    Affairs* 16, no. 2 (Spring 1987): 115–137.
Rosenberg, Alexander. "Prospects for the Elimination of Tastes from Econom-
    ics and Ethics." In J. Paul, F. Miller, and E. F. Paul, eds., *Ethics and Eco-
    nomics*. London: Blackwell, 1985. Pp. 48–68.
Rothbard, Murray. *Power & Market*. Menlo Park, Calif: Institute for Humane
    Studies, 1970.
Scanlon, Thomas. "Utiliarianism and Contractualism." In A. Sen and B.
    Williams, eds., *Utilitarianism and Beyond*. Cambridge: Cambridge Univer-
    sity Press, 1982.
Scruton, Roger. *The Meaning of Conservatism*. Harmondsworth: Pelican Books,
    1977.
Sen, Amartya. "The Moral Standing of the Market." In J. Paul, F. Miller, and
    E. F. Paul, eds., *Ethics and Economics*. London: Blackwell, 1985. Pp.
    1–19.
Shue, Henry. "The Bogus Distinction—'Negative' and 'Positive' Rights." In
    Norman E. Bowie, *Making Ethical Decisions*. New York: McGraw-Hill,
    1985. Pp. 223–231.
Sidgwick, Henry. *The Methods of Ethics*, 7th ed. London: Macmillan, 1961.
Singer, Peter. "The Right to Be Rich or Poor." In Jeffrey Paul, ed., *Reading
    Nozick*. Totowa N.J.: Rowman & Littlefield, 1981. Pp. 37–56.
Sparshott, Francis. *An Enquiry into Goodness*. Toronto and Chicago: University
    of Toronto Press and University of Chicago Press, 1958.
Steiner, Hillel. "How Free: Computing Personal Liberty." In A. Philips
    Griffiths, ed., *Of Liberty*. Royal Institute of Philosophy Lecture Series 15.
    Cambridge: Cambridge University Press, 1983. Pp. 73–90.
Suits, David. "On Locke's Argument for Government." *Journal of Libertarian
    Studies* 1, no. 3 (1977): 195–203.
Tannehill, Morris, and Tannehill, Linda. *The Market for Liberty*. New York:
    Laissez Faire Books, 1984.
Taylor, Richard. *Freedom, Anarchy, and the Law*. Buffalo: Prometheus, 1982.
Thomson, Judith Jarvis. "Some Ruminations on Rights." *Arizona Law Review*

45 (1977). Reprinted in Jeffrey Paul, ed., *Reading Nozick*. Totowa, N.J.: Rowman and Littlefield, 1981. Pp. 130–147.

Tucker, Robert C., ed. *The Marx-Engels Reader*. New York: Norton, 1978.

Wilson, James Q. "Raising Kids." *Atlantic Monthly* (October 1983): 45–56.

Wong, David. *Moral Relativity*. Berkeley: University of California Press, 1984.

INDEX